The Historical Bible

THE LIFE AND TEACHINGS
OF JESUS

ACCORDING TO THE EARLIEST RECORDS

BY

CHARLES FOSTER KENT, Ph.D., Litt.D.

WOOLSEY PROFESSOR OF BIBLICAL LITERATURE IN YALE UNIVERSITY

WITH MAP AND CHART

CHARLES SCRIBNER'S SONS

NEW YORK   CHICAGO   BOSTON   ATLANTA
SAN FRANCISCO   DALLAS

PREFACE

WITHIN the past few years a rapidly increasing body of thoughtful men and women, inside and outside the church, have learned to appreciate and appropriate the practical results that have come from a thorough, constructive application of modern historical and literary methods of study to the Old Testament. Time is demonstrating more and more clearly that these methods, instead of destroying, are revealing anew the beauty and permanent significance of those ancient records.

What is eminently true of the Old is destined, in even larger measure, to prove true of the New Testament. The gospels, like the historical books of the Old Testament, embody older oral and written sources which reflect the earliest impression that Jesus' personality and words made on the minds of his followers. The first step, therefore, in the quest of the real Jesus is to distinguish and to separate these oldest records from the later variant accounts which blur or conceal the original portrait. The more vital the questions involved, the more important is it that the records be carefully studied and tested by the most thorough methods known to modern historical research. Men rightly demand to-day a definite rational basis for their faith. Before Christianity can make the appeal which it should to the individual and to society, it must rest on firm, unassailable historical foundations.

Jesus was so many-sided that no one of the gospels gives a complete or proportionate portrait of him. A harmony of the gospels, with its widely divergent readings, is a most unsatisfactory text-book for a constructive study of the life and teachings of Jesus. Even more confusing and misleading is a composite gospel which, like Tatian's *Diatessaron*, combines all the variant statements of the four gospels. Practical experience is demonstrating that what is demanded to-day is a single narrative that will embody the oldest records embedded in the four New Testament gospels. This must be so arranged that it will give a simple, logical, and, as far as possible, a chronological view of Jesus' life and teachings.

The primary aim of the present volume is to meet this need in the most direct and practical way. The vividness and consistency of the

v

PREFACE

portrait of Jesus furnished by what are recognized as the oldest records in the gospels are the best demonstration that we have here the testimony of the earliest eye-witnesses whose words have been preserved. Through their eyes we can again look upon the divine Friend and Teacher of men. As we listen to his words, as they have recorded them, we are captivated anew by their irresistible truth and charm. Involuntarily we echo the words of an early auditor: "Surely never man taught as he taught." Here is the eternal Jesus, practically unobscured by later philosophies or doctrines. He is it who is surely destined again to draw to himself, as he did in the days of his flesh, the busy men of affairs, who are "bound to the wheel of things" or who are blinded by ignorance or prejudice; for he has for each of them a plain, practical message that means freedom and happiness and the fulness of life.

In the Introduction and in connection with each chapter, the most important data, which enable the student to distinguish between the older and later records, have been presented and the significant gospel parallels noted. The detailed references in the Appendix will guide the student to the larger literature, as well as suggest my indebtedness to previous writers. The conclusions and convictions presented in this volume have been gradually wrought out in the classroom and in the larger school of experience. The constant aim has been to present in clear, non-technical form the essential facts and thus to enable the reader to draw his own conclusions regarding the many vital questions involved.

To five men, who have read the manuscript and from their knowledge of the Bible and of life have contributed valuable suggestions, especially regarding the best form in which to present the results, I owe a large debt: Professor Jeremiah W. Jenks, of New York University; Henry A. Sherman and Harold B. Hunting, of the house of Charles Scribner's Sons; and William D. Murray and Harrison S. Elliott, of the International Committee of the Young Men's Christian Association. I am also under obligation to two of my colleagues in the University, Professors Frank C. Porter and Benjamin W. Bacon, for the light they have thrown, both in their published works and in private discussion, upon the interpretation of the life and teachings of Jesus.

C. F. K.

YALE UNIVERSITY,
Christmas, 1912.

CONTENTS

INTRODUCTION

THE RECORDS OF THE LIFE AND TEACHINGS OF JESUS

CHAPTER   PAGE

I. THE RECORDS OUTSIDE THE GOSPELS............... 1

    I. Christianity at Work in the World.—II. The Roman Historians.—III. The Jewish Writers.—IV. Evidence Found in the Catacombs.—V. The Uncanonical Gospels.—VI. The Recently Discovered Sayings of Jesus. —VII. The Writings of the Church Fathers.—VIII. The Apocryphal Gospels.—IX. Acts and Revelation.—X. Paul's Epistles.—XI. The Value of the Extra-Gospel Testimony.

II. THE CONTENTS AND CHARACTERISTICS OF THE FOUR GOSPELS... 10

    I. The Contents of the Gospel of Mark.—II. Its Plan. —III. Its Characteristics.—IV. Aim of the Gospel.— V. The Contents of Matthew.—VI. Characteristics and Aims of the Gospel of Matthew.—VII. The Contents of the Gospel of Luke.—VIII. Characteristics of This Gospel.—IX. Aim of the Gospel.—X. The Contents of the Fourth Gospel.—XI. Characteristics and Aim of the Fourth Gospel.—XII. A Comparison of the Four Gospels.

III. THE WRITTEN SOURCES UNDERLYING THE GOSPELS..... 19

    I. The Relation of the First Three Gospels to Each Other.—II. Their Agreement in Substance and Verbal Detail.—III. The Synoptic Problem and Its Solution. —IV. The Important Variations of the Fourth Gospel. —V. The Early Tradition Regarding the Origin of the Gospel of Mark.—VI. Mark's Sources.—VII. The Earliest Record of Jesus' Work and Teachings (Q).— VIII. Characteristics and Value of the Earliest Source.

IV. THE LITERARY HISTORY AND DATE OF THE GOSPELS.. 28

    I. The Period of Oral Transmission.—II. Influences that Gave Rise to the Gospels.—III. The Earliest Records.—IV. The Gospels of Matthew and Luke.— V. The Gospel of John.—VI. Conclusions.

vii

CONTENTS

CHAPTER PAGE

V. The Historical Background of Jesus' Life and Work.   34

I. The Division of Palestine After the Death of Herod the Great.—II. Judea under the Rule of Rome.—III. Duties of the Procurators.—IV. The Organization and Authority of the Jerusalem Sanhedrin.—V. The Rule of the Procurators.—VI. The Character and Rule of Herod Antipas.—VII. Rome's Strength and Weakness.—VIII. The Needs of the Roman World.

THE EARLY LIFE AND WORK OF JESUS

§ CXXI. Jesus' Birth, Boyhood, and Early Training.   43

Luke 2¹⁻⁷, ²¹ᵃ, ⁴⁰⁻⁵².
I. The Account of Jesus' Birth.—II. The Place and Date of His Birth.—III. His Home.—IV. The Life at Nazareth.—V. Jesus' Educational Opportunities.—VI. His Visit to the Temple at the Age of Twelve.—VII. His Acquaintance with the Scriptures of His Race.—VIII. The Young Master Builder.

§ CXXII. The Personality and Teaching of John the Baptist   57

Luke 3¹, ², Matt. 3⁴⁻⁶, Luke 3⁷⁻¹⁷ (cf. Matt. 3¹⁻⁸, Luke 3³, Matt. 3⁷⁻¹²).
I. The Records of John's Birth and Work.—II. His Character and Aims.—III. His Teachings.—IV. His Symbol of Baptism.—V. The Results of His Work.

§ CXXIII. Jesus' Baptism and Temptation   62

Mark 1⁹⁻¹¹ (cf. Matt. 3¹³⁻¹⁷, Luke 3²¹, ²²), Matt. 4¹⁻¹¹ (cf. Luke 4¹⁻¹³, Mark 1¹², ¹³).
I. The Reasons Why Jesus Went to John.—II. Literary Form of the Record.—III. The Significance of the Baptismal Vision.—IV. The Meaning of the Account of Jesus' Temptation.—V. The Different Phases of Jesus' Temptation.

§ CXXIV. Jesus and John the Baptist   69

Matt. 14³⁻⁵ (cf. Luke 3¹⁹, ²⁰, Mark 6¹⁷⁻²⁰), Mark 1¹⁴, ¹⁵, Matt. 11²⁻¹⁹ (cf. Luke 7¹⁹⁻³⁵), Matt. 14⁶⁻¹² (cf. Mark 6²¹⁻²⁹).
I. The Gospel Evidence That Jesus Worked First in Judea.—II. John's Arrest.—III. His Later Message to Jesus.—IV. Jesus' Estimate of John.—V. The Account of John's Death.

§ CXXV. Jesus' Early Work in Galilee   75

Matt. 4¹²ᵃ, Mark 1¹⁶⁻²⁰ (cf. Matt. 4¹⁸⁻²², Luke 5¹⁻¹¹), John 1⁴³ᵇ⁻⁵⁰, Mark 1²¹⁻³⁸ (cf. Luke 4³¹⁻⁴³, Matt. 8¹⁴⁻¹⁷).

CONTENTS

PAGE

I. The Record.—II. Reasons Why Jesus Went to Capernaum.—III. The Aims and Methods in the Early Galilean Work.—IV. The Call of the Six Fishermen.—V. The Site of Capernaum.—VI. A Sabbath in Capernaum.—VII. Jesus' Significant Decision.

§ CXXVI. Jesus' Popularity and the Beginning of the Pharisaic Opposition 84

Mark 2$^{1-17}$ (cf. Matt. 9$^{2-13}$, Luke 5$^{17-32}$), Luke 5$^{29-39}$, 7$^{36-50}$, Mark 2$^{18-36}$ (cf. Matt. 9$^{14-17}$, 12$^{1-14}$, Luke 5^{33}–6^{11}, 13$^{10-17}$, 14$^{1-6}$).
I. The Record of the Growing Opposition.—II. The Causes of the Pharisaic Opposition.—III. The Charges Which the Pharisees Made against Jesus.

§ CXXVII. The Gospel Miracles 93

Matt. 12$^{38, 39, 41, 42}$ (cf. Luke 11$^{29-32}$, 12$^{54-56}$, Matt. 16$^{1-4}$), Mark 3$^{7-12}$ (cf. Matt. 4$^{24, 25}$, 12$^{15-21}$, Luke 6$^{17-19}$), Mark 4^{35}–5^{43} (cf. Matt. 8$^{18, 23-34}$, 9$^{18-26}$, Luke 8$^{22-56}$), Matt. 8$^{5-10, 13}$ (cf. Luke 7$^{1-10}$), Mark 6$^{1-6}$ (cf. Matt. 13$^{54-58}$, Luke 4$^{16-30}$), Mark 1$^{39-45}$ (cf. Matt. 4^{23}, 8$^{1-4}$, Luke 4^{44}, 5$^{12-16}$).
I. The Significance of the Gospel Miracles.—II. Jesus' Attitude toward Miracles.—III. Miracles in the History of Early Religions.—IV. The Canons of Interpretation Employed by Critical Historians.—V. The Different Types of Recorded Miracles.—VI. The Significance of the Illustrations of Jesus' Power Over Nature.—VII. Conclusions.

§ CXXVIII. The Call and Training of Jesus' Disciples 108

Mark 3$^{13-21, 31-35}$ (cf. Luke 6$^{12-16}$, 8$^{19-21}$, 11$^{27, 28}$, Matt. 10$^{2-4}$, 12$^{46-50}$), Luke 9$^{57-62}$ (cf. Matt. 8$^{19-22}$), Luke 14$^{25-35}$, 39, 40, 43-45 (cf. Matt. 10$^{37, 38}$, 5^{13}, 15^{14}, 10$^{24, 25}$, 12$^{33-35}$, 7$^{16-20}$, Mark 9^{50}), Mark 9$^{38-40}$ (cf. Luke 9$^{49, 50}$), Luke 8$^{1-3}$, 10$^{38-42}$, Matt. 9$^{35-38}$ (cf. Luke 10$^{1, 2}$), Luke 10$^{3-12}$ (cf. Matt. 10$^{1-16}$, Mark 6$^{7-11}$, Luke 9$^{1-5}$), Matt. 7^{6}, Luke 10^{16} (cf. Matt. 10^{10}), Mark 6$^{30, 31}$ (cf. Luke 9^{10}, 10^{17}), Matt. 11$^{25-27}$ (cf. Luke 10$^{18-20}$).
I. Jesus' Purpose in Calling His Disciples.—II. The Personnel of the Twelve.—III. The Conditions of Active Discipleship.—IV. Jesus' Fellowship with His Disciples.—V. The Ministering Women.—VI. Jesus' Commission to the Twelve.—VII. Jesus' Reason for Sending Out the Twelve.—VIII. The Return of the Twelve.

JESUS' FUNDAMENTAL TEACHINGS

§ CXXIX. The Aims and Methods of the Great Teacher 122

Matt. 5$^{1, 2, 17-20}$, 11$^{28-30}$, 7$^{24-29}$ (cf. Luke 6$^{47-49}$, Mark 1^{22}), Mark 4$^{1-25, 33, 34}$ (cf. Luke 8$^{4-18}$, Matt. 13$^{1-9, 18-23, 10-15, 53}$).

CONTENTS

PAGE

I. Jesus the Teacher.—II. His Attitude toward the Earlier Teachers of His Race.—III. His Aims as a Teacher.—IV. The General Characteristics of His Teaching Methods.—V. The Literary Form of His Teachings.

§ CXXX. GOD'S ATTITUDE TOWARD MEN.............. 134

Luke 15 (cf. Matt. 18$^{12-14}$), Matt. 7$^{7-11}$ (cf. Luke 11$^{9-13}$).
I. Current Jewish Ideas of God.—II. The Growth of the Belief in the Fatherhood of God.—III. Jesus' Teaching Regarding the Nature of God.—IV. God's Readiness to Forgive the Sinner.—V. Jesus' Teaching Regarding God's Readiness to Answer Prayer.

§ CXXXI. MAN'S ATTITUDE TOWARD GOD............. 142

Matt. 5$^{33-37}$, 6$^{1-6, 16-18, 7, 8}$, Luke 11$^{1-8}$ (cf. Matt. 6$^{9-15}$), Luke 18$^{1-14}$, 17$^{5, 6}$, Mark 11$^{22-25}$ (cf. Matt. 21$^{21, 22}$), Matt. 6$^{25-27}$ (cf. Luke 12$^{22-25}$), Matt. 6$^{28-34}$ (cf. Luke 12$^{26-32}$).
I. Jesus' Conception of Man.—II. The Importance of the Right Attitude in Worship.—III. Jesus' Type of Prayer.—IV. The Value of Persistency and Humility in Prayer.—V. The Invincible Power of Faith.—VI. Trust That Leaves No Place for Worry.

§ CXXXII. THE KINGDOM OF GOD 156

Matt. 13$^{31, 32}$ (cf. Mark 4$^{30-32}$, Luke 13$^{18, 19}$), Luke 13$^{20-21}$, Mark 4$^{26-29}$, Matt. 13$^{24-30, 43-50}$, Luke 17$^{20, 21}$, 14$^{1a, 15-24}$, Mark 10$^{13-27}$ (cf. Matt. 19$^{13-26}$, Luke 18$^{15-27}$), Matt. 13$^{44-46}$, Mark 9$^{43-47}$ (cf. Matt. 6$^{29, 30}$).
I. The Different Conceptions of the Kingdom of God in the Old Testament.—II. Jesus' Description of the Characteristics of the Kingdom of God.—III. Conditions of Entrance into the Kingdom.—IV. Riches a Barrier to Entrance into the Kingdom of God.—V. The Place and Meaning of the Kingdom in Jesus' Teachings.

§ CXXXIII. THE OBLIGATIONS OF CITIZENSHIP IN THE KINGDOM OF GOD.............................. 167

Matt. 6$^{19-24}$ (cf. Luke 12$^{33, 34}$, 11$^{34-36}$, 16^{13}), Luke 12$^{12-21}$, 16, Matt. 25$^{14-29}$ (cf. Luke 19$^{11-26}$, Mark 4^{25}).
I. Single-Minded Loyalty to God.—II. The Right Use of Wealth.—III. The Improving of Present Opportunities.—IV. The Use of Natural Gifts.

§ CXXXIV. MAN'S DUTIES TO HIS NEIGHBOR AND TO HIMSELF................................... 176

Matt. 5$^{21-26}$, 18^{15}, Luke 17^4 (cf. Luke 17^3), Matt. 18$^{21-35}$, 7$^{1-5}$ (cf. Luke 6$^{37-42}$), Matt. 5$^{38-48}$ (cf. Luke 6$^{29, 30, 27, 32-36}$), Matt. 7^{12} (cf. Luke 6^{31}), Luke 10$^{25-37}$ (cf. Mark 12$^{28-31}$, Matt. 22$^{35-40}$), Mark 12$^{32-34}$.

CONTENTS

PAGE

I. The Fatal Crime of Wrong Thinking.—II. Reverence and Regard for the Person of Another.—III. Forgiveness.—IV. Charitable Judgment.—V. Jesus' Law of Love.—VI. The Expression of Love toward a Neighbor.

§ CXXXV. MAN'S RESPONSIBILITY TO SOCIETY 188

Mark 10² ⁻¹² (*cf.* Matt. 19³ ⁻⁹, 5³¹, ³², Luke 16¹⁸), Matt. 19¹⁰ ⁻¹², 17²⁴ ⁻²⁷, Mark 12¹³ ⁻¹⁵ ᵃ (*cf.* Matt. 22¹⁵ ⁻²², Luke 20²⁰ ⁻²⁶), John 7⁵³ ⁻8¹¹, Luke 17¹, ² (*cf.* Mark 9⁴², Matt. 18⁶, ⁷), Matt. 18¹⁰.
I. Jesus' Method as a Social Teacher.—II. His Teachings Regarding the Family.—III. Obligations of the Individual to the State.—IV. Treatment of the Criminal.—V. Care of the Poor.—VI. Protection of the Weak and Ignorant.

§ CXXXVI. THE REWARDS OF THE CHRISTIAN LIFE 202

Luke 14¹, ⁷ ⁻¹⁴, Matt. 20¹ ⁻¹⁶, Luke 17¹ ᵃ, ⁷ ⁻¹⁰, Mark 10²⁸ ⁻³¹ (*cf.* Matt. 19²⁷ ⁻²⁹, Luke 18²⁸ ⁻³⁰), Matt. 5³ ⁻⁶ (*cf.* Luke 6²⁰, ²¹), Matt. 5⁷ ⁻¹² (*cf.* Luke 6²², ²³).
I. Jesus and the Jewish Doctrine of Rewards.—II. The Rewards of Faithful Service.—III. The Place of Happiness in Jesus' Teaching.—IV. The Original Form of the Beatitudes.—V. The Conditions of True Happiness.

THE CULMINATING EVENTS OF JESUS' LIFE

§ CXXXVII. THE CRISIS IN GALILEE 216

Luke 9⁷ ⁻⁹ (*cf.* Mark 6¹⁴ ⁻¹⁶, Matt. 14¹, ²), Mark 6³² ⁻⁴⁴ (*cf.* Matt. 14¹³ ⁻²¹, 15²⁹ ⁻³⁹, Luke 9¹⁰ ᵇ ⁻¹⁷, Mark 8¹ ⁻¹⁰), Mark 6⁴⁵ ⁻⁵¹ (*cf.* Matt. 14²² ⁻³³), Mark 7¹ ⁻²³ (*cf.* Luke 11³⁷ ⁻⁴¹, Matt. 15¹ ⁻²⁰), Luke 11¹⁴ ⁻²⁶ (*cf.* Matt. 12²² ⁻³², ⁴³ ⁻⁴⁵, Mark 3²² ⁻²⁷), Luke 12¹, ², Matt. 10²⁷ ⁻³³ (*cf.* Matt. 10²⁴ ⁻²⁶, Luke 12³ ⁻⁹), Luke 12¹⁰, Matt. 11²⁰ ⁻²⁴ (*cf.* Luke 10¹² ⁻¹⁵).
I. The Attitude of Herod Antipas toward Jesus.—II. The Culmination of Jesus' Popularity.—III. The Grounds on Which Jesus Condemned the Scribes and Pharisees.—IV. His Warnings to His Disciples.—V. The Influence of This Crisis upon His Method of Work.

§ CXXXVIII. JESUS IN RETIREMENT WITH HIS DISCIPLES . . 227

Mark 7²⁴ ⁻³⁰ (*cf.* Matt. 15²¹ ⁻²⁸), Mark 7³¹, 8²² ⁻9³² (*cf.* Mark 7³² ⁻³⁷, Matt. 16¹³ ⁻17²², Luke 9¹⁸ ⁻⁴⁵).
I. The Request of the Syro-Phœnician Woman.—II. Peter's Confession.—III. Jesus' First Prediction of His Passion.—IV. The Story of the Transfiguration.—V. The Healing of an Epileptic.

CONTENTS

PAGE

§ CXXXIX. INCIDENTS OF THE LAST JOURNEY TO JERUSALEM   239

Mark 9[33-37, 41] (*cf.* Matt. 18[1-5], Luke 9[46-48]), Luke 9[51-56], Mark 10[1], Luke 13[22] (*cf.* Matt. 19[1, 2]), Matt. 7[13, 14], Luke 13[24-35] (Matt. 7[21-29], 8[11, 12], 23[37-39]), Mark 10[32-44], Luke 22[27b] (*cf.* Matt. 20[17-28], Luke 18[31-34], 22[24-27a], Mark 10[45]), Luke 19[1-10], Mark 10[46b-52] (*cf.* Luke 18[35-43], Matt. 20[29-34]).
I. Jesus Facing Jerusalem.—II. The Narrow Way of Salvation.—III. The Request of James and John.—IV. The Blind Man and the Tax-Collector at Jericho.

§ CXL. THE RENEWAL OF JESUS' PUBLIC ACTIVITY IN
JERUSALEM   250

Mark 11[1-10] (*cf.* Matt. 21[1-11], Luke 19[29-44]), Mark 11[11], Luke 13[6-9] (*cf.* Mark 11[12-14, 20, 21], Matt. 21[18-22]), Mark 11[15b-19] (*cf.* Matt. 21[12-17], Luke 19[45-48]), Mark 11[27-33] (*cf.* Matt. 21[23-27], Luke 20[1-8]), Matt. 21[28-42, 46a], Luke 20[19b] (*cf.* Mark 12[1-12], Luke 20[9-17, 19a]), Luke 13[1-5], Mark 12[18-27] (*cf.* Matt. 22[23-33], Luke 20[27-40], Mark 12[35-40] (*cf.* Matt. 22[41-23[3, 5-7], Luke 20[41-47]), Luke 11[46] (*cf.* Matt. 23[4]), Matt. 23[13, 23a, 25, 27, 29-32] (*cf.* Luke 11[52, 47, 48]), Luke 11[49-51] (*cf.* Matt. 23[34-36]), Mark 12[41-44] (*cf.* Luke 21[1-4]).
I. The Triumphal Entry into Jerusalem.—II. The Story and Parable of the Fig Tree.—III. The Public Rebuke of the Temple Authorities.—IV. Public Discussions with the Leaders of Judaism.—V. The Arraignment of the Scribes and Pharisees.

§ CXLI. JESUS' PREPARATIONS FOR HIS DEATH   265

Mark 13[1-4a, 32] (*cf.* Matt. 24[1-4a, 36], Luke 21[5-7]), Matt. 25[1-12], 24[37-51] (*cf.* Mark 13[4b, 31, 33-37], Luke 12[35-48], 17[22-37], 21[34-36]), Mark 14[1-9] (*cf.* Matt. 26[3-13], Luke 22[1, 2]), Luke 21[37, 38], Mark 14[10-21] (*cf.* Matt. 26[14-25], Luke 22[3-13, 21-23]), I Cor. 11[23-25], Mark 14[26-31] (*cf.* Mark 14[22-25], Matt. 22[26-35], Luke 22[14-20, 39, 31-38]).
I. The Prediction of the Temple's Destruction.—II. Jesus' Warnings to His Disciples.—III. The Anointing at Bethany.—IV. Judas' Bargain with the High Priests.—V. Jesus' Last Supper with His Disciples.—VI. Jesus' Farewell Words to His Disciples.

§ CXLII. JESUS' ARREST AND TRIAL   278

Mark 14[32-52] (*cf.* Matt. 26[36-56], Luke 22[39-53]), Luke 22[54-23[25] (*cf.* Mark 14[53a, 66-72, 65, 55b-64], 15[1-15], Matt. 26[57a, 69-75, 67, 68, 57b-66], 27[1, 2, 11-26]).
I. The Struggle in Gethsemane.—II. The Arrest of Jesus.—III. His Examination before the High Priests.—IV. His Trial before Pilate.

§ CXLIII. JESUS' DEATH AND BURIAL   288

Mark 15[16-47] (*cf.* Matt. 27[27-66], Luke 23[26-55]).
I. The Record of Jesus' Crucifixion.—II. His Last

CONTENTS

PAGE

Words.—III. The Place and Manner of the Crucifixion.—IV. Jesus' Burial.—V. The Date of His Death.
—VI. The Meaning of His Death.

§ CXLIV. THE LIVING CHRIST.......................... 297

I Cor. 15$^{1-8}$ (cf. Mark 16, Matt. 28, Luke 23^{56}–24^{53},
Acts 1$^{1-11}$).
I. The Immediate Effect of Jesus' Crucifixion upon
His Disciples.—II. Their Sudden Recovery of Faith
and Courage.—III. Paul's Testimony.—IV. A Com-
parison between the Current Conceptions of the
Resurrection from the Dead and that of Paul.—V. A
Comparison of the Different Gospel Records of the
Resurrection.—VI. The Naturalistic Interpretations
of the Resurrection Stories.—VII. The Supernatural
Explanations.—VIII. The Spiritual Interpretation.

§ CXLV. JESUS THE SAVIOUR OF MANKIND............ 310

John 3$^{14-21}$, 4$^{23, 24}$, 6$^{27, 33}$, ^{35}, 8$^{12b-d, 31b-d, 32, 34b-36}$, 10$^{14-16}$,
11$^{25b-26a}$, 12^{44b-50}, 13$^{13-16, 34, 35}$, 14$^{6b-7, 10-17, 21}$, 17$^{11c-12a, 15-26}$.
I. The Fourth Gospel's Conception of Jesus as Teacher
and Saviour.—II. Jesus' Self-Designation.—III. His
Interpretation of the Extent of His Mission.—IV. Why
Jesus Is the Universal Saviour of Mankind.—V. The
Reasons Why Christianity Is a Conquering World
Religion.

APPENDIX I. A PRACTICAL BIBLICAL REFERENCE LIBRARY 323

APPENDIX II. GENERAL QUESTIONS AND SUBJECTS FOR SPE-
CIAL RESEARCH....................... 326

MAP AND CHART

PALESTINE IN THE TIME OF JESUS...................._Frontispiece_

CHART INDICATING THE ORIGIN AND APPROXIMATE DATES OF
THE GOSPELS ....to face page 33

INTRODUCTION

THE RECORDS OF THE LIFE AND TEACHINGS OF JESUS

I

THE RECORDS OUTSIDE THE GOSPELS

I. Christianity at Work in the World. Christianity is not a dead but a living religion. The most convincing and universally valid testimony to the historical reality and divine nature of Jesus' personality and work is the effect of his life and teachings upon the world to-day. Though often misinterpreted and misrepresented, they are slowly but surely transforming the life, the ideals, and the thought of humanity. Christianity is unquestionably the most potent moral and religious force in human history. The child, even before he reaches self-consciousness, feels the all-pervading influence of Christian civilization. Throughout his life this force surrounds him and gives to him all that is best and richest in his thought and experience.

In the final analysis, Christianity is a personal attitude toward God and man—a way of living that finds its present inspiration, as well as its historical illustration, in the personality, spirit, and teachings of Jesus. During the intervening centuries it has received additions from many sources; but the only satisfactory explanation of the unique elements in Christianity is the historical Christ. His own standard, "By their fruits you shall know them," applies equally to himself. If we had no written records, we should know his ideals and methods through the mighty inspiration that he has imparted to humanity. By the calm faith in the heavenly Father that sustains his followers in the presence of trials and temptations, we know the faith of the Master. By the spirit of love and fidelity that inspires them to perform deeds of heroic self-sacrifice, we know the spirit of the modest, tireless, courageous Man of Nazareth. By the ever-deepening social consciousness that recognizes the responsibility of the strong to help

1

the weak, we know the Shepherd of men who devoted not only his energies but his life to "saving lost sheep." Not in perishable books, but in the life and ideals of men Jesus wrote the imperishable and universally intelligible record of his work and teachings.

II. **The Roman Historians.** From the point of view of imperial Rome the brief career of Jesus in a distant and despised province was so insignificant that to find even an incidental allusion to it in contemporary Roman history is surprising. Four of the Roman writers of the second Christian century, however, refer either to Jesus or his followers. By far the most significant statement is that of Tacitus, the well-known Roman historian, who wrote between 115 and 117 A.D. In his *Annals* he affirms (XV, 44) that "in order to suppress the rumor [that the Emperor himself had set fire to Rome in 64 A.D.] Nero falsely accused and punished with most acute torture persons who, already hated for their shameful deeds, were commonly called Christians. The founder of that name, Christus, had been put to death by the procurator Pontius Pilate, in the reign of Tiberius; but the deadly superstition, though suppressed for a time, broke out again, not only throughout Judea, where this evil had its origin, but also through the city (Rome), whither all things horrible and vile from all quarters flow and are encouraged. Accordingly, first those were arrested who confessed; then on their information a great multitude was convicted, not so much of the crime of incendiarism as of hatred of the human race." The passage reflects the proud, supercilious attitude of Rome toward the Jews. But it also establishes definitely the outstanding facts regarding Jesus and suggests the numbers and character of his followers, who were found in Rome as early as the middle of the first Christian century.

The historian Suetonius, writing about the same period, states that Claudius "expelled the Jews from Rome because they were constantly raising a tumult at the instigation of Chrestus." The popular error which led Suetonius to believe that the founder of the Christian sect was still in their midst does not invalidate this incidental reference to the presence of Christians at Rome. More exact and informing is the letter which Pliny the younger, while governor of Bithynia, in northern Asia Minor, about 112 A.D., wrote to the Emperor Trajan. In his official communication the cultured Roman official describes in detail the Christians, whom he found in his distant province, and asks for advice as to how to deal with them. Witnesses "affirm that the sum of their guilt or error was to assemble on a fixed day before daybreak, and sing responsively a hymn to Christ, as to a god, and to bind themselves with an oath not to enter into any wickedness, or to commit thefts, robberies, or adulteries, or to falsify their work, or to repudiate trusts committed to them. When these things were ended, it was their custom to depart, and, on coming together again to take food, men and women together, yet innocently."

The satirist Lucian, writing between 165 and 170 A.D., speaks of the founder of the Christian religion as "a man who had been fixed to a stake in Palestine, and who was still worshipped for having introduced a new code of morals in life." Speaking of the followers of Jesus, he declares that their master has persuaded them that they are brothers, and they believe that they will live forever. Thus, before the end of the second Christian century the followers of the humble Nazarene had become so prominent in the Roman Empire that the leading historians and writers of the day, although despising them, could not pass them by without at least a brief mention.

III. **The Jewish Writers.** The references in the Jewish writings which come from the first Christian century are equally significant. In his *Antiquities* (XX, 9¹) Josephus records the condemnation and death of "James, the brother of Jesus, the so-called Messiah (or Christ)." Josephus also apologizes for this act, saying that it was inspired by the Sadducees, whose judgment is always harsh, and that the milder Jews would not have approved it. Origen in three different passages confirms this reference of Josephus to Jesus (*Contra Celsum*, I, 47; II, 13; *Matt.* X, 17). The famous passage in his *Antiquities*, XVIII, 3³, in which Josephus is made to assert that Jesus was a wise man, a worker of miracles, a teacher of such men as receive the truth with joy, that he was, indeed, the Christ, and that, although crucified, he rose again on the third day, is clearly a later Christian addition. Although found in all the extant Greek manuscripts of Josephus, it was unknown to Origen and was first referred to by Eusebius. Hence it was probably inserted between 250 and 300 A.D. Josephus's reference to the work of John the Baptist still further supplements and confirms the biblical narrative. Otherwise the Jewish writers of the period simply establish the fact that Jesus lived; but they furnish no detailed information regarding his life and work. In all their references the later hostility between Jews and Christians is clearly reflected. Jesus is referred to as "that man," "the one hung," "the Nazarene," "the fool," and "Absalom ben Stade" (son of the stake).

IV. **Evidence Found in the Catacombs.** Very different is the pathetic but effective testimony which comes from the Roman catacombs. Over ten thousand inscriptions have thus far been deciphered. Tradition states that in these underground quarries the bodies of a hundred and seventy-four thousand Christians, many of them martyrs, found their final resting-place. From the days of Hadrian, the phrase "In Christ" became a constant recurring element in burial inscriptions. Even more significant are the symbolic pictures which decorate the walls of the catacombs. Over a hundred and thirty-two themes are thus treated. As a result of the careful work of the German scholar Wilpert (published in his Corpus), these are now dated with reasonable certainty. Twenty of these pictures come from the first Christian century and are found in the famous room of Domitilla of the Flavian family. The influence of Græco-Roman art was still strong. Three symbolic pictures, however, have biblical themes: (1) Daniel among the lions, symbolizing God's protection of the faithful in danger. (2) Noah, also symbolizing God's protection of his people. (3) The Good Shepherd, represented by Cupid, the Roman god of love, as a shepherd. In the paintings of the second century a great variety of themes are introduced, such as the incarnation, represented by the adoration of the wise men; the annunciation; and the divine nature of Christ, illustrated by the healing of the paralytic and the woman with the issue of blood. Christ's work as Saviour is illustrated by many different symbols, as, for example, the sacrifice of Isaac, the Good Shepherd, Noah, and Daniel among the lions, the last judgment, the resurrection, and the life of the blessed in paradise. Even such sacramental themes as baptism and the eucharist are represented by Moses striking the rock, the breaking of bread, the multiplication of loaves, and other symbolic scenes. These pictures reflect, more clearly than any contemporary literature, the popular religious thought of the early Christians. They strongly confirm the main facts of the gospel story and illustrate the beliefs of the early church. Above all, the heroism and devotion which inspired them testify to the invincible power of the spirit and teachings of Jesus.

V. The Uncanonical Gospels. During the first three centuries many accounts of Jesus' life and teachings were written, but were so legendary and of so little value that they were not included in the canon, that is, the final authoritative edition of the New Testament; but were known as uncanonical gospels. More than twenty-five such gospels are referred to either by title or in quotations preserved by the early Christian writers. Many of these writings bear the names of Jesus' disciples, as, for example, the Gospel of Andrew, the Gospel of Bartholomew, and the Gospel of the Twelve. Of these many attempts to record the life and teachings of Jesus, the majority were clearly later than the canonical gospels, and possess little intrinsic value. Three uncanonical gospels, however, are of especial interest. The first is the Gospel of the Hebrews. It was probably first written in Syriac, not earlier than the second century. Among the early Christians of Palestine it ranked in authority with the Fourth Gospel. It was frequently quoted by the early Church Fathers, who were the authoritative interpreters of the beliefs of the Christians during the second and third centuries. About twenty-five of these quotations survive. Among other things they tell of how Jesus' mother and brothers urged him to go with them and be baptized by John. They also present a variant account of Jesus' baptism, of his temptation, and of the story of the rich young man. The value of this lost Gospel of the Hebrews is very differently estimated by scholars. Its point of view is in many ways similar to that of Luke. The apologetic aim is also prominent. It may possibly have preserved certain fugitive facts; but recent discoveries show that it is inferior in almost every respect to the canonical gospels, and especially to the Gospel of Matthew, upon which it is evidently based.

In 1886 there was discovered in upper Egypt a fragment of the Gospel of Peter, which comes from the second Christian century. This fragment tells of the trial, crucifixion, and death of Jesus. It also contains two resurrection stories. Its reference to Jesus as preaching to those in the underworld is closely parallel to the corresponding passage in I Peter 3¹⁹. The book contains little supplemental historical data, but is simply a fanciful version of the earlier gospel history. It illustrates, however, the development of Christian thought during the second century, and marks the transition from the canonical to the distorted apocryphal gospels. The Gospel of the Egyptians, which is known only through a few unimportant quotations, doubtless possessed the same general characteristics as the Gospel of Peter. The earliest references to it come from about 200 A.D. Apparently during the third and fourth centuries it enjoyed a certain authority among the Christians of Egypt.

VI. **The Recently Discovered Sayings of Jesus.** It is not improbable that many of the sayings of Jesus which have recently been discovered in Egypt are derived from the Gospel of the Egyptians. In thought and form they are closely related to the Gospel of John, upon which they appear to be based. It is doubtful whether any of them may be dated earlier than the second century. While they suggest the fascinating possibility that almost contemporary records of the life and teachings of Jesus may yet be discovered, those thus far unearthed add little to our knowledge of his original utterances. One or two may contain the actual words of Jesus, as, for example: "Jesus saith, 'Wherever they are . . . and there is one . . . alone, I am with him. Raise the stone and there thou shalt find me; cleave the wood and there am I.'" The following utterance: "Jesus saith, 'Let not him who seeks . . . cease until he finds, and when he finds, he shall be astonished, and astonished, he shall reach the kingdom, and having reached the kingdom, he shall rest,'" probably reflects an original saying It is preserved by the Church Fathers in the briefer form: "He who wonders shall reign, and who reigns shall rest." Several of these sayings are colored by that ascetic and ritualistic spirit which is the exact opposite of that which Jesus taught and did: "Jesus saith, 'Except you fast to the world, you shall in no wise find the kingdom of God; and except you keep the Sabbath, you shall not see the Father.'" Most of these utterances seem but the reverberating echoes of the sayings which the canonical gospels present in their more nearly original form.

VII. **The Writings of the Church Fathers.** It is natural to expect that in the voluminous writings of the learned and devoted Church Fathers many facts and teachings not preserved in the New Testament would be found. This expectation, however, is unfulfilled, and the reason is because the data were no longer available. The possession of written gospels evidently led the Christians of the second and third generations to relax their zeal in preserving current oral traditions. Justin Martyr, the successor of the apostles, adds a little information regarding Jesus, as, for example, the statement that in his home in Nazareth he made yokes and ploughs; yet it is not clear whether even in this case the basis was not a conjecture drawn from Jesus' command, "Take up my yoke," rather than the memory of an actual fact. Of the sayings of Jesus reported by the Church Fathers, practically all, in form and content, resemble the teachings found in the gospels. The most significant are: "Be approved money-changers; disapproving some things, but holding fast that which is good." "Never rejoice except when you have looked upon your brother in love." "They who wish to behold me and lay hold on my kingdom must receive me by affliction."

VIII. **The Apocryphal Gospels.** Far more barren than the writings of the Church Fathers are the so-called apocryphal gospels. These fanciful accounts of supposed incidents in the life of Jesus, like the apocryphal books of the Old Testament, were written too late to be included among the New Testament writings. They deal for the most part with the birth and infancy of Jesus, and supply by the aid of pious imagination the answers to the popular questions which were raised with increasing insistency by the later church. Two of them, the Proto-Evangelium of James and the Arabic Gospel of the Infancy, may come from the latter half of the second Christian century. The remainder cannot be dated earlier than the third, fourth, and fifth centuries. Most of them have survived and are highly esteemed in the Roman Catholic and Greek churches. They not only reiterate in greater detail the stories found in the opening chapters of Matthew and Luke, but state that the Virgin Mary was also immaculately conceived and guarded from all that might defile. The Gospel of Thomas contains grotesque and almost blasphemous stories regarding Jesus' boyhood, attributing to him miracles that are purposeless and unethical. The titles suggest the contents of the following gospels: Concerning the Birth of Mary, History of Joseph the Carpenter, and the Passing of Mary. The Acts of Pilate contains a popular tradition regarding the trial of Jesus and makes the Roman procurator bear testimony to the innocence and divine character of the great Teacher. These gospels have practically no historical value, but they reveal the tendencies later at work in the church, and the profound impression that Jesus' personality and work made upon the world.

IX. **Acts and Revelation.** The New Testament books, other than the four gospels, like the writings of the Church Fathers, supply surprisingly little supplemental data. Acts 20[35] has preserved this priceless and undoubtedly original teaching of Jesus: "It is more blessed to give than to receive." The apostolic sermons found in Acts are valuable, however, not so much for the information regarding Jesus' life and teachings, as for the evidence which they furnish regarding the trend of early Christian thought and teaching. The chief aim of the early apostles was to convince their hearers that Jesus was, indeed, the Messiah, and to interpret the shame of the cross in the light of the older scriptures. Similarly, the book of Revelation is of historical value because it shows how prominent were the Jewish apocalyptic ideas in the Christian church during the latter half of the first Christian century. These Jewish messianic and apocalyptic tendencies strongly influenced the writers of the New Testament gospels and explain why so much attention is given in these narratives to Jesus' crucifixion and resurrection.

X. Paul's Epistles. The writings of Paul contain the oldest biblical reference to the life and teachings of Jesus. His earliest epistles, those to the Thessalonians and Galatians, were written only about two decades after the death of Jesus. Before the close of the first quarter-century following that event the great apostle to the Gentiles completed his work and probably sealed it by martyrdom at Rome. If Paul did not himself stand among the crowds to whom Jesus spoke, he associated closely with his disciples and had ample opportunity, first as a zealous persecutor and later as a devoted follower, to learn from the lips of eye-witnesses the details regarding his Master's life and work. The facts which Paul preserved are, therefore, profoundly significant; yet they are also exceedingly meagre. The reason for his comparative silence regarding the events of Jesus' life is obvious. Paul, as he frequently states (II Thess. 2⁵ I Cor. 11²³ 15³), was writing to those who had already been instructed in the main facts of the Christian faith. In his letters he was also dealing with specific problems that had arisen in the churches. He, in common with those to whom he wrote, was looking for the speedy return of Christ. Hence his gaze was fixed on the present and future rather than on the past. Above all, he was interested in the death and resurrection of Jesus as Messiah and Saviour, rather than in the details of his life and teaching.

Paul speaks of Jesus as born of the seed of David (Rom. 1³), under the Mosaic law (Gal. 4⁴). He also describes Jesus as meek and gentle (II Cor. 10¹) and as a man who knew no sin (II Cor. 5²¹). He refers to Jesus' preaching ministry (Gal. 1⁹ Rom. 15⁸) and to his sending out apostles (Gal. 2⁸ I Cor. 9¹⁴). He declares that he lived the life of obedience (Rom. 5¹⁹), for the sake of mankind endured poverty (II Cor. 8⁹), and suffered the death of the cross (Rom. 4²⁵ 5⁶⁻¹⁰). Paul refers repeatedly to Jesus' crucifixion. In I Corinthians 11²⁰⁻²⁶ he gives a detailed account of the Lord's supper, and in 15¹⁻⁸ is found the oldest and clearest description of the visions of the risen Jesus that came to his disciples after his death. The centre of Paul's interest is shown by the fact that he refers to the resurrection thirteen times. These scattered references in Paul's epistles represent the oldest New Testament records of the life and teachings of Jesus. While this earliest gospel is exceedingly brief, it confirms the more important incidents reported in the gospel histories.

XI. The Value of the Extra-Gospel Testimony. If our four canonical gospels had been lost, the main facts regarding Jesus' life would nevertheless have been preserved: his serene trust in God, his kindliness and friendliness toward all men, his life of poverty and service, his dauntless spirit, his work as a teacher, the date and manner of his death, the rapid increase of his followers, and their devotion, which, like that of their Master, flinched not in the presence of death. The extra-gospel sources tell also of the beliefs, as well as the spirit, which Jesus inculcated in the minds of his followers. This testimony is not that of one but of many groups of writers. Supercilious Roman historians, hostile Jews, ardent apostles like Paul, learned Church Fathers, and heroic martyrs all unite in testifying to the historical certainty of Jesus' life and work. This army of witnesses is reinforced by the innumerable heroes and heroines of the commonplace who, touched by the spirit of Jesus, bear uncontrovertible testimony to the potency of his personality and ideals. In establishing the historicity of Jesus and in conforming the data underlying the New Testament records, the testimony of these many Roman, Jewish, and Christian witnesses is invaluable; but the fact remains that, beyond one or two clearly authentic sayings, they add practically nothing to what is found in the canonical gospels. Evidently the New Testament gospel writers garnered the field so thoroughly that no important gleanings were left. In the writings of the second and following centuries pious imagination or dogmatic philosophizing vainly sought to supply what memory had failed to retain. For the historical details of Jesus' life and teaching we must turn to the New Testament gospels, and especially to the older records embodied in the first three, as our chief and practically only sources.

II

THE CONTENTS AND CHARACTERISTICS OF THE FOUR GOSPELS

1. **The Contents of the Gospel of Mark.** The Gospel of Mark is to-day recognized by all authorities as the oldest of the gospels. It is pre-eminently the narrative gospel. It falls naturally into three great divisions, with an introduction and an epilogue. Inasmuch as it furnishes the chronological framework for both Matthew and Luke, a detailed analysis of its contents is essential to a use of the gospel data in reconstructing the life and teachings of Jesus. The following outline suggests its structure:

Introduction: Summary of John's work and of Jesus' baptism and temptation, 1^{1-13}.

A. Jesus' Work in Galilee, $1^{14}-7^{23}$.
    1. Beginning of his work of teaching and healing, 1^{14-45}.
    2. Growth of pharisaic opposition, $2^{1}-3^{6}$.
    3. The call of the Twelve, 3^{7-35}.
    4. The teaching by parables, 4^{1-34}.
    5. Confirmation of his authority by miracles, $4^{35}-6^{13}$.
    6. The fate of John the Baptist, 6^{14-29}.
    7. Miracles illustrating Jesus' power over nature, 6^{30-56}.
    8. Conflict with the scribes and Pharisees, 7^{1-23}.

B. Jesus in Retirement with His Disciples, $7^{24}-10^{52}$.
    1. Miracles of healing, $7^{24}-8^{26}$.
    2. Revelation of his coming death, $8^{27}-9^{32}$.
    3. Glory through service, 9^{33-50}.
    4. The spirit of renunciation, 10^{1-31}.
    5. The rewards in the kingdom, 10^{32-45}.
    6. Healing the blind beggar at Jericho, 10^{46-52}.

C. The Closing Scenes at Jerusalem, $11^{1}-16^{8}$.
    1. Assertion of his God-given authority, $11^{1}-12^{12}$.
    2. Teaching in the temple, 12^{13-44}.
    3. Warning of coming judgment, 13.
    4. Events leading to the betrayal, 14^{1-52}.

    5. Peter's denial, 14$^{53,\ 54,\ 65-72}$.

    6. Jesus' trial and crucifixion, 14$^{55-64}$ 15$^{1-39}$.

    7. The burial and the empty tomb, 15^{40}–16^{8}.

Epilogue: The resurrection experiences, 16$^{9-20}$.

II. Its Plan. The general order of the Gospel of Mark is both chronological and geographical. The chronological data, however, are exceedingly vague (cf. 2^{1} 8^{1}, "in those days"). They become definite only in the detailed account of passion week. Within the main subdivisions the narratives appear to be arranged, not chronologically, but topically, so as to conserve the evangelist's purpose. A detailed study of the contents of this gospel confirms the conclusion that when it was written the exact sequence of many of the events in the life of Jesus was so far forgotten that to record them in the exact order in which they occurred was no longer possible.

The brevity of Mark's introduction reveals his purpose. His interest centred in the active work of Jesus rather than in his childhood and in the experiences that led up to his public activity. In this respect Mark is typical of the first generation of Christians. Unfortunately the original conclusion of the gospel has been lost, for it breaks off abruptly in the middle of the eighth verse of the sixteenth chapter. The present epilogue in 16$^{9-20}$ is apparently a later addition. Its vocabulary, literary style, and representation are all different from those found in the body of the gospel. It is in reality a composite of verses taken from other gospels. By an early tradition it was attributed to the presbyter Aristion, who lived about 110 A.D.

Jesus' statement in Mark 14^{28} that "after I am raised up I will go before you into Galilee" implies that the original conclusion told of Jesus' appearance in Galilee. It was probably lost either through an accident that befell the last leaf of the manuscript or else because its contents were not in accord with the tradition which later won the chief place in the teaching of the church.

III. Its Characteristics. The characteristics of the Gospel of Mark are clearly defined and throw much light upon its purpose as well as upon its historical value. It is the most vivid of all the gospels. The different incidents are portrayed with great detail and rich local color. The words are chosen because of their strength and fitness to portray action. The present tense is frequently employed and is often abruptly introduced into the context where Greek and English usage demand the past tense. The constant recurrence of the adverb "immediately" adds greatly to the vividness of the narratives.

CHARACTERISTICS OF THE FOUR GOSPELS

Simplicity and clearness are also characteristic of the gospel. It con-tains few involved sentences. "And" is the common connection, as in the simple narratives of the Old Testament. The presence of certain Latin words and idioms and the author's habit of constantly reckoning in Roman money impart to it a Roman atmosphere. The author often uses colloquialisms and words drawn from the common speech of the people, for which the cultured Luke, when he quotes from the Gospel of Mark, substitutes more classic synonyms. In many cases the syntactical constructions are loose and the antecedents indefinite. These characteristics all suggest that Mark gathered his material from popular sources and from the lips of those who were in close touch with the humblest classes in the early Christian community.

The spirit of this gospel is modest and joyous. It portrays clearly the humanity of Jesus. Thus in 6^5 it states that he was unable to do any mighty works in his home town. It records the many early morning hours spent by Jesus in earnest prayer (1^{35}). It tells how his family and friends attempted to put a stop to his activity, thinking him rash, if not insane ($3^{20, 21}$). In its accounts of certain miracles, as, for example, that of the healing of the blind man (8^{24-26}), the different stages in the cures are described. Nowhere else in Christian literature do we find more interesting and illuminating flash-light pictures of the real Jesus, whose sincerity and charm were irresistible. These artless reminiscences, far better than a formal biography, introduce us to the energetic, tireless worker, devoted to his God-given task of helping men to find their true goal in life. He is fond of children (9^{36} 10^{16}); he loves the rich young man (10^{21}), as well as the shepherdless masses. He is stirred by indignation and torn by grief (3^5). He yearns for the intelligent appreciation of his friends (8^{27-29}). He is profoundly distressed by the evidences of their disloyalty (14^{34-37}). Through these earliest pictures we look upon the face of Jesus and realize why he drew all men to himself.

IV. **The Aim of the Gospel.** The Gospel of Mark is more than a mere historical record. Like all the gospels it was written for a practical, evangelistic purpose. That purpose was evidently to provide a gospel for the guidance and use of the early Christians and especially of the missionaries, as they went forth, like Paul, to proclaim Jesus to the Gentile world. For this reason the author rarely refers to the Old Testament. Whenever he introduces references to Jewish customs or Jewish places he explains them. As in the sermon attributed to the apostle Peter in Acts 10, its aim was to lead the heathen to a faith in

Jesus by showing how "God anointed Jesus of Nazareth with the Holy Spirit and power and how he went about doing good and curing all oppressed by the devil: for God was with him" (Acts 10³⁸). This practical purpose explains the prominence given to miracles and especially to the cure of demoniacs. The method of the author was objective and dramatic. He sought to kindle faith and to lead the Gentiles into loyal discipleship, not so much by telling what Jesus taught as by vividly portraying what he was and by recounting the miracles which he performed. This hand-book for the use of early Christian evangelists was well fitted to inspire personal devotion and loyalty to that marvellous healer of men's bodies and minds and souls.

V. **The Contents of Matthew.** The German scholar Jülicher has called the Gospel of Matthew "the most important book ever written." In the early church it was certainly the most influential and popular of all the gospels. Its contents fall into five main divisions:

A. **Introduction,** 1¹⁻⁴¹⁷.
    1. Birth and childhood of Jesus, 1, 2.
    2. The work of John the Baptist, 3¹⁻¹².
    3. Jesus' baptism and temptation, 3¹³⁻⁴¹⁷.

B. **Jesus' Work in Galilee,** 4¹⁸⁻¹³⁵³.
    1. His teachings, 4¹⁸⁻⁷²⁹.
    2. His miracles, 8¹⁻⁹³⁵.
    3. Call and mission of the Twelve, 9³⁶⁻¹⁰⁴².
    4. Effects of his work upon the people, upon the Pharisees, and upon his methods, 11–13.

C. **The Crisis and Rejection in Galilee, and the Founding of the Church,** 14–18.

D. **Activity in Perea and Jerusalem,** 19–25.

E. **The Passion and Resurrection,** 26–28.

The general plan of the Gospel of Matthew is closely parallel to that of Mark; but there is a strong tendency to arrange the material within the divisions in groups of five or ten. Thus the section 8¹⁻⁹²⁵ contains ten examples of Jesus' work of healing. The great body of his teachings is massed in the "Sermon on the Mount" (5–7), and is classified logically rather than chronologically. In contrast to the order and plan of Mark the teachings are assigned the central place, and the narratives are introduced simply to give them an effective setting.

VI. **Characteristics and Aims of the Gospel of Matthew.** In Mark Jesus is presented as the Healer and Friend of men; in Matthew he is pre-eminently the great Teacher. In contrast to the Gospel of

Mark, the atmosphere of Matthew is distinctly Jewish. References to Jewish customs and Palestinian places are common and the interpretation of their meaning for Gentile readers is rare. The one custom that is interpreted, that of releasing a prisoner at the Passover, was Roman rather than Jewish in its origin. This gospel contains over forty quotations from the Old Testament. Apparently one of the chief aims of the author was to demonstrate that Jesus and his work were the fulfilment of the older messianic prophecies. These facts imply that the author had Jewish Christians primarily in mind. There is also a marked tendency to idealize the disciples and to ignore the incidents that present them in an unfavorable light. The passages in the Gospel of Mark which illustrate Jesus' humanity are, as a rule, not quoted. Jesus' prophetic and miraculous power is emphasized. The later church and its problems are far more prominent. There is also a strong tendency to adjust the teachings of Jesus to the needs and customs of the growing Christian communities; but the spirit of the gospel is thoroughly broad and catholic. Jesus' mission is by no means limited to the Jews. Their opposition and rejection of the great Teacher are denounced in strongest terms. What the Jews have rejected is here offered to all mankind. The lessons learned by the Christian church during the half-century following the death of Jesus are woven into the gospel. The word "church" is here found on the lips of Jesus (16[18] 18[17]), even though it would seem that the term was first used long after his death.

In the light of these characteristics it is clear that the Gospel of Matthew aims primarily to prove that Jesus is the promised Messiah, not only of the Jews, but of all the human race, and to establish the fact that his kingdom is universal. The contents and arrangement of the material also indicate that the author was seeking to present the teachings of Jesus fully and systematically in order to provide for the use of converts and the instruction of the young a practical manual of Christian faith and conduct.

VII. **The Contents of the Gospel of Luke.** Renan has called the Gospel of Luke "the most beautiful book ever written," and few will question this statement. Its literary unity is more complete than that of the other gospels. The following is its general plan:

A. **Introduction:** Birth and childhood of Jesus and the work of John the Baptist, 1–3.

B. **The Beginnings of Jesus' Work,** 4–6.

C. **The Height of His Galilean Activity,** 7[1]–9[50].

D. Incidents and Teachings in Connection with His **Journey to Jerusalem**, 9^{51}–19^{27}.

E. **Activity at Jerusalem**, 19^{28}–21^{38}.

F. **The Passion and the Resurrection**, 22–24.

Luke follows in general the order of Mark, but adds the account of the birth and boyhood of Jesus. He omits, for the most part, Mark's account of Jesus' period of retirement and inserts instead a large group of teachings, chiefly parables, which are peculiar to this gospel. He also distributes the teaching material, adjusting it to the historical setting. Thus he combines in balanced proportion the narratives which are primarily emphasized in Mark with the teachings which are made central in Matthew.

VIII. **Characteristics of This Gospel.** The Gospel of Luke contains from beginning to end illustrations of its author's finished literary style. The quotations from the simple Gospel of Mark are often recast and replaced by classic Greek words and phrases. The sentences are balanced and closely knit. The vocabulary is large and rich. Many medical terms and phrases are used. The style is fluent and refined. At times the language is hyperbolic and is thus rendered exceedingly impressive. Striking contrasts abound, for example, between light and darkness, the rich and poor, God and Satan. Its tone is supremely joyous and happy. Prayer and praise resound throughout it from beginning to end. Children frequently appear on its pages. It is pre-eminently the gospel for the young. Women occupy an especially prominent place in this gospel. Its opening chapters contain the songs of Elizabeth and Mary. It alone introduces us to the home of Mary and Martha and to the ministering women who, like the disciples, shared in Jesus' work. It recounts the parable of the quest of the housewife for the lost piece of money and the story of the healing of a sadly afflicted woman.

It is also the gospel of repentance. Forgiveness and faith are characteristic notes. The poor and afflicted are frequently mentioned. The humanitarian motive is strong. The author's interest is with the needy rather than with the rich and powerful. Luke alone has preserved the wonderful parables of Dives and Lazarus and of the good Samaritan. It is evident that when the book was written the narrow Jewish bonds had been broken and the gospel message had become universal. Thus the Gospel of Luke adds many beautiful and essential elements to the portrait of Jesus. It reveals, as does no other gospel, his love for the poor and needy, and emphasizes those broad so-

CHARACTERISTICS OF THE FOUR GOSPELS

cial principles which give his teachings their pre-eminent value in this modern social age.

IX. **Aim of the Gospel.** The author of the Gospel of Luke, with the truly scientific spirit that characterizes his writings, has clearly stated in his opening paragraph the motive that impelled him to write. "Inasmuch as many have undertaken to compose a narrative, upon the themes that are a matter of conviction among us; even as they were transmitted to us by those who were eye-witnesses and servants of the word from the beginning, I also determined, as I have accurately investigated all from the very first, that I would write for you in order, most excellent Theophilus, to enable you to understand the reliable truth about the affairs of which you have been informed." The contents of the gospel confirms the author's statement of his aim. It was designed to give a systematic and complete picture of both the life and teachings of Jesus. It aimed to point out thereby to all men the way of life; for the needs of Luke's Greek friend Theophilus were felt by every one who had been touched by the spirit and ideals of Jesus. The aim of the gospel was, therefore, in a true sense historical; but in common with all the gospels it was primarily religious and practical.

X. **The Contents of the Fourth Gospel.** In passing from the first three gospels to the fourth, a marked change in plan as well as atmosphere is at once recognized. This gospel contains three great divisions, with a brief introduction and an appendix:

Introduction: The word Incarnate, 1^{1-18}.

A. **Jesus' Activity in Galilee, Judea, and Samaria,** 1^{19}–6^{71}.

B. **His Work in Judea and Perea,** 7–12.

C. **The Final Scenes at Jerusalem, and His Self=Revelation to His Disciples,** 13–20.

Appendix, 21.

The Fourth Gospel lacks the literary as well as the general chronological unity of the first three. The connection at many points is suddenly broken. For example, a more satisfactory logical order is obtained if chapter 7^{15-24} is placed after 5, and 15 and 16 after 13^{31a}. It is possible that, in the process of transmission, these sections have been disarranged and that the order suggested is the original. While there are evidences of a general chronological plan, the detailed incidents and teachings are grouped so as to conserve the practical aims of the gospel. Seven great signs or miracles are recorded, beginning with the changing of the water into wine at Cana and concluding with the raising

16

of Lazarus. These signs are introduced to illustrate the main teachings of the gospel. Thus, for example, the feeding of the five thousand introduces the teaching that Jesus is the bread of life. The raising of Lazarus is the prelude to the memorable utterance, "I am the resurrection and life." The Fourth Gospel presents universal principles and truths rather than mere historical facts. Different witnesses to the character and claims of Jesus are marshalled in their turn: John the Baptist, the disciples, the multitudes, the typical miracles, Jesus' own declarations, and last of all the account of his resurrection.

XI. **Characteristics and Aim of the Fourth Gospel.** The Gospel of John is in diction the simplest but in thought the profoundest of all the gospels. Its vocabulary is even more limited than that of Mark. Only a few of the most prominent connectives are employed; and yet in this seemingly most lucid of gospels are found the deepest and most complex theological doctrines. The same teachings are presented with the aid of a great variety of allegorical figures, as, for example, the bread of life, the living water, and the vine. The thought is philosophical, although the illustrations are concrete, and the figures are exceedingly vivid. The tone of the gospel is richly spiritual. It is obviously the product of mature meditation and wide experience. The point of view is that of the later church. The chief themes are the great problems which, near the end of the first century, stirred it to its very foundations. To meet these problems and to deliver the church from the perils which beset it the author of the Fourth Gospel wrote. His purpose was also personal and practical. He definitely states his aim in 20[31]. It is "that you may believe that Jesus is the Messiah the Son of God, and that believing you may have life in his name." In the author's mind, belief is the chief essential for man's salvation, and the two essential beliefs are that Jesus was the Messiah and that he was in a unique sense the Son of God. All the details of this marvellous gospel are shaped to prove this thesis. Its object, therefore, is not to give, as do the first three gospels, a picture of what Jesus actually did and taught, but rather to substantiate the beliefs regarding him that were held by a growing body of Christians and so to reveal the soul of the Master that men may find their true life through him.

XII. **A Comparison of the Four Gospels.** There are certain characteristics common to the four gospels. The first is their absolute sincerity. The second is their intense devotion to him whose life and teaching they seek to record or to interpret. The third is their recognition of his divine character and authority. They were all inspired by intensely practical aims and were intended to meet certain definite needs, which arose in the early history of the church.

Each has its own marked individuality. The brief, simple, vivid narrative of Mark may be described as the popular, evangelistic gospel. It presents those dramatic personal facts in which the common people were intensely interested. It relegated to the background detailed teachings and doctrinal questions which concerned only the learned. Matthew is pre-eminently the teaching gospel. The prominence given to the teachings of Jesus and the topical arrangement of its material made it the manual that was most widely used in the early church for instruction regarding the work and teachings of Jesus. Luke is the humanitarian, social gospel. It makes sharp distinctions between the rich and the poor, the ruling classes and the masses. It defines the fundamental obligations of the individual, not only to God, but to his fellow-men, in terms of love and sympathy and service. It is the gospel which presents most clearly Jesus' teachings regarding the way along which society must proceed in order to solve its social problems. The Fourth Gospel is the doctrinal gospel, for its avowed and dominant aim throughout is to establish the fundamental doctrines of the early church and to interpret in universal, philosophical terms the significance of Jesus' character and work.

Although in many details the gospels contradict, yet, as a whole, they richly supplement each other. The character and work of Jesus were so many-sided that in order to interpret and appreciate them it is necessary to consider them from many different points of view. Each gospel represents a different and indispensable point of approach. The task of the historian is first to determine the point of view of each of these witnesses and then to estimate and combine their testimony so as to gain a true impression of what Jesus actually was and did and taught. That the gospels contain the data for the satisfactory accomplishment of this most vital of all tasks is the conviction of all constructive biblical scholars.

III

THE WRITTEN SOURCES UNDERLYING THE GOSPELS

I. The Relation of the First Three Gospels to Each Other.
The first and most important step in the study of the life and teachings
of Jesus is to distinguish the older historical sources incorporated in the
gospels, to determine their date and point of view, and to estimate
their historical value. In accomplishing this task two guides are available: (1) A careful study of the contents of the gospels and of their relation to each other. (2) The testimony of early Christian tradition.
In many ways this problem is similar to that presented by the earlier
historical books of the Old Testament, only it is more complex. The
same historical and literary methods are applicable and lead to similar
constructive results.

The comparison of the contents of the first three gospels has shown
that they agree in the general order of events. Even such a disconnected incident as the healing of the paralytic appears in the same
relative position in all three gospels. Matthew, on the whole, shows
greater freedom in departing from the order of Mark than does Luke,
but in both the first and third gospels these divergences are rare. It
is only in chapters 22 and 23, which contain the account of passion
week, that Luke departs radically from the narrative of Mark. Material not found in Mark is usually grouped together in Matthew and
Luke, as, for example, in Matthew 5–7 or Luke 6^2–8^3 or 9^{51}–18^{14}.

II. Their Agreement in Substance and in Verbal Detail. A
comparison of the first three gospels shows that they agree not only
in general order but also in contents. Three-fourths of the gospel of
Matthew is practically a duplicate of Mark, and eleven-twelfths of the
entire Gospel of Mark is reproduced in the same or in a slightly variant
form in Matthew. With three or four exceptions, Matthew quotes,
either wholly or in part, every narrative found in Mark. If the Gospel of Mark were to be lost, nearly three-fourths of it could be found
in or reconstructed from Luke. The material found in Mark but not
in Matthew or Luke represents less than an ordinary chapter. This

original Marcan material includes the parable of the seed of corn in 4^{26-29} and the reference to the flight of the young man at the time of Jesus' arrest ($14^{51, 52}$). Furthermore, the Gospel of Matthew has practically no narrative material not found in Mark, except the stories of infancy, the account of the healing of the centurion's servant, and of the way in which Jesus paid the temple tax (17^{24-27}), and certain minor incidents in his trial before Pilate. Luke, on the other hand, has considerable narrative material not found in the other gospels. It includes such stories as the raising of the widow's son at Nain (7^{11-17}), the anointing of Jesus' feet (7^{35-50}), Jesus at the home of Mary and Martha (10^{38-42}), the healing of the crooked woman (13^{10-17}), the account of the ten lepers (17^{11-19}), the conversion of Zaccheus (19^{1-10}), Jesus before Herod (23^{6-12}), the penitent thief (23^{39-43}), and the journey to Emmaus (24^{13-35}).

The gospels of Matthew and Luke contain an exceedingly large number of the sayings of Jesus which are not found in Mark. In many passages the agreement both in narratives and teachings between these two gospels amounts to practical identity (cf., e. g., Matt. 11^{2-19} and Luke 7^{18-35}). This verbal agreement extends through verses and sometimes through long paragraphs. Peculiar words and phrases and even the detailed order of sentences are thus reproduced, proving beyond doubt that the two gospel writers drew not from oral but from the same written sources. Frequently in one of the gospels, as, for example, Matthew, the parallel narrative found in Mark is condensed or expanded (cf., e. g., Mark 6^{14-29} Matt. 14^{3-12}). Luke as a rule recasts the material which he quotes from Mark or the teaching source more freely than does the author of Matthew. More rarely, one of the gospel writers combined a narrative found in Mark with a variant account of the same incident evidently taken from the teaching source common to Matthew and Luke (e. g., Matt. 10^{5-42} 23^{1-39}). In the Fourth Gospel, on the contrary, close parallels, such as are found between the first three gospels, are almost unknown. In a few cases the author of this gospel has freely paraphrased a story found in a preceding gospel, as, for example, the description of the feeding of the five thousand (cf. 6^{1-13}); but ordinarily the narratives and teachings of the Fourth Gospel are fundamentally different from those found in the first three.

III. **The Synoptic Problem and Its Solution.** These significant coincidences and variations between the different gospels are the basis of what is technically known as the synoptic problem. From the closing years of the eighteenth century the first three gospels, because of their striking similarity in order, contents, and point of view, have been known as the synoptic gospels. The energy and acumen of New Testament scholars during the past two centuries have been devoted to examining the coincidences and variations between the gospels with the practical purpose of determining their origin and relative historical value. Every verse and phrase has been subjected to the most careful study and comparison. While there is yet no general agreement regarding minor questions, in its significant aspects the synoptic problem may be said to have been practically solved. Without discussing the detailed evidence, we may accept two points as established: (1) The Gospel of Mark is the source from which Matthew and Luke derived their order of events and their common narrative material. The theory that Mark was derived from Matthew and Luke is no longer regarded as tenable, for both Matthew and Luke share in common with Mark certain material which is found there in a fuller and evidently the original form. Moreover, as has been noted, Mark contains certain narratives not found in either Matthew or Luke. (2) For their accounts of the work of John the Baptist, the baptism and temptation of Jesus, and for most of their reports of Jesus' teachings, Matthew and Luke drew from a common written source or sources no longer extant (ordinarily designated as Q, from the German word, *Quelle, source, cf.* VII).

IV. **The Important Variations of the Fourth Gospel.** The wide and fundamental variations of the Fourth Gospel present another exceedingly complex but vital problem. At certain points this gospel agrees with the other three, especially in regard to Jesus' trial, crucifixion and resurrection; but in general it follows its own order and presents a radically different picture of Jesus' life and teachings. The chief scene of Jesus' activity is not Galilee, but Judea and Samaria. The proclamation of his messiahship and his cleansing of the temple are placed, not at the end, but at the beginning of his work ($1^{41-45, 49}$ 2^{13-20}). His relation to the Jews is represented as being from the first one of bitter opposition and denunciation. Even the miracles differ widely from those recorded in the first three gospels. The changing of water into wine in Cana of Galilee and the raising of Lazarus to life after he had been four days in the grave are nowhere mentioned in the synoptic gospels, even though the latter miracle falls in the period which they record most fully. The Fourth Gospel adds many details, as, for example, Jesus' words to Judas at the last supper (13^{27}) and his proclamation of his kingly authority before Pilate (18^{33-37}). Like the Gospel of Matthew, it omits most of the narratives which illustrate his human traits.

The literary form of Jesus' teachings in the Gospel of John is also very different. The same vocabulary and idioms appear throughout and strongly indicate that the teachings, as well as the narratives, come from the same pen. Long discourses and allegories, as, for example, that of the vine and branches, replace the brief epigrammatic proverbs, paradoxes, and parables of the synoptic gospels. In general, Jesus is represented as emphasizing, not the character of the kingdom of God and how it can be entered, but his own personal claims and men's obligations to him. The earlier doctrine of repentance almost entirely disappears, and individual salvation is defined primarily as a recognition of Jesus' divine authority. Paul's doctrine of the pre-existence of Jesus and of his right of divine homage takes the place of the simple synoptic portrait of the divinely gifted Teacher and Friend of sinners who knew and satisfied men's deepest spiritual and moral needs. These wide variations indicate that, while the Fourth Gospel is of the greatest importance in interpreting the broad significance of Jesus' work and in revealing the point of view and beliefs of the early Christian church, it is only of secondary and supplemental historical value. The one important exception is the priceless story of Jesus' treatment of the woman taken in adultery, which in certain versions is appended to John 7. Otherwise the oldest and chief historical sources for both the life and the teachings of Jesus are found in the synoptic gospels.

V. The Early Tradition Regarding the Origin of the Gospel of Mark. Inasmuch as both Matthew and Luke depend chiefly upon Mark for their narrative material, the origin and history of the Second Gospel are questions of great importance. Papias, the bishop of Hierapolis, in Phrygia, who wrote between 130 and 160 A.D., states that "Mark, who was Peter's interpreter, wrote down accurately, though not in order, all that he recollected of what Christ had said or done. For he was not a hearer of the Lord, nor a follower of his; he followed Peter, as I have said, on a later date, and Peter adapted his instructions to practical needs, without any attempt to give the Lord's word systematically. So that Mark was not wrong in writing down some things in this way from memory, for his one concern was not to omit or falsify anything he had heard." The Mark to whom Papias refers was John Mark, the son of Mary of Jerusalem and a nephew of Paul's missionary companion Barnabas. He must have been a young man at the time of Jesus' death. The fact that the Gospel of Mark alone preserves the obscure statement regarding the young man who fled away on the occasion of Jesus' arrest ($14^{51, 52}$) suggests, although it does not absolutely prove, that the one thus introduced was John Mark. In any case, he appears to have been little more than a boy when the events which he records transpired. He therefore cannot properly be counted as an eye-witness, although it is not improbable that certain details regarding the passion week are the report of his own personal observation.

Mark accompanied Paul and Barnabas on their first missionary journey (Acts 13^5). Later, Paul refused to take him with him, although afterward he was reconciled to him. Colossians 4^{10} refers to a visit Mark was soon to make to the Colossian church. These few historical facts indicate that Mark, though a Jew by birth, was intimately acquainted with the Gentile world. He fully understood the problems and need of the Christians outside Palestine and the necessity of placing in the hands of the missionaries of the second generation a popular, vivid account of those incidents which illustrated Jesus' character and method. Mark's residence in Jerusalem also brought him into close personal touch with Peter and the other apostles; in fact, his home from the first was an important meeting-place of the early Christian community. Hence, of all the Christians of his generation, Mark was in many ways uniquely fitted to write the gospel which bears his name.

VI. **Mark's Sources.** The contents of Mark's gospel in general substantiates Papias's statement that it was based on the memory of incidents related by Peter, although it contains additional matter. It is made up of loosely connected memorabilia. Its strong Aramaic flavor is probably derived from the original language which Jesus used and in which Peter doubtless preached to his Jewish hearers. It contains precisely the material which a popular preacher like Peter would naturally use to impress the people. Further evidence that Peter speaks through this gospel is the fact that up to 8^{27} (where he comes to the forefront) the narrative is disjointed; after that the arrangement is systematic. In the list of disciples found in 3^{16-19} Peter is mentioned first, even though the important sons of Zebedee are introduced immediately after him, and Peter's brother Andrew is given fourth place, indicating that the arrangement is not accidental but deliberate. Peter is unquestionably, next to Jesus, the most important character in the book, and details are recorded which at first were only known to him. The frankness with which his faults and mistakes are set forth is probably due to his spirit of self-effacement—a characteristic that we naturally expect to find in a true disciple of Jesus. It is not entirely clear whether the present order in the Gospel of Mark is due to Mark or to a later editor. At first glance Papias's statement suggests that the arrangement is not the work of Mark. But Papias evidently had in mind the order of the teachings in the Gospels of Matthew and Luke, which were regarded much more highly by the early church; for he refers to the lack of systematic arrangement of words rather than of incidents. It is probable, therefore, that the gospel, practically in its present order, comes from Mark, and that in this form it was used by the authors of Matthew and Luke.

The clearest evidence of editorial work is in 13. The nucleus of this chapter seems to have been certain original utterances of Jesus regarding the fate of Jerusalem; but the passage as a whole voices the popular beliefs regarding Jesus' second coming that were current in the later church (cf., e.g., II Thess. 2). A discourse extending through a long chapter is without parallel elsewhere in the Gospel of Mark. The language of the passage is also different from that of the rest of the gospel. The statement in 13[14]: "Let him who reads understand," implies that this apocalypse was in written form when it was introduced into the Second Gospel. It was apparently intended to restrain the fanatical hopes of the Christians in the troublesome days that marked the destruction of Jerusalem and the scattering of the Jewish race in 70 A.D.

In addition to the information derived from Peter, Mark appears to have incorporated some of the doctrines of Paul. An educated Christian, living after the middle of the first Christian century, and closely associated with the great apostle to the Gentiles, could not fail to feel the influence of that master of men. Yet in comparison with the Fourth Gospel, the Gospel of Mark contains surprisingly few traces of Paul's peculiar ideas and phrases. Its broad universalism is characteristic of the church of the day. The earliest apostles, as well as Paul, were interested in the problem presented by Jesus' crucifixion and found in his resurrection its satisfactory solution. Jesus' humanity, as well as his divine character, is fully recognized by Mark; but there is no trace of Paul's doctrine of Jesus' pre-existence. Withal, the influence of Paul is here exceedingly small compared with that of Peter and the early disciples. Thanks to Mark's concrete rather than philosophical type of mind and his early associations, he has given us a marvellously faithful record of that unique impression which Jesus made upon his first disciples.

There are indications that he was also acquainted with a part, if not all, of the common teaching source (Q), quoted by both Matthew and Luke. In the account of John the Baptist, of Jesus' temptation, of his commission to his disciples, and in the allusions to other incidents and teachings, Mark shows a familiarity with a fuller narrative and teaching source than his actual quotations indicate. Thus, for example, he simply epitomizes Jesus' directions to his disciples which are quoted in fuller form from their common teaching source by Matthew and Luke (cf., § CXXVIII[vi]).

VII. The Earliest Record of Jesus' Work and Teachings (Q).

The exact extent of the older source that lies back of the synoptic gospels and constitutes one of the two chief foundations of Matthew and Luke is still an open question. There are certain data that may be interpreted as evidence that it originally consisted not of one but of several independent written documents. Furthermore, it is not clear whether or not a majority of the teachings of Jesus found only in Matthew or in Luke come from this common source. Their use of Mark indicates that neither of them quoted all of their available material, and that some themes interested one gospel writer more than another. The analogy is still further instructive. As a rule, Matthew quotes Mark more literally than does Luke, while Luke is more careful to preserve the original order of incidents. The same habits probably governed them in their use of the common teaching source or sources. Whether or not this common material was found in one or in two or more originally independent documents is comparatively unimportant, It possesses literary, doctrinal, and historical characteristics which indicate that all was written from the same general point of view, if not by the same hand, so that it may be treated as one collection of Jesus' sayings. Furthermore, if Luke's order be accepted as representative of the original, these quotations together constitute a more or less closely knit literary unit; but it is practically impossible to reconstruct a writing simply from later citations.

The testimony of Papias confirms the internal evidence furnished by the gospels; for, after describing the work of Mark, he adds: "Now Matthew composed the sayings [of the Lord] in the Hebrew [Aramaic] language and every one interpreted them as he was able." The Matthew thus referred to is in all probability the disciple of Jesus who bore that name. Papias's statement implies that this early Aramaic gospel consisted chiefly of utterances of Jesus. The general character of the teaching material common to Matthew and Luke accords so well with this description that its identification with Matthew's original Aramaic collection of Jesus' sayings is reasonably certain. Minor errors, found in both Matthew and Luke and due to translation, indicate, however, that the authors of these gospels did not have the original Aramaic text but Greek translations of these sayings before them. Papias's statement, "Every one interpreted them as he was able," suggests such versions. These were probably larger than the original Matthean collection. In addition to the sayings of Jesus, this earliest source appears to have contained accounts of the work of John the Baptist, of Jesus' baptism and temptation, of the healing of the centurion's servant, and possibly of the feeding of the multitudes.

As in the case of Mark, the author of Matthew appears to have quoted the common teaching source more exactly and fully than did Luke. It is difficult to determine how many of the teachings peculiar to the Third Gospel were derived from this source, for Luke freely recasts his material and readjusts it to his aims and point of view. In any case the original collection was probably larger than the quotations indicate. Its great intrinsic value would, however, lead the gospel writers to neglect no important teaching, so that it is not impossible that we know it practically in its entirety.

VIII. Characteristics and Value of the Earliest Source. The literary characteristics of the sayings thus quoted are distinctive. Even though they are obscured by oral transmission and the exigencies of translation from a Semitic to an Aryan tongue, they undoubtedly introduce us, more nearly than do any other writings in the New Testament, to the leading characteristics of Jesus' style and thought. Here the poetic parallelism of the earlier prophets and sages reappears. The literary style is simple, concise, and direct. Dramatic contrasts abound. The figures are forcible and thought-compelling. They appeal to the reason, the feelings, and to the will. The geographical horizon is practically limited to Galilee. The point of view is distinctly Jewish; but the hypocrisy and unreasonable ceremonial demands of the Pharisees are sternly and uncompromisingly opposed. God's kingdom or rule, in the present as well as the future, in the human heart as well as in organized society, is made the goal for which every man should strive. Here the whole emphasis is placed, not on what later generations thought of the messenger, but on his message.

There are few traces of a nationalistic, apologetic, or ecclesiastical bias. The influence of Paul's pervasive thought has not touched it. Here it is that we gain the clearest insight into the purposes and ideals of Jesus. Although two decades may lie between the days when Jesus delivered his revolutionary message to the men of Galilee and the hour when one of his disciples attempted to commit it to writing; yet, by the aid of this oldest source, it is possible to hear his life-giving words as they fell from his lips; even as through the eyes of Peter and his faithful interpreter Mark, we may see the Friend of sinners healing the sick and teaching the eager crowds beside the Sea of Galilee.

IV

THE LITERARY HISTORY AND DATE OF THE GOSPELS

I. The Period of Oral Transmission. In the light of the preceding inductive study of the data, it is now possible to trace tentatively the history of the gospel records. There is no evidence that Jesus ever wrote down any of his teachings. Like the rabbis of his day, he depended entirely upon his disciples to preserve and transmit them. On their minds and characters he inscribed his priceless message to humanity. The ideal disciple of that age was "one quick to hear and slow to forget" (*Sayings of the Jewish Fathers*, 5¹⁸). Another favorite maxim of the scribes was "when a scholar of the scribes sits and forgets a word of his Mishna, they account him worthy of death" (*Sayings of the Fathers*, 3¹²). Jesus' personality and work were calculated to make an indelible impression upon the minds of his followers. His teachings were cast in a form both easy to understand and difficult to forget: the pointed proverb, the picturesque metaphor, the epigrammatic precept, the thought-provoking paradox, and the familiar parable. Justin Martyr, the earliest of the Church Fathers, truly declares: "Short and concise came words from Christ, for he was no sophist, but his word was a mighty work of God." Not only was the attitude of Jesus' disciples toward his teaching receptive, but these teachings were fixed in their memories by constant repetition as they went about teaching and preaching. With true intuitions the Christian church has recognized that the Spirit of God was at work in the minds of his followers helping them to retain and proclaim the truth (John 16¹³⁻¹⁵ 14²⁶).

There is every reason, therefore, to believe that during the two decades following the death of Jesus they retained a remarkably faithful impression of his life and teachings. While eye-witnesses survived who could tell of what they themselves had heard and seen, there was no need of writing. Those to whom the disciples spoke also had little acquaintance with books, while the widespread expectation of the speedy coming of Jesus left little incentive to write. That which the disciples orally transmitted included their reminiscences of the more important incidents in his public activity, disconnected teachings, and the stories that illustrated his teachings. To these were soon added the doctrines which rapidly gained acceptance in the early church.

The homely, personal incidents in Jesus' life were first forgotten. Of his ordinary intercourse with the people and with the disciples there are but a few priceless reminiscences. Most of these human touches, which are of especial interest to modern students, have largely faded from the portrait. A few have survived in Mark; but they have almost completely disappeared in the later gospels. But the great outstanding facts and the most important teachings were evidently transmitted during the two decades following the death of Jesus with marvellous vividness and detail.

II. Influences That Gave Rise to the Gospels. The impulse that produced the earliest gospels came from both within and without the church. The characteristics of these earliest gospels, as well as the conditions amidst which Christianity expanded, indicate that they were written to meet the growing need of records adapted to the instruction of the young and of newly converted Christians. The death of many of those who had themselves seen and heard Jesus led certain scholars of the second generation, as Luke plainly states in his preface, to collect from surviving eye-witnesses those facts and teachings which they were still able to recall. The needs of the missionaries and of the Greek-speaking Christians strengthened this tendency. While there is every reason to believe that Jesus and his disciples originally taught in Aramaic, by 60 A.D. a large proportion of his followers were either Gentiles or Jews who lived in Egypt and the other lands of the dispersion and so were unacquainted with that language. They therefore required records of Jesus' life and teachings translated into Greek. As early as 50 A.D. Paul began to write his epistles, and through them a large section of the early church became acquainted with the use and value of written records. This fact doubtless further intensified the demand for written gospels.

III. The Earliest Records. Between 50 and 65 A.D. the influences just considered became exceedingly strong. If Papias's statement that the apostle Matthew made an Aramaic collection of the sayings of Jesus be accepted, it may be dated a little before—certainly not long after 50 A.D. It was, therefore, practically contemporary with Paul's earliest writings. Whether or not Luke and the author of the present

Gospel of Matthew used the same translation of this older Aramaic source is uncertain, but the internal evidence favors the conclusion that the Greek version used by Luke was slightly different in detail, if not in quantity, from that known to the author of Matthew. Possibly Luke knew the earlier collection of the sayings of Jesus, simply as it had been incorporated in one or more of the fragmentary gospels to which he refers in his preface.

Mark's gospel must have been issued some time between 55 and 75 A.D. Ancient Christian tradition dates it after the death of Peter (64–65 A.D.) and confirms the evidence within the gospel that it was written at Rome. As has already been noted, the earlier collections of the sayings of Jesus, probably in their Aramaic form, were already in existence and known to Mark. If it was also accessible to his readers, many of Mark's significant omissions are at once explained. To Peter's reminiscences he doubtless added data drawn from his own observation and from the rapidly growing body of Christian traditions. That his gospel might be adapted to the growing needs of the church outside Palestine, he probably wrote in Greek, although the influence of his earlier Aramaic oral sources are evident at every point and have led some scholars to conclude that he must have written originally in Aramaic. The Christian apocalypse quoted in Mark 13 and Matthew 24 must have been written about a decade later, soon after the destruction of Jerusalem, for it reveals an intimate familiarity with that event. Many New Testament scholars hold that this apocalypse, and probably extracts from certain other written sources (e. g., Mark 7³¹–8²⁶) were added by Mark or a later editor of the gospels. At least the detailed allusions to the destruction of Jerusalem seem to indicate that the present Gospel of Mark was not completed until after 70 A.D. The memory of the great catastrophe was still fresh in the mind of its final reviser, so that there is every reason to believe that at least by 75 A.D. the gospel was current in its present form.

IV. The Gospels of Matthew and Luke. The obvious dependence of the Gospel of Matthew upon Mark in its final form indicates that it must have been completed after 70 A.D. In addition to copious quotations from Mark, it incorporated passages from the Christian apocalypse quoted in Mark 13. It also drew largely from the earlier collection of Jesus' sayings by the apostle Matthew. Not only the sayings which it shares with Luke, but also the majority of the teaching peculiar to it, probably came from this early source. This fact doubtless explains why the first gospel bears the name Matthew. Side by side with the waning current of direct oral tradition, which had been largely incorporated in the writings of Mark and the earlier collections of Jesus' teachings, there appeared an increasing volume of ecclesiastical tradition. This aims, on the authority of Jesus' teaching and example, to solve the new problems that confronted the Christian community, to establish the doctrines which were being widely accepted, and to reduce the principles laid down by the Master to definite rules of conduct (cf., e. g., Matt. 18[16-19]). From this same source the author of Matthew may have derived the stories of the infancy, which he tells in his own characteristic literary form. There will doubtless always be a difference of opinion as to how long a period these later additions represent. Fortunately the question is comparatively unimportant. The essential fact is that the heart of the gospel comes from Jesus' own generation. The Gospel of Matthew in its final form may, in the light of all the evidence, be dated between 75 and 80 A.D.

Contemporaneous with the original Gospel of Mark, that is, between 55 and 80 A.D., the early fragmentary gospels, to which Luke refers in his preface, must have been written. They appear to have contained both narrative and teaching material. Possibly the author of the Gospel of Matthew was acquainted with one or more of these shorter gospels. It is probable, if not practically certain, that Luke, as he implies in his preface, derived from them a large part of the narratives and teachings found in chapters 9[51]–18[14] of his gospel and peculiar to it.

Luke's quotations indicate that his main sources were the Greek version of the early sayings of Jesus and the Gospel of Mark. In addition, like Mark, he probably drew from the testimony of eye-witnesses and from popular oral traditions. His account of Jesus' birth, which stands at the beginning of his gospel, still retains the simple idioms and the poetic figures that characterized the speech and thought of the common people. Luke's dependence upon Mark, his possible acquaintance with the Gospel of Matthew, and his apparent familiarity with Josephus's writings are regarded by many as convincing evidence that he did not write his gospel before 80; although a recent writer (Harnack, *Neue Untersuchungen zur Apostelgeschichte*, 86) would date it as early as the sixth decade of the first century. A date about 80 A.D. on the whole best accords with the internal evidence. That Luke, the physician and friend of Paul, who later wrote the book of Acts as a sequel, is the author of this gospel is now established beyond reasonable doubt.

V. The Gospel of John. The author of the Gospel of John was acquainted with all three of the synoptic gospels, so that he must have written some time after 85 A.D. One of his chief sources is the teaching of the apostle Paul, whose influence was becoming ever stronger in the Christian church during the second half of the first century. Another source was the peculiar Græco-Roman philosophy that exerted a powerful influence upon the Christian church during the second and third centuries. This influence is revealed in the opening chapter, where Jesus is declared to be the incarnation of the Logos or Word of early Greek and Stoic philosophy. The problems with which the Fourth Gospel deals and the beliefs which it sets forth are those which filled the minds of the Christians of Alexandria and Ephesus during the last decade of the first century and the opening years of the second century.

Notwithstanding the Palestinian atmosphere, the geographical references, the intimate personal touches, and the implications that the author of the Fourth Gospel was an eye-witness of at least the closing events in Jesus' life, modern students find it increasingly difficult to hold, in the light of all the facts, that he was John, the son of Zebedee. Even those who maintain that he was, frankly confess that the fiery, ambitious "son of thunder," who figures in the gospel records, must have undergone such a fundamental transformation and have drunk so deeply at the fountain of Greek philosophy that he was in every sense another man. The evidence is also becoming cumulative that John, the son of Zebedee, early met a martyr's death. This event is attested by the prophecy attributed to Jesus in Mark 10[39] (before 75 B.C., *cf.* Matt. 20[23]). Papias also states clearly that "John was killed by the Jews, thus plainly fulfilling, along with his brother, the prophecy of Christ concerning him." This testimony has been still further confirmed by the recently discovered Chronicle of Philip Sidetes, which asserts that "Papias, in his second book, says that John the Divine and James, his brother, were killed by the Jews." In the earliest church calendars John and James are also commemorated as martyrs. The ecclesiastical tradition that John, the son of Zebedee, lived to an old age, seems to have arisen because he was confused with John the Presbyter whom Papias mentions in connection with the son of Zebedee and other prominent apostles. This confusion may also explain the origin of the corresponding tradition, of which there is no trace earlier than the second half of the second century, that John, the son of Zebedee, was the author of the Fourth Gospel. The prominence of John

SOURCES AND APPROXIMATE DATES OF THE GOSPELS

A.D.	Rome	JESUS' LIFE AND DEATH		IMPORTANT EVENTS
30	Tiberius	PETER'S T E S T I M O N Y		18-36 Caiaphas High Priest 26-36 Pontius Pilate procurator 20-42 Literary activity of Philo 37 Banishment of Herod Antipas 38 Persecution of Jews at Alexandria
40	Caligula / 37 41 Claudius			41-44 Reign of Herod Agrippa I. 44 Rebellion led by Theudas
50	54	PAUL'S E P I S T L E S	MATTHEW'S COLLECTION OF THE SAYINGS OF JESUS (Q) GREEK VERSION OF SAYINGS	50 Jews banished from Rome 50-60 Paul's missionary work 50-100 Agrippa II. 52-66 Rebellions in Palestine
60	Nero		BRIEF GOSPELS GREEK VERSION OF SAYINGS	64 Burning of Rome Nero's persecution of Christians 66 Jews declare war against Rome
70	68 69 Vespasian	GOSPEL OF MARK GOSPEL OF MATTHEW		70 Jerusalem and Temple destroyed 70-80 Building of Colosseum 75-79 Josephus' Jewish War
80	79 Titus 81 Domitian	GOSPEL OF LUKE		80 Founding Rabbinical School at Jamnia
90		GOSPEL OF JOHN		90 Synod at Jamnia and the completion of O.T. canon 93 Josephus' Antiquities 95 Persecution of Christians at Rome
100	96 Nerva 98 Trajan			

the Presbyter favors the conclusion, held by certain scholars, that he was the author of the Gospel of John. The description, in John 21[24, 25], of the disciple who was the author of the Fourth Gospel, also applies to him with singular appropriateness, for he was one of the two, outside the ranks of the Twelve, whom Papias calls a "disciple." From the evidence furnished by the Fourth Gospel and ecclesiastical tradition it seems probable that he was a Jewish Christian, originally from Jerusalem, who spent the latter part of his life in Asia Minor, making his home at Ephesus. There he held a position of high authority, and through his teaching and writings exerted an influence on the thought of the Christian church that was only surpassed by that of Jesus and Paul.

VI. **Conclusions.** The history of the gospel records, as told by the Church Fathers and revealed by the internal evidence, is far from simple. The four canonical gospels do not represent parallel and distinct lines of tradition. Instead, they and their sources interlace at many points. The accompanying diagram aims to represent graphically their complex relationship. Back of the earliest written sources was a rich body of local traditions, preserved by those best fitted to retain and transmit the treasures intrusted to their keeping. The motives that led the earliest gospel writers to undertake their tasks were natural and sincere. An earnest zeal faithfully to present the facts characterizes all their work. Three primary written sources may be distinguished: (1) the early collection of the sayings of Jesus, (2) the original gospel of Mark, and (3) the other early fragmentary gospels from which Luke, and possibly Matthew, quotes. It is generally agreed that these sources are the foundations of our four gospels.

The excellence and authority of the four gospels explain why the stream of oral tradition dried up so quickly, for when once the early Christians could turn to written records, they became independent of the testimony of eye-witnesses. Furthermore, between 60 and 70 A.D. these eye-witnesses began rapidly to pass away. These facts suggest the reason why so few of the details regarding Jesus' life and teachings have been preserved outside the gospel records. Fortunately the data found in the gospels, although not so complete as we might wish, are sufficient to give a faithful and life-like picture of what Jesus actually was and did and of the immortal principles that he proclaimed.

V

THE HISTORICAL BACKGROUND OF JESUS' LIFE AND WORK

I. The Division of Palestine after the Death of Herod the Great. The year 4 B.C. marks a great transition in the political history of the Jews and of Palestine. Hitherto the Maccabean kingdom had been preserved practically in its integrity. Under Herod the Great its bounds had been extended; but in 4 B.C. it was finally dismembered. After a disastrous period of anarchy the details of Herod's will were confirmed by Augustus, except that Archelaus was appointed tetrarch rather than king. To this incompetent son of Herod were given Judea, Samaria, and Idumea; to Herod Antipas, Galilee and Perea; to Philip, the territory east of the upper Jordan (including Auranitis, Gaulonitis, Trachonitis, Batanea, Banias, and Iturea). Of these three subdivisions the territory of Archelaus was by far the richest. Geographically it was the most unified, but the different races within its bounds were bitterly hostile to each other. Archelaus unfortunately possessed the evil, not the redeeming, characteristics of his father. His rule, according to Josephus, was barbarous and tyrannical. He succeeded in arousing the hatred of the chief men of Judea and Samaria, so that in 6 A.D., after a reign of less than a decade, he was accused by them of mismanagement and banished by the imperial court to Vienne in Gaul.

Quirinius was then sent to Judea to make a census of the population and an estimate of the value of the property as a basis for taxation. The bitter opposition aroused among the Jews suggests that it was the first census imposed upon them by Rome. They resented it not only because of their traditional superstition of being numbered, but also because it was evidence of subjection to the hated heathen, and made the payment of the Roman tax unavoidable. It was at this time that the Zealots first appear in Jewish history. Although Galilee was not affected by this census, these Zealots instituted there a revolt which spread through Judea. They were the embodiment of the narrow Jewish nationalistic spirit. Their watchword was: "No Lord but

Jehovah; no tax but that to the temple; no friend but the Zealot."
Their ambition was to throw off the yoke of Rome, and to realize it,
they showed themselves ever ready to unsheath the sword and to attempt the impossible. They were the extreme expression of that rest-
lessness and bitter hatred of authority which increased rather than
diminished under the rule of Rome.

II. **Judea under the Rule of Rome.** Under Herod Jerusalem
had been transformed into a city of marble palaces and large public
buildings. Here were gathered the accumulated wealth and power of
the Jewish kingdom. Although, when Archelaus was deposed, the
capital of the Roman province had been transferred to Cæsarea, beside
the Mediterranean, Jerusalem retained its old prestige. In their treatment of the Jews the Romans aimed to give as much freedom as possible and to guard against stirring up their religious prejudices. The
image of the emperor was not placed on the coins that circulated
in Judea. The Roman standards were kept outside Jerusalem. The
Sabbath was regularly observed, and the Jews were permitted to slay
any foreigner who entered the inner precincts of their temple court.
Inasmuch as Judea was one of the eastern outposts of the empire and
subject to frequent revolts, it was placed under the immediate direction
of the emperor rather than that of the senate. Over it was appointed
a procurator, or governor, who was chosen from the ranks of the eques-
trian or military class, and who reported directly to the emperor. Thus,
Judea was subjected to a type of military rule which was rigorous
although not onerous as long as its inhabitants submitted peaceably.

III. **Duties of the Procurators.** The duties of the procurators
were of three kinds. Their first duty was to maintain order and to
administer the government of the province. In performing these functions they had the support, not of the regular Roman soldiers, but of
the auxiliaries. These were recruited from the Samaritans and the resident Greeks, for the Jews were not compelled to serve in the army.
The second duty of the procurators was to supervise the collection
and disbursement of the taxes. Of these the major tax was probably
levied by the local sanhedrin in each of the eleven townships or to-
parchies into which Judea was divided. It was then turned over to
the procurator, who, after making the necessary expenditures for im-
provement and administration, sent the balance to Rome. The poll-
tax was probably collected in the same way.

Far more burdensome was the customs tax, for, in keeping with the
ancient oriental usage, it was farmed out, the "farmer" paying to the

treasury a fixed sum, but collecting much more. This tax included export and import duties levied on goods transported from city to city or to or from the province, market taxes, taxes on necessities such as salt, and tolls levied on bridges and harbors. The publicans, as they are called in the English translations, were the men who bought these local rights from the Romans and ultimately collected the customs taxes. They were subject to peculiar temptations and were the victims of an iniquitous system. They had to pay the exorbitant prices imposed by those from whom they bought the privilege. On the other hand, they were able, by threats and underhanded methods, to extort outrageous sums from all classes in the community. Hence they were the object of intense hatred, and were ordinarily classed, not without reason, with sinners and outcasts. Jews, tempted by cupidity to take up this occupation, were especially despised and hated, for they were regarded not only as unprincipled robbers, but also as the allies and agents of the heathen conquerors.

The third duty of the procurators was to administer justice in all cases in which Gentiles were involved. Ordinary civil and even criminal cases, in which only Jews were concerned, were apparently decided by each local Jewish sanhedrin or else referred to the national sanhedrin at Jerusalem. The right of capital punishment was taken from the sanhedrin some time before 30 A.D., so that to carry out this extreme sentence the approval of the procurator was required. Questions involving both Jews and Gentiles were also decided by this Roman official or by his representatives. In all ordinary cases he was the court of final appeal. Roman citizens, however, possessed the right of appealing directly to the emperor. Thus, Rome, in keeping with its usual wise provincial policy, introduced as far as possible its principles of justice and systematic administration, but at the same time, for politic reasons, recognized local customs and institutions.

IV. **The Organization and Authority of the Jerusalem Sanhedrin.** The sanhedrin first emerged into prominence as a national institution during the Maccabean struggle. It was clearly the successor of the older Gerousia or assembly of the elders. Herod the Great deprived it of most of its power, but this was restored under the procurators. Its chief task was to administer the Jewish law. Hence, its functions were civil, criminal, moral, and religious. Its civil authority was limited to Judea, but its religious influence extended to the farthest bounds of the Jewish world. It not only administered the laws, but also enacted them. The statement in Josephus's *Jewish*

War, II, 7¹, implies that it collected the Roman tax both in Jerusalem and throughout the province of Judea. It was also the municipal council that administered the affairs of the city. According to the Mishna, it had seventy-one members. At its head sat the high priest. Vacancies were apparently filled by the sanhedrin itself. New members were chosen from the leading Jewish families. Although the high priestly or Sadducean party was represented in the sanhedrin, the Pharisees were in the majority, and through this representative national assembly they ruled the Jewish world.

V. The Rule of the Procurators. Little is known regarding the rule of the first three procurators, Coponius (6–9 A.D.), Ambivius (9–12), and Rufus (12–15). Gratus was appointed by the Emperor Tiberius the year following his accession in 14 A.D. According to Josephus, Gratus deposed Annas, and appointed his son Eleazer in his stead. After a year the procurator placed a certain Simon at the head of the temple priesthood, and a little later Caiaphas, who figures in the gospel story. Tacitus (*Annals*, IV, 42, 43) states that while Gratus was procurator (15–26 A.D.), the Zealots kept the people in a ferment, and that there was much discontent because of the heavy taxation. Gratus was succeeded in 26 by Pontius Pilate, who held the office of procurator for a decade. He is described by Agrippa I as a man "of unbending and recklessly hard character" (*Ad Caium*, 38). His chief faults were his failure to understand the Jews, his rashness in stirring up their prejudices, and his weakness in yielding ultimately to their demands. Thus, contrary to the well-established Roman usage, he attempted to bring the Roman flags into Jerusalem by night. He also made the creditable attempt to bring water to Jerusalem by means of an aqueduct; but in each of these instances he yielded to the storm of protest which his action aroused. Later, when he set up certain votive shields in the temple, the emperor himself, in response to a petition of the Jews, condemned the act. He was finally dismissed in disgrace because of his cruel treatment of certain deluded Samaritans who attempted to follow a false Messiah. Thus Pilate's reputation with contemporary Roman writers corresponds to the tragic rôle which he played in the gospel records.

VI. The Character and Rule of Herod Antipas. Herod Antipas, in contrast to his father, might well have been called Herod the Little, for he inherited most of his ancestor's characteristics; but his achievements and his vices were small in comparison. His building ambitions found expression in the rebuilding of his first capital, Sepphoris. This

Galilean village, situated on a hill a few miles west of Nazareth, he surrounded by a strong wall and adorned with public buildings. Attracted by the beauty and the tropical climate of the Sea of Galilee, Herod later selected as a site the narrow stretch of coast plain along the western side of the lake and there built a new capital, which he named, in honor of his imperial patron, Tiberias. This city he also surrounded by a strong wall and built within it a palace and a stadium Through it ran a street with colonnades; the general plan and appear ance of the city was Græco-Roman rather than Jewish. It was also organized as a Greek city, with a council of six hundred and a committee of ten with an archon at its head. The other two scenes of Herod's building enterprise were Bethharan, across the Jordan from Jericho, and the castle of Machærus at the extreme southern end of Perea. On this wild, picturesque site he also built a royal palace or castle, which commanded a marvellous view of the Dead Sea and the Judean hills on the west.

Jesus' designation of Herod as a fox well characterizes his fundamental weakness. The term must, of course, be interpreted in the light of the biblical conception of the fox—the skulking, treacherous animal that destroyed or undermined the results of honest labor. This characteristic is well illustrated by Herod's treachery in secretly reporting a victory won by the Roman general Vitellius before the real victor could gain the favor of Tiberius. By this act Herod incurred the bitter enmity of Vitellius, who, when governor of Syria, retaliated by bringing charges against him which resulted in his banishment by Caligula in 37 A.D. Herod's failure to restrain his passion also led him to divorce his wife, the daughter of the Arabian king Aretas. This base act influenced his former father-in-law to join later with Vitellius in charges against him. His evil genius was Herodias, the wife of his half-brother Herod Boethus, who left her former husband to share Herod's throne.

Notwithstanding his despicable personal character, Herod Antipas appears to have given his subjects on the whole a peaceful and prosperous rule. Galilee and Perea, with their broad valleys and rounded, well-watered hills, supported a dense and active population. Here farmers, shepherds, fishermen, and tradesmen lived side by side. Across Galilee ran the many highways which brought to it the products of the outside world and in turn opened favorable markets. Herod's subjects were for the most part the descendants of the Jewish colonists who had settled in Galilee and Perea under the rule of the later Maccabean kings. While they were loyal to the laws of their race, they were not priest-ridden as were the Jews of Judea. They were a simple, liberty-loving people, easily stirred to action by popular leaders, as is shown in the history of the many uprisings led by the Zealots. Among them were cherished the nobler ideals of Israel's earlier prophets and sages. Nowhere in all the Roman world were men to be found who were freer from heathen superstitions or narrow fanaticisms. Hence it was not because of the mere accident of birth that Jesus turned to Galilee as the most promising field for his work.

The province of Herod's third son, Philip, joined that of Herod Antipas on the east. Of the three sons of Herod, Philip was by far the best. Although the rocky, diversified territory over which he ruled contained the greatest variety of population—Jews, Greeks, Syrians, and Arabs —he established a strong and equitable government. His chief aims seem to have been to develop the resources of his province and to conserve the cause of justice and the best interests of his subjects. On the fertile, well-watered plain south of Mount Hermon he established his capital and named it Cæsarea Philippi. Here he built a strong Græco-Roman city, the ruins of which still remain. At the northern end of the Sea of Galilee, where the Jordan breaks through the Galilean hills and runs with many windings through a delta into the Sea of Galilee, he built another Roman city. This he named Bethsaida Julias, in honor of the daughter of Augustus. As its Jewish name ("House of Fish") indicates, it was the centre of the great fishing industry that flourished at the northern end of the lake. This was the Bethsaida which, with Capernaum and Chorazin, was the scene of most of Jesus' public activity and the object of his saddest and severest denunciations.

VII. Rome's Strength and Weakness. The larger background of Jesus' work is the great Roman Empire. At the beginning of the Christian era Rome represented two things: (1) the practical unification of the civilized world and (2) the universal establishment of law and order. Rome's geographical position fitted her to be the mistress of the lands encircling the Mediterranean. By gradual conquests the Roman Empire had extended its bounds until under Augustus its power was absolute throughout this favored centre of the world's earliest civilization. Its unity was in part due to its strong military policy, which enlisted in its armies men of all races, and taught them to fight, not against each other, but for Rome. It was also considerate of the customs and interests of the local peoples, and jealously guarded their peace and prosperity. Broad, well-built highways were constructed over rivers, mountains, and deserts. These roads bound even the most distant provinces closely to the home city. Over them passed not only Rome's armies, but traders bearing from one part of the empire to another the ideas as well as the products of many different peoples. Upon the conquered races Rome left the stamp of that powerful Græco-Roman civilization which had reached its highest development under Augustus. To the beauty of Greek art and architecture Rome added strength and utility. In connection with magnificent temples and other public buildings there were constructed paved streets, aqueducts, and sewers. These constructions were carried on even in the most distant parts of the empire. On the borders of the desert east of the Jordan the travellers still find many most impressive illustrations of Rome's marvellous power to lift a semi-barbarous people to a level of material civilization almost equal to that of the parent city. Rome was also able to impress upon the conquered that high regard for law and order which was the corner-stone of the empire. The result was that the reigns of Augustus and of his immediate successors were characterized by almost uninterrupted peace.

Notwithstanding her strength, Rome was pitiably weak at many points. The old republican form of government had yielded to what soon became an almost absolute despotism. Men like Tiberius, Caligula, and Nero proved unworthy of this great trust. About them they gathered a nobility which grew more and more corrupt and profligate, as it preyed upon the helpless masses. Even the senate and Tiberius himself were appalled by the luxury and profligacy of their day, and confessed their inability to check the glaring evils. Imperial Rome, with its population of over a million and a half, was the centre of this corruption. More than half of its inhabitants were paupers or slaves. Slavery in Rome was far different from the mild institution found in early oriental countries. The lot of these slaves, who were the victims of the refined cruelties which only a highly developed but brutal civilization is able to inflict, was pitiable and practically hopeless. They were also a grave menace to the integrity of the empire. Above all, the old religions, which in the earlier days had developed personal strength and virtue, had become degenerate. Their priesthoods connived to prey upon the masses. Among the ruling class the worship of the emperor was rapidly taking the place of the older cults. The religions of the East, especially the seductive cults of Egypt and Phœnicia, attracted a wide following, even in the imperial city, and exerted a pernicious and degrading influence.

VIII. The Needs of the Roman World. Already, in the first Christian century, the more thoughtful in the Roman Empire were beginning to appreciate keenly the needs which the civilization of the day failed to meet. One of these needs was a more powerful and permanent unifying force than Roman arms and rule. A philosophy or religion was also demanded that would satisfy the requirements of all the varied elements in the empire. Each individual, whether a ruler or subject, needed a standard of morals, enforced by religion, which would enable him to strive for and obtain that which is of abiding value in life. Of the current philosophies, Stoicism in many ways held up the highest ideals. It taught the importance of virtue. Virtue alone is good, for welfare and happiness depend entirely upon virtuous action. Every man has a natural capacity for virtue. Hence Stoicism sought to inculcate habits of sobriety and self-restraint and to lead its followers to live in accordance with the laws of nature. It emphasized man's duties to himself, to God, and to all men. It enjoined consideration even for slaves. Epictetus taught that all men have God as their father and are therefore by nature brothers. "Wherever one man is, there is the place to do a good deed." But Stoicism was cold and self-centred. It lacked enthusiasm and devotion to an heroic personality that embodied its ideals. It failed to appreciate the joy that comes from the complete giving of one's self to service. Above all, it was the religion simply of the favored classes, and offered little hope and inspiration to the toiling masses. Stoicism, however, was one of the great pioneers that preceded Christianity, and, like Judaism, it prepared the way for the new and greater force that was soon to be felt in the life of the world.

Already Judaism had entered upon that proselyting movement which, during the centuries immediately preceding and following the beginning of the Christian era, attracted many thoughtful Gentiles to the religion of Israel's prophets and lawgivers. In Hillel, who died about 6 B.C., Judaism found in many ways its noblest exponent. He was a brilliant and ardent student of Israel's scriptures. He was broad, tolerant, and kindly in his attitude toward men and their problems. Among his famous sayings was that one which recalls the corresponding teaching of Jesus: "What you do not like yourself do not to another. This is the whole law. All else is but amplification." He also taught: "Be among the pupils of Aaron, who loved peace and pursued peace, who loved all creatures and guided them to the law." Equally noble was his precept: "If you are where no men are, show yourself a man." He was keenly alive to the importance of teaching, and gathered about himself a large and enthusiastic body of disciples. His influence was doubtless still strong in Jerusalem when Jesus, as a boy of twelve, visited the capital city. Judaism as a whole, however, was inclined to follow the leadership of Hillel's conservative contemporary Shammai. The prevailing trend was toward ceremonialism. Religion was made something austere and cold. For the ordinary sinners and even the common toilers, who by virtue of their occupations could not conform to the exacting demands of the ritual, the Pharisees had no comforting or saving message. The Sadducean, high-priestly party, which was in control of the temple and influential in the sanhedrin, was grasping and unprincipled. Furthermore, Judaism was still only a national religion. The spiritual heritage received from its earlier prophets and sages was to a great extent forgotten or ignored. Instead, hatred for Rome, contempt for everything not Jewish, emphasis on the obligations of the ceremonial law, and impossible messianic hopes occupied the attention of the great majority of the race. Judaism needed a great spiritual leader to loose its bonds, to single out what was eternal and universal in its teachings, to adapt it to human needs, and by his personality and life, as well as by his words, to interpret clearly and concretely man's divine possibilities.

THE EARLY LIFE AND WORK OF JESUS

§CXXI. JESUS' BIRTH, BOYHOOD, AND EARLY TRAINING

Now it came to pass in those days that a decree came from Cæsar Augustus that a census should be taken of the whole world. This was the first census when Quirinius was governor of Syria, and all went to have themselves registered, everyone to his own city. Now Joseph also went up from the city of Nazareth in Galilee into Judea, to the city of David, which is called Bethlehem, because he belonged to the house and family of David, to have himself registered, with Mary his wife, who was great with child. And while they were there, the days were fulfilled that she should be delivered, and she brought forth her first-born son. And as there was no room for them in the inn, she wrapped him in swaddling clothes and laid him in a manger.

1. The Roman census (Luke 2¹, ²)

2. Jesus' birth (³⁻⁷)

And when eight days had elapsed for circumcising him, his name was called Jesus.

3. His name (²¹ᵃ)

Now the child Jesus grew, and became strong; and the grace of God was upon him.

4. Development (⁴⁰)

And his parents went every year to Jerusalem at the feast of the Passover. And when he was twelve years old, they went up to the feast as usual. And when the days were completed and they were on their way back, the boy Jesus remained behind in Jerusalem. And his parents knew it not; but supposing him to be in the caravan, they went a day's journey; and they sought for him among their kinsfolk and acquaintances. And when they did not find him, they returned to Jerusalem, seeking for him. And it came to pass, after three days they found him in the temple, sitting in the midst of the teachers, both listening to them, and asking them questions; and all who heard him were amazed at his understanding and his answers. And when Joseph and Mary saw him, they were astonished; and his mother said to him, Child, why have you treated us in

5. First visit to Jerusalem and his zeal for religious instruction (⁴¹⁻⁵⁰)

43

this way? Behold, your father and I sought you sorrowing. And he said to them, Why was it that you sought me? Did you not know that I must be in my Father's house? But they did not understand the saying that he said to them.

6.
Intel-
lectual,
spirit-
ual,
and
physi-
cal
growth
(⁴¹-⁵²)

And he went down with them and came to Nazareth; and he was subject to them. And his mother kept all these sayings in her heart. And Jesus kept on advancing in wis-dom and stature, and in favor with God and men.

I. The Accounts of Jesus' Birth. The interest of the oldest gos-pel writers was focused, not on the place or manner of Jesus' birth, but upon his personality and his teachings. Mark and the early teaching source (Q) began their narratives with an account of the work of John the Baptist; but Luke, in pursuance of his purpose to give a compre-hensive and chronological account of Jesus' life, gathered the current accounts of his birth and lineage. The Gospel of Matthew, interpret-ing the sign by which Isaiah sought to convince the vacillating Ahaz (7¹⁴) as a messianic prediction, gives an account of the birth that is quite independent of that of Luke. Thus, for example, in Luke the angel that announces the birth of Jesus appears to Mary, but in Mat-thew, to Joseph. In Luke the announcement of the birth of the child was made by the angels to the shepherds near Bethlehem; but in Mat-thew it was to the Magi by the star. In Luke the child is first taken by his parents to the temple to be presented before the Lord. There they find the aged Simeon and Anna the prophetess. "After they had accomplished all things that were according to the law of the Lord, they returned to Galilee to their own city, Nazareth" (Luke 2³⁹). But Matthew states that they fled at once to Egypt to escape the merciless persecution of Herod.

Notwithstanding the wide variations, both gospels agree (1) that Jesus' Davidic descent was through Joseph, and (2) that he was born amidst the most humble surroundings. All these stories emphasize the profound, world-wide significance of his birth. For Jew and Gen-tile, king and shepherd, the wise and the lowly it meant indeed:

> Glory to God in the highest,
> And on earth peace among men.

Men's conclusions regarding the exact manner of Jesus' birth will probably always differ, for there is strong biblical evidence to support

44

the belief in his natural as well as in his supernatural genesis. Only Mary could decide absolutely that much-debated question, and none of the gospels claim to present her direct testimony. Jesus nowhere referred to the manner of his birth. Instead, he declared, when his mother and brothers came to turn him aside from his mission: "Who is my mother and my brother? He who does the will of God is my brother and sister and mother" (Mark 3[33, 35]). In all his teachings he asserted that spiritual kinship was infinitely more important than mere physical relationship.

Paul, the oldest witness and interpreter of Jesus, says nothing about a supernatural birth. He employs idioms which would naturally be used to describe the ordinary process of generation. Thus, in Romans 1[3], he states that Jesus was "born of the seed of David according to the flesh"; in 8[3] that he was "born in the likeness of sinful flesh"; in 9[5] he refers to the fathers of the race "of whom Christ was according to the flesh" (cf. Gal. 4[4]). The Epistle to the Hebrews makes the fact that Jesus was "tempted in all points even as we are" the basis of his work as the Friend and Saviour of men. Matthew, Mark, and Luke, except in one verse (1[34], which many scholars regard as an interpolation that destroys the unity of the context), constantly speak of Jesus as the son of Joseph the carpenter. In so doing they support the unmistakable implication of the genealogies and of the Old Syriac version of Matthew 1[16] which reads: "Joseph begat Jesus." The context of Luke 2[5] also favors the Old Latin translation, based on Greek manuscripts of the second century, that reads "wife," instead of the variant readings of the later Greek texts, "betrothed" and "betrothed wife."

On the other hand, the Christian church, since the second century, has held tenaciously to the belief that Jesus was not born in the ordinary way. That belief appears to have been in part the popular expression of a profound consciousness of Jesus' uniqueness and divinity. It aimed to define that divineness in terms of origin rather than of personality and teaching. It also reflects the influence of the prevailing attitude toward physical generation. The ancient Canaanites and Phœnicians regarded the process of reproduction as a sacred mystery; but in time, through their licentious religious practices, they so degraded it that Jews and Christians alike, in their horror and revulsion, ceased to appreciate its divine significance and sanctity. Hence, in contemporary Judaism the belief was widespread that, as Philo expresses it (1[13, 215]), "Every child of promise was born miraculously."

45

Elsewhere he states that "the Lord begat Isaac" (1^{137}). The real husband of Leah was "the unnoticed." Zipporah was found by Moses "pregnant, but not by man" (1^{147}). Samuel was born of a human mother who became pregnant on receiving divine seed. The tendency was also general throughout the ancient world to regard the fleshly nature as inherently sinful. This was one of the fundamental beliefs of the Gnostic sects of the second century, and it permeated to a considerable extent the thought of the orthodox Christian writers. Later it led to the development of monasticism, and the error still prevails in many minds and many quarters. The creeds formulated during the early Christian centuries teach that Jesus "was conceived of the Holy Ghost and born of the Virgin Mary." The apocryphal gospels which come from the same period still further develop this doctrine and teach that Mary was likewise miraculously conceived, and that her birth and life were attended by a series of prodigious portents.

Inasmuch as the biblical testimony is inconclusive, the question regarding the manner of Jesus' birth is naturally answered according to each man's individual training and point of view. The significant fact, however, is that, whichever answer be accepted, Jesus remains as unmistakably the Son of God as he is the Son of man. To all thoughtful Christians the fact is self-evident that their conception of God is almost wholly derived from the life and teachings of Jesus. As the revealer of the divine Father he is divine. His life-giving words, his heroic deeds, and his invincible power over the lives of men attest convincingly to this scientific age, as they did to his earliest disciples, his divine character and authority. To the men of to-day this uncontrovertible testimony of practical experience is even more satisfactory and convincing than the angels' songs and the supernatural portents that strengthened, as well as expressed, the faith of the early church.

In a humble peasant village, amidst the insignia of poverty and toil, Jesus was born. His birth and early training allied him with the countless army of humble toilers whose physical, mental, and moral burdens he sought to take from their weary shoulders. The beautiful narratives that have gathered about his birth will always continue to have a large religious value and to hold an important place in the thought of his followers, for they reflect humanity's ultimate appreciation of his God-given mission and its world-wide meaning. Yet the fact should never be overlooked that the marvellous charm of these narratives lies in those inimitable touches which link him with our common experiences and needs. This element is especially strong in Luke's peerless account of the humble peasant father and mother and of the birth in the lowly manger-cradle. Born "according to the flesh under the law," "tempted in all points like as we are," Jesus set out on the narrow way that led to complete oneness with his heavenly Father. As our elder brother, he calls upon us to follow him along the same narrow path, and thus to become perfect as he became perfect.

II. The Place and Date of Jesus' Birth. The answer to the often mooted question, whether Jesus was a native of Nazareth or Bethlehem, depends largely on the accuracy of Luke's detailed chronological note in 2[1-4]. The historical difficulties presented by his statement regarding the enrolment under Quirinius have long been recognized. Contemporary records indicate that Quirinius was not governor of Syria until 6–9 A.D. and that Herod the Great died in 4 B.C. The evidence is conclusive that there was no universal census throughout the empire under Augustus between 6 and 4 B.C. Although Josephus's account of the closing years of Herod's reign is detailed, he makes no reference to a local or imperial census in Palestine at this time; but in 6 A.D. Quirinius was governor of Syria and instituted a census in Judea. It aroused such widespread opposition that it would seem to have been the first taken in that province. The aim of an imperial census was to establish the basis for a local property and poll-tax. It is, therefore, not entirely clear why, as Luke implies, each Jew was required to return to the home of his family or clan. In the light of these facts many scholars hold that Luke here made a mistake in dating the census of Quirinius in 6 B.C. rather than 6 A.D.

On the other hand, it is urged in the light of a recently discovered inscription that, as early as 6 B.C., Quirinius was serving under the legate of Syria and might have been despatched to conduct a census in Judea at that time. Evidence has also been found that the Romans carried through a census in the province of Egypt a little before 6 B.C. This may have extended to the neighboring territory of Herod. His subserviency to the will of Augustus is well known. If the census had been taken under his direction, it would doubtless have been arranged so as not to arouse Jewish prejudices. Luke's historical accuracy, as illustrated elsewhere in his writings, lends weight to his detailed statement in 2[1-4]. Acquainted, as he was, with many of those who had themselves known eye-witnesses of these early events, he was apparently in a position to verify his facts. His assertion, therefore, that Jesus was born at Bethlehem carries large weight. Certain recent writers have endeavored to identify Jesus' birthplace with the Galilean

Bethlehem, about ten miles from Nazareth, the modern Bet-Lahm (cf. Rix, *Tent and Testament*). The early church traditions, however, as does Luke's narrative, point unmistakably to the Judean Bethlehem, the home of David.

Outside the opening chapters of Matthew and Luke the implication is that Jesus was born in Nazareth. In Mark 6^{1-4} Galilee is spoken of as his own country (cf. also Matt. 13^{54}). The question in John 1^{46}, "Can any good come out of Nazareth?" carries the same implication. If the author of the Fourth Gospel had known that Jesus was born in Bethlehem he would probably have stated that fact in his reply to the objections of the Jews who raised the question, "Does the Christ come out of Galilee?" For it was in keeping with the popular belief that the Messiah must come "of the seed of David and from Bethlehem, the village where David was." It has been urged that the stories which associate Jesus' birth with Bethlehem were the logical outgrowth of the Jewish belief that the Messiah must be of Davidic descent and therefore born at the home of Israel's early king (cf. Micah 5^2). In view of the conflicting evidence the Christian church will continue to think of Bethlehem as Jesus' birthplace until more conclusive proof to the contrary is discovered.

The biblical evidence regarding the date of Jesus' birth is also not entirely clear. There is little doubt that it occurred before the death of Herod the Great in 4 B.C., but not long before that event. The German scholar Oefele has recently published an Egyptian papyrus roll, now found in the British Museum, which gives the position of the planets from 17 B.C. to 10 A.D. He computes on the basis of this document that between April 15th and December 27th of 6 B.C. there were repeated conjunctions of the planets Jupiter and Saturn, and that on the 27th of December the planet Jupiter became stationary only once in many thousand years, they undoubtedly attracted widespread attention throughout the ancient world and furnish the most natural explanation of the story of the visit of the Magi. In the light of all the evidence the birth of Jesus may be dated with considerable assurance in 6 B.C.

As is well known, the present system of reckoning time is due to an error of mediæval scholars. The exact day of Jesus' birth is, of course, unknown. The early church celebrated it on the same day as the Epiphany, on January 6. The Armenian church still follows this ancient custom. It is definitely known that in the fourth century the Roman church began to observe the anniversary of Jesus' birth on the 25th of December. As in the case of many minor questions in the life of Jesus, the details have long since been forgotten; but fortunately the great facts of his work and teaching are established beyond all doubt.

III. Jesus' Home. Jesus was probably the oldest of five brothers. He had at least two, and possibly more, sisters. The names of his brothers alone are given: James, Joses, Judas, and Simeon. The house in which the peasant family lived was doubtless similar to the houses found in Nazareth to-day: square, built of stone or brick, with a dirt floor and a single door. The house was intended as a protection from the heat of summer, the cold of winter, and the marauder by night. Therefore there were few, if any, windows. In these narrow quarters the family ate their frugal meal and, wrapped in their blankets, slept at night on the cold floor or on mats. The level house-top, reached by a stairway on the outside, was the common place of gathering in the daytime. There they often slept during the hot summer nights. Within these same narrow quarters Joseph and his sons probably plied their carpenter trade.

Jesus' high conception of fatherhood strongly suggests that Joseph was wise, just, and considerate, and that he knew how to "give good gifts to his children" (Matt. 7[11]). Unlike many oriental fathers, he apparently took his children, and especially his eldest son, Jesus, into his confidence, and thus established that relation of paternal comradeship which is prominent in Jesus' teachings. That he died before Jesus entered upon his public activity is a well-established tradition, confirmed by the reference in Mark 3[32] to Mary, where Joseph would naturally be mentioned, if he were living. The spirit of Jesus' home was strongly religious. Three times a year the family probably went up together to Jerusalem to the great feasts. According to John 7[3-10] Jesus' brothers on one occasion urged him, apparently against his inclination, to go with them to the Passover at Jerusalem. The motive which led his kinsmen to seek to stop his public preaching was probably their horror because he questioned the teachings of the learned scribes and Pharisees. How early the responsibilities, which in an oriental home rest heavily on the eldest son at the death of his father, devolved upon Jesus we do not know. It was probably in early manhood, and, if so, these responsibilities were important factors in the training of the future Friend and Teacher of men.

IV. The Life at Nazareth. The town of Nazareth lay on a hillside sloping to the southeast. The hill above it, on the west, rose to the height of fifteen hundred feet above the level of the sea and fully a thousand above the Plain of Esdraelon to the south. This hill, easily accessible from the town which lies in the hollow below, commands a marvellous view of the historic scenes of central Palestine. To the northwest, five miles across the rolling hills, was Sepphoris, the early capital of Herod Antipas and the strongest military centre in Galilee. To the west were the blue waters of the Mediterranean and the sharp outlines of Mount Carmel, jutting far out into the Plain of Esdraelon. This scene recalled the courageous work of Elijah and the great victory in early Hebrew history won through the inspiring leadership of Deborah. On the southeast rose the elevated plateau of Mount Gilboa, the scene of Saul's last battle. Beyond were the hills of Samaria, with Mount Ebal in the distance. Eastward the view extended across the Sea of Galilee to the bold headlands of Gilead and the Jaulan. In the nearer eastern horizon stood the rounded top of Mount Tabor, only an hour and a half away. Near it ran the main highway through the heart of Palestine from Egypt to Babylonia. Other roads ran directly from Nazareth to the southwest, joining the great coast highways from Egypt to Phœnicia. On the northern horizon rose in majestic succession the lofty plateaus of upper Galilee crowned by the snow-clad summit of Mount Hermon. On the near-by hill-top the boy Jesus must have spent many hours meditating on the picturesque and significant world spread before his vision.

The town of Nazareth to-day has a population of about ten thousand. In antiquity it was probably considerably smaller, for it was not fitted by nature to be a large city. One copious spring furnishes the water supply for the entire town. Here the men and women and children gather as they doubtless did in the days of Jesus. In a small town like Nazareth the life resembles that of a great family rather than that of our modern cities. The weddings, with their glad songs and dancing, the funerals, with their sad laments, the losses and good fortunes of each citizen are shared by all. The page of human life is opened wide so that here he who will may read. Nazareth, with its slaves, its laborers, its poor beggars, its just and unjust judges, was an epitome of Galilee; and Galilee with its varied population was a type of the larger Græco-Roman world. In Nazareth, therefore, Jesus had ample opportunity to study intimately the varied phases of human life, so that in time it was unnecessary that any one should tell him, "for he knew what was in the heart of man."

V. Jesus' Educational Opportunities. The training of every Jewish child began in the home at the age of five and six, and his first teacher was his mother. Before he could understand the meaning of the words he was taught the Shema, Israel's impressive creed, found in Deuteronomy 6[4, 5] 7[7]: "Hear, O Israel. The Lord thy God is one Lord. Thou shalt love the Lord, thy God, with all thy heart and with all thy soul and with all thy might. The Lord did not set his love upon you nor choose you because ye were more in number than any people, for ye were the fewest of all peoples; but because the Lord loveth you." As a child grew he was taught to write down these words and thus he learned his letters. Later his mother interpreted their meaning and told him the stories of Israel's heroes. At the age of six he was probably sent to the synagogue school, where, in the common meeting-room, the man who kept the synagogue further instructed the children in the law and how to read and write. Cross-legged they sat in a circle about their teacher, reciting aloud the Shema. These nineteen verses, taken from Deuteronomy 6[4-9] 11[13-21] and Numbers 15[37-41], were the confession of faith which every Jew throughout the world repeated each morning and night. The training in the synagogue school was supplemented by the daily prayers and reading in the home. A prayer was offered before and after each meal. At the first glimpse of the rising sun the boy was taught to stop and give thanks. Probably even at this period in the development of Judaism a metal box containing the opening words of the Shema was placed at the door of the house. This the boy was to touch whenever he left or entered his home. In the Sabbath service at the synagogue he also listened to the reading of the law and to the interpretation of a passage of the prophets by the leader of the service or by some wandering scribe. In addition to Aramaic, which was the language of his home, Jesus probably had a reading acquaintance with both Hebrew and Greek. Hebrew and Aramaic were but variant dialects of the same Semitic language, so that the opportunities of the home and of the synagogue school were sufficient to give him this working knowledge. The Greek version of the Old Testament was also used by the Jews of Palestine as much, if not more than the Hebrew version. A majority of the quotations, even in the gospels, are from this later translation. In the larger cities of Galilee and Judea Jesus constantly came into contact with a Gentile population who spoke Greek, so that he had an opportunity to acquire a certain familiarity with that language. It is not probable that his family possessed a roll of the law or the prophets. At the synagogue, in charge of the Chazzan, who cared for the building, were kept rolls of the law, the prophets, and the other sacred writings. To these Jesus doubtless had access. His words to the scribes, for example, in Mark 2²⁵: "Have you never read what David did?" or in Mark 12¹⁰⁻²⁶: "Have you not read even this scripture?" (*cf.* also Matt. 12⁵ 19⁴) imply that he, like them, had not only read but carefully studied these ancient scriptures.

VI. Jesus' Visit to the Temple at the Age of Twelve. Another great door of opportunity was opened to Jesus by the repeated journeys which, after the age of twelve, he made to Jerusalem on the occasion of the three great annual festivals. His first visit was an epoch-making event in his life. It occurred at about the time when Archelaus was deposed and Quirinius was instituting his hated Roman census. All Judea was in a ferment. The impression made upon the mind of Jesus is, perhaps, reflected in the parable of the nobleman who left his estates to his servants and went into a far country, for Archelaus appears here to have been the ruler that he had in mind. If the venerable Hillel was not still living, his disciples doubtless thronged the temple courts and the echoes of his broad ethical teaching must have fallen upon the receptive ear of the boy Jesus. Shammai at this time probably stood at the head of the temple teachers, and his emphasis upon the ceremonial rites of the temple and the traditions of the past determined the accepted tenets of Phariseeism. This first visit was made at an eventful moment in the development of the boy Jesus, for the age of twelve marked the transition from boyhood to young adolescence. It was the period of the first spiritual awakening when every normal boy begins to feel strongly the stirrings of the social and religious impulse. The journey to Jerusalem was the culmination of the preceding years of training in his home and in the synagogue at Nazareth, for now he assumed the full religious responsibilities that devolved upon every faithful Jew. Henceforth he was under obligation to resort to the temple three times a year (Ex. 34²², ²³) and to observe all the exacting demands of the law.

It requires little imagination to follow the boy from his home at Nazareth, as he with his parents made his first pilgrimage to Jerusalem. Three highways were open: one ran southwest across the Plain of Esdraelon to the Plain of Sharon, and thence up over the Pass of Bethhoron to Jerusalem. The second and most direct road ran almost due south along the great plains of central Samaria. Large companies of pilgrims made this journey in safety, but, as a rule, all Jews avoided the hated Samaritans. The route probably followed by Jesus' parents ran first to the southeast, across the great central highway, along the

Plain of Jezreel to Scythopolis, the ancient Bethshean, and thence along the western side of the Jordan Valley. A journey of four days brought the pilgrims to Jericho. Thence they ascended four thousand feet from the low tropical plain of the lower Jordan over the rounded, barren, robber-infested hills of the wilderness of Judea up to Jerusalem. Jesus' later reference to this road in the parable of the good Samaritan indicates that he was intimately acquainted with it. At last, passing through Bethany and over the southern spur of the Mount of Olives, the pilgrims gained their first glimpse of the Holy City. Then passing across the Valley of Kedron, they probably entered the temple area through the sheep gate on the northwest. Here they would find in the great Court of the Gentiles, with its encircling colonnade, a medley of races, Jew and Gentile. Their ears would be deafened by the cries of the money-changers and those who sold animals for sacrifice. Proceeding toward the temple to the east, they next would ascend the steps that led to the higher platform and enter the Court of the Women. Leaving Mary here, Joseph and his son doubtless entered the court of the Israelites and stood before the great rock-cut altar, on which the priests were offering sacrifices, and listened to the songs of the temple singers. Their attention was also attracted by the gilded façade of the famous temple, which symbolized Jehovah's abiding presence.

Later, in the hush of Friday evening, either in the temple courts or, more probably, at the home of some friend on the Mount of Olives, or possibly at Bethany, Jesus, with his parents, kinsmen, and friends, celebrated the solemn Passover meal. The introductory prayers, the impressive formulas, the dramatic attitudes of the participants, and the historic associations all aroused the patriotic and religious impulses latent within the young boy of Nazareth. The Passover recalled Jehovah's past deliverances of his people and the sacred obligations which they owed to him and to all the needy members of their race. The feasts and ceremonies of the seven ensuing days were joyous as well as impressive. They gave large leisure for social intercourse and for personal contact with the acknowledged teachers of the nation. That Jesus improved this opportunity to gain satisfactory answers to the many questions that were already stirring in his mind is plainly recorded in Luke's vivid narrative. It is only the Arabic Gospel of the Infancy that represents him as a prodigy, instructing the rabbis in the statutes of the law and the mysteries of the prophets. Jesus' attitude was rather that of an eager learner whose earnest, searching questions and answers amazed the by-standers. It reveals a child who had improved in the fullest degree his earlier opportunities and who was already intently studying and meditating upon the scriptures of his race.

His zeal for knowledge was so strong that it kept him in Jerusalem even after the seven days of the feast were over. The departure of his parents, leaving him behind, shows, incidentally, how complete was their confidence in him. His mother's words on returning are also an index of that strong, sincere affection which they felt for their eldest son. Jesus' reply to their question has been variously interpreted. It certainly is not a rebuke to his mother. The literal words are, "Did you not know that I must be in the things of my Father?" The meaning seems to be clear. The aim of all Jewish education and the purpose of their visits to the temple was to learn about God, his commands, and how to keep them. The boy of twelve, as often in his later public activity, answered a question by propounding another: Am I not doing that for which we made our pilgrimage to Jerusalem? The incident reveals the presence at this early age of those interests which in maturer years became the commanding motives in his life. Viewed from one point of view, this simple story discloses to us what for the lack of a better term we are wont to call a genius; but from another point of view Jesus was simply a normal boy. Luke declares that Jesus grew in wisdom even as he grew in stature, and that in increasing measure he won the favor both of God and man. Luke strongly emphasizes the fact that his development was gradual, progressive, and normal. It illustrated Jesus' own words, "first the blade, then the ear, then the full corn in the ear." These long years of natural intellectual and spiritual growth are often forgotten; and yet they are of supreme importance in interpreting his character and work.

VII. **His Acquaintance with the Scriptures of His Race.** It is significant that Jesus spent from twenty-eight to thirty years in preparation for a ministry which lasted not more than three years and possibly only one. His world-transforming work was the culmination of prolonged experience, observation, meditation, and thorough study. From the records of his later teachings it is possible to distinguish the ancient writings with which he was especially familiar. Although doubtless acquainted with the legal writings as a whole, such deeply spiritual passages as Deuteronomy 5[13-16] or 8[2, 3] or Leviticus 19[18] appealed to him most strongly. With the marvellous stories that fill the pages of the Old Testament he was thoroughly familiar. Noah, the Sodomites, David, Solomon, the Queen of Sheba, Elijah and the poor widow, Elisha and Naaman, and the prophet Jonah, all figure in his teaching.

Jesus was well acquainted with the great statesman prophet Isaiah, from whom he drew the outlines of his parable of the vineyard keepers, and the figure of the people who worship God with their lips but not with their hearts (cf. Isa. 29¹³ Mark 7⁶). Hosea's memorable words (6⁶), "I desire mercy and not sacrifice," were fundamental to all of Jesus' teachings. In Jeremiah's arraignment of the religious leaders of his nation (Jer. 7¹¹) he found the inspiration for his bold attack upon the rulers of the temple who had made it again a den of thieves. From Ezekiel, Daniel (7¹³), and the book of Enoch, he appears to have derived his favorite self-designation "the Son of man." In the II Isaiah's marvellous portrait of the suffering servant of Jehovah, Jesus found the clearest formulation of his own ideal of service and of the way in which it was to be realized.

The words of the psalmists were eagerly read by the youth of Nazareth. He had committed to memory many passages from the Psalms, for he repeatedly quotes them in his discussions with the scribes or to express the deepest emotions of his soul (e. g., Ps. 22, 91, 102, 110¹, 118²², ²⁵). The Psalms, as no other Old Testament book, reveal the simple, natural, deeply spiritual atmosphere in which Jesus' faith developed.

Although the fact is often overlooked, Jesus was also intimately acquainted with the teaching of Israel's wise men or sages, and especially with their pointed proverbs. Repeatedly he identifies himself with these earlier teachers of men (cf. Matt. 11¹⁹ Luke 7³⁵). Many of his parables are based on figures suggested in the proverbs of the Jewish sages. In one instance, at least, he reiterates a teaching of that noble friend of humanity Ben Sira (cf. Luke 12¹⁶⁻²¹ and Ben S. 5¹). The evidence is convincing that he singled out and assimilated all that was best in the message of Israel's earlier teachers and made it the basis of his own.

VIII. The Young Master Builder.

In the gospel narratives Jesus is called a carpenter and the son of a carpenter. The Greek word used in Mark 6³ suggests one who not only used the tools of this trade but also planned and even directed constructive work. That Jesus' occupation was limited to making yokes, as Justin Martyr states, is nowhere confirmed by the implications of the older records. His interest in the foundations of the temple, his parable of the houses built on a rock or on the sand, his allusions to the destruction of the temple and to its being rebuilt, to the man who pulled down his granaries that he might build larger, and to the builder who exhausted his resources before completing his work (Luke 14²⁸⁻³⁰) all imply that Jesus was a master builder. The skill with which he trained and sent forth his disciples indicates that he was accustomed to directing men. Several of the parables, as, for example, that of the talents, or of the equally paid laborers, or of the two sons who were asked to work for their father, represent the point of view of the employer rather than that of the employed. So also does his quick appreciation of the words of the centurion who was accustomed to issuing commands. At the same time, it is clear that Jesus worked with his own hands, as well as directed others. His task was doubtless to build the roofs and the simple woodwork required in the square houses of Nazareth. It may have also included the building of the stone and mud foundations and walls and the rude furniture and tools required by the citizens of the upland village. But the main occupation of a carpenter in a settled town like Nazareth was to rebuild the houses or barns that had fallen into disrepair. In the rigorous climate of Galilee the mud walls and roofs must constantly be restored, so that the chief task of the many that fell to the local builder was to rebuild. If these conclusions are correct, they throw much light upon Jesus' training for his life-work. Amos as a shepherd, accustomed to be on a constant watch against Arab marauder or wild beast, was thereby trained to be the watchman who proclaimed to northern Israel the advance of the Assyrian lion. Even so Jesus' work as a master builder led him to see the possibilities in those whose moral character needed fundamental repair. His interests and methods, in contrast to those of the earlier teachers of his race, were thoroughly constructive. He was pre-eminently a re-builder and upbuilder. Under his powerful, positive influence diseased bodies were restored to health, disordered minds became clear and normal, men and women, held captive by the sinister power of their past sins and wrong habits, were freed from their fetters. Jesus, with trained insight, not only perceived the divine possibilities in each human being, however humble, but also showed him how to realize those possibilities. Thus the Master Builder, by study, by meditation, and practical experience, was trained in God's own way to become the master builder of men. Moreover, he was able to train those who in turn became builders of men so skilfully that through them his influence has gone forth throughout all the world.

§ CXXII. THE PERSONALITY AND TEACHING OF JOHN THE BAPTIST

Now in the fifteenth year of the reign of Tiberius Cæsar, Pontius Pilate being governor of Judea, and Herod being tetrarch of Galilee, and his brother Philip tetrarch of the region of Iturea and Trachonitis, and Lysanias tetrarch of Abilene, in the high priesthood of Annas and Caiaphas, the word of God came to John, the son of Zacharias, in the Wilderness of Judea: Repent, for the kingdom of Heaven is near. Now this John had a garment of camel's hair and a leather girdle about his loins, and his food was locusts and wild honey. *1. The message of John the Baptist (Luke 3¹, ², Matt. 3⁴, cf. Matt. 3¹⁻³)*

Then Jerusalem and all Judea and all the country around about the Jordan began to go out to him, and to be baptized by him in the River Jordan, confessing their sins. *2. Its effect (Matt. 3⁵, ⁶, cf. Luke 3³)*

He said, therefore, to the crowds that went out to be baptized by him, You offspring of vipers, who warned you to flee from the wrath to come? Bring forth, therefore, fruits worthy of repentance and do not say to yourselves, 'We are descendants of Abraham'; for I tell you, that God is able of these stones to raise up children to Abraham. Already the axe is laid at the foot of the trees; every tree therefore that does not bring forth good fruit is cut down, and cast into the fire. *3. His call to repentance (Luke 3⁷⁻⁹, cf. Matt. 3⁷⁻¹⁰)*

And the crowd kept asking him, saying, What then must we do? And he answered and said to them, He who has two coats, let him give to him that has none; and he who has food, let him do likewise. And there came also tax-collectors to be baptized, and they said to him, Teacher, what must we do? And he said to them, Extort no more than is assigned to you. Soldiers also asked him, saying, And we, what must we do? And he said to them, Use violence toward none, neither accuse any one wrongfully; and be content with your wages. *4. His practical counsel to different classes (Luke 3¹⁰⁻¹⁴)*

Now as the people were in expectation and all were arguing in their minds about John, whether possibly he were the Christ, John answered, saying to them all, I indeed baptize you with water; but one is coming mightier than I, the latchet of whose shoes I am not worthy to untie. He will baptize you with the Holy Spirit and with fire. His fan is *5. His predictions regarding his successor (Luke 3¹⁵⁻¹⁷, cf. Matt. 3¹¹,¹²)* in his hand and he will thoroughly cleanse his threshing floor, and gather the wheat into his barn; but the chaff he will burn up with unquenchable fire.

I. The Records of John's Birth and Work. John the Baptist, except in Luke, appears in the gospel narrative entirely without introduction. The birth stories in Luke indicate how deep was the impression that the personality and work of John made upon later generations, for they believed that his birth was announced by an angel and attended by miraculous signs. These beautiful stories, preserved by Luke, who was skilful in detecting the heart-beat of the people, indicate that John was a Judean and born in a God-fearing, priestly family. His home was in a village outside Jerusalem. The name of the town has disappeared from the gospel story, and the later conjectures of pious pilgrims apparently have no historical basis. His home was probably near Jerusalem. His father's occupation often took him to the temple and gave him an insight into the inner life of his nation which he doubtless imparted to his son. The one fixed date in gospel history is the year of John's first appearance as a public preacher. Luke (3^{1-3}) states that John the Baptist began his work in the fifteenth year of the Emperor Tiberius. Inasmuch as Tiberius began his reign in 14 A.D., John must have entered upon his public activity either during the latter part of 28 or the beginning of 29 A.D.

The few details that have been preserved by the synoptic gospels regarding the work of John the Baptist are well attested. The underlying source is the early collection of Jesus' sayings (Q) from which Matthew and Luke drew much of their data. The brief summary of John's work at the beginning of Mark's gospel also appears to have been based upon the same source. In the account of John's public preaching, Matthew and Luke have quoted almost verbatim from this teaching source. In 3^{10-14} Luke adds a quotation, either from this source or else from another known only to him. Its literary form, its contents, and its agreement with the facts given by both Matthew and Luke all confirm its historical accuracy. To this account Luke has added in $3^{15, 16a}$ a statement in his own words regarding the impression which John's teaching made upon the multitudes. From a detailed comparison of the texts it is possible to reconstruct with assurance the original narrative.

II. John's Character and Aims. In his character and teachings John closely resembled the early Hebrew prophets. The content of his message was in many respects similar to that of Amos. Like the princely Isaiah, he stepped out of his class. Like Jeremiah, he sacrificed all personal interest to the realization of his God-given mission. His conviction that a new and nobler era was about to dawn reflected the buoyant hopefulness of the II Isaiah. His habits and costume, as well as his boldness, reminded the people of the prophet Elijah. It is not strange, therefore, that they regarded John as the fulfilment of the prediction of the second coming of that pioneer prophet recorded in the closing verses of the prophecy of Malachi. Jesus also recognized in the spirit and methods of John the essential fulfilment of the earlier prediction.

In the light of the earlier prophetic analogies and of contemporary conditions, it is possible to understand John and his work. Already there were many indications of a widespread reaction against the cold formalism and deep-rooted corruption that prevailed throughout Palestine and even in Jerusalem under the shadow of the temple. The sect of the Essenes represented one phase of this reaction. While they retained the ceremonialism of Judaism, they sought through asceticism and the observation of certain rules to realize their high ideals of personal purity. Although he did not subscribe to their tenets as a whole, it is practically certain that John knew and came into contact with this peculiar sect. Many of them found their homes in the deep ravines which ran through the wilderness to the lower Jordan, the scene of John's public activity. In his emphasis upon personal morality, upon deeds of justice and mercy, and upon sharing possessions with the needy, John was in perfect accord with the Essenes, although in other respects he differed widely from them. John stood for three things: (1) as a link between what was best in Israel's past and present; (2) as a protest against existing conditions; and (3) as the herald of a new era.

III. **His Teachings.** The gospel record is silent regarding John's prophetic call. It introduces the prophet in the full tide of his public activity. Like the earlier prophets, he addressed his nation as a whole and strove to prepare it for the new era which he declared was about to dawn. The phrase "kingdom of Heaven" was variously interpreted by the Jews of his day. It meant literally the reign or rule of God, for, since the days of the Maccabees, Heaven was commonly used as a synonym for God. John manifested no sympathy with the popular, nationalistic hope of his race. Possibly the current apocalyptic expectations which included a supernatural overthrow of existing conditions, the exaltation of the pious and faithful to positions of highest authority, and the inauguration of a new political and social organization, in which the people of Jehovah would rule supreme over all mankind, may have been present in John's thought; but this belief is not implied by the gospel records. John held fast to the ethical ideals of the pre-exilic prophets like Amos and Isaiah. His statement that "God is able of these stones to raise up children to Abraham" indicates that in his mind God's reign was not limited to the Jews. Instead, he declared that the axe was laid at the root of the trees, that Judaism was threatened with immediate destruction. Furthermore, he taught that only by bearing good fruit could the individual or the nation escape the impending judgment. Among those who came out to hear him were not only Jews, but also Gentiles and Samaritan soldiers, and for them all he had the same practical, ethical message. A characteristic and surprising element in John's teaching was his declaration that his own work was incomplete. He fully recognized his limitations as a reformer. He was able to help men to break free from the influence of their past habits and life and wrong motives; but he also saw the need for a greater teacher who would completely destroy the corrupt elements in the nation, conserve all that was good, and, above all, so inspire men with the spirit of God, the Holy One, that their motives and characters would be fundamentally changed. In the belief that this greater teacher was soon to come John was influenced not only by his clear recognition of the insistent needs of his age, but also by the predictions of earlier prophets, like the author of Malachi 3^{1-3}, and, above all, by the portrait of the servant of Jehovah in Isaiah 42–53. It was regarding this servant of Jehovah that the earlier prophet had declared in the name of Jehovah:

> I have put my spirit upon him,
> That he may set forth law to the nations (42¹).

IV. **John's Symbol of Baptism.** Although John reacted against the current ceremonialism, he made use of the symbol of baptism, and because he used this he was commonly known as "the Baptizer." Symbolic purification by the use of water was no new idea in Judaism. In Ezekiel 36²⁴, ²⁵ Jehovah declares to the scattered Jewish exiles: I will gather you from the nations "and I will sprinkle clean water upon you and you shall be cleansed from all your filthiness." In the same connection the prophet adds, speaking for Jehovah, "I will put my spirit within you and cause you to live according to my statutes." Possibly from this context John gained his idea of the Greater One who would baptize the people with the spirit of the Holy One. Isaiah's words: "Wash you, make yourselves clean" (1^{16}), must have deeply influenced John. Washing was also required by the Jewish ritual to remove various types of ceremonial pollution (cf. Ex. 19^{10} Lev. 15$^{5-8,}$ $^{10-21,}$ ^{27} 17^{16} 22^6). A ceremonial bath was necessary if a Gentile desired to become a proselyte. John, however, made it the chief symbol in his work, not because of its ceremonial associations, but because it was the universally recognized symbol of cleansing from filth. His aim was to provide a simple, direct means whereby the common people, and especially those burdened with sin, could find access to God and be assured of his forgiveness. Immersion of the entire man was doubtless the type of baptism which John employed, for it is adapted to his spirit and purpose. He sought by word and symbol to bring about in each man, not partial but complete moral purification. It is obvious that to a man like John, whose emphasis was entirely moral and spiritual, this outward act was but a convenient sign used to symbolize a deeper reality. For the men who were baptized by John it meant three things: (1) public confession of guilt and renunciation of past sins; (2) a prayer for divine forgiveness and for consecration to a purer life; and (3) preparation for God's coming rule in the life of the individual and the nation.

V. The Results of John's Work. John appears for a time to have shaken the foundations of Judaism's self-assurance. Pharisees, as well as the masses, came to him as he taught and baptized on the banks of the lower Jordan. Men of all classes, including those far beyond the pale of Phariseeism, were attracted to him. Jews and Gentiles alike went out to hear this uncompromising preacher of justice and ethical religion. What for them was John's charm? His appearance, and what might be called sensational methods, doubtless attracted many, for his generation ran eagerly after every new religious enthusiast; but the foundation of John's power lay deeper. The boldness and intense earnestness of the man proclaimed his absolute sincerity. The more thoughtful Jews recognized in him the spirit and message of the ancient prophets. Many were attracted by the note of expectancy, and hoped that he was but the herald announcing the early realization of their own peculiar type of messianic hope, whether national and kingly or apocalyptic and catastrophic. The majority went to John because his words stirred their consciences and promised release from the burden of sin that oppressed them. His dramatic symbol of baptism at once suggested that he had a message fitted to meet those needs.

The Jewish writer, Josephus, bears strong testimony to the character of the man and the impression that he made upon his race: "He was a good man and commanded the Jews to exercise virtue, both as justice toward one another and piety toward God, and so to come to baptism; for baptism would be acceptable to God, if they made use of it; not in order to expiate some sin, but for the purification of the body, provided that the soul was thoroughly purified beforehand by righteousness" (*Ant.*, XVIII, 5²). John, like the rabbis of his day, gathered about him a group of disciples whose fidelity is attested not only by their devotion at the death of their master, but also by the fact that they evidently disseminated his teachings widely throughout the Græco-Roman world. A quarter of a century later Paul found in distant Ephesus a body of John's followers who believed and lived in accordance with the teachings of their martyred master (Acts 19¹⁻⁷). From certain passages in the Fourth Gospel it would appear that as late as the close of the first Christian century many were found who still followed the teachings of John and in some cases were inclined to regard them as more authoritative than those of Jesus. The influence which John exerted upon Jesus marks, however, the culmination of his work.

§ CXXIII. JESUS' BAPTISM AND TEMPTATION

1. His baptismal vision (Mark 1⁹⁻¹¹, *cf.* Matt. 3¹³⁻¹⁷ Luke 3²¹, ²²)
Now it came to pass in those days that Jesus came from Nazareth of Galilee and was baptized by John in the Jordan. And at once, as he came up from the water, he saw the skies part asunder and the Spirit, like a dove, come down upon him. And a voice out of the skies said, Thou art my Son, the beloved, in thee I delight.

2. Temptation to self-gratification (Matt. 4¹⁻⁴, *cf.* Mark 1¹²⁻¹³ Luke 4¹⁻⁴)
Then Jesus was led up by the Spirit into the wilderness to be tempted by the devil. And when he had fasted forty days and forty nights he afterwards hungered. And the tempter came and said to him, If thou art the Son of God, command that these stones become bread. But he answered, It is written: 'Not on bread alone is man to live, but on every word that proceeds from the mouth of God.'

3. To use unfair means (Matt. 4⁵⁻⁷, *cf.* Luke 4⁹⁻¹²)
Then the devil takes him to the holy city and, setting him on the pinnacle of the temple, says to him, If thou art the Son of God, throw thyself down; for it is written, 'He will give his angels charge concerning thee and in their hands they will bear thee up, that thou mayest never dash thy foot

against a stone.' Jesus said to him, Again it is written, ' Thou shalt not tempt the Lord thy God.'

Once more the devil takes him to a very high mountain and shows him all the kingdoms of the world and their glory. And he said to him, All these things will I give thee if thou wilt fall down and worship me. Then Jesus says to him, Begone, Satan, for it is written, ' Thou shalt worship the Lord thy God and him only shalt thou serve.'

4. To compromise his ideal (Matt. 4⁸⁻¹¹, *Cf* Luke 4⁵⁻⁸, ¹³)

Then the devil leaves him.

I. The Reasons Why Jesus Went to John. The Gospel of the Hebrews states that Jesus was induced by his brothers to go and listen to the stirring sermons of John the Baptist. Possibly there was a certain historical basis for this statement, but in any case the reasons why Jesus went to John were more fundamental. In such a small country as Palestine it was practically inevitable that the works and teachings of John should be well known, and they were of a character to attract the Master Builder of Nazareth. Jesus recognized in John one who, like himself, had seen through the hollowness and superficiality of Phariseeism and was eager to bring life and joy to those who were unable to fulfil the narrow, impossible demands of the Jewish religion. Both were spiritual disciples of the great ethical prophets of their race, so that they met on common ground. Jesus' later utterances regarding John indicate that he was attracted by the charm of the Baptist's personality. His boldness, his moral earnestness, and his interest in all classes drew the Nazarene to him. John was the first to voice that new, divine humanism that found not only its echo but its full expression in Jesus. John apparently crystallized feelings and convictions already in the mind of the young Master Builder.

II. Literary Form of the Record. Each of the synoptic gospels records Jesus' baptismal vision. They all appear to have drawn their material from the older teaching sources. In the Marcan version the vision of his divine calling comes only to Jesus. Luke adds the important and impressive fact that it came while he was praying. Luke also implies that the multitudes were present. In Matthew the divine proclamation is to all mankind; while in the Fourth Gospel it comes not to Jesus but to John the Baptist.

Some scholars hold that these various narratives represent simply the attempt of the early church to trace back Jesus' messianic call to the baptism; but it seems far more probable that each gospel writer, in his characteristic way, records Jesus' endeavor to make clear to his disciples his inner experience at the critical moment when he openly allied himself with John. Other analogies in the gospels indicate that the vision was the usual literary form in which Jesus and the evangelists were wont to describe a subjective experience. Thus, according to Luke 10¹⁸, Jesus said, on the successful return of the disciples after their preaching mission: "I saw Satan fall as lightning from heaven." According to Matthew 16¹⁷ he declared after Peter's confession: "Flesh and blood have not revealed it to you, but my Father who is in heaven." Obviously it is impossible and misleading to interpret the account of the baptism and temptation with absolute literalness. The phrase, "the heavens are opened," is the regular idiom by which the New Testament writers introduce a spiritual vision (cf., for example, Stephen's vision in Acts 7⁵⁵). The physical impossibility of seeing all the nations of the world at one glance has long been recognized. The narrative also reflects the universal belief of the ancients that the world was flat. The bold suggestion that Jesus should bow down to Satan was in itself too repulsive to constitute for him a real temptation.

In its literary form the account of the temptation is closely akin to such a narrative as that in Genesis 3, in which the struggle within the mind of woman is made objective by means of the dialogue with the serpent. It illustrates Jesus' superlative skill as a teacher. Even if he had described his inner struggle in the abstract terms of philosophy and psychology, he would have conveyed little to the untrained minds of his disciples. Told in the form of a narrative, full of vivid pictures, this account not only suggested to their intuitive and imaginative minds the nature of his temptation, but also enabled them to remember and transmit the essential facts, so that they may to-day be interpreted in the light of their historical setting and the larger knowledge and experience that has come to the race.

In character and purpose the narrative is similar to the visions by which Amos, Isaiah, and Jeremiah each communicated to his disciples the nature of the inner struggle which culminated in his prophetic call. Thus, for example, in the sixth chapter of his prophecy Isaiah tells of the vision which came to him in the temple on the death year of King Uzziah, when his consciousness of Jehovah's character and the needs of his nation led him to the great decision expressed in the words, "Here Lord, send me." The close of the narrative reflects his later experiences and indicates that the story was not told to his disciples until many years had elapsed. Jesus likewise appears to have described his own decisive struggle not until later in his ministry, when the minds of his disciples had been in part prepared to understand it. The occasion was probably after Peter had openly declared at Cæsarea Philippi his belief that Jesus was the Messiah. Jesus' quick rejoinder, "Get thee behind me, Satan," with which he met Peter's protest against the thought that his master was about to face death, indicates that Peter voiced one phase of the temptation which was present with his master throughout his public and private activity (*cf.* Luke 22[28]). In the accounts of his baptism and temptation Jesus was also endeavoring to make clear to this inner group of followers the lofty spiritual ideal that guided him in all his work and teaching.

III. **The Significance of the Baptismal Vision.** Jesus' baptism clearly marks a great turning-point in his life. It was the moment when he gave up his former occupation for his new vocation. The baptism represented not the decision of a moment but the culmination of all his previous training and thought. He had lived in closest touch with the people of Nazareth and had moved among the throngs that filled the crowded cities of Galilee. He recognized their deep need of a spiritual guide who would lead them to their divine Father and reveal to them the forgiveness and the inspiration which God was eager to give. In his own experience Jesus had found that eternal source of peace and strength. His clear consciousness that his own personal knowledge of God and of the way of life alone would satisfy the needs of the people was the compelling force in his call. When he left his shop at Nazareth and took his stand beside John, who with splendid courage and success was addressing himself to these moral and spiritual needs, Jesus publicly signified his response to that divine call. The message which came to him was expressed in the language of Psalm 2[7]:

> Jehovah said to me, "Thou art my son;
> This day have I begotten thee,"

And Isaiah 42[1]:

> Behold my servant whom I uphold,
> My chosen, in whom I take delight;
> I put my spirit upon him,
> That he may set forth the law to the nations.

It was an absolute assurance of his divine sonship and of God's approval of his act. With it came an overwhelming sense of responsibility. The fact that the words of the II Isaiah were in his mind suggests the way in which he interpreted that responsibility. It is also significant that when he later returned to his home at Nazareth and attempted to make clear to his fellow-townsmen the nature of his mission, he quoted, according to Luke 4[17-19] (*cf.* Isa. 61[1, 2]), one of the memorable passages from the same prophet who had defined in most spiritual terms God's eternal purpose and the way in which it was to be realized. The oldest gospel records imply that Jesus' full messianic consciousness came at his baptism. How far that consciousness was removed from the popular expectations of his day is indicated by the story of the temptation, as well as by his later teaching and work. In a far deeper sense than any Old Testament prophet had predicted, Jesus realized that he was the Son of God, called to do a work so personal, so revolutionary, and so spiritual that it would fail completely to meet the narrow, materialistic, impossible expectations of his people.

IV. The Meaning of the Account of Jesus' Temptation. Many questions gather about the story of Jesus' temptation: Does it concern the character or the method of his work, or both? Does it represent the temptations of a brief period or of a lifetime? Are the common human temptations begotten by passion and ambition the basis, or does it represent a conflict between Jesus' own spiritual ideal, as it had been in part defined by the II Isaiah, and the material expectations of the people? Do the different incidents of the narrative represent different phases of the temptation, or are they but varied illustrations of the same inner struggle?

Psychologically a period of struggle and decision was practically inevitable after a moment of great spiritual exaltation. Persian tradition states that Zarathustra (Zoroaster), at the beginning of his work as a prophet, was tempted by an evil spirit to renounce the good law and so gain power over the nations. Confucius spent three years in solitude before he took up his work as a teacher. Paul of Tarsus, after his vision on the way to Damascus, spent months, if not years, in meditation and readjustment apart from men, in the solitude of the Arabian desert. The traditional setting of Jesus' temptation was the wilderness of Judea, which, with its rounded, barren, treeless hills and deep, rocky ravines, rises abruptly on the west of the Jordan Valley. It offered the same quiet seclusion that Jesus later sought and found on the hilltops north of the Sea of Galilee. Here he meditated on his God-given task and the way in which it was to be accomplished. The different incidents in the gospel account apparently represent different phases of temptation that came to him as he faced his life-work. That he might have yielded to the temptations that assailed him is definitely implied. In the gospel story there is little trace of the baser passions that attack men most strongly during the adolescent period. This fact does not prove that Jesus had failed to feel their influence. His profound sympathy with sinners suggests that he had; but, if so, they had been overcome in the thirty or more years of struggle, training, and growth in quiet Nazareth. The temptations which now came to Jesus are those which appeal to a strong man in the full flush of his manhood. In many respects they are typical and, as such, constitute one of the strongest bonds that bind the perfect son of man to his fellows.

V. The Different Phases of Jesus' Temptation. The background of the first temptation is the hunger begotten by the protracted sojourn in the barren, uninhabited wilderness; but the real motive is evidently something far deeper than mere physical hunger. Jesus' answer, quoted from Deuteronomy 8³, "Man shall not live by bread alone, but by every word that comes from the mouth of God," indicates that it was primarily a struggle between his higher conception of his task and the natural desire for ease and quiet and popularity. He loved men and society. Should he use his power for his own self-gratification? It is the insidious temptation that comes to every man after the first burst of youthful enthusiasm has spent itself. It was the temptation that mastered the man whom Jesus portrays with superlative insight in the parable of the rich and successful landholder who said to himself, I will tear down my barns and build larger, and then settle down to a life of ease and luxury. It was because Jesus knew the deadly power of this temptation that he declared, "If any man will come after me, let him deny himself." He knew that self-indulgence was a deadly foe to efficiency and that it would never meet his deeper moral and spiritual needs or those of the men who looked to him for leadership. He recognized that no man could live by bread alone. Not material ease or luxury, but an intimate acquaintance with God and a consciousness of doing his will, whatever be the cost, could alone satisfy man's deep hunger.

The background of the second phase of the temptation is the popular, apocalyptic, messianic hopes that were strong in the minds of the men whom he wished to reach. These hopes voiced the political, social, and religious ideals of his race. Whether he spoke to the masses, to the Pharisees, or to his own disciples, these popular messianic expectations confronted him at every point throughout his ministry. To a pious, patriotic son of Abraham they presented a temptation that was strong and insistent. Repeatedly the scribes and Pharisees in his later ministry came to him demanding miraculous proofs of his divine authority. In every case he sternly refused to grant their request. His reply to this temptation is voiced in the language of Deuteronomy 6[16], "Ye shall not test Jehovah, your God." Tersely it expresses the profound truth that man has no right, even if he could, to force the hand of the Almighty. It illustrates the superb poise and sanity which characterized Jesus' attitude toward the current apocalyptic hopes and toward the subtle temptations that they presented to one eager to gain the ear of the people. He knew that by performing some portent, or by even publicly proclaiming that he was the Messiah, he might gain a large and immediate following. Expressed in modern terms, it was the temptation to yield to the lure of selfish and base ambition and to seek to attain quick popularity and success by unfair means. Jesus saw clearly the selfishness and the ultimate futility of these sensational and questionable methods. Work that abides is not so done; least of all a work that is to touch and transform the beliefs, the motives, and the lives of men.

The third phase of the temptation was an appeal, not merely to Jesus' natural ambition for power, but also to his noble desire to extend widely the influence of his personality and message. In its essence it appears to have been the temptation to lay aside for the moment those severe, seemingly impossible spiritual ideals that in time transformed the natural leaders of his race into enemies, and thus by a specious compromise to broaden his field of service. Satan was represented by the powerful Pharisees and by the corrupt hierarchy which, with the grafter Annas as its virtual head, ruled enthroned in the temple at Jerusalem. Should he contend against this mighty power, as he did practically alone until it treacherously slew him, or should he bow before it and by thus compromising his ideals mount to public favor and influence? It is in many ways the most insidious temptation that can assail a strong man intent on attaining success and on doing a noble work. The author of Matthew has rightly made this the culminating phase of the temptation. Jesus, however, saw clearly the pitfall into which every man inevitably stumbles who compromises the ideal which God reveals to him and allies himself with injustice and graft, even though such an alliance may seem to be the only road that leads to large success and service. He whose supreme aim was to bring men into intelligent, loyal relation to God knew that he could not perform his mission if disloyal in the slightest to the promptings of the divine voice within him. It was his single-eyed, unswerving devotion to the service of God that made Jesus the universal Saviour of men.

This marvellous story of the temptation is apparently also an epitome of Jesus' inner struggle and victory during his public ministry. It reveals at the beginning of the gospel narrative the ideals, the motives, and the heroism that guided him to his final triumph on the cross. It is the open window of his soul, through which it is possible to study the simple yet divine principles that found expression in all that he taught and did. It reveals the one absolutely normal and therefore perfect man. It shows that Jesus regarded life and humanity with eyes that had looked into the very heart of the Father, and that he recognized that he was therefore in a unique sense called to reveal God to his fellow-men. The fulfilment of this divinest of all missions led Jesus to disappoint almost every hope that in the minds of the people was associated with the magic word "Messiah." And yet in the sense in which he interpreted that ancient hope and in the higher meaning which he gave it, he knew, with growing conviction, that he was indeed the Servant of Jehovah, the One anointed and called to do God's work, Israel's true Messiah.

§ CXXIV. JESUS AND JOHN THE BAPTIST

Then Herod seized John the Baptist and bound him, and put him in prison for the sake of Herodias, his brother Philip's wife. For John had said to him, It is not lawful for you to have her. And although Herod wanted to put him to death, he feared the people for they held John to be a prophet.

Now after John was put in prison Jesus came into Galilee preaching the good tidings of God, and saying, The kingdom of God is near. Repent and believe in the good tidings.

When John heard in prison about the deeds of Jesus, he sent by his disciples and said to him: Are you he who is to come, or are we to look for some one else? And Jesus in answer said to them, Go and report to John what you see and hear: the blind regain their sight, and the lame walk, the lepers are cleansed and the deaf hear, and the dead are

1. John's imprisonment (Matt. 14³⁻⁵, cf. Luke 3¹⁹, ²⁰ Mark 6¹⁷⁻²⁰)
2. Jesus' early preaching (Mark 1¹⁴, ¹⁵)
3. His reply to John (Matt. 11²⁻⁶, cf. Luke 7¹⁹⁻²³)

raised up, and the poor have good tidings preached to them. And blessed is he who shall find no cause of stumbling in me.

4. His estimate of John (Matt. 11:7-19, cf. Luke 7:24-35)

And as these men went away, Jesus began to speak to the people about John: What did you go out into the wilderness to see? A reed shaken by the wind? But what did you go out to see? A man clothed in soft robes? Behold, those who wear soft robes are in kings' houses. But why did you go out? To see a prophet? Yea, I say to you, and much more than a prophet! This is he of whom it is written,

> Behold I send my messenger before my face,
> Who shall prepare thy way before thee.

Verily I tell you, Among those born of women, no one hath arisen greater than John the Baptist; but he who is least in the kingdom of Heaven is greater than he. For all the prophets and the law prophesied until John: yea, if you are willing to receive it, this is Elijah who is to come. He who has ears to hear, let him hear. And from the days of John the Baptist until now the kingdom of Heaven suffers violence, and the violent seize it. To what shall I compare this generation? It is like children sitting in the market places, who call to their playmates and say, We piped to you but you did not dance. We lamented, but you did not beat your breast. For John came, neither eating nor drinking, and men say, 'He has a demon.' The Son of man came eating and drinking, and men say, 'Here is a glutton and a wine-drinker, a friend of tax-collectors and sinners.' Yet wisdom is vindicated by her deeds.

5. John's death (Matt. 14:6-12, cf. Mark 6:21-29)

Now when Herod's birthday came, the daughter of Herodias danced before them, and pleased Herod. Whereupon he promised with an oath to give her whatever she should ask. And she, being prompted by her mother, said to him, Give me here, on a dish, the head of John the Baptist. And although the king was sorry, yet because of his oath, he commanded that it be given her. So he sent and beheaded John in the prison. And John's head was brought on a dish, and given to the girl; and she brought it to her mother. And John's disciples came and carried away the body, and buried him. Then they went and told Jesus.

THE GOSPEL EVIDENCE OF JESUS' WORK IN JUDEA

I. The Gospel Evidence that Jesus Worked First in Judea.
The synoptic gospels are singularly silent regarding Jesus' activity immediately after his baptism and temptation. Mark, however, records the fact that immediately after John was imprisoned "Jesus came into Galilee preaching." This statement implies that he had remained for a time with John. That he did not return to his work as a carpenter at Nazareth is probable, for the exalted vision of his mission which he had received at his baptism made that practically impossible. Judea, already aroused by John's stirring message, seemed to furnish the most promising field in which to enter upon his work. John 3²²⁻²⁶ refers definitely to a Judean ministry, although the tradition bears the marks of the later point of view. From John 1⁴⁰⁻⁴² it may also be inferred that the two brothers, Andrew and Peter, were numbered among the disciples of John the Baptist, and that Jesus first met them during his work in Judea. If so, the readiness with which they later, beside the Sea of Galilee, responded to his call is fully explained.

The exact nature of Jesus' activity in Judea is not clear. Apparently he at first took up the message and methods of John the Baptist. Mark 1¹⁵ states that, even when Jesus returned and began to preach in Galilee, his words were an echo of John's: "The kingdom of God is near. Repent." The Fourth Gospel adds that Jesus, while still in Judea, baptized and gathered about him disciples, as did John, and that the reason for his return to Galilee was that he might not eclipse John's work. Even though the tradition is late, and is intended to magnify the work of Jesus in comparison with that of John, it strengthens the evidence for a brief Judean ministry. That Jesus made any superior claims for himself or sought to rival the work of John is disproved by the spirit and conception of his mission revealed in the account of the temptation and also by John's later message to him. Jesus' sojourn in Judea must have been primarily a period of training and testing. It also made clear to him the difficulties of the Judean field, and probably led him finally to choose Galilee as the chief scene of his activity. His later lament over Jerusalem (Luke 13³⁴) also implies that he seriously attempted to gain a hearing and a following in Judea and failed. There is no evidence regarding the length of Jesus' sojourn in Judea, but it was probably short, for John's imprisonment appears to have come soon after Jesus' baptism.

II. John's Arrest. Mark's gospel implies that the event which led Jesus to turn from Judea to Galilee was John's arrest and imprisonment. Josephus states that Herod's reason for making the arrest was that the multitudes followed the Baptist and listened to him so gladly that the suspicious tetrarch "feared lest the great influence John had over the people might put it in his power and inclination to raise a rebellion, for they seemed to do anything that he advised. Accordingly John was sent a prisoner, because of Herod's suspicious character, to Machærus," the gloomy castle on the heights east of the Dead Sea. The three synoptic gospels give more detailed reasons for John's arrest. It was in keeping with the spirit of the intrepid John that he should publicly—possibly in the presence of Herod—protest against his unjust and immoral act in marrying the divorced wife of his kinsman, Herod Bœthus. John's protest was all the more distasteful to Herod because it voiced incensed public opinion. This courageous act of the Baptist undoubtedly deepened the popular impression that he was, indeed, the Elijah whose coming was predicted in the closing verses of Malachi. Even as Elijah of old had publicly condemned Ahab's despotism and murderous cruelty in seizing Naboth's vineyard at the suggestion of Jezebel, so John, according to the gospel narratives, raised his voice in stern protest against Herod's crime that had been prompted by the wiles of Herodias. John himself absolutely repudiated the title of Messiah, but the popular reception of his teachings tended to confirm Herod's fears that he was a religious enthusiast who might stir the people to rebellion. Josephus's reference to John is also significant, for it reveals the popular beliefs then rife and Herod's attitude toward them.

John's arrest must have made a deep impression upon Jesus. His departure from Judea was evidently not prompted by fear, for in leaving Judea and Perea for Galilee he came more directly under Herod's power and surveillance. John's imprisonment must have struck dismay into the minds of the people of Judea and chilled their enthusiasm so that they had little desire to listen to disciples of the Baptizer or to teachers like Jesus. He therefore sought a more familiar and favorable field; but he who at this time proclaimed himself a teacher and champion of the common people, even in Galilee, faced from the first the danger of imprisonment and death.

III. **John's Later Message to Jesus.** The records of Jesus' later contact with John are taken from the oldest teaching source (Q). The quotations in Matthew and Luke are practically identical. Luke expands the narrative in $7^{21, \ 22a}$, stating in his own language, by way of explanation, the effect of Jesus' work upon the multitudes. This vivid, early narrative contains a remarkable illustration of Jesus' superlative skill in dealing with men. Evidently a rumor of his work and teaching had reached the ears of John through his disciples. With tense interest John sent them to ascertain whether Jesus was, indeed, that greater one whom he hoped was soon to come. It was a critical moment in Jesus' ministry, when these devoted followers of John, probably in the presence of the multitude, put to him their eager question. If Jesus had attempted to answer John's definite inquiry, he would undoubtedly have been misunderstood. In a sense he was not the realization of John's hope, for the reality was far greater than the expectation. If he had proclaimed himself the Messiah, he would not only have thwarted his purpose, and involved himself with Herod, but would also have given the people and John a wrong impression. Instead, with rare pedagogical skill, he asked the disciples of John to stand by and witness with their own eyes the work he was doing. The words of Jesus as he describes his work are at many points an echo of those in Isaiah 61$^{1-3}$ (cf. also Isa. 42^7), which, according to Luke 4$^{16-21}$, he read and applied to himself on the occasion of his memorable visit to Nazareth. To one like John, familiar and in fullest sympathy with the teachings of the earlier prophets, Jesus' reply was equivalent to saying, "I am not the Messiah of the popular expectation, but I am doing the work of Jehovah's servant as defined by his most spiritual prophet." To an ethical teacher like John, who looked for one who would do a greater and more profoundly spiritual work than himself, Jesus' reply must have been in the highest degree satisfactory. Jesus' concluding words, however, "Blessed is he who shall find no cause of stumbling in me," implies that already he had met many who were dissatisfied with the interpretation which he was giving to his task. Possibly he also spoke as he did because he feared that John's disciples would fail to grasp the deeper significance of his work.

IV. **Jesus' Estimate of John.** In the ancient narrative, preserved practically verbatim in both Matthew and Luke, we have a clear statement of Jesus' estimate of John. It also well illustrates the clarity, vigor, and compelling power of the language with which Jesus clothed his thoughts. In a series of brief questions he prepared the minds of his hearers for a true appreciation of John. His words reflect the deep impression that the Baptist's unflinching courage, his disdain of luxury, and his spiritual message made on Jesus. He also declared that John realized the hope expressed in Malachi 3^1: "Behold, I am about to send my messenger, and he shall prepare the way before me." Mark, who begins his gospel with the statement that John was the fulfilment of this prophecy, may well have had in mind this utterance of Jesus. Without hesitation, Jesus placed John among the greatest teachers of the human race. And yet Jesus recognized that John failed to appreciate the full significance and possibilities of God's rule. With that calm assurance which came from conviction and experience, Jesus declared that whoever stood in the full light of his own more spiritual interpretation of God's relation to man and of man's larger life in God was greater than the latest and most heroic of all the long line of Israel's prophets.

The words which follow have all the characteristics of Jesus' epigrammatic style. Their meaning has been variously interpreted. Luke gives their logical if not their original order, but Matthew has the more exact form. The thought seems to be that the teachings of Israel's earlier lawgivers and prophets were the guides of the nation until John appeared. He presented a simpler and more spiritual conception of the kingdom of God. But Jesus' later experience had convinced him that what the people demanded was not the rule of God in their hearts and lives, but an actual material kingdom which they were ready, if necessary, to establish by violence. Thus, the older prophetic conception of the kingdom, or rule, of God had suffered violence at their hands. This interpretation is confirmed by Jesus' further statements regarding the unreasonable demands of the generation to whom he spoke. He likened them to children sitting in the marketplaces complaining of all who attempted to entertain or interest them. The austere John they characterized, in the language of their day, as insane. Jesus, who met all classes on the common basis of friendship and good-fellowship, they called a glutton and a friend of the disreputable classes. At the same time he expressed the firm conviction that the fruits of his work would justify the wisdom of his method and demonstrate the divine origin of his spiritual ideal.

V. The Account of John's Death. Mark's record of the closing scene in the life of John the Baptist shows in certain minor details the influence of popular transmission. Herodias, Herod's evil genius, was not, as it states, the former wife of Philip, but of Herod Boethus. Herodias's daughter Salome, who is represented as dancing before Herod and his assembled guests, and is spoken of as a young girl, must have been at least twenty-eight years of age at the time, for her second husband (the Philip the tetrarch mentioned by Luke) died in 34 A.D. It was also contrary to all known precedents for a Jewish or Roman ruler to permit one of the members of his family to dance at a public feast. Herod's promise that he would give to the maiden whatever she asked, even to the half of his kingdom, is more in keeping with the language and spirit of the book of Esther than with the habits and authority of a tetrarch like Herod, who was but an agent of Rome. Luke's keen historical sense led him to omit the story. Matthew's briefer and more conservative version has been followed in the text adopted above. Even though a later generation may have embellished the Marcan version of the story, the fact that John the Baptist paid for his courage by death at the hand of Herod is a tragic but well-established fact.

The news of John's death undoubtedly made a profound impression upon Herod's subjects, and most of all upon Jesus. It revealed clearly to him the forces with which he must deal and the fate that awaited an intrepid herald of God's truth. Viewed in the light of history, the chief significance of John's work is that he was, as he declared, the forerunner of the one greater than he, the latchet of whose shoes he was unworthy to loosen. John was the forerunner of Jesus in that he aroused the conscience of his nation and taught them the comparative insignificance of form and ceremonial and the pre-eminent value of righteous deeds and of loyalty to God. He also attracted an earnest group of disciples and so trained them that some of them became faithful followers of Jesus. Above all, he taught his hearers to look for the speedy inauguration of God's reign. Finally, through contact with him, Jesus gained a clearer consciousness of his own divine task; and where John the Baptist laid down his work, the Master Builder of Nazareth took it up.

§ CXXV. JESUS' EARLY WORK IN GALILEE

Leaving Nazareth, Jesus went and dwelt in Capernaum, which is by the sea.

1. At Capernaum (Matt. 4¹³ᵃ)

Now Jesus was passing along beside the Sea of Galilee; and he saw Simon, and Andrew the brother of Simon casting a net into the sea; for they were fishers. And Jesus said to them, Come with me, and I will make you fishers of men. Then at once they left the nets and followed him. And going on a little further, he saw James the son of Zebedee, with John his brother, who also were in the boat mending the nets. And immediately he called them; and they left their father Zebedee in the boat with the hired servants, and went with him.

2. Call of the four fishermen (Mark 1¹⁶⁻²⁰, cf.Matt. 4¹⁸⁻²², Luke 5¹⁻¹¹)

Then Jesus found Philip and said to him, Follow me. Now, Philip was from the city of Andrew and Peter. Philip

3. Of Philip and Nathanael (John 1 43b-50)

finding Nathanael, said to him, We have found him of whom Moses in the law, and the prophets wrote, Jesus of Nazareth the son of Joseph. And Nathanael said to him, Can anything good come out of Nazareth? Philip said to him, Come and see. Jesus saw Nathanael coming to him and said of him, Look, an Israelite indeed, in whom is no guile! Nathanael said to him, How is it that you know me? Jesus answered and said to him, Before Philip called you, when you were under the fig tree, I saw you. Nathanael answered him, Rabbi, thou art the Son of God; thou art King of Israel. Jesus answered and said to him, Believest thou, because I said to thee, I saw thee beneath the fig tree? Thou shalt see greater things than these.

4. Jesus' authority (Mark 1 21, 22, cf. Luke 4 31, 32)

Now Jesus and his disciples entered Capernaum; and on the next sabbath day he went into the synagogue and began to teach. And the people were astonished at his teaching, for he taught them as one who had authority, and not as the scribes.

5. His ability to cure the insane (Mark 1 23-28, cf. Luke 4 33-37)

Now there was in their synagogue a man with an unclean spirit; and he cried out, saying, What business have you with us, Jesus of Nazareth? Have you come to destroy us? I know who you are, the Holy One of God. And Jesus rebuked the unclean spirit, saying, Silence! Come out of him! So after the unclean spirit had shaken the man, and had made him cry with a loud voice, it came out of him. And the people were all so amazed that they talked about it among themselves, saying, What is this? A new teaching with authority? He commands even the unclean spirits and they obey him! And the news regarding Jesus went out at once in all directions throughout Galilee.

6. Peter's mother-in-law (Mark 1 29-31, cf. Luke 4 38, 39 Matt. 8 14, 15) 7. Acts of healing (Mark 1 32-34, cf. Luke 4 40, 41 Matt. 8 16, 17)

And immediately after going out of the synagogue, they came into the house of Simon and Andrew, with James and John. Now the mother of Simon's wife lay sick of a fever; and immediately they told Jesus about her. And he came, and taking her hand, he raised her up; and the fever left her, and she ministered to them.

Now in the evening, when the sun had set, they brought to him all who were sick, and possessed by demons. And all the people of the city were gathered at the door. And he healed many who were sick with various kinds of diseases, and cast out many demons.

JESUS' EARLY WORK IN GALILEE

And very early the next morning, long before day, he rose and went out into a desert place, and there prayed. And Simon and they who were with him followed after him, and found him; and they said to him, All are seeking thee. And he said to them, Let us go elsewhere into the next town, that I may preach there also; for that is why I came out. Then he went through the whole of Galilee, preaching in the synagogues and casting out demons.

8. His retirement to pray and preach (Mark 1 35-38 cf. Luke 4 42, 43)

I. The Record. The basis of the gospel account of the beginning of Jesus' work in Galilee is the vivid narrative of Mark. The incidents gather about Peter's home at Capernaum and imply that his direct testimony is here the chief source. Mark's narrative reveals at every point a remarkable insight into Jesus' aims and methods. At this period, when Jesus touched Peter so intimately, there is every reason to believe that the chief disciple has recounted events in their original order. The description of the cleansing of the leper in Mark 1 40-45 is, however, loosely connected with its context. Matthew and Luke have a simpler and probably a more exact account. Matthew inserts it immediately after the so-called Sermon on the Mount, intending, perhaps, to illustrate thereby Jesus' careful observation of the Jewish ceremonial law. Luke adjusts it to its implied setting in Mark, and places the scene of the event in one of the cities outside Capernaum.

John 1 35-51 contains an account of the call of Philip and Nathanael. The incident is introduced by the author of the Fourth Gospel to illustrate his thesis that Jesus' messiahship was publicly recognized from the beginning of his ministry. While this position is contrary to the clear testimony of the synoptic gospels, which make Peter the first to call him Messiah, the narrative itself has probably preserved a nucleus of fact.

II. Reasons Why Jesus Went to Capernaum. Jesus' transfer of his home and the centre of his activity from Nazareth to Capernaum reveals the aim of his early work in Galilee. He fully realized that a prophet is not without honor save in his own country. The fact that the home of Peter and Andrew was in Capernaum may also have attracted him to that city; but the more fundamental reason was probably because Capernaum was to Galilee what Jerusalem was to Judea. Unlike the other cities about the Sea of Galilee, which were strongly Greek in population and civilization, Capernaum was Jewish. It was the centre of an active, teeming population. Past it ran the central highway from Egypt to Babylonia. Another highway from the east of the Jordan ran through it, along the northern end of the Sea of Galilee and across the broad valleys to the west, until it reached the great coast road from Egypt to Phœnicia. It was, therefore, in close communication with the other important cities of Palestine and with the commercial capitals of southwestern Asia. It was also, by virtue of its geographical and commercial position, one of the cities in which the Jews of Palestine came in closest touch with the Græco-Roman civilization and its corrupting influence. The resulting luxury and immorality furnished the dark background of Jesus' healing and teaching ministry. In and about Capernaum he found in largest numbers "the lost sheep of the house of Israel," whom he sought to shepherd. The insistent needs of the broad field, therefore, drew him thither, even as similar needs have attracted his heroic, devoted followers to the darkest spots on the face of the earth.

III. The Aims and Methods in the Early Galilean Work. As Jesus plainly declares, he came, "not to call the righteous, but sinners," the outcasts from the synagogue upon whom the Pharisees looked only with contempt and disapproval. His aim was to find and to heal those who were morally and spiritually sick. He sought not only to lead them to repent and to break their past habits, but to teach them how to live a richer, more joyous life. He endeavored to do so by bringing them into vital touch with God and by awakening in them a sense of their divine sonship and their human brotherhood. Thus, as an experienced master builder, he aimed to rebuild the ruined lives of men according to the plan of the divine Architect, and to make them effective members of God's kingdom. He aimed, also, to free that most democratic of Jewish institutions, the synagogue, from the dogmatic and ceremonial restrictions with which the scribes and Pharisees had surrounded it, and to restore it to the common people to whom it rightfully belonged.

His methods were carefully adapted to the realization of these definite aims. He depended primarily upon personal touch and friendship. Rejecting the ascetic habits of John the Baptist, he associated closely with all classes: with the fishermen along the shore, with the crowds in the market-places and on the streets, and with the multitudes assembled in the synagogues on the Sabbath day. His method was not so much that of the preacher as that of the teacher. It was only as the crowds gathered in large numbers about him that he resorted to preaching, and even then he always held himself open to questions and in turn propounded questions to the people, after the manner of the teaching rabbis. There are suggestions in the gospel records that he regarded his healing ministry as incidental and in many ways a hindrance to the realization of his main purpose. He sought to restore the rights of the synagogue to the people, not by denouncing the cold formalism of the scribes, but by making it the open court in which the vital questions of the daily religious life should be frankly and helpfully discussed. As ever, his method was constructive rather than destructive. Thus, his aim and his method in his earlier Galilean ministry were first, by public address and by mingling with all classes, to spread wide the net that he might draw to himself those who were needy and ready to listen to his message; then to teach them by word, by example, and by close personal contact the principles that were essential to the larger fellowship with God and man.

IV. **The Call of the Six Fishermen.** The account of the beginnings of Jesus' work is so meagre that we are dependent in part upon inferences drawn from the gospel records. John the Baptist had evidently attracted many followers from the cities about the Sea of Galilee, as was natural, for they were situated in the Jordan Valley that had been the scene of his work. These men were the nucleus of a larger following which Jesus soon drew to himself. The quick response of the two brothers, Andrew and Peter, and of the two sons of Zebedee to Jesus' invitation to join in his work indicates that they already were personally acquainted with him and partially understood him and his aims. The way in which Jesus calls them reveals that rare tact which characterizes all his dealings with men. From the first he set before them a large task, but one for which they were fitted and which therefore appealed to them individually. Their response to Jesus' call does not necessarily mean that they abandoned entirely their occupation as fishermen. The famous Jewish rabbis and their followers had their regular vocation as well as their avocation. After Jesus' crucifixion the disciples apparently returned at once to their work as fishermen. Jesus may have at first demanded only a part of their time. He simply requested that they aid in the work which he had undertaken. It is not stated whether or not they all followed him in his first preaching and teaching throughout Galilee. Mark 1[38] implies that Peter at least accompanied him.

John 1[35-51] indicates that the two brothers, Philip and Nathanael, early joined the growing ranks of Jesus' followers. They, like Simon Peter and Andrew, were natives of Bethsaida. Philip bore a Greek name, that of the tetrarch who had recently made their fishing town a centre of Greek culture, and had named it, in honor of the daughter of Augustus, Bethsaida Julias. It was situated on the left bank of the Jordan, on a slight eminence which rose about fifty feet above the surrounding plains. At this point the Jordan, after its rapid descent through the northern hills, begins to twist and wind more leisurely through the delta by which it enters the Sea of Galilee. Ruins of Roman structures still mark the spot. Below it, where the Jordan enters the Sea of Galilee, is the best place for fishing in all the lake. This was without reasonable doubt the only Bethsaida on the shores of the Sea of Galilee.

V. **The Site of Capernaum.** The much-debated site of Capernaum, which was probably the home of James and John, is at last practically determined. The identification with Khan Minyeh is disproved by an overwhelming weight of evidence. Most decisive of all is the complete absence of any Græco-Roman ruins in its vicinity. The ruins found there come clearly from the later Arab period. It was not until the seventeenth century that Capernaum was identified with this site. The confusion arose from the assumption that the northeastern limit of the Plain of Gennesaret was the hill now known as Tel Ormeimeh, rather than the famous spring which bears the name Tabighah. It was this spring which, according to Josephus, was called Capernaum. It clearly marked the western bounds of the city by that name, which therefore lay, as Josephus states, on the border of the Plain of Gennesaret.

The early pilgrim, Bishop Arculf, about 670 A.D. visited this region and gives detailed descriptions of different sacred sites. Standing near the spring of Tabighah, he thus pictures the Capernaum of his day: "It had no wall, and, being confined to a narrow space between the mountain and the lake, it extended a long way upon the shore from west to east, having a mountain on the north and a lake on the south." This description corresponds exactly with the topography of the northwestern end of the lake. Immediately to the east of the spring Tabighah the hills come down close to the shore, but gradually recede, leaving an ever-widening plain in the midst of which is found to-day the Græco-Roman and Arab ruins of Tel Hum. The Dominican monk Burkhard, near the close of the thirteenth century, in describing the spring Tabighah, says: "Josephus calls this fountain Capernaum because the whole land from the fountain to the Jordan—a distance of two hours—belonged to Capernaum."

THE SITE OF CAPERNAUM

The adopted home of Peter and of Jesus, therefore, extended for miles along the northern shore of the Sea of Galilee. The synagogue, which marked the centre of the town, was two miles to the east of the famous spring. Where the home of Peter was situated is, of course, only a matter of conjecture. It is a significant fact that to-day, as in the past, with the exception of the Jordan delta, the best place for fishing is just below the spring of Tabighah, which sends its warm waters into the lake and attracts the fish. Here, perhaps, where fishermen would most easily follow their trade, and away from the din of the great city, Peter and his family found their adopted home.

Just above this spring rises the abrupt hill where Jesus could find quiet for meditation apart from the noisy life of the city. This near-by vantage-point, which commanded a marvellous view of the fertile plain of Gennesaret on the west and southwest, of the towering hills of Galilee on the northwest, of the widely extended town of Capernaum on the northeast, and of practically the entire coast line of the Sea of Galilee on the south, was probably one of the places to which Jesus often retired alone or with his disciples.

VI. **A Sabbath in Capernaum.** Mark has preserved in the latter part of the first chapter of his gospel a detailed and suggestive picture of a Sabbath day's work in Capernaum. It opens in the synagogue. From the context it would appear that there was but one central synagogue in the great city. This conclusion is confirmed by the results of excavations at Tel Hum. While the ruins of the great synagogue that has been excavated by the Franciscan brothers may be dated not later than the second Christian century, they probably represent an earlier, first-century synagogue and suggest its general character and structure. According to Luke 7[5] the older synagogue was built by a rich centurion, and it is not impossible that the present ruins are a part of the original structure. It stood a few hundred feet from the lake, which it faced, and commanded a superb view of its blue waters and the many-colored hills which enclosed the Sea of Galilee on the east, south, and west. On the right bank, close to the water's edge, rose the splendid buildings of Herod's capital, Tiberias. On the heights to the south was the great Græco-Roman city of Gadara. On the heights to the east of the lake were the heathen cities and villages over which the tetrarch Philip ruled. Thus, while the synagogue at Capernaum was the centre of a strongly Jewish population, the tangible evidences of heathen culture and dominance were visible on every side. In front of the synagogue was a great platform approached by steps which led up from the east and west. From this platform three doors led into the synagogue. The central door was six feet wide and the other two four and one-half feet wide. The building itself was seventy-eight feet long and fifty-nine feet wide. The interior was surrounded on three sides by rows of Corinthian columns which supported the galleries. In its size and the character of its architecture the original synagogue of Capernaum was doubtless superior to those found in the other towns and villages of Galilee.

The synagogue was the most democratic of all the institutions of Judaism. It was wholly under the control of the people, who appointed certain rulers chosen from the elders to direct its services. Its objects were twofold: (1) public worship and (2) study of the scriptures. It stood, therefore, for inspiration and instruction. The congregation took part in reciting the shema, or public confession of faith, and in certain of the prayers, which preceded and followed the reading of the passages from the law. Itinerant scribes, rabbis, or any who were able to interpret and exhort, were invited to address the people. These addresses usually followed the reading of the passage from the prophets, and this passage was ordinarily used as a text. In the early synagogue an opportunity was probably given for questions and discussion, for its service was exceedingly informal. It was entirely different from the temple ritual, which it was intended to supplement. Jesus was naturally invited to speak in the synagogues, as were Paul and the later apostles on their missionary tours. In a very true sense, the Jewish synagogue was the birthplace of Christianity. This democratic institution, with its strong emphasis on teaching, explains many of the fundamental characteristics of early Christianity. Its essential elements are still preserved in the modern Christian prayer-meeting and Sunday-school, the essential functions of which it combined.

Mark simply records the effects of Jesus' teaching upon the people and especially upon a "man with an unclean spirit." The term was used by Jesus' contemporaries to describe a moral degenerate who was the victim of his own evil acts and habits. Whether these were revealed by a deranged mental condition or simply by his depraved appearance, words, and action is not clear. The man was sufficiently possessed of his reason to be deeply affected by the personality and words of Jesus. His exclamations reveal the powerful impression that Jesus had made upon him. The title, "the Holy One of God," is not necessarily messianic but simply describes his exalted conception of Jesus' sanctity. Jesus' calm words of authority not only freed the man from his derangement, but also from the bondage of his past sins and habits, thereby revealing the divine possibilities latent within him. Mark chiefly emphasizes the effect of this scene upon the people. The Jews were accustomed to acts of healing by their famous rabbis and especially by those who were renowned for their sanctity. What most astonished the people of Capernaum was the new, ringing note of authority that distinguished Jesus' teaching, and his remarkable influence upon men of depraved minds and morals. This incidental testimony contributes much to the portrait of Jesus. Unlike the scribes, he did not draw his authority from Moses and the interpretations of the earlier rabbis. Its ultimate basis was his profound appreciation of the needs of the lost sheep of the house of Israel and his absolute conviction that God was able and eager to meet those needs. It was an authority expressed in countenance, in manner, in act, in words, and in personality. Learned Pharisees, moral degenerates, and self-respecting fishermen, the strong and helpless alike, recognized it, and resented it or bowed before it.

Jesus' sympathy made it impossible for him to resist the many appeals which came to him from the sick and needy in their extremity. His words in the Matthew version of the parable of the talents (25[40]), "Even as you have done this to the least of these my disciples, you have done it unto me," voiced the spirit that actuated him in his work. He who uttered the parable of the good Samaritan could not turn a deaf ear to the cry of distress. His work, therefore, was necessarily a healing as well as a teaching ministry. In the home of Simon and Andrew he found Peter's mother-in-law afflicted by one of the fevers which still prevail along the low-lying northern shores of the Sea of Galilee and explain why to-day it is almost without inhabitants. Under the influence of Jesus' presence and encouragement the sick woman quickly rose and ministered to him and his followers.

As was inevitable, the report of what Jesus had done for the poor demoniac and for Peter's mother-in-law quickly spread throughout Capernaum, so that by nightfall he found himself surrounded by a horde of those afflicted by physical and mental disorders who had come to be healed by the holy rabbi. The narrative does not say that all were restored to health, but simply that many went away healed. Mark or a later editor adds the comment that Jesus did not permit the demons to speak "because they knew him."

VII. **Jesus' Significant Decision.** That the experiences of this eventful Sabbath in Capernaum represented a new stage in Jesus' work is clearly shown by the testimony of the gospels. Apparently his reputation as a healer and wonder-worker had come to him unexpectedly and without his having sought it. The statement that "very early the next morning, long before day, he went out into a desert place and there prayed" suggests that the new situation presented to him a grave problem, if not a temptation. Should he remain in Capernaum and gratify the desires of the people, as his sympathies prompted? It meant immediate popularity and a wide extension of his influence; but it also meant that his time would be largely, if not wholly, occupied in the mere work of physical and mental healing. The report of Simon Peter and his other followers that "all are seeking you" brought the issue to a climax. Even Mark, who is especially interested in the miracles as evidences of Jesus' divine authority, has preserved the decisive answer which Jesus made to this popular cry. Leaving the waiting multitudes behind, he sought a new field where he would not be thus handicapped, for, as he plainly declared, his primary object was not to heal but to preach. He desired by public address and private teaching to satisfy the deeper moral and spiritual needs of the people. Thus, from the very first, by act as well as word, he proclaimed the broader spiritual aim of his mission. Incidentally he healed men's bodies and minds; but his larger task was "to seek and to save the lost."

§ CXXVI. JESUS' POPULARITY AND THE BEGINNING OF THE PHARISAIC OPPOSITION

1.
Jesus'
assurance
that
the
paralytic's
sins
were
forgiven
(Mark
2¹⁻⁷, cf.
Matt.
9²˒³
Luke
¹)

Now when Jesus entered Capernaum again, after some days, it was reported that he was at home. And many people gathered together, so that there was no longer room for them, not even about the door; and Jesus preached to them. And four men came, carrying a man who was paralyzed, and trying to bring him to Jesus. And when they could not come close to Jesus on account of the crowd, they uncovered the roof where he was. And when they had torn it up, they let down the bed on which the paralytic was lying. And on seeing their faith, Jesus said to the paralytic, Son, thy sins are forgiven. But certain of the scribes were sitting there and saying to themselves, Why does this man speak thus? He blasphemes! Who can forgive sins but God alone?

And Jesus at once perceived that they were saying such things to themselves and said to them, Why do you say such things to yourselves? Which is easier: to say to the paralytic, 'Thy sins are forgiven'; or to say, 'Rise and take up thy bed and walk'? But that you may know that the Son of man has authority on earth to forgive sins (he said to the paralytic), I say to thee, Rise, take up thy bed, and go to thy house. Then the man rose, and immediately took up his bed and went out before them all. So they were all amazed and glorified God, saying, We have never seen anything like this.

Then Jesus went forth again by the sea side; and all the crowd came to him, and he taught them. And as he passed by, he saw Levi, the son of Alphæus, sitting at the custom house; and he said to him, Follow me. And he arose and followed him.

Now it came to pass that Jesus was eating dinner in his house and many tax-collectors and sinners sat down with Jesus and his disciples. And the scribes and Pharisees, seeing that he ate with the sinners and tax-collectors, said to his disciples, Does he eat with tax-collectors and sinners? And when Jesus heard it, he said to them:

They who are well have no need of a physician, but they who are sick;
I came not to call the righteous, but sinners to repentance.

And one of the Pharisees invited him to eat with him. And he entered into the Pharisee's house, and reclined at the table. And behold a woman that was a sinner in the city found out that he was reclining at table at the Pharisee's house, and she brought an alabaster flask of ointment. And as she stood behind at his feet, she began to wet his feet with her tears and to wipe them with the hair of her head. And she kept tenderly caressing his feet and anointed them with the ointment.

Now when the Pharisee, who had invited him, saw it, he said to himself, If this man were a prophet, he would know what kind of woman this is who is touching him; for she is a sinner. And Jesus answering, said to him, Simon, I have something to say to thee. And he replied, Say it, Teacher.

2. The physical cure (Mark 2⁸⁻¹², cf. Matt. 9⁴⁻⁸ Luke 5²²⁻²⁶)

3. Call of Levi, 2¹³, ¹⁴, cf. Matt. 9⁹ Luke 5²⁷, ²⁸)

4. The nature of Jesus' mission (Mark 2¹⁵⁻¹⁷, cf. Matt. 9¹⁰⁻¹³ Luke 5²⁹⁻³²)

5. A woman's tribute of gratitude (Luke 7³⁶⁻³⁸)

6. The parable of the two debtors (39-43)

A certain money lender had two debtors; one owed him five hundred denarii (about $90.00) and the other fifty denarii (about $9.00). As they were not able to pay, he forgave them both. Now which of them will love him the more? Simon answered and said, He, I suppose, to whom he forgave the more. And he said to him, Thou hast rightly judged.

7. Jesus' declaration that the woman's sins were forgiven (44-50) And turning to the woman, he said to Simon, Seest thou this woman? I came into thy house; thou gavest me no water for my feet, but she has wetted my feet with her tears and dried them with her hair. Thou gavest me no kiss, but she, since the time I came in, has not ceased tenderly caressing my feet. Thou didst not anoint my head with oil, but she has anointed my feet with ointment. Therefore, I say to thee, Her sins, which are many, are forgiven, for she has loved much; but he to whom little is forgiven, loves little. And he said to her, Thy sins are forgiven. And his fellow-guests began to say to themselves, Who is this who even forgives sins? And he said to the woman, Thy faith has saved thee; go in peace.

8. His reason for not following the detailed injunctions of the Jewish law (Mark 2¹⁸⁻²², cf.Matt. 9¹⁴⁻¹⁷ Luke 5³³⁻³⁹) And John's disciples and the Pharisees were fasting; and they came and said to him, Why do the disciples of John and the disciples of the Pharisees fast, but thy disciples fast not? And Jesus said to them, Can the bridal guests fast, while the bridegroom is with them? As long as they have the bridegroom with them they cannot fast. But the days will come, when the bridegroom shall be taken away from them, and then will they fast in that day. No one sews a piece of unshrunken cloth on an old garment, else the piece tears away from it, the new from the old, and a worse tear is made. And no man puts new wine into old wine skins; else the wine will burst the skins, and both the wine and the wine skins be destroyed. Instead one puts new wine into fresh wine skins.

9. His interpretation of the Sabbath (Mark 2²³⁻²⁸, cf.Matt. 12¹⁻⁸ Luke 6¹⁻⁵) And it came to pass that he was going on the sabbath day through the grain fields; and his disciples began, as they went, to pluck the ears. And the Pharisees said to him, Behold, why do they do that which is not lawful on the sabbath day? And he said to them, Have you never read what David did, when he had need and both he and those with him were hungry? How he entered into the house of God,

when Abiathar was high priest, and ate the show-bread, which only the priests may eat, and gave also to those with him? And he said to them, The sabbath was made for man, and not man for the sabbath; and so the son of man is also lord of the sabbath.

And he entered again into the synagogue. And a man was there who had a withered hand. And they watched Jesus to see if he would heal him on the sabbath day, that they might accuse him. And he said to them, Is it lawful on the sabbath day to do good or to do harm? to save a life or to kill? But they remained silent. And when he had looked around on them with anger, grieved at the hardening of their heart, he said to the man, Stretch forth thy hand. He stretched it forth; and his hand was restored. And the Pharisees went out and at once began to take counsel with the Herodians against him, how they might destroy him.

10. His works of healing on the Sabbath (Mark 3¹⁻⁶, cf. Matt. 12⁹⁻¹⁴ Luke 6⁶⁻¹¹ 13¹⁰⁻¹⁷ 14¹⁻⁶)

I. **The Record of Growing Opposition.** The narrative of Mark is still the principal guide. Historical scholars find here, however, several difficult problems. Chief among them is how far later Christian thought has shaped the gospel story. It was natural that the evangelists who lived in the midst of the bitter conflicts between Jew and Gentile should be eager to prove by the authority of Jesus that his followers were not under obligation to observe the strict ceremonial laws of Judaism. Are the sayings regarding old and new cloth, for example, simply put into the mouth of Jesus as some scholars claim, or do they represent his original teachings? The vigorous, epigrammatic form of these utterances is certainly characteristic of the great Teacher of Nazareth rather than of his later followers. These teachings are in perfect harmony with his acts and words during his early Galilean ministry. Mark 2¹–3⁶ also records the beginnings of that almost inevitable breach between Jesus and the narrow leaders of Judaism to whom these figures of speech refer. Hence there are strong grounds for regarding them as his original words.

At the same time, the influence of the later point of view is traceable at several points in the Marcan narrative. Thus, for example, Mark 2⁶⁻¹⁰ states that Jesus proclaimed the forgiveness of the poor paralytic on the basis of his unique authority as the Son of man. Luke, however, in his parallel version (7³⁶⁻⁵⁰) simply records Jesus' statement, "Your sins are forgiven." An important element in Jesus' work, like that of

John the Baptist, was not only to proclaim to these outcasts God's readiness to forgive, but also to assure them, if they manifested true penitence, that their individual sins were forgiven. John the Baptist dramatized this vital truth by means of his symbol of baptism. Jesus depended upon his simple, direct assurance or else, as in the parable of the prodigal son, emphasized the great truth by means of graphic illustrations. His authority, like that of the earlier Hebrew prophets, was his personal knowledge of God's character and of his attitude toward the penitent sinner.

II. **The Causes of the Pharisaic Opposition.** At first Jesus was apparently regarded by all classes as a self-taught rabbi who had gained his knowledge from study, meditation, and practical experience. In many respects he closely resembled the itinerant scribes and rabbis who were familiar figures to the men of his day. Like them, he aimed to reach, teach, and help the people. His teaching methods were also practically identical with theirs. He preached and taught in the synagogues and wherever opportunity offered. He never turned away from those who came to him privately for information and counsel. The literary forms in which he cast his teachings were likewise those of the rabbis (cf. § CXXIX^v). He, like them, emphasized the importance and authority of the earlier scriptures of the race, and sought to interpret them clearly and practically. He and his disciples made pilgrimages to Jerusalem to observe the great feasts, in accordance with the spirit, if not the detailed commands, of the Jewish law. In all his preaching he taught the necessity of repentance as the basis for divine forgiveness. Above all, he sought, like the rabbis, to give the people a clear conception of the character and demands of God and to teach them how to live moral lives. It is not strange, therefore, that at first the scribes and Pharisees were frequently found among Jesus' attentive listeners and that many of them invited him into their homes.

The differences between Jesus and the Pharisees were, however, equally fundamental. His mission and appeal were primarily to the classes who were beyond the pale of orthodox Judaism. His aim was not to make servants of the law, but intelligent, devoted sons of God. He was not dreaming, as were the Pharisees, of a nation that would for at least one day completely meet the demands of the ritual, but of true happiness and the fulness of life for each individual. While many of them longed to see a supernatural demonstration of their racial prerogatives, he labored to establish a great fraternity in which all should be bound together by common love and devotion to the divine Father.

He either ignored or rejected the later traditions that were so jealously guarded by the Pharisees. His message was one of good tidings for all who in penitence sought God's forgiveness. Like the early prophets, he taught that the right attitude toward God and one's fellow-men, expressed in unselfish service, was infinitely more important than the observance of detailed ceremonial laws. But Jesus never sought to irritate the Pharisees; indeed, he endeavored to conciliate and to meet them on common ground; but they could not long remain blind to the fundamental difference between their aims and teachings and those of the Master Builder of Nazareth.

III. The Charges Which the Pharisees Made against Jesus. Mark has clearly indicated the four or five reasons why the Pharisees took exception to the work and teaching of Jesus, and has presented them in what is probably their original chronological order.

The first charge was precipitated by the healing of the paralytic. Contemporary Judaism had not entirely forgotten the broader teachings of its spiritual prophets, but the narrow ritualists held that there was no forgiveness without requital (Weber, *Alt Synag. Theologie*, 267–300). This doctrine meant that true repentance and contrition were not sufficient to secure Jehovah's immediate forgiveness, but that some form of penance was required. Upon those who had sinned, therefore, and especially upon those who were unable to meet the extreme requirements of the Jewish law, there continued to rest a burdening sense of guilt long after they had truly repented. To these Jesus declared unqualifiedly, "Your sins are forgiven." His words to the woman who anointed his feet in the house of Simon the Pharisee were simply an echo of the teachings of Israel's earlier prophets and sages regarding God's character and attitude toward the penitent wrong-doer. In reviving this forgotten truth and in freeing the penitent outcasts from a painful burden imposed upon them by a false theology, Jesus tore down the barriers men had reared between the loving Father and his children. His calm, authoritative assurances naturally aroused that immediate and bitter opposition of the Pharisees which was practically inevitable in an age when religious tolerance was almost unknown.

A second charge which they brought against him was that he associated constantly with sinners. These included those who had lived or were living immoral lives and also those who, like many of the toilers of the land, were unable to satisfy the impossible demands of the Pharisees. Many of these sinners were the women of the street and the detested tax-collectors. For the strict Pharisees, mere association with them meant ceremonial uncleanness. The result was that, as far as possible, the Pharisees left them strictly alone. Jesus, however, not only preached to them and taught them, but made them his friends, and even entered into their homes as a guest. To them he devoted himself pre-eminently, and from their ranks he drew many of his followers. When the murmurs of the Pharisees became audible, Jesus explained his action by declaring that his mission was to heal those who were morally maimed or sick.

The third charge was that, unlike John and his disciples, Jesus failed to observe the detailed ceremonial laws, and especially those which commanded fasting on certain fixed days. He made no attempt to refute this charge, but at once set forth the broader principle that guided him: "For him who came to proclaim good tidings, fasting was as unseemly as for guests at a wedding." From the concrete illustration he rapidly passed to the broader generalization, as he contrasted his teachings with the demands of Judaism. With quiet humor he declared that to try to combine them was like sewing a piece of unshrunken cloth on an old garment. To restrict his teaching regarding the larger meaning and use of life to the narrow bounds fixed by Judaism was like putting new and unfermented wine into old and weak wine-skins. Jesus refused to allow his joyous, hopeful message to be constricted by Jewish ceremonialism. Even John had found it impossible to respect these limitations and had been compelled to develop a new rite. Jesus, ignoring all rites, sought simply to lead each man to develop his divine gifts under the limitations and in the immediate surroundings in which God had placed him. The new and glorious truth which Jesus proclaimed must needs be expressed in new ways. By such teachings as these he not only revealed the independence and breadth of his own vision, but also made evident that deep chasm between legalistic Judaism and Christianity which later generations of his followers were destined to appreciate still more keenly.

The fourth and, from their point of view, the strongest charge which the Pharisees brought against Jesus was that he disregarded the elaborate Sabbath laws which they deemed fundamental. Indeed, the later Jewish law went so far as to make work on the Sabbath a capital crime, and a large proportion of the time and energies of the scribes were devoted to guarding and interpreting these regulations. The result was that in reality they made the Sabbath for themselves and for the people a day of anxiety and strenuous mental labor. As with the extreme Puritans who followed their guidance, the close of the Sabbath day marked the beginning of a much-needed period of rest and relaxation. The faithful were but slaves of the institution, in constant fear lest they should offend Jehovah by failing to keep all its regulations. It is true that the Talmudic teachers taught that "the Sabbath was made for man and not man for the Sabbath." This saying, attributed to Jesus in Mark, but lacking in one of the most important texts (B), may be a later insertion in the gospel narrative. It voices, however, Jesus' conviction, which is reiterated in different language in the succeeding verse (cf. Mark $2^{27, 28}$). It was his teaching and example that revealed the impossible inconsistencies in the prevailing Jewish interpretation of the Sabbath and brought again before his followers the truer content of that noble institution.

As has already been noted (I § XXV) the earlier prophets had declared that the Sabbath was for man's rest and that each man owed this rest not only to himself, but also to all dependent upon him, including even the toiling ox and ass. As the context implies, Jesus in his original utterance declared, not that he, the Son of man, alone possessed divine authority to interpret the significance of the Sabbath, but that every man was master of the Sabbath. This statement, as the parallel passage clearly indicates, meant that the Sabbath was God's good gift to man. Man was under obligation, therefore, to use it like all other good gifts for his best physical, mental, and spiritual re-creation. He was master of the Sabbath, not only in that he was to use it for his own best development, but also for that of society as a whole. This social and humanitarian interpretation of the meaning of the Sabbath is illustrated repeatedly by Jesus' own example. Not only did he abstain from involving others in unnecessary labor, but also constantly aimed on the Sabbath as on other days to serve men as opportunity offered. Indeed, the narrative of Mark implies that, if possible, he was even more active in his work of preaching and healing on the Sabbath than on other days.

Luke, in 13^{10-17} and 14^{1-6}, has preserved two illustrations, one of the healing of the sick woman on the Sabbath in a synagogue and the other of a man afflicted with dropsy in the house of one of the rulers of the Pharisees. These acts naturally brought upon him the open condemnation of the Pharisees. Jesus' recorded reply reveals his innermost convictions regarding Sabbath observance. It implies that, like every Jew of his day, he aimed to conserve its sanctity, that is, to keep it distinct from other days, but distinct in a new and larger sense. He appealed to their humane instincts which prompted every man to lead his thirsty ox or ass from the stall to give it water, or to draw and relieve from its distress any animal which may have fallen into a well. Even so he claimed the right, indeed, insisted upon the obligation, to relieve any human being who might then appeal to him for help. One of the best Western texts (D) preserves in connection with Luke 6⁵ a saying which may be original: "Observing a man at work on the Sabbath, he said to him, 'Man, if thou knowest what thou art doing, happy art thou; but if thou knowest not, thou art cursed and a transgressor of the law.'" The same teaching appears among the sayings of Jesus recently discovered in Egypt. It expresses his attitude toward the Sabbath: The man who had in mind the principle underlying the Sabbath regulations and responded to the call of necessity or service to the needy was a law to himself; but he who did not have that higher consciousness was still under obligation to observe the ancient law of his race.

In the eyes of the stricter Pharisees, Jesus was a heretic, a law-breaker, and a man ceremonially defiled. Their attitude toward a true prophet and new truth is not without many analogies in human history. It is only fair to note that some of the Pharisees were doubtless at first sincere in their opposition, for they failed to see that Jesus was but insisting on principles already proclaimed by their earlier prophets. During the intervening centuries the law, with all its detailed ceremonial regulations, had been consecrated by the blood of martyrs and exalted to a position of highest authority, so that every orthodox Jew loved and revered it as the absolute word of God. Little wonder that they strenuously opposed the peasant teacher who quietly ignored many of the commands that they held to be infallible. The supreme tragedy of Israel's tragic history is that they did not recognize the truth of his assertion that he was not destroying but simply freeing them from the narrow bondage of the law by giving to its fundamental principles a fuller and diviner interpretation.

§CXXVII. THE GOSPEL MIRACLES

Then some of the scribes and Pharisees addressed Jesus, saying, Teacher, we would see a sign from thee. But he answered and said, It is an evil and adulterous generation that craves a sign, and there shall be no sign given it, but the sign of Jonah, the prophet. The men of Nineveh shall stand up at the judgment along with this generation and condemn it; for they repented at the preaching of Jonah, but behold, a greater than Jonah is here! The queen of the south shall rise up at the judgment along with this generation and condemn it, for she came from the ends of the earth to hear the wisdom of Solomon, but behold, a greater than Solomon is here!

1. Jesus' refusal to gratify the popular demand for a sign (Matt. 12³⁸, ³⁹, ⁴¹, ⁴². cf.Luke 11²⁹⁻³² 12⁵⁴⁻⁵⁶ Matt. 16¹⁻⁴)

And Jesus withdrew to the sea with his disciples. And a great multitude followed from Galilee, Judea, Jerusalem, from across the Jordan, and about Tyre and Sidon—a great multitude, on hearing all that he was doing, came to him. And because of the crowd, he told his disciples to have a small boat ready for him, that he might not be crushed; for he had healed many, so that all who had plagues were pressing on him to touch him. And whenever the unclean spirits saw him, they fell down before him and cried out, Thou art the Son of God. But he charged them repeatedly not to make him known.

2. His work of healing and his endeavor to avoid publicity (Mark 3⁷⁻¹², cf.Matt. 4²⁴, ²⁵ 12¹⁵⁻²¹ Luke 6¹⁷⁻¹⁹)

Now on that day at evening he said to them, Let us cross over to the other side. So leaving the crowd, they take him with them in the boat just as he was, and other boats were with him. And a great squall of wind arose and the waves began to beat into the boat so that the boat was already filling, and he was in the stern asleep on the cushion. So they wake him and say to him, Teacher, carest thou not that we are perishing? Then awakening, he rebuked the wind, and said to the sea, Peace, be still! And the wind ceased and there was a great calm. Then he said to them, Why are you anxious? Have you no faith yet? And they feared greatly and said to one another, Who then is this, that even the wind and the sea obey him?

3. Jesus in a storm on the Sea of Galilee (Mark 4³⁵⁻⁴¹, cf.Matt. 8¹⁸, ²³⁻²⁷ Luke 8²²⁻²⁵)

4. His meeting with the demoniac east of the Sea of Galilee (Mark 5¹⁻¹⁰, cf. Luke 8²⁶⁻³¹ Matt. 3²⁸, ²⁹)

And they came to the other side of the sea, into the country of the Gerasenes. And as he stepped out of the boat, he was at once met by a man from the tombs, with an unclean spirit, who had his dwelling in the tombs. And no man could bind him any longer, not even with a chain; for he had often been bound with fetters and chains, and the chains had been torn apart by him and the fetters broken in pieces and no man had strength to tame him. And constantly, night and day, in the tombs and in the mountains he kept crying out and cutting himself with stones. And when he saw Jesus from afar, he ran and threw himself down before him, crying out with a loud voice, What have I to do with thee, Jesus the son of the most high God. I adjure thee, by God, torment me not. For Jesus was saying to him, Evil spirit, leave the man. Then he asked him, What is thy name? And he said to him, My name is Legion, for we are many. And they repeatedly besought him not to send them away from the country.

5. His cure of the demoniac (Mark 5¹¹⁻²⁰, cf. Luke 8³²⁻³⁹ Matt. 8³⁰⁻³⁴)

Now a large drove of swine were there, feeding on a mountain side; so they besought him, saying, Send us into the swine, that we may enter them. And he gave them permission. And the unclean spirits went out and entered the swine; and the drove, about two thousand in number, rushed down the steep slope into the sea, and were drowned in the sea. And they who fed them fled and told it in the city and in the villages. And the people came to see what had happened. And they came to Jesus and saw the man who had been possessed of demons, sitting clothed and in his right mind, even he who had had the legion. And they were afraid. And they who had seen it described to them what had happened to the man who had been possessed by demons and to the swine. And they began to beg of Jesus to depart from their territory. And as he was entering the boat, the man who had been possessed by demons besought him that he might accompany him. But Jesus would not allow him, but said to him, Go home to thy friends, and tell them how great things the Lord hath done for thee, and all his mercy on thee. So he went his way and began to proclaim in the Decapolis region how great things Jesus had done for him. And all marvelled.

And when Jesus again crossed over in a boat to the other side, a large crowd had gathered to meet him. And there comes one of the rulers of the synagogue, Jairus by name; and on seeing Jesus, he falls at his feet, and beseeches him insistently, saying, My little daughter is at the point of death; I pray thee, come and lay thy hands on her, that she may be made well, and live. And Jesus went with him; and a great crowd followed him, and they pressed about him.

6. Jairus's appeal in behalf of his daughter (Mark 5²¹⁻²⁴, *cf.* Luke 8⁴⁰⁻⁴² Matt. 9¹⁸, ¹⁹)

And there was a woman who had had an issue of blood twelve years, and had suffered many things, under many physicians, and had spent all her money, yet was none the better, but rather had grown worse. Having heard about Jesus, she came in the crowd behind him and touched his garment. For she kept saying, If I touch but his garments, I shall be made well. And immediately the flow of her blood was dried up, and she felt in her body that she was healed of her plague. And Jesus knew immediately that power had gone out from him, and he turned around in the crowd, and said, Who touched my garments? And his disciples said to him, Thou seest the crowd pressing around you, and yet thou sayest, 'Who touched me?' And he looked round about to see her who had done this thing. But the woman knowing what had been done to her, came and fell down before him in fear and trembling, and told him all the truth. And he said to her, Daughter, thy faith hath made thee well. Go in peace, and be healed of thy plague.

7. The cure of an afflicted woman (Mark 5²⁵⁻³⁴, *cf.* Luke 8⁴³⁻⁴⁸ Matt. 9²⁰⁻²²)

While he was still speaking, messengers came from the house of the ruler of the synagogue, saying, Your daughter is dead; why trouble the Teacher any further? But Jesus, without heeding the word spoken, said to the ruler of the synagogue, Fear not, only have faith. And he would not let any man go with him, except Peter and James, and John the brother of James. And they came to the house of the ruler of the synagogue. And seeing a tumult, and many persons weeping and wailing loudly, Jesus said to them, Why make a tumult and weep? The child is not dead, but asleep. And they laughed him to scorn. But after putting them all out, he takes the father of the child, and her mother, and those who were with him, and goes into the room where the child was. And taking the child by the hand, he says to her,

8. The recovery of Jairus's daughter (Mark 5³⁵⁻⁴³, *cf.* Luke 8⁴⁹⁻⁵⁶ Matt. 9²³⁻²⁶)

Talitha cumi, which means, Little girl, I say to thee, Arise.
And immediately the little girl rose up, and began to walk.
(She was about twelve years old.) Then they were immediately filled with great amazement. But Jesus charged them
earnestly that no man should know of this. And he told
them to give her something to eat.

9.
Healing the centurion's servant (Matt. 8⁵⁻¹⁰,¹³, cf. Luke 7¹⁻¹⁰)

Now when he entered Capernaum, a centurion came to him
and besought him, saying, Lord, my servant is lying at home
sick with paralysis, terribly tormented. Jesus said to him, I
will come and heal him. But the centurion answered and
said, Lord, I am not worthy to have you come under my
roof. Only say the word and my servant will be cured.
For indeed I am a man under authority, with soldiers under
me: I say to this man, 'Go,' and he goes; to another, 'Come,'
and he comes; to my slave, 'Do this,' and he does it. When
Jesus heard it, he marvelled and said to his followers,
Verily, I tell you, I have not found such faith as this with
anyone in Israel. And Jesus said to the centurion, Go, be it
done to thee as thou hast believed. And the servant was
healed in that hour.

10.
Jesus' inability to perform miracles at Nazareth (Mark 6¹⁻⁶, cf. Matt. 13⁵⁴⁻⁵⁸ Luke 4¹⁶⁻³⁰)

And he went out from there and entered into his native
city; and his disciples followed him. And when the sabbath
day came he began to teach in the synagogue. And many on
hearing him were astonished, saying, Whence has this man
these things? And what wisdom is this which has been
given to him? And have such miracles been wrought by
his hands? Is not he the carpenter, the son of Mary and
brother of James and Joses and Judas and Simon? And
are not his sisters here with us? And they were offended
because of him. But Jesus went on to say to them, A
prophet is not without honor except in his own city and
among his kinsmen and in his own house. And he could
not perform there a single miracle except that he laid his
hands on a few sick people and healed them. And he marvelled because of their unbelief. So he went about the surrounding villages, teaching.

11.
The cleansing of a leper (Mark 1³⁹⁻⁴⁵, cf. Matt. 4²³ 8¹⁻⁴ Luke 4⁴⁴ 5¹²⁻¹⁶)

Then he went and preached in their synagogues throughout all Galilee, and cast out demons. And a leper comes to
him, beseeching him and kneeling down to him, and saying to
him, If thou wilt, thou canst make me clean. Being moved

with compassion, he stretched forth his hand and touched him, and said to him, I will; be clean. Then at once the leprosy left him and he became clean. But Jesus strictly charged him and immediately sent him off, saying to him, See thou tell no one anything; but go, show thyself to the priest and offer for thy cleansing what Moses commanded, as a proof to them. But he went away and began to proclaim it widely and to spread the matter abroad, so that Jesus could no longer enter a city openly. But he stayed outside in desert places; and the people came to him from every quarter.

I. The Significance of the Gospel Miracles. To understand the miracles recorded in the gospels it is necessary to have a clear conception of the conditions in the Galilee of Jesus' day and of his character and aims. Since the days of Alexander the vice of the East and West had poured into Palestine. Wrong living and thinking had distorted the bodies and minds and souls of men. At every turn beggars, afflicted with all kinds of loathsome diseases, cried for help and healing. Oriental charity then, as now, was lavish; but it pauperized rather than permanently relieved the needy. The lot of the insane was especially pitiable. The current scientific explanation of most types of insanity attributed it to malignant demons that took possession of those abnormally afflicted. The victims of insanity also shared this ancient theory, and it only added to the horrors of their hallucinations.

Into this life Jesus entered, with a robust, wholesome body, with a mind that was clear and sane and that recognized many of the hidden causes that lay back of the guilt and suffering which confronted him. He was inspired by a divine pity and an intense passion not only to relieve but to heal and save the ignorant, shepherdless, suffering masses that crowded about in the eager hope that he could help them. Joyously, confidently, he met the human needs that appealed to him, for he knew that life and health and happiness were the good gifts that the heavenly Father was eager to bestow upon his needy children. Viewed in the broad perspective of history, it is incredible that a teacher and lover of men like Jesus could have lived and worked in the Galilee of his day and not healed men's bodies and minds, as well as their souls.

The miracles of Jesus have a fourfold significance: the first is their evident influence on his thought and methods of work. In the second place his power to heal aided him greatly in fulfilling his mission, for it was necessary first to remove the physical and mental barriers before he could deal effectively with men's deeper moral and spiritual problems. His work of healing established between himself and those whom he wished to reach a basis of gratitude, friendship, and absolute trust which were essential before he could implant in their minds his higher spiritual teachings and stir their wills to noble and persistent action. In the third place Jesus' miracles, as the gospel narratives clearly state, made a profound impression not only upon the crowds who gathered about him, but also upon his own disciples. Men learned far more readily through the eye than through the hearing of the ears. The deeds which they beheld confirmed their convictions regarding his character and mission. The memory of the miracles that their Master performed was ever in the mind of the early Christians and carried the church through the perilous crises that overtook it during the second and third centuries.

In the fourth place, Jesus, by his acts of healing, set an example to his followers throughout all the ages. His representatives in the present, as well as in the past, are called to deal not merely with the intellectual and spiritual problems of the people, but in solving these to contribute that which is indispensable to men's mental and physical well-being. The man of to-day, as in the past, needs, even more than he does the ordinary physician, one who can, like the Physician of souls, teach him how to think and live aright. Modern science is beginning to appreciate how powerful is the influence of mental and moral states upon the health of the individual. Following the example of Jesus, many are seeking to enlist these potent forces in healing mental and physical maladies. Jesus' example also gave the impetus to that movement which, under the influence of Christianity, has established dispensaries and hospitals and asylums throughout the civilized world, and, through the heroic work of medical missionaries, is bringing help and healing to thousands suffering under the dark shadow of heathenism.

II. **Jesus' Attitude toward Miracles.** The striking contrast between the attitude of Jesus toward miracles and that of the people of his day is well illustrated by the conversation recorded in Matthew 12^{38-42}. The narrative comes from the earliest collection of the sayings of Jesus and is reproduced practically verbatim in Luke 11^{29-32}, where Jesus' words are addressed to the assembled crowds rather than to the Pharisees. Mark simply states that the Pharisees came seeking a sign from heaven, that is, from God, in order to test Jesus. It was the same popular demand that had come to him at his first great temptation. Pharisees, Zealots, and the common people all expected that the one who was to realize their messianic ideals and to do Jehovah's work was to be attested by miraculous signs. A few years later even the Samaritans followed in great numbers an impostor, who, claiming that he was the Messiah, led them forth to the top of Mount Gerizim, where he promised to perform mighty miracles. Mark has preserved one significant fact unrecorded in the other gospels: Jesus' first reply to the request of the Pharisees was a deep sigh which revealed the depth of his disappointment and showed that he realized the difficulties of the task which confronted him. Then with his usual directness he declared plainly to the Pharisees that no miraculous signs would be given them. He even condemned them on the ground that their demand was unreasonable.

The author of the Gospel of Matthew, in 12⁴⁰, recalling the miracle recorded in the book of Jonah, offers an explanation of Jesus' statement that no sign would be given except that of the prophet Jonah, which obscures the original teaching. He, like the Pharisees, still clings to the popular belief that the Messiah must be attested by a miracle: "For as Jonah was three days and three nights in the belly of the sea-monster, so the Son of man shall be three days and three nights in the heart of the earth." Luke's silence suggests that this explanation was not found in the common teaching source (Q). Matthew, however, has, with this exception, preserved what appears to be the logical and probably the original order of Jesus' words. Their meaning is clear. His message, like that of Jonah, was a plain call to repentance. The Ninevites, heathen though they were, heeded and repented at the teaching of Jonah. Therefore their ready response to an appeal to their consciences was a rebuke to the irresponsive Pharisees and leaders of Judaism who were listening untouched to the greater message of John the Baptist and of Jesus. Even the heathen queen of Sheba put to shame the men of Galilee, for she came from afar to hear the teaching of Solomon, who represented Israel's wise men, but Jesus' contemporaries rejected the teachings of him who was greater than the wisest man of Israel's past. In this figurative way Jesus declared to the men of his race that his mission was spiritual, and that his authority was attested, not by signs and miracles, but by the appeal which his message made to the human conscience. His words but confirm the evidence already noted regarding his attitude toward miracles. Not only did he early turn his back upon the sick of Capernaum, that he might carry on unimpeded his larger work of teaching and preaching, but also, according to Mark, he constantly commanded those whom he had healed not to report what had been done to them. Whenever he made a statement regarding the object of his work, he asserted that it was primarily to seek and to save not the sick but sinners.

The absence of any reference in Paul's writings to the miracles of Jesus is also significant. He himself believed in works of healing, as the book of Acts abundantly testifies. The only satisfactory explanation of his silence is that he deemed miracles merely incidental and not essential to Jesus' work and to the interpretation of his character. Mark's narrative implies that Jesus' power to work miracles came to him unexpectedly. The fact that he continued to heal men's physical maladies indicates that he appreciated and used this gift, not as an attestation of his divine authority, but as an important aid in his work.

III. **Miracles in the History of Early Religions.** It is significant that miracle stories are associated with practically all the great religious leaders of the past. Gautama, the famous Buddha, who lived about 500 B.C., is in many respects the best illustration of this fact. The miracle stories told about him come from northern India and cannot be dated earlier than 300 B.C. Probably some of them are much later. They state that Gautama was descended from heaven and was miraculously incarnated in his mother's womb. Mighty portents marked his birth; on the day on which he received his name a Brahmin foretold his future greatness. After seven years of spiritual struggle he gained that insight which made him a blessed Buddha. Before entering upon his work he was tempted by Mara, the spirit that represented the lust of the world. Many miracles are attributed to him. He gave sight to the blind, and at one time fed five hundred monks out of a basket of cakes with a little milk and ghee. On another occasion one of his disciples was made to walk on the water. He predicted his death three months before it took place. Later he was translated in the presence of two of his disciples.

As a rule the miracle stories found in the Jewish scriptures also gather about certain great characters, such as Moses, Samuel, Elijah, and Elisha, who lived before written records became common. About the prophets of the classical period, such as Amos, Hosea, Jeremiah, and Ezekiel, no miracles are recorded. Isaiah is the only prominent exception, and the miracles associated with his name are found only in late writings. Furthermore, the different strata of narratives, as for example, those which record the opening events in Israel's history, differ widely in this respect. The oldest accounts of the Egyptian plagues, the exodus, the crossing of the Jordan, and the work of Samuel, as a rule, trace the various events which they record to natural causes. In the later accounts of the same events the explanation is almost universally miraculous. For example, the Hebrew escape from Egypt as the result, not of a series of natural calamities, as in the early records, but of seven miracles that take place at the command of Moses. Instead of being driven back by the east wind, or held temporarily by a landslide, the waters of the Red Sea and the Jordan stand on either side as a wall, while the Israelites march through the depths dry-shod. In contrast to the simple, direct, natural narrative of Samuel and Kings, the later stories of the Chronicler represent the development of Israel's history as due to a succession of miracles. The spirit of I Maccabees is deeply religious and the history probably comes from an eye-witness of the events, yet it contains no miracle stories; but in the later parallel narrative of II Maccabees they appear at every point. These familiar facts illustrate the tendency of the later Jewish writers to emphasize and magnify the physical miracles in their national history and in the careers of their great leaders, rather than those elements which were of deeper moral and religious import.

IV. The Canons of Interpretation Employed by Critical Historians. On the whole, the simplest and most satisfactory definition of a miracle is that it is a phenomenon not explained by known natural laws. According to its derivation the word miracle describes that which seems wonderful to those who witness it. Hence the miracles of one generation may be the common events or at least the scientifically accepted facts of a succeeding generation. Although the realm of the known is constantly being extended, it is still relatively insignificant compared with that which is unknown. Even as many of the miracles of yesterday are explained by the science of to-day, so, beyond doubt, many present-day mysteries will be explained in the future and the laws which govern them definitely formulated. What we call natural laws, however, are merely certain uniform modes of behavior which we observe in our study of natural phenomena. To explain an event in accordance with these laws is merely to classify it under one or another of these prevailing modes of behavior; but this does not explain the ultimate cause. There are certain phenomena which in their essential character are miracles, that is, they are not subject to explanation in accordance with natural laws. These phenomena are the result of free choices of moral personalities. The supreme miracle in the life of Jesus and in human history is his transcendent moral character and its effect upon men.

It is sometimes said that there is a tendency among modern scientists to eliminate entirely the miraculous or supernatural. In a certain sense this statement is true. There are some students of human history who would reduce it to the mere interplay of economic and social laws. Others deny the freedom of the will and regard human life as governed entirely by physical laws. Against this type of scientific theory all our innermost convictions and our higher interests revolt. But the best corrective of this extreme materialism is not a blind, dogmatic conservatism, but rather a willingness to accept the results of sane and reasonable scientific investigation in the biblical as well as in other fields of research.

Inasmuch as the gospels themselves contain widely variant accounts of the same miracle, the demand of the historical critics that certain well-established canons, equally applicable to the Old and New Testaments, be carefully applied, in order to ascertain the ultimate basis of historic fact underlying these accounts, seems reasonable. These canons may be formulated as follows:

1. Of several accounts the oldest should ordinarily be followed. Two centuries of New Testament scholarship have demonstrated that certain strata of the narrative are older than others. For example, as has already been noted, the older collection or collections of the sayings of Jesus, quoted by Matthew and Luke, evidently antedate Mark's narrative. Mark's gospel, in turn, represents a record probably several decades earlier than that of the Fourth Gospel. In some rare cases a later account preserves important facts; but ordinarily the narrator who stands nearest to the incidents which he records is the most reliable.

2. Of several different accounts or possible interpretations of the same incident, the simpler or more natural should be adopted. Thus, in the narratives of Mark (1^{16-20}) and Matthew (4^{18-22}), Jesus simply called his earlier followers and they without hesitation responded; but in the parallel account of Luke (5^{1-11}) their call is preceded by a miraculous draught of fishes. In the account of the recovery of Jairus's daughter most earlier interpreters were inclined to find a miracle. As a matter of fact, according to the oldest record, Jesus himself declared, "The child is not dead, but asleep."

3. Due allowance must be made for popular ignorance of natural laws and for the tendency to interpret with mechanical literalness

what was originally simply a figure of speech. It must be remembered that the gospel writers lived in an age when it was customary to regard that which was marvellous, or even that which to us seems natural, as supernatural. To the ancients an eclipse was even a greater miracle than the raising of the dead to life. All forms of insanity and mental derangement were attributed to the influence of personal demons. The gospel writers rarely describe the therapeutic methods which Jesus employed in his work of healing. They were naturally more interested in the result than in the process. In a few instances Mark has suggested the ways in which Jesus reinforced the faith of those whom he sought to heal, as, for example, touching the sick or the wetting of the eyes of the blind with saliva from his own mouth. In certain instances even Jesus' disciples interpreted his expressive figures with misleading literalness. A familiar example of this is their failure to understand his allusions to his coming death and his warnings to beware of the leaven of the Pharisees. Luke has fortunately preserved the parable of the fig tree, by which Jesus describes the fate awaiting the Jewish people; but in Mark the original parable has been transformed into an account of the cursing of a barren fig tree and the miracle of its sudden withering (cf. § CXL³, ᴵᴵ).

4. The historical value of each miracle story must be determined largely by whether or not it is consistent with Jesus' character, acts, and teachings as revealed by the oldest sources. Only one or two miracles appear to have been recorded in the earliest collection of Jesus' teachings, although this fact may be due to the peculiar purpose of these writings. The primitive source, however, together with the earliest narrative in Mark, gives a vivid, consistent picture of what Jesus was and did. It is reasonable to use this as a standard by which to test the historical value of the later narratives. Thus, for example, in the popular account of the healing of the demoniac east of the Sea of Galilee, Jesus is represented as wantonly destroying a herd of swine. It was a region peopled not by Jews but by heathen. Even if the swine belonged to Jews, it is difficult to believe that Jesus' point of view was so narrowly Jewish that he would for a moment have justified on ceremonial grounds the destruction of that which inevitably meant serious loss to the owners. Many hold that we have here the popular interpretation of what was originally simply a coincidence; for, if a herd of swine, terrified by the wild cries of the demoniac, rushed into the lake, their strange actions would naturally have been attributed to the influence of the great Wonder-Worker.

THE GOSPEL MIRACLES

V. The Different Types of Recorded Miracles. The gospels attribute to Jesus four distinct types of miracles: (1) those of moral and spiritual healing; (2) of mental healing; (3) of physical healing, and (4) those illustrating his power over natural forces. The transformations in the character of such men as Levi and Zaccheus, the corrupt tax-collectors, were as unmistakable miracles as any recorded in the gospels. To-day we are so familiar with such transformations that their miraculous character often escapes us. Psychology also helps us in part to fathom the mental states which result in these marvellous transformations, but they are still shrouded with mystery. On the other hand, the reason why this type of miracle did not impress the contemporaries of Jesus nearly as deeply as did the other wonders that he performed was because it was less concrete and objective. Mark was chiefly impressed by Jesus' ability to heal disordered minds. Whether or not Jesus himself accepted the popular explanation of insanity as due to demoniacal possession, he adopted it for practical reasons as a basis for the cures which he worked, even as he did the prevailing conceptions of the universe. In the thought of the gospel writers and the Church Fathers, who held the current beliefs regarding the causes of disease and especially of insanity, these acts of healing were regarded as the most convincing proof of Jesus' power and authority over Satan, who they believed controlled these evil spirits.

As might be expected, it was in the field of moral and mental disorders that Jesus' powerful personality was able to accomplish most. It is significant that his first recorded act of healing was a cure of the demoniac in the synagogue at Capernaum, and that the great majority of his miracles appear to have been of this character. His growing reputation inspired ever greater faith in the minds of the crowds and of the afflicted, so that in the regions about Capernaum it became increasingly easy for him to effect these cures. On the other hand, Mark states that when Jesus returned to his home at Nazareth and was surrounded by those who knew him as a boy and youth, he failed to find that faith or, in the language of modern psychology, that suggestible attitude which was absolutely necessary in order to effect cures, so that there he was able to heal only a few. Matthew 12[43-45], which apparently here records a saying of Jesus preserved in the earliest collection, possibly suggests that certain of these acts of mental healing were only temporarily effective, and that a recurrence of their maladies sometimes left the poor victims in a more pitiable state than before. It may have been that among the growing number of followers who accompanied

Jesus there were some who remained with him because they realized that only in his presence could they find permanent relief.

Many of the recorded miracles of physical healing are in certain respects paralleled by well-authenticated analogies to-day. The scientists who investigated the miracles effected by the Holy Coat of Treves, after eliminating all cases which could be explained by other causes, found well-attested cures of the atrophy of the optic nerve, of paralysis of the arm due to dislocation, of the complete loss of the use of arms and legs as a consequence of rheumatic gout, of Saint Vitus's dance, of blindness of one eye and of paralysis of one arm as the result of brain-fever, of a chronic intestinal disorder, of a cancerous tumor, of caries of the spine, and of chronic inflammation of the spinal marrow. (See Korum, *Wunder und göttlicher Gnaderweiss bei der Austellung des heiligen Rockes zu Trier im Jahre* 1891.)

Striking illustrations of the power of the mind over physical states are now so common that they are recognized by medical science, and the laws which govern them are beginning to be formulated. Modern scientists and historians, therefore, approach the gospel accounts of physical healing with an entirely new attitude. They simply ask that the established canons of historical interpretation be faithfully applied to each narrative. As a rule, the historical accuracy of these records is signally confirmed by critical investigation. In many cases the natural laws lying back of them are also revealed. For example, the account of the healing of the woman afflicted with an issue of blood is regarded by many medical authorities as a case of auto-suggestion. It has commonly been held that Mark 1[40-45] records the cure of a case of real leprosy, which has hitherto proved incurable; but Jesus' command that the man go to the priest and perform the ablutions provided in Leviticus 14[1-32] for certain types of skin affections, which were popularly called leprosy but were in reality curable, suggests the nature of the disease.

VI. **The Significance of the Illustrations of Jesus' Power over Nature.** There are many who feel that their religious faith must stand or fall with the nature miracles of Jesus. They contend that if these are rejected, Christianity must be regarded as a mere human development rather than as a unique and supremely divine revelation. This conservative position is worthy of the utmost sympathy and respect, nor can it be denied that it is logically tenable, for many able thinkers hold it to-day. They maintain that the unique personality of Jesus was to a certain extent unfettered by ordinary human limitations. More progressive thinkers, on the other hand, believe that the moral grandeur of Jesus is obscured by certain of the nature miracles popularly attributed to him; that without genuine human limitations to surmount and conquer, heroism and noble self-sacrifice are impossible. They believe that Jesus is only the more truly divine because he was so completely human, being "tempted in all points even as we are." In any case it seems clear that the great essentials of our faith remain unshaken whatever view we hold regarding these nature miracles, for, since the days of Horace Bushnell, it is universally agreed that the corner-stone of the Christian faith is the moral and spiritual character of Jesus.

Measured by critical historical canons, two miracle stories stand in a very different category from most of those found in the gospels. The one is the story of the raising of the widow's son at Nain. It is recorded only by Luke (7[11-17]) and bears on its face the marks of late origin. Thus, for example, Jesus is designated here for the first time in Luke as "the Lord," and he is later called a prophet. The close analogies between this narrative and the ancient story of the healing of the boy by Elijah and the variant form of the same story in II Kings 4 have been noted by many interpreters. The account of the raising of Lazarus from the dead is recorded only in the Fourth Gospel. The silence of the synoptic writers would be more easily explained if the miracle had been performed in some remote village, but according to the Fourth Gospel it took place at Bethany, a near suburb of Jerusalem, and during Jesus' last week at Jerusalem, when every day and almost every hour of his activity is recounted with unparalleled detail by the early evangelists. This silence suggests that the story of the raising of Lazarus was unknown, not only to Paul and the Twelve, but also to the first generation of gospel writers. It is also important to recall that the Fourth Gospel is to a great extent allegorical—more so than we ordinarily realize in this matter-of-fact age. It is quite probable that the evangelist never intended his account of the raising of Lazarus to be understood as literal history, but rather as an allegorical illustration of Jesus' spiritual power. This interpretation brings the narrative into harmony with the implications of the earliest evangelists that Jesus healed only those to whose faith he could personally appeal.

There are relatively few nature miracles recorded in the synoptic gospels. The account of the changing of the water into wine at Cana is not found in the older gospels. It appears for the first time in the Fourth Gospel, where it is in all probability to be interpreted allegorically. In this connection it is important to note how frequently that gospel disparages mere physical signs as the ultimate basis of personal faith in Jesus (*e. g.*, 2^{23-25} 4^{48} $6^{2-14, 63}$ 11^{47} 20^{29}). The account of Jesus stilling the tempest on the Sea of Galilee is recounted in Mark and reproduced almost verbatim in the parallel passages in Matthew and Luke. To interpret the incident rightly, it is important to study it in the light of its physical setting. Squalls on the northern end of the Sea of Galilee are famous for the quickness with which they sweep down over the lake and the equal suddenness with which the waters become calm when the storm is past. Jesus' words, "Peace, be still," are even more appropriate, if originally addressed to his perturbed disciples rather than to the troubled sea. The words which follow in Mark 4^{20}, "Why are you fearful? Have you not yet faith?" are, in fact, addressed to them. It is easy to see how the sudden passing of the squall and the almost immediate quieting of the waves would be attributed to Jesus' divine power, so often revealed in dealing with the fears and passions that perturbed the spirits of men. It is also possible that a familiar Old Testament passage (Ps. 89^9) was in the mind of Mark when he described the incident:

> Thou rulest the pride of the sea,
> When its waves arise thou stillest them.

The most familiar of the four or five stories that are told by the gospel writers to illustrate Jesus' power over natural forces is the account of how he fed the multitudes beside the Sea of Galilee. Like the account of the stilling of the waves, it has a powerful hold on the artistic and poetic imagination of the Christian world and on the heart of humanity. Jesus' use of the figure of bread in the Fourth Gospel, nevertheless, raises the question whether the food with which he fed the waiting multitudes was physical or spiritual. The details of the narrative differ widely in the various gospel accounts. They all agree, however, that the multitudes stayed long with Jesus, yet went away fed. Historical students call attention to the fact that the inhabitants of Palestine, in the past as to-day, rarely set out on a journey, even of a few hours, without placing some of the soft, easily transported oriental bread in their wallets. Jesus certainly allayed the spiritual hunger of the multitudes. As he did so he aroused their desire to remain and hear him. He also inspired in them the spirit of unselfish giving which would lead each to share what he had with his neighbor. Hence, in giving them the bread of life, Jesus satisfied both their physical and their spiritual needs.

VII. **Conclusions.** Thrown into the crucible of historical criticism, the great majority of the gospel miracles emerge unscathed. This is pre-eminently true of the miracles which are the expression of Jesus' strong love and compassion for men. It is the miracle stories cited by the evangelists to illustrate his power over natural forces that fail to meet the tests of the critical historian. This result is in complete accord with Jesus' own assertion that he was not a wonder-worker whose authority was to be attested by miraculous signs, such as turning stones into bread or throwing himself down from a height. The miracles which Jesus performed were of a diviner, more spiritual character. The abiding value of the narratives of the storm at sea and of his feeding the multitudes is that they illustrate his complete devotion to his followers and his marvellous control of their fears and of their naturally selfish impulses. From the modern point of view, as well as from that of Jesus, the gospel miracles are not so much his divine credentials as they are the revelation of his Godlike spirit and of his truly miraculous power over the bodies and minds and souls of men. Thus interpreted, the gospel miracles possess an increasing value for each succeeding generation, for only as our experience and knowledge broaden and deepen can we fully appreciate the many-sided personality and work of him who healed men's bodies and minds and souls.

§ CXXVIII. THE CALL AND TRAINING OF JESUS' DISCIPLES

1. The appointment of the Twelve (Mark 3¹³⁻¹⁹ᵃ, cf. Luke 6¹²⁻¹⁶ Matt. 10²⁻⁴)

Then Jesus went up into the mountain, and called to him those whom he would; and they went with him. And he appointed twelve that they might be with him, and that he might send them out to preach, and to have authority to cast out demons: Simon, to whom he also gave the name Peter; and James the son of Zebedee and John the brother of James; and to these two he gave the name Boanerges, which means, Sons of thunder; and Andrew, and Philip, and Bartholomew, and Matthew, and Thomas, and James the son of Alphæus, and Thaddeus, and Simon the Cananean, and Judas Iscariot, who also betrayed him.

Then he came home and again the crowd gathered, so that they were not able so much as to get their food. And when his relatives heard it, they went out to seize him, for they said, He is out of his mind. And his mother and his brothers came and, standing outside, they sent to him and called him. And the crowd was seated around him. And they said to him, Here are your mother and your brothers outside seeking you. And he said to them in reply, Who are my mother and my brothers? And looking around on those who were sitting in a circle about him, he said, Behold, my mother and my brothers! Whoever does the will of God, that one is my brother, and sister, and mother.

2. Jesus' definition of true kinship (Mark 3¹⁹ᵇ⁻²¹, ³¹⁻³⁵, cf. Matt. 12⁴⁶⁻⁵⁰ Luke 8¹⁹⁻²¹ 11²⁷, ²⁸)

And as they journeyed on the way, a certain man said to him, I will follow thee wherever thou goest. Then Jesus said to him, The foxes have holes and the birds of the heavens have their resting places, but the Son of man hath nowhere to lay his head. He said to another, Follow me; but the man said, Let me first go and bury my father. But Jesus said to him, Let the dead bury their own dead. Go thou and proclaim the kingdom of God. Another also said, I will follow thee, Lord, but first let me bid farewell to those of my household. But Jesus said to him, No man who looks back after having put his hand to the plow is fit for the kingdom of God.

3. The insistent demands of discipleship (Luke 9⁵⁷⁻⁶², cf. Matt. 8¹⁹⁻²²)

Now large crowds were journeying along with him. And he turned and said to them, If any one comes to me and hates not his father and mother and wife and children and brothers and sisters, yes, and his own life also, he cannot be my disciple. And he who does not carry his own cross and come after me cannot be my disciple. For which of you, wishing to build a tower, does not first sit down and count the cost, to see if he has money to complete it? Lest after he has laid the foundation and has not the means to finish, all those looking on begin to mock him, saying, 'This man began to build, but was not able to finish.' Or what king, on going to war with another king, will not first sit down and take counsel whether he is able with ten thousand men to meet him who is coming against him with twenty thousand? And if not, when the other is still far away, he sends an embassy and asks for terms of peace. So then every one of you, who does not renounce all his possessions, cannot be my disciples.

4. The importance of counting the cost (Luke 14²⁵⁻³³, cf. Matt. 10³⁷, ³⁸)

Salt indeed is good, but if even salt has lost its savor,

5. Uselessness of the faithless
(Luke 14³⁴, ³⁵, cf. Mark 9⁵⁰ Matt. 5¹³)

wherewith shall it be seasoned. It is fit neither for the land nor for the dunghill: men throw it out. He who has ears to hear, let him hear.

He also spoke to them a parable:

6. The ideal of discipleship
Luke 6³⁹, ⁴⁰, cf. Matt. 15¹⁴ 10²⁴, ²⁵)

Can a blind man guide a blind man?
Shall they both not fall into a ditch?
For a disciple is not above his teacher;
Yet every finished disciple shall be like his teacher.

7. Character essential for effective teaching
(Luke 6⁴³⁻⁴⁵, cf. Matt. 12³³⁻³⁵ 7¹⁶⁻²⁰)

For there is no sound tree that brings forth rotten fruit,
Nor again is there a rotten tree that brings forth sound fruit;
For each tree is known by its own fruit.
Men do not gather figs from thorns,
Nor do they pluck grapes from a bramble-bush.
The good man from the good store-house of his heart brings out what is good,
And the bad man from the bad store-house brings out what is bad:
For out of the abundance of his heart the mouth of man speaks.

8. The lesson of tolerance
(Mark 9³⁸⁻⁴⁰, cf. Luke 9⁴⁹, ⁵⁰)

John said to him, Teacher, we saw a man casting out demons in thy name, who did not follow us. And we tried to prevent him, because he did not follow us. But Jesus said, Prevent him not. For no one shall work a miracle in my name and then be able quickly to speak evil of me. He who is not against us is for us.

9. The ministering women
(Luke 8¹⁻³)

Now it came to pass soon afterwards that Jesus journeyed about from city to city and village to village, preaching and bringing the good tidings of the kingdom of God. And he was accompanied by the Twelve and certain women, who had been healed of evil spirits and illnesses: Mary, who was called Magdalene, from whom seven demons had gone out, Joanna, the wife of Chuzas, Herod's steward, Susanna and many others were ministering to them out of their possessions.

Now in the course of their journey Jesus entered a village, and a certain woman named Martha received him in her house. And she had a sister named Mary, who seated herself at the Lord's feet and listened to his words. But Martha was distracted with much serving. And she came to him and said, Lord, carest thou not that my sister has left me to serve all by myself? Bid her, therefore, help me. But the Lord said to her, Martha, Martha, thou art anxious and troubled about many things, yet few things are needed—or only one; Mary has chosen the good portion, which shall not be taken away from her.

And Jesus went about, through all the cities and villages, teaching in their synagogues, preaching the good tidings of the kingdom, and healing all kinds of disease and sickness. But when he saw the crowds he was moved with compassion for them, harassed and scattered, like sheep without a shepherd. Then he said to his disciples, The harvest is plenteous, but the laborers are few. Beseech, therefore, the lord of the harvest to send forth laborers into his harvest.

Go on your way. Behold, I send you forth as lambs in the midst of wolves. Carry no purse, no wallet, no sandals, and salute no man on the road. And whatever household you enter first say, Peace be to this household. And if the son of peace be there your peace shall rest upon him; but if not, it shall return to you again. Stay in the same house, eating and drinking what they provide, for the laborer is worthy of his hire. Go not from one house to another. Also whatever city you enter and the people receive you, eat the things that are set before you, heal the ill in it, and tell them: 'The kingdom of God is near you.' But whatever city you shall enter and the people receive you not, go out into its streets and say, 'Even the dust from your city, which clings to our feet, we wipe off against you. But know this, "The kingdom of God is near." ' I tell you, on that day it shall be more tolerable for Sodom than for that city.

> Give not that which is holy to the dogs,
> And throw not your pearls before swine;
> Lest they trample them under their feet,
> And turn again to devour you.

> He who hears you hears me,
> And he who rejects you rejects me,
> And he who rejects me rejects him who sent me.

111

10. The pre-eminent importance of the attitude in discipleship (Luke 10³⁸⁻⁴²)

11. Jesus' reasons for sending out his disciples (Matt. 9³⁵⁻³⁸, cf. Luke 10¹, ²)

12. His directions to his disciples (Luke 10³⁻¹², cf. Matt. 10¹⁻¹⁶ Mark 6⁷⁻¹¹ Luke 9¹⁻⁵)

13. To consider the attitude of their hearers (Matt. 7⁶ Luke 10¹⁶, cf. Matt. 10⁴⁰)

14.
Their
return
(Mark
6[30, 31]**,**
*cf.***Luke**
9[10]
10[17]**)**

And the apostles gathered to Jesus, and they told him all that they had done and all that they had taught. And he said to them, Come by yourselves into a desert place in private, and rest a little.

At that season Jesus answered and said,

15.
Jesus'
prayer
of
thanks-
giving
(Matt.
11[25-27]**,**
cf.
Luke
10[18-20]**)**

I praise thee, Father, Lord of heaven and earth,
That thou didst hide these things from the wise and prudent,
And didst reveal them to babes;
Yea, Father, for so it pleased thee.

All things have been intrusted to me by my father,
And no one knows the Son but the Father,
Nor does anyone know the Father but the son,
And he to whom the Son may wish to reveal him.

I. Jesus' Purpose in Calling His Disciples. In his choice of disciples Jesus reveals the aims and methods of a teacher. Most of the great teachers of his race had gathered about them a group of disciples. When Isaiah's counsels were rejected by king and people in the crisis of 735 B.C. he turned to his disciples as the agents through whom to ultimately communicate his teachings to his nation: "Binding up the admonition and sealing the instruction among my disciples, I will wait for Jehovah, who is hiding his face from the house of Jacob, and in him will I trust" (Isa. 8[16]). Baruch and the other faithful scribes, from whom has come the present book of Jeremiah, were devoted disciples of that prophet of Judah's decline. All the famous rabbis of Jesus' day had disciples who sat at their feet, drank in the teachings that fell from their lips, and in turn transmitted them to their own followers. For fully two centuries the doctrines of Hillel and Shammai were thus treasured, for the Jews were strongly opposed to committing to writing anything that might rival the sacred written law of the Old Testament. Like Isaiah, Jesus chose a definite group of disciples. The formal choice came at the critical moment when the opposition of the leaders and the inability of the masses fully to appreciate his teachings were becoming more and more evident. His first object, therefore, in choosing disciples was to impress upon their minds and characters the truths which he desired to impart to the needy of his race. As the earliest records of his work and teachings, they proved far more effective than cold, impersonal writings.

The Gospel of Mark states that Jesus chose his disciples that "they might be with him." It is evident that Jesus felt strongly the need of friendship and enjoyed exceedingly the companionship of men. This side of his nature has been often overlooked. But it was not merely to supply his social needs that he drew these busy men from their daily tasks. It was because of what this companionship meant to them. In doing some worthy task together men learn best to know each other's inner thoughts and motives. Jesus taught his disciples by action and association, as well as by words. From the first he appears to have set before them that missionary ideal which they later recognized in even larger measure than he had anticipated. "Follow me and I will make you fishers of men," were the kindly, almost playful, and yet richly suggestive words with which he first summoned Peter and Andrew. He saw how plenteous was the harvest and how great the need of effective reapers. It was, therefore, to make men who would in turn become makers of men that Jesus called and trained his disciples.

II. **The Personnel of the Twelve.** The scene of the formal call of the Twelve appears to have been the quiet table-land that rose abruptly from the narrow plain on the northwestern end of the Sea of Galilee. Their call marked an important moment in Jesus' career. Henceforth his attention was devoted largely to teaching and training them. Why he chose exactly twelve is not quite clear. Matthew 19[28] and its parallel in Luke 22[30] imply that it was because there were twelve tribes of Israel and that each of the disciples might later sit on a throne judging one of these tribes. The idea, however, is apocalyptic and cast in the characteristic Jewish terminology adopted by the later church. The explanation of his choice of twelve appears to be much simpler. As he sent them out two by two he naturally chose an even number. In the lists in Matthew and Acts the disciples are arranged in pairs. Of those who gathered about him there were twelve who gave large promise of future helpfulness.

Four lists have been preserved; all differ in minor details. They go back, however, to two original lists. The one is that of Mark 3[13-19a], which Matthew follows in 10[2-4] with only minor changes in order. The other is that of Luke 6[12-16], which is reproduced in Acts 1[13, 14] in a slightly different order. The only fundamental variations between these two independent lists is that in Mark the name of Thaddeus appears, while in Luke the name of Judas the son of James takes its place.

In the gospel narratives the personality and work of Jesus are made so prominent and commanding that the individual portraits of the Twelve are exceedingly dim. Peter's is by far the clearest. This rough, energetic fisherman of Capernaum is a surprising combination of strength and weakness. The explanation of the seeming contradictions in his character lies in his mercurial disposition. Confidence and despondency, insight and obtuseness, boldness and cowardice mark his career. Jesus, almost at the same moment, called him a rock and Satan. Paul, likewise, in the same chapter called him a pillar and a dissembler (Gal. 2⁹, ¹³). John's character has been popularly interpreted by the Fourth Gospel which bears his name. The sharp contrasts between this portrait and the few allusions to him in the synoptic gospels have long been recognized, so that the convincing evidence that he was not its author removes a cause of confusion. He and his brother James are called "the sons of thunder," and the few facts that are recorded of them confirm the impression that they were men with strong, impulsive, ambitious natures. They and Peter were the three disciples who proved Jesus' closest friends and associates.

Simon, the Cananean, came from the ranks of the Zealots. The appellation Cananean in Mark and Matthew is the Aramaic equivalent of Zelotes in Luke and Acts. He represented, therefore, that enthusiastic, intemperate body of Zealots who were especially strong in Galilee and who were ever ready to take up the sword against Rome. His presence among the Twelve still further illustrated the type of men that Jesus drew about him. They stood close to the common people and reflected their needs and hopes. They came neither from the aristocracy nor the rabble, but from the respectable middle class. It is an astonishing fact that apparently they were all mature men whose occupations and manner of thinking were already fixed. Although far removed from the narrow dominance of the priests, they were accustomed to bow before the authority of the scribes and Pharisees. They were better acquainted with deeds than with creeds. They were also familiar with the teachings of the earlier Hebrew prophets and were looking for a new and better era. Above all, they were enthusiastic, impressionable, and responsive to an exacting call to service. Their ignorance of the subtle requirements of the scribal law rendered them more teachable than the more learned Jews of Judea. Their close, practical touch with real life made them appreciative of the simple, practical message which Jesus brought them.

III. **The Conditions of Active Discipleship.** The surprising incident recorded in Mark 3¹⁹ᵇ, ²⁰ and in its immediate sequel (³¹⁻³⁵) shows that Jesus had broken away completely from his inherited Semitic point of view which placed supreme emphasis upon the ties of blood relationship. The failure of his family to appreciate his aims and methods may have strengthened this tendency; but it was in keeping with his spirit and attitude toward men. It was a dramatic moment when he publicly declared that the bonds of a common loyalty to God were far stronger than those of kinship. Mark is probably right in introducing this sweeping declaration immediately after the account of the formal choice of the Twelve. Henceforth Jesus regarded them and the larger group of disciples who gathered about him as his true kinsmen. For over thirty years he had faithfully performed the duties imposed by birth. Now he recognized as paramount the obligations of that larger family relationship in which God is the Father and all men are kinsmen.

The strenuous emphasis that he placed on the necessity that a true disciple be ready to break all home ties that might retard him in his larger service suggests the struggle through which Jesus himself had passed. His words are hyperbolic. Never was the hypocrisy of making the demands of the ceremonial law an excuse for neglecting personal duty to parents more scathingly denounced than by Jesus. We have every reason to believe that there was never a more loyal son than he. The assertion, therefore, that a man must hate his own kinsmen is but his characteristically effective way of proclaiming the principle that, to become his active disciple, a man must be ready to forego everything. It was the readiness that he demanded, not necessarily the act. Peter certainly remained loyal to his home ties. This was probably true of the other disciples. For the mighty task that Jesus essayed he required the help of heroic men who, like himself, were ready to sacrifice all and to dare all. He asked each man at first to sit down and with absolute sincerity count the cost. As subsequent events proved, a selfish, calculating disciple (Judas) was fatal to his cause. Men who were to sweeten and to purify the corrupt life of Palestine must have tested courage, a spirit of complete self-sacrifice, and enthusiasm. The experiences of the opening days of his public activity had made clear to Jesus the magnitude of his task. That knowledge, instead of daunting him, led him to perfect his plans and to select his followers more carefully. Nowhere is Jesus' heroic purpose and spirit more clearly revealed than in the conditions which he imposed upon his immediate followers. It is no vague, impractical dreamer that is here disclosed, but an heroic, practical, resourceful leader who knows conditions and men. His methods are as definite as his aims. The conditions that he imposes upon others—personal purity and sincerity —he has already accepted for himself.

IV. Jesus' Fellowship with His Disciples. Jesus told his disciples from the first that he had nothing to offer of those things which men ordinarily strove to attain, and that to follow him meant not only the giving up of many of the things which they held dearest, such as home, calling, friends, and possessions, but it meant also a life of danger and privation. Why did these mature, practical men follow him? Beyond the opportunity for self-sacrifice and service, he made them no definite offers. Their later words and actions show that they had a very imperfect conception of his real aims. Clearly that which led them to leave all and follow him was primarily the charm of his personality. They accepted the Teacher long before they did his teachings. His courage, optimism, enthusiasm, good-fellowship, and practical idealism were irresistible.

The Gospel of Mark gives a few vivid illustrations of the nature of the relation that existed between Jesus and his disciples. More and more Jesus himself recognized the importance of this companionship. Even during the strenuous days at Capernaum he found time to withdraw with them to the quiet of the near-by heights or out upon the lake or to the solitudes on the eastern side of the Sea of Galilee. "The first steps toward a new life of brotherhood were taken here in stillness and privacy; it was the first wonderful stirrings of a new humanity" (Bousset, *Jesus*, 64). It is a side of Jesus' activity that is almost overlooked by the later gospel writers, who were intent upon reporting his teachings and deeds and upon interpreting the larger meaning of his work; but the older sources record the priceless truth that the corner-stone of Christianity was a noble brotherhood that found its inspiration in Jesus' personality.

Jesus was the close personal friend of each of his disciples; but he also maintained his dignity as their teacher and master. Ordinarily in their journeys he appears to have gone ahead and they to have followed a short distance behind (Mark 9[33, 34] 10[32]). When they wished to ask a question or he desired to communicate with them, they came forward and then fell back again. There are repeated references in the earlier gospels to their coming to him and to his summoning them (Mark 8[1] 9[35] 10[32] 12[43]). Usually, as he preached and healed in public, they were grouped behind him (10[23]). Frequently he took three of them (Peter, James, and John) with him, leaving the others behind (*e. g.*, 5[37]). This natural reserve and dignity only enhanced the significance of the friendship between Jesus and his followers.

V. The Ministering Women. Luke alone of all the gospel writers has preserved a detailed record of the presence of ministering women among the larger group of Jesus' disciples and followers. Mark 15[40, 41], however, confirms Luke's valuable information, for it states that among the timid, heart-broken witnesses of the crucifixion were Mary Magdalene, Mary the mother of James the younger and Joses, and also Salome, who, when he was in Galilee, followed him and ministered to him, and many other women who came up with him to Jerusalem. These statements show how little sympathy Jesus had with the contemporary asceticism—for example, that of the Essenes. All classes who sought his help received it impartially and unstintingly. None needed it more than the women of his day, and especially the type which gathered about him.

Prominent in this group was Mary of Magdala. This city lay on the western shore of the Sea of Galilee and on the southern side of the Plain of Gennesaret. It was at this point that the great highway from Egypt to northern Syria and Babylonia reached the Sea of Galilee and joined the road that came up along the Jordan and the western shore of the lake. About it were broad, fertile fields, so that its situation made it in Jesus' time famous for its wealth and corruption. Here the atmosphere was Græco-Roman, with all the social immorality that characterized this civilization in its Eastern setting. Tradition is, therefore, probably right in saying that the woman out of whom Jesus "cast seven devils" was a victim of the immoral life of Magdala, although it is well to remember that this is only a conjecture.

The other women whose names are given evidently came from quite a different class. Joanna was the wife of Herod's steward. Possibly her husband is the royal official, mentioned in John 4[46-53], who believed with his whole household. Mary, the mother of James and of Joses, and Salome also appear to have been women of high standing in the Christian community. In the account of Jesus' visit to the home of Mary and Martha, Luke had given a vivid picture of the great Teacher amid domestic scenes. Even during his short sojourn there he found an opportunity to instruct the family and to commend Mary's wisdom in listening to his words. Although none appreciated genuine hospitality more highly, he mildly rebuked Martha's zeal, which led her to neglect his teachings in order to provide for his entertainment, by protesting that his physical needs were few (following what appears to be the original reading). These two sisters are representatives of that larger group of unknown followers who realized Jesus' ideal of discipleship in the quiet of the home and in their daily tasks, even though they did not actually leave all to follow him in his itinerant ministry.

VI. Jesus' Commission to the Twelve. The sending out of his disciples was apparently but an incident in Jesus' brief ministry. Inasmuch as it has no close connection with the rest of the narrative, its historical character has even been questioned. It is recorded, however, in the two oldest sources, and these are quoted in each of the synoptic gospels. It is also in complete harmony with Jesus' purpose as revealed at this period in his activity. Mark has possibly abridged the earlier teaching source. Matthew has apparently combined the material which he found in his two sources. Luke has dealt with the variant accounts which he found in his two sources (Q and Mark) in a bold and characteristic way. In 9^{1-6} he follows Mark in the description of the sending forth of the Twelve. In 10^{1-12} he introduces the account of the sending out of the apostles, which he found in the early teaching source (Q), to describe a mission of the seventy (or, as it appears in certain texts of 10^{17}, seventy-two). This account, however, is almost identical with the description of the sending out of the twelve disciples which Matthew evidently drew from the same teaching source and which he has preserved in its original setting. Luke's object in substituting "seventy" for "the disciples" may have been to establish a traditional basis for the subsequent mission of the Christian apostles to the heathen nations. The number seventy corresponds to the number of the nations mentioned in the table of Genesis 10; the number seventy-two to the number found in the Greek version of that chapter. The command that they should go forth two by two corresponds to the custom followed by the early Christian missionaries. The Gospel of Matthew, on the other hand, in keeping with its characteristic point of view, inserts a command not found in Luke: "Take no road to the Gentiles, and enter no city of the Samaritans; rather go to the lost sheep of the house of Israel." While these words represent the practice of the Twelve, as well as that of the early Jerusalem church, they reflect a problem which did not arise until after Jesus' death. This command was, perhaps, introduced by the author of Matthew as a preparation for that broader command which he introduces in 28^{19}: "Go then and make disciples of all the nations." Aside from his radical alteration at the beginning of the narrative, Luke has apparently preserved the more nearly original order and version of Jesus' directions to his disciples. Mark, familiar with the customs of the later Christian missionaries, gives a different version of the original command; the disciples are here permitted to take a staff and a pair of sandals. Otherwise Mark confirms Luke's order.

VII. Jesus' Reason for Sending Out the Twelve. According to the gospel record Jesus sent out his disciples because he felt strongly the limitations of time and space, which prevented him from satisfying the needs of the many whose suffering and ignorance appealed to him. Matthew, in 9[35, 36], prefaces his quotation from his older source with a description of Jesus' teaching and healing work throughout Galilee, and of his deep compassion for those who were like a scattered, shepherdless flock. Jesus' words also imply that his deeper reason for sending out his disciples was thereby to train the laborers for their task. He realized that only in the laboratory of actual experience could their training be completed so that "they would be like their teacher." The report of their actual work is meagre, but sufficient to indicate that it was similar to his own, namely, healing and preaching. Mark adds that their message, like that of John and of Jesus in his earlier ministry, was to call the people to repentance. This is also implied by the words found in Matthew: "The kingdom of heaven is at hand." Thus their primary task was to preach; but, like the later Christian apostles, they also performed acts of healing.

In the light of oriental custom the practical wisdom of Jesus' detailed directions are obvious. In the Semitic world hospitality was regarded as a fundamental virtue. Jesus fully appreciated the psychological principle that they who give readily are the most ready to receive. On the other hand, oriental customs, and especially those followed in salutations, were so elaborate that they consumed a vast amount of time. Expressed in modern terms, Jesus commanded his disciples to do their work in the simplest and most direct way, to avoid unnecessary hindrances, and to work only where conditions were favorable. He also sought to impress them with the supreme importance and dignity of their task and to prepare them for the misunderstandings and affronts which they were sure to meet. The later church has rightly found in the principles which underlie these commands the incentives for its world-wide missionary activity.

VIII. The Return of the Twelve. The gospel records are strangely silent regarding the results of the mission of the Twelve. Luke, in 10[17-20], contains a brief account which is clearly colored by the language and thought of the later missionary period in which he lived and wrote. Mark's account of the return of the disciples is much simpler and apparently more historical. Luke, however, has introduced, in connection with his account of the return of the disciples, a remarkable utterance of Jesus. It was evidently derived from the teaching source (Q), for Matthew has preserved it practically verbatim, although in a slightly different setting. The words fit that period in Jesus' activity when the inability of the multitudes and the refusal of the learned scribes and Pharisees to accept his teachings had become plainly manifest. The thought is expressed in poetic form and reveals strong emotion. Appreciating this fact, Luke prefaces them with the words, "At the same time, Jesus rejoiced in the Holy Spirit and said." This brief prayer of thanksgiving is another of the open windows through which it is possible for us to look into the depths of Jesus' soul. Experience had taught him the profound significance of that insight into God's character and purpose which had been revealed to him. At the same time it had taught him how difficult it was to make clear to the learned but prejudiced and self-satisfied leaders of his race the simple and yet all-important truths that filled his soul and made him and his work unique. Possibly in desperation he had turned to the ingenuous group whom he gathered about him as his disciples, in the hope that by virtue of their individual needs and freedom from prejudice they might understand and accept him and his teachings. The result of this experiment had given promise that his hope would yet be fulfilled. Jesus' actual words are too hyperbolic to admit of exact translation. The word translated "babes" means, literally, those who, like infants on their mothers' breasts, were still unable to speak.

In its present form the second stanza of Jesus' prayer would seem to be the later form in which the teachings regarding his personality and mission were expressed by his followers. An earlier and more logical form of the utterance is preserved in Christian writings which come from the second and third centuries:

> All has been intrusted to me by my Father,
> And no one has known the Father except the Son,
> Nor the Son except the Father,
> And those to whom the Son reveals [himself].

Attractive and on the whole convincing is the suggestion in *Die Schriften des Neuen Testaments* (I, 322) that the original Aramaic word, *Abba*, which elsewhere in the gospels is translated, according to the context, father, the father, and my father, be here rendered as a vocafive, thus preserving the same type of prayer as is found in the preceding stanza. Following this suggestion the passage may be rendered:

> All is now revealed to me, O Father,
> And no one knows thee, O Father, except thy Son;
> No one knows thy Son, O Father, but thou,
> And those to whom the Son reveals himself.

JESUS' FUNDAMENTAL TEACHINGS

§ CXXIX. THE AIMS AND METHODS OF THE GREAT TEACHER

1. Jesus' aim to perfect the ancient teachings (Matt. 5¹, ², ¹⁷, ²⁰)

Now on seeing the crowds Jesus went up into the mountain. And when he sat down, his disciples came to him. Then he opened his mouth and taught them, saying:

Think not that I came to destroy the law or the prophets:
I came not to destroy but to fulfil.
For I tell you, unless your righteousness shall excel that of
the scribes and Pharisees,
You shall not enter the kingdom of Heaven.

2. The advantages of his way of living (Matt. 11²⁸⁻³⁰)

Come to me all you who are weary and heavy laden,
And I will give you rest.
Take my yoke upon you, and learn from me,
For I am meek and lowly in heart,
And you shall find rest for your souls;
For my yoke is useful and my burden light.

3. Its value as a basis of life (Matt. 7²⁴, ²⁵, cf. Luke 6⁴⁷, ⁴⁸)

Everyone who hears these words of mine and does them
Shall be compared to a wise man, who built his house upon
a rock;
And the rain fell, and the floods came,
The winds blew and beat upon that house;
Yet it fell not, for it was founded upon a rock.

4. The peril of failing to adopt it (Matt. 7²⁶, ²⁷, cf. Luke 5⁴⁹)

And everyone who hears these words of mine and does them
not
Shall be compared to a thoughtless man who built his house
upon the sand;
And the rain fell, and the floods came,
The winds blew and beat upon that house;
And it fell, and great was its downfall.

And it came to pass when Jesus finished these words that the crowds were astonished at his teaching, for he taught them as one who had authority, and not like their scribes.

5. Effect of Jesus' teachings (Matt. 7²⁸, ²⁹, cf. Mark 1²²)

And again on another day, Jesus began to teach by the seaside. And a great crowd gathered about him, so that he entered a boat, and sat in it on the sea. And all the crowd were by the sea on the land. And he taught them many things in parables, and said to them in his teaching, Listen! The sower yonder went out to sow, and as he sowed some seed fell along the road, and the birds came and ate it up. And some fell on the rocky ground, where it had not much earth; and it sprang up at once, because it had no depth of earth; and when the sun rose, it was scorched by the heat, and because it had no root, it withered away. And some seed fell among the thorns, and the thorns grew up and choked it, and it bore no fruit. And some fell on the good soil, and came up and grew and bore, some thirty-fold, some sixty-fold, and some a hundred-fold. And he said, He who has ears to hear, let him hear.

6. The parable of the sower (Mark 4¹⁻⁹, cf. Luke 8⁴⁻⁸ Matt. 13¹⁻⁹)

And when he was alone his companions and the Twelve questioned him about the parables. And he said to them, Do you not understand this parable? Then how are you to understand all the parables. The sower sows the word. And these are they who are along the road where the word is sown; and when they have heard, Satan immediately comes and takes away the word sown among them. And in the same way, these are they who are sown upon the rocky places: the ones who, when they have heard the word, receive it immediately with joy; yet have no root in themselves, but survive for a time; then when distress or persecution arises because of the word, they at once fall away. And others are those who are sown among the thorns; they are the ones who have heard the word, yet the anxieties of the world, the deceitfulness of riches, and the desires for other things enter in and choke the word, and it becomes unfruitful. And these are they who are sown upon the good soil; the ones who hear the word and accept it, and bear fruit, thirty-fold, sixty-fold and a hundred-fold.

7. The varied reception of Jesus' teachings (Mark 4¹⁰⁻²⁰, cf. Luke 8⁹⁻¹⁵, Matt. 13¹⁸⁻²³)

8. The
obliga-
tion to
impart
the
truth
(Mark
4²¹⁻²⁵,
cf.
Luke
8¹⁶⁻¹⁸)

And he said to them:

Is the lamp brought to be put under the bushel or under
the bed?

Is it not to be put on the lamp stand?

For nothing is hidden, except to be disclosed,

And nothing is concealed, but that it should come to light.

If anyone has ears to hear, let him hear.

And he said to them:

Take heed what you hear.

With what measure you measure, it shall be measured to
you, and more shall be given to you.

For he who has, to him shall be given,

And he who has not, from him shall be taken even that
which he has.

9.
Jesus'
use of
para-
bles
(Mark
4³³, ³⁴,
cf.
Matt.
13¹⁰⁻¹⁵,
⁵³)

And with many parables like these he spoke the word to
them as they were able to hear it; except in parables he did
not speak to them; but in private he explained everything
to his own disciples.

I. Jesus the Teacher. Jesus was pre-eminently a moral and religious teacher. This side of his activity is most clearly set forth in
the two earliest sources (Q and Mark) which underlie the gospel records. By his contemporaries and disciples he was addressed most
frequently as Rabbi, or Teacher. In this rôle he can best be understood. Jesus combined the divine passion and enthusiasm of Israel's
prophets with the moral purpose and didactic skill of the scribes and
of their forerunners, the Hebrew sages. He sprang from a race of
teachers and inherited and utilized the results of the experience gained
during a thousand years, in which the best energies of Israel's spiritual
leaders had been devoted to interpreting and making effective the will
of God in the life of the nation and of the individual.

That which primarily distinguished Jesus from the scribal teachers
of his day was the quiet note of authority that characterized all his
teachings. This quality was one of the chief sources of his charm and
effectiveness. It was the authority, not of dogmatism, but of deep
conviction born of personal experience. He manifested at every point
a profound reverence for the teachers of Israel's past; but there was
no need for him to cite their authority, when the truths which he proclaimed were daily attested by his own observation and consciousness.

For this reason he constantly called upon his hearers to use their own good sense and moral judgment. Thus, for example, one of his important teachings regarding the delicate question of Sabbath observance was based upon a matter-of-fact comparison of the relative value of men and beasts.

Jesus' greatness as a teacher was due, in the first place, to that intimate knowledge of God which was the mystery and yet the inspiration of all that he did and taught. This possibility of a personal acquaintance with God was the supreme reality which he was endeavoring, with all the skill of an inspired teacher, to make clear to his disciples; and out of the fulness of his heart his mouth spoke. A second source of Jesus' skill as a teacher was his knowledge of men. He knew the ideals and hopes, as well as the joys and sorrows, in the minds of his hearers. Although he only rarely, as in the case of the hostile scribes and Pharisees, expressed his judgments publicly, yet it is clear that he knew intimately the different classes with which he came into contact and analyzed with unerring instinct their motives as well as their acts. Above all, his judgments were prompted by love and sympathy and the strong desire to help rather than to criticise. Described in modern terms, Jesus was the great psychologist, as well as the prophet and philanthropist of his age.

The third reason for Jesus' greatness as a teacher was the clarity and concreteness of his method of teaching. It was in marked contrast to the verbose, complex methods of reasoning employed by the rabbis of his day. He undoubtedly thought as he taught, in figures drawn from nature or from the every-day life of the people. No complicated theology or philosophy obscured his vision of the eternal verities. For the unsophisticated fishermen and for the fallen women of the street, as well as for the learned Pharisees, he had a clear, concrete message. The fourth reason why Jesus was pre-eminently a great teacher was that his aims were definite and his methods intensely practical. He knew what were the needs of the people and what would satisfy those needs. With unprecedented skill, he adapted his methods to the realization of his aims. The principles which he employed are the shibboleths of modern pedagogy. To his marvellous message he added the marvellous charm of his personality, so that it is not strange that wherever he went, during his Galilean activity, he was surrounded by crowds of listeners who plied him with eager questions.

Spontaneously and unreservedly he gave himself to all who came to him, whether in public or private. He did not even wait for men to come to him, but went forth to find them. In the bazaars and on the streets he taught them. In the synagogues he sought and found attentive audiences. Later, when the people were ready to follow him, he led them forth to the quiet spots along the northern shore of the Sea of Galilee or else upon the upland plateaus, which at points rise a few yards from the shores of this sunken, inland lake. A comparatively late Christian tradition has fixed upon one of these heights, the Horns of Hattin, to the south of the Plain of Gennesaret, as the scene of the so-called "Sermon on the Mount." The earliest Christian tradition, however, which comes from the seventh century, identifies the scene with the hill to the north of the famous fountain of Tabighah, and therefore just north of the western suburbs of ancient Capernaum. It is exceedingly probable that many of the sayings which the author of Matthew has grouped together in chapters 5–7 were first uttered on this spot. As Jesus in time turned from the multitudes and devoted himself to the training of his disciples, he sought retired places like this, in which they would be free from the distractions that were peculiarly characteristic of the city and village life of the ancient East.

II. **Jesus' Attitude toward the Earlier Teachers of His Race.** As has already been noted, the foundation of much of Jesus' thought and teaching was laid on the earlier scriptures of his race; but he accepted as authoritative, not the detailed laws, but the principles underlying them. He recognized that the Jewish scriptures represented simply a stage in Israel's moral and religious evolution. This fact explains his own broad statement regarding his attitude toward them: "I came not to destroy the law and the prophets, but to fulfil." As a matter of fact, he quietly rejected practically all the religious institutions upon which the pharisaic scribes placed chief emphasis: fasting, rigid Sabbath observance, and the laws of ceremonial cleanliness. To circumcision and similar Jewish institutions he apparently never referred. While he did attend the great feasts, there is no evidence that he ever brought offerings to the temple. In the passage recorded in Matthew 9[13] (cf. also 12[7]) he reiterated the words of Hosea, "I desire mercy, not sacrifice." By example as well as word he declared that "love was more than burnt-offering and sacrifice" (Mark 12[33]). In a well-authenticated passage (Matt. 5[23, 24]) he advised his followers to go and right any wrongs which they had committed against their associates before bringing offerings to Jehovah's altar. These familiar examples illustrate the meaning of his words regarding his relation to the ancient scriptures. He was not an iconoclast; but his profound reverence for the truth led him to distinguish clearly between the universal and the national, between the eternal and the temporal, between the spirit and the letter.

Jesus appears to have accepted the current traditions regarding the origin and authorship of the Old Testament books, even as he did the scientific and unscientific ideas of his age. Nowhere does he claim to speak with authority except in the fields of morality and religion. At the same time, as has been truly said, "Jesus was the higher critic of his day." With that quiet note of conviction and authority that amazed the assembled multitudes, he set aside the commands that had come down from the "men of old." For the time-honored laws regarding murder, adultery, and oaths, which dealt simply with external acts, he substituted his own fuller statements of the principles which underlie them. By his teaching and example, Jesus rendered obsolete much that is found in the Old Testament; but in so doing he did not destroy; rather he brought to full fruition and expression the germinal principles contained in the old law and the prophets. To the scribes and Pharisees, whose eyes were fixed on the letter of the law, he seemed, indeed, a destroyer of their sacred scriptures. Jesus, who saw through the letter to the spirit, knew that he was the true champion and fulfiller of the law and the prophets. Regarding certain fields of thought and teaching, he was silent, because he realized that here the utterances of the earlier teachers were sufficient. Earlier prophets, like Amos and Isaiah, had set forth the social and political principles that govern society so fully that Jesus quietly accepted them as the basis of his own teachings. These earlier teachers of Israel had spoken to the nation, but Jesus spoke, above all, to the individual. He sought to make their words simple and practically applicable to the needs of each and every man. In his use of the older scriptures he was governed, not by the casuistical laws of rabbinical interpretation, nor by a blind reverence for the text, but by a keen appreciation of the moral and spiritual needs of the crowds who gathered about him and by the desire to bring to them that which was really valuable in the records of God's earlier revelation through the life of his people.

III. **Jesus' Aims as a Teacher.** Jesus' work was so many-sided and comprehensive that it is difficult to define his aims in a few brief statements. He declared repeatedly that he "came not to save the righteous, but sinners." The record of his activity confirms the conclusion that his primary aim was to deliver men from the effects of wrong beliefs, motives, and habits of living, and to restore them to complete physical, mental, moral, and spiritual health. He desired that they "might have life, and that abundantly," that they might "know the truth, and that the truth might make them free." Jesus aimed not only to present a clear and true conception of God, but to establish a vital personal relation between him and each individual, and to inspire a childlike faith that would leave no place for anxiety or uncertainty regarding the tasks and problems of life. He desired to give each of his fellow-men that knowledge of the Father which was the inspiration of his own thought and activity. This was the mystery which Jesus sought to reveal to his disciples. In this way Jesus aimed to teach men how to live—not under the compulsion of a rigid set of rules, but guided by a genuine, commanding love for God and man. His yoke, which he invited men to place upon their shoulders, was not a burden, but was intended to relieve those who were laden, not only with their own sins, but also with the heavy load that Jewish legalism placed upon their shoulders. It was the same yoke that had enabled him serenely and joyously to bear the heavy burdens which had rested upon him during the responsible days at Nazareth, in the stress of his early Galilean activity, and amidst the turmoil of pharisaic persecution. It was a yoke which had been tested and had proved not only easy, but also supremely useful—as the exact meaning of the Greek words suggests—because it had made those burdens light. Furthermore, Jesus aimed to give men a worthy goal for which to strive, and so to train them as disciples that they might surely attain it. Finally, he endeavored, by leading all men into common allegiance to the common Father, to unite them in the universal fraternity, which he described as the kingdom or reign of God, and thus to develop a perfect social order.

IV. The General Characteristics of Jesus' Teaching Methods. Jesus endeavored to realize his aims in the most natural and direct way. At first glance it would appear that he had no distinctive method. This impression, however, is due to the fact that he adapted his method with marvellous versatility and skill to the person or class which he wished to reach. If they were fishermen, he drew illustrations and figures from the common life and experiences of that class. If it was a woman, he spoke, for example, of the loss of the coins which had been received as a part of the marriage dowry. When a learned disciple of the scribes came to him, he began to discuss the law. In every case he first established a point of contact by using a figure or a story that aroused the interest of his hearers. More than that, Jesus always endeavored to establish from the first a basis of personal friendship between himself and those whom he sought to help and teach. Some were bound to him by gratitude for an act of healing, others by the charm of his personality and friendliness. With the eye of a skilled teacher, Jesus saw, behind the immoral lives or petty acts of those who gathered about him, the real man that each aspired to be or could be. With intense zeal and superlative skill he strove to develop that true manhood. Sometimes he appealed to their reason and sometimes to their feelings, but always to their wills, for he was never contented unless he stirred men to action and thus developed their character.

Another characteristic of Jesus' method was its simplicity and directness. Even the imperfect records show clearly that he never employed unnecessary words. By his use of familiar figures he was able to express by a word or phrase more than otherwise could be stated in many sentences. After having established a point of contact, he quickly led his hearers from the atmosphere of the petty and the commonplace to the highest moral and spiritual points of view. Then he directed their vision to that which was universal and eternal. Sometimes he himself formulated the principle after he had fully illustrated it. He also appreciated the high, didactic value of concrete illustration. To teach the attitude of trust he placed a child in their midst. Many of his most important teachings, as, for example, those regarding Sabbath observance and the forgiveness of sins, were called forth by experiences in connection with his disciples. Many incidents illustrate the fact that he fully appreciated the value of the laboratory method in teaching moral and spiritual truth. By his own example, by their life together, and by the work which they performed under his direction, even more than by precept, Jesus trained his followers so that they, as "finished disciples, should be like their master."

Another marked characteristic of Jesus' teachings is their positive rather than negative quality. The earlier teachers of his race had expressed their message largely in the form of denunciations and warnings. "Thou shalt not" rings through the Old Testament; but almost completely disappears in the gospels. On rare occasions Jesus denounced the Pharisees and the mercenary high priests, but ordinarily he was content to commend the good rather than to denounce the evil. He called men's attention to the great truths of life and experience, and trusted that the errors and falsehoods would be speedily recognized and so disappear. It was because his message was simple, positive, and constructive that he succeeded in drawing all classes to himself and has held them through the succeeding ages. By virtue of the example of its founder, Christianity has from the first been a teaching religion. Its success in the past has been determined by the fidelity with which it has adhered to this ideal; its conquests in the future depend upon the thoroughness with which Jesus' followers make his teaching aims and methods their own.

V. The Literary Form of Jesus' Teachings. The exquisite beauty of literary form which characterizes Jesus' recorded teachings was evidently not the result of accident but of careful thought. Undoubtedly much of their literary beauty has been lost in transmission; but enough has been preserved to indicate that Jesus almost universally employed the balanced parallelism of Hebrew poetry in expressing his teachings. Frequently he repeated the same thought in slightly different form in the second line of a couplet. Thus, for example, he taught:

> Nothing is hidden, except to be disclosed,
> And nothing is concealed but that it should come to light.

Often he used the element of contrast by bringing out in the second line of a couplet the antithesis of the thought expressed in the first. More often the second and succeeding lines completed and supplemented the thought presented in the first. A favorite type was the enveloping or introverted parallelism. Here the first and fourth lines are closely related, and the second and third are not only parallel to each other but also supplement the thought of the first line. This type is illustrated by the familiar teaching:

> Take my yoke upon you, and learn of me,
> For I am meek and lowly in heart,
> And you shall find rest for your souls;
> For my yoke is useful and my burden light.

In certain cases a close parallelism is traceable between succeeding stanzas. Thus, in the description of the house built upon a rock each of the first five lines is closely paralleled by the corresponding lines in the succeeding stanza, which describes the house built upon the sand. By these artistic methods Jesus not only appealed to the æsthetic sense of his hearers, but also imparted to his teachings a marvellous clarity and impressiveness.

THE LITERARY FORM OF JESUS' TEACHINGS

Mark's assertion that Jesus spoke only in parables must be interpreted in accordance with the larger meaning of the Hebrew word for parable, *maschal*. This type of literature was frequently used by Israel's sages, and included not only that which is to-day known as the parable, but also the proverb, the metaphor, the didactic simile, the paradox, and even the allegory. Thus interpreted, Mark's assertion is true, for it is difficult to find a discourse, or even a brief saying of Jesus, which is not adorned and illuminated by some one of these figures of speech. They are the matchless word pictures which give beauty and variety to the gospel narratives. Mark's statement in 4^{12} that their aim was to conceal rather than to reveal the thought is, however, misleading, and is evidently based upon a wrong application of the words used by Isaiah in describing his mission (Isa. $6^{9, 10}$). The large use of these figures of speech is in perfect harmony with Jesus' teaching aims and methods. They imparted to his sayings a picturesqueness and suggestiveness otherwise unattainable. Above all, they enabled him to present abstract truths in simple, concrete form, and in language equally intelligible to all ages and all races. The figures are most of them drawn from the simple peasant life of Palestine. Their atmosphere and setting is that of the home and, above all, of nature, but the themes possess a universal human interest.

Jesus was the master of the effective metaphor. In concise phrases, as, for example, "the leaven of the Pharisees," or "the lost sheep of the house of Israel," or "the salt that has lost its savor," he expressed truths which commentators cannot set forth with equal clarity in many pages. By means of the didactic simile, also, he associated his teachings with the common objects and experiences in the daily life of his hearers. In this way he not only made clear his thought and commanded the interests of his disciples, but also provided a constant reminder of his message. For example, they who had listened to his teachings regarding the wise and the foolish man could never again discuss the foundations on which they should build their houses without being reminded of that abiding foundation on which he exhorted them to build their faith. Jesus also appreciated the importance of making his hearers think and of directing their thoughts so that of themselves they would arrive at right conclusions. Like the great teacher of Greece, he frequently used what is known to-day as "the Socratic method." To impress upon them the responsibility of transmitting the teachings which they had received, he plied them with homely questions: "Is the lamp brought to be put under the bushel or under the bed? Is it not to be put on the lamp stand?" Having thus prepared their minds for the answer, he formulated it for them: "No truth is imparted in secret, except that it may be publicly proclaimed."

One of the most effective ways in which Jesus compelled his disciples to think was by use of the paradox. The seeming contradiction aroused their curiosity. In discovering the solution, they fixed in their minds the underlying truth. Certain of Jesus' profoundest teachings are thus expressed: "Many who are first shall be last, and the last first."

> "He who has found his life shall lose it,
> And he who has lost his life for my sake shall find it."

The literary form which Jesus used most often was the parable proper. It may be defined as a narrative drawn from nature or common experience to suggest or illustrate a moral or religious truth. The rabbis had long employed this effective type of teaching, but there is a simplicity and naturalness in Jesus' parables which is largely lacking in those which have come down from other Jewish teachers. They are suffused with the personality of the great Teacher. He alone opened wide the great storehouse of nature and drew from it those suggestive parables which remain for all time our best guides to the vivifying thoughts in the mind of the Master. Frequently these illustrations appear to have been suggested by something at the moment before the eyes of his hearers. The graphic "Behold," or "Yonder," which introduces the parable of the sower implies that Jesus, as he uttered it, pointed to a man sowing grain beside the lake.

Ordinarily, Jesus' parables were intended to illustrate one central truth. To endeavor to find in each element an underlying symbolism leads to serious error. At the same time many of his parables approach the allegory, in which the parts as well as the whole are typical. In Jesus' interpretation of the parable of the sower, which Mark records, not only does the story, as a whole, illustrate the importance of the right attitude on the part of the hearer, but it also describes in detail the four types of hearers. The first represents those whose habits and inclinations are so thoroughly perverse that they are utterly irresponsive to the truth. The second includes those who are not devoid of good impulses, but who lack courage and persistency, so that their faith is quickly destroyed by trouble or opposition. The third, represented by the seed thrown among thorns, includes those who hear but are under the control of base ambitions and the false standards of the social class in which they live, and whose time is so absorbed in the pursuit of material things that the truth bears no fruit. The fourth type comprises the faithful disciples, who not only hear but heed, and apply the truths in their own lives. While there are only traces of the allegory in the synoptic gospels, it is the prevailing form in which the teachings of Jesus are presented in the Fourth Gospel. "The light of the world," "the bread of life," and "the vine and its branches" are figures which have become the common possessions of Christendom.

Rarely Jesus used irony and satire, but usually these were tempered by a kindly humor. An excellent illustration is his reference to the Pharisees as "those just persons who need no repentance!" (Luke 15⁷). No careful student of the gospels can fail to appreciate that quiet vein of humor which runs through many of Jesus' teachings. An example is his reply to the preposterous charge of certain of his foes that "in the name of Beelzebub, the ruler of the demons, he was casting out demons," that, "if Satan is divided against himself how shall his kingdom stand: if I am casting out demons with the help of Beelzebub, with whose help do your sons cast them out? Therefore shall they be your judges." He makes the proud Pharisees ridiculous in the picture of those who place themselves in the chief seats in the synagogue and then are compelled to their shame to retire to the position which rightfully belonged to them. The saying, "Cast not your pearls before swine," contains an unmistakable element of humor.

The intense earnestness of Jesus' purpose is also illustrated by his frequent use of hyperbole. The instincts and enthusiasm of the teacher led him to put those teachings, which might have otherwise been misunderstood or neglected, in a form well calculated to arrest attention. The necessity of exaggeration is an accepted principle in elementary education. If Jesus sometimes indulged in an overstatement, he trusted to the sense of his hearers and to his teachings on other occasions to correct it. It is important to recognize this characteristic in order to interpret rightly Jesus' message as a whole. Familiar illustrations of his use of hyperbole are the statements that "it is easier for a camel to go through the eye of a needle, than for a rich man to enter the kingdom of Heaven," or that a man, in order to become his disciple, must leave his own father and mother. An example of his humorous use of hyperbole is his charge that the scribes "strain out a gnat and swallow a camel."

Like the scribes, Jesus taught the spirit and manner of worship by means of prayers, of which the familiar Lord's Prayer survives as the classic example. Another effective literary form in which Jesus presented his teachings was the beatitude. Occasional examples of the beatitude are found in the Psalms, but Jesus appears to have employed this literary form very frequently. In reality it is an exclamatory sentence. It expresses an axiomatic truth based on observation and experience. Without arousing opposition or inviting discussion, it admirably voices those profound convictions which impart to Jesus' teachings their distinctive note of authority. Of the many literary forms which Jesus employed, the most characteristic are the metaphor, the proverb, the didactic simile and parable, and the beatitude. These gave to his teachings that variety and adaptability which to a great extent explain their perennial charm and effectiveness. In form as well as in content, the great Teacher of Nazareth, indeed, "taught as never man taught before."

§ CXXX. GOD'S ATTITUDE TOWARD MEN

1. God's eagerness to reclaim the sinner (Luke 15¹⁻⁷. *cf.*Matt. 18¹²⁻¹⁴)

Now all the tax-collectors and the sinners were drawing near to Jesus to hear him, but the Pharisees and scribes were complaining, saying, This man receives sinners and eats with them. So he spoke to them this parable: What man of you, who has an hundred sheep and has lost one of them, does not leave the ninety and nine in the wilderness and go after the lost one until he finds it. And after finding it he lays it on his shoulders rejoicing. And on coming home, he calls his friends and neighbors together and says to them, Rejoice with me, for I have found my sheep that was lost. I tell you that even so there shall be joy in heaven over one sinner that repents more than over ninety-nine righteous people who have no need of repentance.

2. His quest for the lost (Luke 15⁸⁻¹⁰)

Or what woman, having ten pieces of silver, if she has lost one piece of silver does not light a lamp, sweep the house clean, and search diligently until she finds it; and after finding it she calls her women friends and neighbors together, saying, Rejoice with me, for I have found the piece which I lost. So I tell you there is joy in the presence of the angels of God over one sinner who repents.

And he said, A certain man had two sons. And the younger of them said to his father, Father, give me the part of your property that belongs to me. So the father divided his property between his two sons. And not many days after, the younger son gathered all his possessions together and went away into a distant country, and there he wasted his money in riotous living. Now when he had spent it all, it came to pass that there was a great famine in that country; and he began to be in want. And he went and worked for one of the citizens of that country, who sent him into his fields to feed swine. And he used to be so hungry that he was ready to fill himself with the pods that the swine were eating; but no one ever gave him anything. But when he came to himself he said, How many of my father's hired servants have bread enough and to spare, while I am perishing here with hunger! I will arise and go to my father, and will say to him, 'Father, I have sinned against God, and against thee. I am no longer worthy to be called your son; make me as one of your hired servants.' So he arose and went to his father. But while he was still a long way off, his father saw him and took pity on him, and ran and fell on his neck and kissed him again and again. And the son said to him, Father, I have sinned against God and against you; I am no longer worthy to be called your son. But the father said to his servants, Quick, bring the best robe and put it on him, and put a ring on his hand and shoes on his feet. And bring the fatted calf and kill it, and let us eat and make merry; for my son here was dead and has come back to life; he was lost and has been found.

Now his elder son was in the field. And when he came and drew near to the house, he heard music and dancing. And he called to him one of the servants, and inquired what was the meaning of these things. And the servant said to him, Your brother has come; and your father has killed the fatted calf, because he has him back safe and sound. But he was angry and would not go in. So his father went out and pleaded with him. But he answered and said to his father, See, all these years have I worked for you, and I never disobeyed one of your commands; and yet to me, you never gave a kid that I might make merry with my friends.

3. The father's forgiveness of the repentant prodigal (11-34)

4. The protest of the older son (25-32)

But when your son here came, who has wasted your possessions with wicked women, you killed for him the fatted calf.
And the father said to him, Son, you are always with me,
and all that is mine is thine. But it was right to make merry
and be glad, for your brother here was dead and has come
back to life; though lost, he has been found.

5.
God's
readi-
ness to
answer
prayer
(Matt.
7⁷, ⁸,
cf.
Luke
11⁹, ¹⁰)

Ask, and it shall be given you,
Seek, and you shall find,
Knock, and it shall be opened to you:
For every one who asks, receives,
And he who seeks, finds,
And to him who knocks, it shall be opened.

6. To
give
the
best
gifts
to his
chil-
dren
(Matt.
7⁹⁻¹¹,
cf.
Luke
11¹¹⁻¹³)

Or what man of you will give his son a stone, if he ask him
for a loaf?
Or will give him a serpent, if he ask him for a fish?
If you then, evil as you are, know how to give good gifts to
your children,
How much more shall your Father which is in heaven give
good things to those who ask him?

I. Current Jewish Ideas of God. Jesus was not a theologian;
yet his conception of God was fundamental to all that he taught. The
passages which record his teachings regarding God are so familiar that
their original meaning and significance have been largely obscured.
Only by comparison with the current Jewish ideas regarding God can
their full meaning and originality be appreciated. The Judaism of
Jesus' day had departed far from the teachings of its earlier prophets.
The reasons for this departure were in part historical. Prolonged contact with the oriental despotisms of Babylonia and Persia, and later
with the vast Greek and Roman empires, had transformed the early
simple faith of Israel. Jehovah was no longer thought of as ever-
present in their midst, revealing himself personally to his prophets
and priests, but as a mighty potentate dwelling in the distant heavens,
ruling his people from afar, and communicating with them through
angelic messengers. Like the oriental kings who had ruled over the
Jews for centuries, he was conceived of as rigorous in his insistence on
the external proofs of man's allegiance. Sacrificial offerings, prayer,
fasting, and the strict observance of the Sabbath were the gifts which

the Jews of Jesus' day felt compelled to present to their divine king as evidence of their loyalty. The logic of legalistic Judaism seemed simple and irrefutable: the divine king was also the great lawgiver. Man's primary duty, therefore, was to show his loyalty to Jehovah by keeping all the commands of the divine law. Since God was just, each man, if not here, in the life beyond, would receive his just deserts. Ceremonial legalism was a cold, logical, pitiless religion which divorced the individual from personal contact with God and imposed upon him a burden heavy to bear, for no one was able to meet each and every demand of the law. Upon the poor and lowly and outcast this burden rested most heavily, for they were hopelessly handicapped by virtue of their occupations, their birth, and their lack of education. True, other more spiritual types of faith were current in Judaism, but they were not emphasized or ordinarily taught by the leaders of the nation.

II. **The Growth of the Belief in the Fatherhood of God.** In leading his race back to a simpler, truer conception of God, Jesus expressed the essence of religion in the one all-embracing word, Father. His teaching was the culmination of a process which may be traced from the beginnings of human history. In the early days, when the gods were thought of as supermen, the Babylonian and Egyptian kings claimed physical descent from the chief deity of their nation. Jeremiah denounced his contemporaries for saying to an idol, "Thou art our father" (2^{27}). With the growth of the belief in one supreme Deity, and that he was a God of spirit, the idea of divine fatherhood was spiritualized. According to Exodus 4^{22}, Moses declared, in the name of Jehovah, "Israel is my son, my first-born." With superlative tenderness Jeremiah, in 3^{19}, voices the yearning of Jehovah for the loyalty and love of his people:

But I had thought, "Now I will make thee like sons,
And I will give thee a pleasant land, a noble heritage!"
I had also thought, "You will call me Father, and will not turn away
     from me."

The unknown prophet of Isaiah 63^{16} (cf. also 64^8) prays, "Thou, O Jehovah, art our Father, our Redeemer." That Jehovah was the father of the nation was a familiar teaching of Israel's early prophets. The more intimate belief in him as the father of the individual appears in the Psalms and the writings of Ben Sira, which record the inner life

137

of the more spiritual-minded Jews in the days immediately preceding the Roman period. Closely akin to the teachings of Jesus are the words of the psalmist in 103[13]:

> Like as a father pitieth his children,
> So Jehovah pitieth those who fear him.

In the strong childlike faith of the lowly and afflicted, who have given us the spiritual psalms of the Psalter, we find the religious atmosphere in which Jesus lived and taught. The noble sage, Ben Sira, also addresses God as "Lord, Father, and Master of my life" (23[1, 4]). The same personal faith in God's fatherhood is reflected in Ben Sira 4[9, 10]:

> Be as a father to the fatherless,
> And take the place of a husband to the widow;
> So will God call you his son,
> And be gracious to you and save you from destruction.

III. Jesus' Teaching Regarding the Nature of God. Jesus' teaching regarding the fatherhood of God is none the less significant because it has a historical background extending through thousands of years. He gave to the term, father, a reality and a personal content that made his teaching a new message to men. He divested the term of all national limitations and interpreted it universally. He spoke not only of my Father, but of the Father, your Father, and our Father, and used these titles interchangeably. In Jesus' thought this term expressed concretely that kindred nature of man and God which is taught in the first chapter of the Old Testament. The designation assumed that those qualities which man learns to know in his fellow-men are also found in God; that it is possible for man to communicate with God and to know him intimately, even as he does his fellow-men. The foundation of Jesus' teachings regarding God, therefore, was the supreme mystery, and yet reality, of human experience: the possibility of man's entering into personal relations with his divine Father. Developing the same simple, forceful figure, Jesus taught God's constant care and guidance of each human child who turned to him in the attitude of submission and trust. Not only in the life of man, but also in the world of nature, in the life of the beast and of the flower, Jesus saw the evidence of this fatherly care. For a cold, pitiless law

Jesus substituted the consciousness of the personal presence of a loving Father able and eager, in his infinite wisdom, to guide each individual in his daily life. Jesus taught, therefore, that man was no longer the slave of the law, but a child being trained by a loving parent.

With true intuitions the church is beginning to realize that the ultimate historical foundations of Christian theology are to be found, not in its later creeds, but in the parables of the lost sheep and of the prodigal son. Although Jesus never taught in abstract terms that God was love, as did a later disciple with inspired insight, it is the God of love who is revealed even more clearly than words could describe in these parables. Jesus believed not in the far-distant, exacting, austere Deity of the Pharisees, nor in a transcendental Being who was to reveal himself in some distant future, as did the apocalyptic teachers of the day, but in a personal, immanent, loving Father.

Undoubtedly, the author of John 4²⁴ has also interpreted correctly Jesus' conception of God in the familiar words, "God is a Spirit, and they who worship him must worship him in spirit and in truth." Jesus placed supreme emphasis on the love of God, for this quality was fundamental and largely overlooked by the teachers of his day; but he also appreciated those divine qualities of justice and majesty which earlier prophets, like Amos and Isaiah, had portrayed with convincing power. His earnest words, "There is none good but God," reveal the humility with which he bowed before the God of infinite goodness. In another passage he emphasizes Jehovah's majesty and justice: I tell you, my friends:

> Fear not those who kill the body,
> And after that can do nothing further.
> I will tell you whom to fear:
> Fear him, who, after he has killed,
> Has power to throw into Gehenna—
> Yea, I tell you, fear him (Luke 12⁴, ⁵).

This passage, however, is the prelude in Luke to the illustration of God's constant and tender care for his children, of which the sparrows were an apt illustration.

The other familiar term by which Jesus described God was that of King. It is implied in the phrase so often on his lips, the kingdom of God. In Jesus' use of the two terms, Father and King, they are closely related and supplement each other. The fatherhood of God implies a world-wide brotherhood. The idea of a universal fraternity in which all are united by loyalty to a common King is also the essence of his teachings regarding the kingdom of God.

While the terms which Jesus used and the germs of all that he taught regarding God are to be found in the Jewish scriptures, that which makes it a new message is its simplicity, its concreteness, its personal quality, and its inspirational power. Back of Jesus' teaching regarding God clearly lies his own experience and belief. In the ultimate analysis the potency of his message depends not upon the clearness and beauty with which Jesus expressed his belief, but upon the fact that he was able to lead his disciples into the same transforming personal relation to God, and that they in turn have been able to make other men "one with God even as he was one."

IV. God's Readiness to Forgive the Sinner. Jesus knew the reality of sin. He saw the evidence of it, not only in the distorted lives, but in the diseased bodies of the men and women who crowded about him seeking mental and physical healing. He appreciated the insufficiency of the current Jewish doctrines to meet the needs of these classes. These doctrines raised a hopeless barrier between the penitent sinner and God. This barrier Jesus sought to tear down. To accomplish this he used three methods: (1) he began by declaring that his message was primarily to outcasts, and that he could and would save them; (2) he assured many whom he healed, as, for example, the paralytic, who was let down through the roof of Peter's house, Thy sins are forgiven; (3) by a remarkable series of parables preserved in Luke 16, he substituted for the current conception of a relentless Deity, who had little interest even in repentant sinners, the picture of a forgiving Father. Hosea, Jeremiah, and certain of the psalmists had caught clear visions of Jehovah's forgiving love, but never before was it set forth so beautifully and convincingly. Dickens has truly said of the parable of the prodigal son, "It is the most touching passage in all literature." Each of the three parables in Luke 15 emphasized the one common teaching: God's intense love even for the sinner, and his eager desire to reclaim him. Matthew's version of the parable of the lost sheep limits it to the Christian converts who had fallen away from the faith, but Luke gives it a universal application. The parable of the lost piece of money is peculiar to Luke. It is a companion to the parable of the lost sheep, and illustrates the effective way in which Jesus adapted his teachings to different classes of hearers.

The concluding section presents with marvellous clearness the mercenary pharisaic doctrine of proportionate rewards. Measured by human standards, the older brother, notwithstanding his narrowness and jealousy, deserved all that his father had to give him, and the prodigal nothing. This parable shows how far Jesus had broken away from the doctrine of rewards, and illustrates, as does no other passage in the gospels, the true character of that God who had revealed himself in the great Teacher. The portrait corrects the errors of later Christian theology as well as those of contemporary Judaism. There is no place here for the harsh doctrine of an angry God or need of a vicarious offering in order to propitiate a divine judge. The one essential requirement in the eyes of the father had been met by the full repentance of the son and by his desire to return and ask forgiveness. Quietly, without denunciation or discussion, Jesus thus swept away the casuistry and error which hitherto had concealed the face of the divine Father, and thereby revealed him in his true character to his needy children.

V. Jesus' Teaching Regarding God's Readiness to Answer Prayer. Jesus' teaching regarding prayer is the logical outcome of his conception of the fatherhood of God. He again effectively uses the analogy of the relation between the human father and son to interpret that higher relationship between each man and his divine Father. In his thought it is an axiomatic truth that God is intensely eager to meet every reasonable desire of his children. At the same time Jesus nowhere declares that men's prayers will be answered in the exact form in which they voice their petition. If a man asks for a loaf, he may not receive a loaf, but he certainly will not receive something inferior, as, for example, a stone. Out of his wisdom and love the heavenly Father will "give good things to those who ask him." With effective reiteration, but in purposely general terms, Jesus emphasizes the absolute certainty that he who comes to God in a receptive attitude shall surely receive, and implies that the gift, as human experience constantly demonstrates, will far surpass the request. The form of Jesus' words also suggests that he had in mind, not petitions for material things, but those more abiding gifts, knowledge, insight, peace of mind, and the joys of efficient service, which he constantly set before his disciples as the true goals for which to strive. These, he declares, God is ready to grant in unstinting measure. The only limit is man's lack of faith and zeal and ability to receive them.

§ CXXXI. MAN'S ATTITUDE TOWARD GOD

1. Reverence for God and for one's personal honor (Matt. 5²³⁻³⁷)

You have heard that it was said by the men of old, Thou shalt not swear falsely, but thou shalt pay thy vows to the Lord.

But I tell you, Swear not at all;
Neither by heaven, for it is God's throne,
Nor by earth, because it is the footstool of his feet,
Nor by Jerusalem, because it is the city of the great King,
Nor shalt thou swear by thy head, because thou canst not make one hair white or black.
Let what you say be 'Yes' for 'Yes,' or 'No' for 'No';
Whatever exceeds that is from the evil one.

2. Acts of charity to be done in order to win not man's but God's approval (6¹⁻⁴)

Take care that you do not your righteousness before men, to be seen of them;
Otherwise you have no reward with your Father who is in heaven.
When, therefore, thou givest alms,
Sound not a trumpet before thee,
As do the hypocrites in the synagogues and in the streets,
That they may be honored by men.
I tell you truly, they get their reward.
But when thou givest alms,
Let not thy left hand know what thy right hand is doing,
That thine alms may be in secret;
And thy Father, who sees in secret, shall recompense thee.

3. Prayer to be directed to God not to man (⁵, ⁶)

And when you pray, you shall not be like the hypocrites;
For they love to pray standing in the synagogues and on the street corners,
That they may appear before men.
I tell you truly, they get their reward.
But thou, when thou prayest, go into thine inner chamber, and shut the door,
And pray to thy Father, who is in secret,
And thy Father, who sees in secret, shall recompense thee.

142

Anu when you fast,
Do not look dejected, like the hypocrites,
For they disfigure their faces to appear to be fasting before men.
I tell you truly, they get their reward.
But when thou fastest,
Anoint thy head and wash thy face,
That thou mayest not appear to men as one fasting,
But to thy Father, who is in secret,
And thy Father, who sees in secret, shall recompense thee.

4
Fast-
ing t
be un.
ostenta-
tatious
with
mind
fixed
solely
on
God
(16-18)

In praying do not use vain repetitions, as the Gentiles do,
For they think that they shall be heard for their much speaking.
Now be not like them,
For your Father knoweth what things you need, before you ask him.

5.
Prayer
to be
brief
and di-
rect
(7, 8)

Now it came to pass, while Jesus was praying at a certain place, when he ceased, one of his disciples said to him: Lord, teach us to pray, just as John also taught his disciples. And he said to them, When you pray, say, 'Father, thy name be hallowed. Let thy kingdom come. Give us each day our bread for the coming day. And forgive us our sins; for we also forgive each one who is indebted to us. And lead us not into temptation.'

6.
Jesus'
type of
prayer
(Luke
11 1-4,
cf.Matt.
6 9-15)

And he said to them, Which of you shall have a friend, and shall go to him at midnight, and say to him, 'Friend, lend me three loaves; for a friend of mine has come to me from a journey, and I have nothing to set before him'; and he from within shall answer and say: 'Do not disturb me; the door is now shut and my children are in bed with me; I cannot rise and give you anything.' I tell you, though he will not rise and give him anything because he is his friend, yet because of his friend's persistency, he will arise and give him as much as he needs.

7. Im-
por-
tance
of per-
sist-
ency
in
prayer
11 5-8)

And he spoke a parable to them regarding the necessity of always praying and never losing heart. There was a judge in a certain city, who had no fear of God, nor respect for men; and in that city there was a widow; and she used to

8. The
para-
ble of
the un-
fortu-
nate
widow
(Luke
18 1-8)

come to him, saying, 'Give me a judgment against my adversary.' Yet for some time he would not. But afterwards he said to himself: 'Although I have no fear of God, nor respect for man, yet since this woman troubles me, I will give her a judgment, lest she annoy me by forever coming.' And the Lord said, Listen to what the unjust judge says! And shall not God avenge his chosen ones, who cry to him day and night, though in so doing he is longsuffering? I tell you, he will vindicate them speedily.

9. The right attitude in prayer (Luke 18⁹⁻¹⁴)

He also said this parable to some who were confident of their own righteousness and despised all other people. Two men went up to the temple to pray; one was a Pharisee and the other a tax-collector. The Pharisee stood up and prayed thus by himself, 'O God, I thank thee that I am not like the rest of men—extortioners, unjust, adulterers, or even like this tax-collector. I fast twice a week. I pay tithes upon all my income.' But the tax-collector stood afar off and would not so much as lift up his eyes to heaven, but kept beating his breast, saying, 'O God, be gracious to me, the sinner!' I tell you this man went down to his house justified more than the other.

For every man who exalts himself shall be humbled,
And he who humbles himself shall be exalted.

10. The power of faith (Luke 17⁵, ⁶)

And the apostles said to the Lord, Give us more faith. But the Lord said, Had you faith like a grain of mustard seed, you would have said to this mulberry tree, Be rooted up and planted in the sea, and it would have obeyed you.

11. The importance of attitude of faith Mark 11²²⁻²⁵ cf. Matt. 21²¹, ²²)

And Jesus said to them, Have faith in God. I tell you truly, Whoever says to this mountain, 'Be lifted up and cast into the sea,' and hesitates not in his heart, but believes that what he says shall be done, he shall have it. Therefore, I say to you, believe that you have received all things for which you pray and ask, and you shall have them. And whenever you stand praying, if you have anything against any one, forgive, that your Father who is in heaven may also forgive you your trespasses.

Be not anxious for your life, as to what you eat,
Nor yet for your body, as to what you wear;

144

Is not life more than food,
And the body than raiment?
Look at the birds of the air,
They sow not nor reap, nor gather into barns,
Yet your heavenly Father feedeth them.
Are you not worth more than they?
Which one of you by being anxious can add a cubit to his
    stature?

12. Trust that leaves no worry about food (Matt. 6[25-27], cf. Luke 12[22-25])

Why then be anxious about what you wear?
Consider the lilies of the field, how they grow;
They toil not, neither do they spin.
Yet I tell you that even Solomon
In all his glory was not arrayed like one of these.
Now if God thus clothes the grass of the field,
Which to-day lives and to-morrow is thrown into the oven,
Shall he not much more clothe you, O men of little faith?

13. About clothing (Matt. 6[28-30], cf. Luke 12[26-28])

Be not anxious then and say,
'What are we to eat, or to drink, or how are we to be clothed?'
(For after all these things the Gentiles seek)
For your heavenly Father knows that you require all these.
But seek first his kingdom and his righteousness,
And all these things shall be given to you besides.
Be not anxious, therefore, about the morrow;
For the morrow will be anxious for itself.
Sufficient for the day is its evil.

14. Seeking to know and do God's will the remedy for worry (Matt. 6[31-34], cf. Luke 12[29-32])

I. Jesus' Conception of Man. Jesus was the most democratic
teacher the world has ever seen. His teachings reveal a profound
appreciation of the value of each individual. His deep insight and
sympathy enabled him to see the divine possibilities in every man,
even the humblest. He had no sympathy with the ideas, current both
in Gentile and Jewish circles, that sinners and outcasts were of comparatively little value. His conception of man was the corollary of
his belief regarding God's attitude toward his children. He taught
that man was the crown of God's creation. All that concerned man,
even the hairs of his head, was of deepest interest to his heavenly
Father. No man was outside the pale of his love. At the same time
Jesus recognized that man could barter away his divine birthright.

No one taught the freedom of the will and the resulting responsibility more clearly than did he. No one hated sin more intensely, for he realized that, on the one hand, it thwarted the divine purpose, and on the other tended to destroy the divine possibilities inherent in each individual. Jesus distinguished clearly between the sin and the sinner. He apparently never gave up hope, even of the most perverse wrong-doer. In his treatment of the sinner he spent little time denouncing sin. He sought rather to develop right motives and to put wholesome ideas in the centre of focus. Above all, he aimed to bring each individual into the right relations to his heavenly Father and to his fellow-men, and thus to restore his spiritual and moral health.

Jesus' conception of the dignity of man and of man's proper attitude toward God is concretely illustrated by his teachings regarding oaths. Here he again took direct issue with the laws found in Leviticus 19^{12}, Numbers 30^3, Deuteronomy 23$^{22,\ 23}$, and the customs of contemporary Judaism. From earliest times the vow had occupied a prominent place in the religious life of the individual. It was regarded as a sacred contract with Jehovah, and as such perpetuated that mercenary interpretation of religion which was the weakness of all primitive cults. The early Semitic peoples used oaths almost constantly. The evils inherent in the practice are obvious. It weakens the plain, unadorned statement and is a confession that a promise, to be binding, must be enforced by the fear of divine judgment. This is precisely the effect of the use of oaths among the modern Arabs, whose plain assertions can rarely be trusted. This free and constant use of the divine name is not only in itself irreverent, but by easy stages engenders a habit of profanity. Other teachers of Judaism were awake to these evils and were striving to correct them. Ben Sira was the first openly to protest:

Accustom not your mouth to an oath;
And do not form the habit of calling upon the name of the Holy One;
For as a servant, who is continually scourged, is not without bruises,
So he who swears and takes the name of God continually shall not
    be free from sin.
A man of many oaths shall be filled with iniquity,
And the scourge shall not depart from his house (23$^{9-11}$).

Philo defined the goal to which Jesus was trying to lead his disciples: "In everything so speak that each word will have the value of an oath" (*De Decal.*, 17[84]). The form in which Matthew has preserved the teachings of Jesus is not in harmony with the meaning of the passage as a whole, for, according to the Talmud, the repetition of the words "yes" or "no" was in itself a form of oath. James 5[12] has beyond reasonable doubt preserved the intent, if not the exact form of Jesus' original teaching: "But above all, my brothers, swear not; neither by heaven, nor by earth, nor by any other oath. Let your 'Yes' be a simple 'Yes,' and your 'No' a simple 'No'—that you may not fall under condemnation." The ideal of Christian manhood which Jesus set before his followers was that of a man whose every word should be so true to truth that to embellish it with an oath would be an act of dishonor. He also aimed to develop in the minds of his disciples, not that idolatrous avoidance of the name of the Deity which characterized the Judaism of the day, but such a profound love and reverence for God that it would be impossible for them to use his name irreverently or in connection with the petty transactions of daily life. Here, as elsewhere, Jesus was endeavoring to illustrate a principle rather than to lay down a specific rule. Christian sects, which have interpreted this passage literalistically, have therefore failed to appreciate its real meaning.

II. **The Importance of the Right Attitude in Worship.** The foundation of Jesus' teachings was that the chief thing in a man's life was to realize his divine right and to come into real, vital, constant touch with his heavenly Father. Not to do so was the one great tragedy in human experience. It was to "lose a man's life." Anything, therefore, that stood in the way of that intimacy was disastrous. Jesus sought to guard men against those mistakes which might prevent them from finding God. From this point of view, it is perfectly clear why he taught that worship performed with eyes fixed on one's fellow-men was worse than useless, for it made the intimate personal relation between that man and God impossible. There is a certain humor in Jesus' reference to the hypocrites, "who sound the trumpet before them in the synagogues and in the streets." "These find what they seek," he declared; "but I set before you a higher goal." Again he uses that strong type of hyperbole which he frequently employed to state his profoundest truths: "Let not your left hand know what your right hand is doing" (that is, let not your own self-approval or that of others be your motive), "and thy father, who looks into the hearts of men, will reward thee with that which he alone can give."

In three stanzas, in language and figures that are closely parallel,

147

Jesus deals with the three current conventional forms of worship: alms-giving, prayer, and fasting. None of these did he condemn, although he does not appear to have encouraged fasting among his disciples. He taught that the value of each was entirely dependent upon the motive and upon whether or not it brought the individual into natural living touch with him who was the sole object of all true worship. Jesus himself appears to have usually retired for prayer to some hill-top or upland plateau. The command to go into the inner chamber and shut the door is but the antithesis of the public praying in the synagogues and on street corners which characterized the conventional religious practices of the scribes and Pharisees. Freedom from distraction and an opportunity to enter into spiritual relation with the God of spirit was what Jesus desired for his disciples.

The same strong emphasis on the purity of motive appears in his teachings regarding fasting. It is improbable that he actually expected his disciples, whenever they fasted, to anoint their heads and wash their faces, as in preparing for a wedding feast. Such ostentation was as foreign to his purpose as dejected looks and disfigured faces. Rather, by his emphasis on that which was the direct opposite of current practice, he aimed to guard his disciples against all ostentation in worship. Obviously, many of the elaborate forms and ceremonies which have developed in connection with the worship of the Christian church are contrary to his spirit and teachings. Only in so far as they lead the individual into closer personal touch with God are they justifiable or of real value.

III. **Jesus' Type of Prayer.** It is interesting to note that that prayer which has guided the faith of countless millions throughout the ages was, like Paul's immortal apostrophe of love in the thirteenth chapter of I Corinthians, simply an incident in the work of a great teacher. According to Luke, it was uttered in response to the request of one of his disciples. The context implies that it was given them simply as a type. It illustrates those characteristics which distinguish all of Jesus' prayers: brevity, directness, sincerity, and absolute confidence in the heavenly Father. Two versions of it are preserved, one in Luke and one in Matthew. Both come from the common early teaching source (Q). Luke has retained the older, briefer version. It consists of but five short sentences. The familiar version in Matthew is generally recognized as being later. It illustrates the strong, natural tendency of his followers to expand the original utterances of the Master in order to make their meaning clear. Still another version is found in the Teachings of the Twelve Apostles. The gnostic writer, Marcion, was acquainted with a fourth, slightly variant version.

There are many close points of contact between the Lord's Prayer and those employed in the Jewish synagogue, and especially the eighteen prayers which were used in the ordinary services. "Father" is the common term with which the Deity is addressed. In the third Jewish prayer are found the words: "Let us hallow thy name in this world, as thy name is hallowed in the high heaven." In another synagogue prayer this suggestive phrase is found: "Honored and hallowed be thy great name in the world which He has created according to His will. May He establish His kingdom during your life and during your days, and during the life of all the house of Israel, even speedily and at a near time, and ye say, Amen." This is still used as the mourner's prayer in the morning service at many Jewish synagogues. Five of the eighteen Jewish synagogue prayers are represented in Matthew's version of the Lord's Prayer. The teaching regarding the forgiveness of others is the one altogether new element in the Lord's Prayer; yet, noble as were the prayers with which the Jewish race voiced their faith and aspirations, there is a world-wide difference between them and the type of prayer which Jesus set before his disciples. The Jewish prayers bear the mark of their racial origin and point of view. Jesus' prayer is individual yet universal, concrete and practical, yet deeply spiritual.

The simple word, "Father," is that with which Jesus began his prayer in Gethsemane. The initial petition, "Hallowed (or sanctified) be thy name," is a familiar phrase in the Old Testament. Ezekiel, in 36^{23}, declares, in the name of Jehovah, "I will sanctify my great name." Again, in Isaiah 29^{23} occurs the phrase, "They shall sanctify my great name." The name of Jehovah here, as in the Old Testament, represents Jehovah's character. This petition is not abstract but personal. It was a profession of reverence and individual devotion. The thought is closely connected with that of the second petition, "Thy kingdom come." In praying that God's reign may be established on earth the petitioner thereby commits himself to the task of bringing about its speedy inauguration. In the version in Matthew this theme is developed more fully in the closely parallel petition: "Thy will be done, on earth as in heaven," for the doing of the will of the divine King was the essential element in the establishment of his reign.

The third petition appears in widely different form in the various versions. Luke reads literally, "Give us day by day our bread for to-morrow." This reading is confirmed in part by that of the Gospel to the Hebrews: "Give us to-day our bread for to-morrow." In part it follows Matthew, which reads: "Give us this day our daily bread." In each case the meaning is clear. Here for the first time the petitioner presents his personal, material needs; but the prayer is an expression of confidence in God's provision rather than a mere request for definite gifts. Its meaning is, "Provide for us each day that which thou, in thy fatherly care and wisdom, seest is needful for us." It is probable that Jesus had in mind the very similar petition in Proverbs 30⁸: "Break off for me the bread of my portion."

The fourth petition is also evidently found in its original form in Luke. It is closely parallel to that of Matthew except that in the latter "debts" is substituted for "sin." The necessity of first forgiving others is a teaching which Jesus repeatedly emphasized.

The fifth and last petition in the Lucan version: "Bring us not into temptation," has clearly been expanded by the author of Matthew; but he suggests its true meaning: "Deliver us from temptations which we are unable to withstand." The author of James 1¹³ was probably dealing with the problem presented by these words when he declared: "Let no man, who is being tempted, say, 'My temptation is from God,' for God is not to be tempted himself by evil and he tempts no man, but each man is tempted with evil when he is drawn away by his own lusts and enticed." The subsequent passages, retained in the familiar versions of the Lord's Prayer, are found only in certain later texts of Matthew and in the Teachings of the Twelve Apostles. They are late additions and are the results of the tendency to expand the five brief sentences of Jesus into an elaborate prayer.

Nowhere is man's right attitude toward God expressed more completely and divinely than in the five short sentences that constituted the original prayer, as it came from the lips of Jesus. Reverence, loyalty, trust, contrition for sin, and the sense of the need of constant help in the battle of life are here all plainly voiced. Prayer is also defined, not as the asking for material things, but as that loyal, trustful attitude toward the divine Father which make his good gifts possible. It is man's outreach toward God and his realization of the privileges of sonship. The spirit which characterizes this prayer is that which made possible God's unique revelation through Jesus.

IV. **The Value of Persistency and Humility in Prayer.** By word and example Jesus condemned the long and repetitious prayers of the Pharisees. Yet he emphasized strongly the importance of per-

THE VALUE OF PERSISTENCY IN PRAYER

sistency in prayer. Two parables illustrating this point have been preserved, one by Matthew and the other by Luke. Both illustrations are drawn from the ordinary homely life of the people. One is that of the friend who came late at night and by his insistence succeeded at last in securing that which he sought. As in the majority of Jesus' parables, but one point is emphasized, that of persistency. An allegorical interpretation, which finds in each element in the story a definite symbolism, gives a conception of Jehovah which was entirely contrary to Jesus' teachings elsewhere. Moreover, it is not constant reiteration of the request by the petitioner which Jesus desired to commend, but that intense desire which is the necessary condition, if God is to give his best gifts. The same principle of interpretation may be applied to the parable of the unprincipled judge who ultimately yielded to the request of the widow because, as the Greek literally expresses it, "he feared that in the end she would give him a black eye."

The conclusion of this parable has apparently been revised by Luke. The original probably emphasized, like the preceding parable, the importance of the persistent attitude in prayer. In the conclusion, however, it is God's attitude that is emphasized. "His chosen ones" designates the members of the later Jewish-Christian community. The promise is given them that, although they cry to him constantly in the midst of their persecutions, without any apparent response, he will ultimately punish their Jewish and heathen persecutors. This Lucan ending, therefore, not only anticipates conditions that arose after the death of Jesus, but restricts in its application the teaching which was originally of universal significance. Jesus, as usual, was laying down a principle rather than giving a detailed promise. To this parable Luke, or possibly a later editor, has also appended the question: "But when the Son of man comes, will he find faith on the earth?" It reflects the later Christian belief that the Messiah would come again as judge, and implies that when it was written certain of Jesus' followers had proved faithless.

Among the matchless parables of Jesus, none illustrates the spirit of true prayer more effectively than that of the Pharisee and the publican who went up to the temple to pray. When we recall that it was probably uttered at Jerusalem, when the Pharisees were already taking measures to slay him treacherously, we appreciate the courage which it reveals. In the thought of the people the Pharisees and tax-collectors stood at opposite extremes of the social and moral scale. The picture here presented of Pharisaism is inimitable. Without bitterness, but with that superb realism which is the charm of all his teachings, Jesus pictured the pride and hypocrisy of that class which had largely lost sight of the higher spiritual ideals. The Pharisee, notwithstanding his many words, asks for himself nothing and gets nothing. The tax-collector says little, but asks much and receives much. Jesus here not only teaches that pride and self-righteousness are harmful; he also shows the reason. They are based upon a false assumption, and therefore are equivalent to a lie. More important still, they reveal a low personal ideal. They are usually the sins of men who, like the Pharisees, have good inheritances and a conventional type of morality, but who fail to set before themselves a lofty goal. They are the moral Esaus, whom God himself cannot help, because they are thoroughly satisfied with themselves and contented to drift. No one emphasized more than Jesus the importance of wholesome self-respect. This is the essence of real humility, for the man who respects himself is, like the tax-collector in the parable, not contented with himself until he has attained the highest gifts that God is able to give him. This wholesome type of humility means growth for its possessor, for it makes it possible for God to realize in him his divine ideal.

V. **The Invincible Power of Faith.** Mark has appended to his account of the withered fig tree an important saying of Jesus, which appears to have been originally uttered not at Jerusalem, but in the vicinity of the Sea of Galilee and during his early Galilean activities. Luke, as in the case of many of Jesus' teachings, illustrates the same thought by a different figure: not that of the mountain, but that of the mulberry tree. Both forms of the teaching probably go back to original utterances of Jesus. Both are characterized by the vigorous, hyperbolic language which he was wont to employ in driving home a great truth. Paul, in I Corinthians 13², in the words, "though I have faith enough to remove mountains," probably refers to Jesus' words. The statement, as we have it, is unqualified, but its concreteness is due to Jesus' method. Nowhere did he teach his disciples to ask for material things, except as their daily needs required, or to dictate to God in their prayers. A disciple who followed the injunctions just considered could never ask for that which was impossible or impracticable for God to give. Jesus taught his followers first to pray, "Thy will be done." The two essentials in prayer that he most strongly emphasized were: (1) an absolute childlike trust, which is the only right attitude toward God, and (2) the spirit of forgiveness, which is the right attitude toward one's fellow-men. Jesus' concluding words also imply that, as elsewhere, he had in mind spiritual blessing, not the purposeless removal of mountains and mulberry trees. Also his words, "Believe that you shall receive all things for which you pray and ask and you shall have them," leave no doubt that what he was aiming to do was not to make the fatal mistake of using prayer as a means of realizing their selfish desires, but rather that their faith might make it possible for them to receive what God was eager to give. Underlying these often misinterpreted utterances is the larger truth that the all-wise and all-loving Father "is far more able and willing to give all good things to his children than they are to ask." The chief function of prayer is to create the right attitude in the mind of the petitioner that will make those good gifts possible.

VI. **Trust That Leaves No Place for Worry.** Jesus' words regarding anxiety are among the best attested in the gospels. Both Matthew and Luke quote them from their common teaching source (Q) almost verbatim. Matthew has retained throughout the question form of teaching which Jesus employed so often and effectively. Luke, writing for more cosmopolitan readers, has substituted ravens, the birds that haunted the towns and cities of the East, for the wild birds that made the air of Galilee melodious. At one or two points Luke has abridged the original, thereby destroying its carefully balanced poetic parallelism. Possibly in the concluding verses, where he departs from Matthew, he has preserved the older saying:

> Rather seek his kingdom,
> And these things shall be given you besides.
> Fear not, little flock,
> For it is your Father's good pleasure to give you the kingdom.

The Aramaic flavor of the version in Matthew, however, supports its originality. "And his righteousness" is probably an addition of the author of that gospel, for the phrase is peculiar to him. Origen (*De orat. libell.*, c. 2), Clement of Alexandria (*Strom.*, I, 24[168]), and other Church Fathers have preserved a saying, attributed by them to Jesus, which may be the still older original:

> Ask for the great things,
> And the small shall be added to you,
> Ask for the heavenly things,
> And the earthly shall be added to you.

Each version conveys the same underlying idea and helps to interpret it.

This passage, which teaches childlike trust in God, reveals more clearly than any other Jesus' attitude toward nature and his love for it. The lilies of the field are probably the beautiful red anemones that in the spring-time clothe the hills and fields of Palestine with a sunset splendor. Their stalks and roots were gathered by the peasants for fuel and furnished a quick, blazing fire. Solomon stood in oriental tradition (as he does to-day in the East) as the superlative type of royal pomp and magnificence, overshadowing in popular imagination the glories of Herod's temple and the beauties of the newly built cities, Tiberias and Cæsarea Philippi. Jesus' words imply that in his judgment all these products of man's skill were inferior to God's workmanship as revealed on hill and field. He here discloses the æsthetic side of his nature that rejoiced in the simple and beautiful—in the physical as well as in the moral world. It was the happy, joyous side of nature that impressed him rather than "the groaning and travail of creation" that caught the ear of Paul (Rom. 8^{22}). Like Israel's psalmists, Jesus saw in nature the revelation of God. Like the modern scientists, he was keenly alive to the evidence of order and law.

Interesting in this connection is the recently discovered saying of Jesus (*New Sayings*, §§ 9–14): "[You ask who are these] who draw us to the kingdom which is in heaven? The birds of the air, and all beasts that are under the earth or upon the earth, and the fishes of the sea." While this saying may not be original, it expresses a thought that was inherent in Jesus' teachings. He did not merely say, Do not be anxious, but appealed to the reason of his disciples. The heavenly Father, whose care is plainly revealed in the life of even the humblest things, will surely care for man, the crown of his creation. For life and growth every man must and does perforce trust him. Surely he has equal reason to trust his loving care for the necessities of life, for food and the things required to clothe and protect the body.

Jesus was not disparaging industry and wise provision for the future. The lack of these necessary qualities he condemns in such parables as those of the foolish maidens and of the man who began to build without first counting the cost. Rather he is dealing with that petty worry and apprehension regarding food, clothing, and personal safety which was almost inevitable with primitive man, but which his more civilized descendants have failed to conquer. With our more complicated life and tenser nerves the possible causes of worry have seemingly multiplied, until this minor weakness of the race is undermining its physical, mental, and spiritual efficiency. Anxiety was the insidious sin that preyed upon the common people whom Jesus first addressed. He presented the only antidote to worry known to man, and that is a faith and trust in God so simple and strong that it leaves no place for anxious care regarding those things over which man in the end has no control. To develop this faith requires courage and persistency. Possession of it is the mark of a noble soul. The lack of it is disloyalty to God as well as to one's self. It is essential to all real peace and happiness.

That his followers might win the steadfast faith that under God's protecting care only good can befall them, Jesus first appealed to their reason, so that the most familiar scenes, the birds and the flower-covered fields would remind them of the Father's love; but he also indicated a still more effective way. He commanded them to place loyalty to God's interests in the centre of focus:

> Seek first his kingdom,
> And all these things shall be added to you besides.

Psychology and practical experience demonstrate the eminent wisdom of this command. Only when men are intent on doing the will of God are they in a position to receive the gifts that he is eager to give. Anxious worry is usually due to false perspective. The whole-hearted endeavor to establish God's reign in one's life and in the world restores the perspective. Petty cares cease to harass a man who is absorbed in the larger interests of the kingdom of God. His own burdens slip from his shoulders when he attempts to relieve others of their burdens. Complete trust in the goodness and wisdom of the heavenly Father and single-minded devotion to the realization of his will in the life of the individual and in society are the only and the complete remedies for anxious care and harassing worry, as the experiences of countless millions throughout the centuries have amply demonstrated.

§ CXXXII. THE KINGDOM OF GOD

1. Its growth (Matt. 13³¹, ³², cf. Mark 4³⁰⁻³² Luke 13¹⁸, ¹⁹) Another parable Jesus set before them, saying, The kingdom of Heaven is like a grain of mustard seed, which a man took and sowed in his field. Though smaller than all other seeds, yet when it grows it is greater than herbs and becomes a tree, so that the birds come and lodge in its branches.

2. Its transforming effect (Luke 13²⁰, ²¹) Another parable he spoke to them, The kingdom of Heaven is like leaven, which a woman took and hid in three measures of meal, until the whole was leavened.

3. Its progressive development (Mark 4²⁶⁻²⁹) And he said, So is the kingdom of God, as though a man should cast seed upon the earth and sleep and rise by night and by day, while the seed sprouts and springs up—he knows not how. The earth bears crops of itself, first the blade, then the ear, then the full grain in the ear. But when the crop is ripe, he has the sickle put in at once because the harvest is come.

4. The good and evil that flourish side by side (Matt. 13²⁴⁻³⁰) Another parable he set before them, saying, The kingdom of Heaven is compared to a man who sowed good seed in his field, but while men were asleep, his enemy came and sowed tares also among the wheat and went away. Now when the blade sprouted and brought forth fruit, the tares appeared also, and the servant of the master of the house came and said to him, 'Sir, didst thou not sow good seed in thy field? How then does it contain tares?' And he said to them, 'An enemy has done this.' The servants say to him, 'Wilt thou have us go then and gather them?' But he said, 'No, lest while you are gathering the tares, you might root up the wheat with them. Let both of them grow together until the harvest; then at the harvest time I will say to the reapers, "Gather the tares first, and bind them in bundles for burning; but gather the wheat into my barn." '

5. Their separation to come at the end of the age (⁴⁷⁻⁵⁰) Again the kingdom of Heaven is like a net that was cast into the sea, and gathered fish of every kind; when it was filled, they drew it up on the beach, and sat down and gathered what was good into vessels; but the bad they cast away. So it shall be at the end of the age. The angels shall come forth and separate the wicked from among the

156

righteous and shall cast them into a furnace of fire. **There** shall be weeping and gnashing of teeth.

Now on being questioned by the Pharisees when the kingdom of God was to come, he answered them and said, The kingdom of God comes not with observation, nor shall men say, 'Behold here it is,' or, 'There!' For behold, the kingdom of God is within you. 6. The kingdom unseen and spiritual (Luke 17²⁰, ²¹)

And it came to pass that Jesus went into the house of one of the rulers of the Pharisees to eat and one of the guests said to him, Happy is the man who eats bread in the kingdom of God. But he said to him, A certain man was giving a great supper, and had invited many people. And he sent forth his servants at supper time to say to those who had been invited, 'Come; for things are now ready.' Then they all alike began to make excuses. The first said to him, 'I have bought a field, and must go and see it. I pray thee, excuse me.' And another said, 'I have bought five pair of oxen and I am on my way to try them. I pray thee, excuse me.' And another said, 'I have married a wife and therefore I cannot come.' So the servant came and told these things to his master. Then the master of the house in anger said to his servant, 'Go out quickly into the streets and lanes of the city, and bring in here the poor and the crippled, the blind and the lame.' And the servant said, 'Sir, what thou hast commanded has been done; yet there is still room.' And the master said to the servant, 'Go out into the roads and the hedges and compel the people to come in, that my house may be filled. For I tell you, not one of those men who were invited shall taste of my supper.' 7. Its privileges open to all, but only those who appreciate them will enjoy them (Luke 14¹ᵃ, ¹⁵⁻²⁴)

And they were bringing little children to Jesus, that he might touch them; but the disciples rebuked them. But when Jesus saw it, he was indignant, and said to them, Let the little children come to me, and forbid them not; for of such is the kingdom of God. I tell you truly, Whoever shall not receive the kingdom of God as a little child, shall by no means enter it. Then he put his arms around them and blessed them, as he laid his hands on them. 8. The condition of participation (Mark 10¹³⁻¹⁶, cf. Matt. 19¹³⁻¹⁵ Luke 18¹⁵⁻¹⁷)

And as he came out upon the road, a man ran to him, knelt before him, and asked him, Good Teacher, what shall I do to inherit eternal life? Jesus said to him, Why call me 9. Riches a barrier (Mark 10¹⁷⁻²⁷, cf. Matt. 19¹⁶⁻²⁶ Luke 18¹⁸⁻²⁷)

good? No one is good except God alone. Thou knowest the commandments: Do not murder; Do not commit adultery; Do not steal; Do not bear false witness; Do not defraud; Honor thy father and mother. He said to him, Teacher, all these things have I observed from my youth. And as Jesus looked upon him he loved him, and said to him, One thing thou lackest; go, sell whatever thou hast, and give to the poor; so shalt thou have treasure in heaven. Then come, follow me. But his countenance fell at the saying, and he went away sorrowful, for he was one who had great possessions. Then Jesus looked around and said to his disciples, How difficult it is for the wealthy to enter the kingdom of God! And the disciples were amazed at what he said. But Jesus addressed them again, saying, Children, how difficult it is to enter the kingdom of God. It is easier for a camel to pass through a needle's eye than for a rich man to enter the kingdom of God! And they were exceedingly astonished, and said to themselves, Then who can be saved? Jesus looked at them and said, With man it is impossible, but with God all things are possible.

10. Inestimable value of the kingdom (Matt. 13⁴⁴⁻⁴⁶) The kingdom of Heaven is like treasure hidden in a field, which a man found and hid. Then in his joy over it, he goes, and sells all that he has and buys that field. Again, the kingdom of Heaven is like a merchant, who was seeking fine pearls. On finding a pearl of great price, he went off and sold all that he had, and bought it.

11. All personal considerations to be sacrificed for it Mark 9⁴³⁻⁴⁷, cf. Matt. 5²⁹, ³⁰)
Should thy hand cause thee to stumble, cut it off;
It is better for thee to enter life maimed,
Than with thy two hands to depart into Gehenna, into the
    unquenchable fire.
And should thy foot cause thee to stumble, cut it off;
It is better for thee to enter life lame,
Than with thy two feet to be thrown into Gehenna.
And should thine eye cause thee to stumble, cast it out;
It is better for thee to enter the kingdom of God with one eye,
Than with two eyes to be thrown into Gehenna.

I. The Different Conceptions of the Kingdom of God in the Old Testament. The kingdom of God occupies so prominent a place in the teachings of Jesus that it is essential to trace its earlier meaning and usage. In the primitive Hebrew code of Exodus 23 every Israelite is commanded to appear three times each year before Jehovah with gifts in his hand. These offerings corresponded to the tribute which the Hebrews brought to their tribal chieftains and, after the establishment of the monarchy, to their king. This ancient law indicates that Jehovah was early regarded as Israel's divine King; but the oldest definitely dated passage in which he is so described is found in Isaiah's initial vision (6⁵), where the prophet exclaims:

> I am dwelling among a people with unclean lips,
> Yet mine eyes have seen the King, Jehovah of hosts.

The same conception underlies the protests against the appointment of Saul as king, which were probably placed on the lips of Samuel by a later disciple of Hosea: "You said to me, 'Nay, but a king shall reign over us,' when Jehovah your God is your king" (I Sam. 12¹²). To a majority of the Hebrews, however, the belief that Jehovah was their divine King did not prevent them from paying homage to their earthly king. They also cherished the hope that a human Messiah would come to establish a world-wide kingdom. His chief task was to be to extend Jehovah's authority and glory throughout the whole earth. This expectation, as held by the common people in the days of Jesus, and especially by those who sympathized with the Zealots, is expressed most clearly in the Psalter of Solomon 17²³: "Behold, O Lord, and raise up to them their king, the son of David, in the time which thou, O God, knowest, that he may reign over Israel thy servant. . . . He shall destroy the ungodly nations with the word of his mouth. . . . And he shall gather together a holy people. . . . He shall judge the nations and the peoples with the wisdom of his righteousness. And he shall possess the nations of the heathen to serve him beneath his yoke. And he shall glorify the Lord in a place to be seen by the whole earth; and he shall purge Jerusalem and make it holy even as it was in the days of old."

Among the Pharisees and educated leaders of Judaism, who were fully aware of the impossibility of throwing off the yoke of Rome, the belief prevailed that the kingdom of God would be miraculously established. This expectation is voiced in Daniel 2⁴⁴: "In the days of these kings shall the God of heaven set up a kingdom which shall never be destroyed, nor shall the sovereignty be left to another people; but it shall break in pieces and destroy all these kingdoms and it shall stand forever." The same hope is found in the Sibylline Oracles (III, 7[67]): "Then a kingdom over all mankind for all time shall God raise up. . . . And out of every land they shall bring frankincense and gifts to the house of God. . . . And all pathways of the plain and rough hills and high mountains and wild ways of the deep shall be easy in those days for crossing and sailing; for perfect peace for the good shall come on earth."

In Psalms 24, 29, 47, and 95 to 100 a third conception of the reign of God is presented. The human king and Messiah completely disappear. Jehovah alone reigns over all nations and races. His rule is to be just, merciful, and unending. This lofty ideal of the kingdom or reign of God is the outgrowth of the teachings of the pre-exilic prophets, of the II Isaiah, and of the larger political vision which opened before the Jews in the post-exilic period. It is by far the broadest and noblest conception of the kingdom of God to be found in the Old Testament.

II. Jesus' Description of the Characteristics of the Kingdom of God. Which of these current conceptions of the kingdom of God did Jesus accept? Or did he reject them all and proclaim a new interpretation of the ancient hope? On this point New Testament scholars to-day differ widely. Some hold that Jesus was in every sense a son of his age and race and looked forward, like the majority of his people, to the ultimate establishment of a temporal kingdom with himself enthroned at its head. A greater number of modern scholars maintain that Jesus shared the current apocalyptic hopes and that he expected and taught his speedy second coming and the miraculous establishment of a supernatural kingdom. Others are convinced that he expected and labored for the establishment of a world-wide spiritual kingdom in which God alone should rule. While our faith in Jesus does not depend upon the answer to this question, the conclusions adopted will inevitably affect our conception of his character and work. It is a question which can be answered only in the light of a most careful analysis of the historical sources and a scientific weighing of the evidence, for the gospels contain many passages to support each of these views. Due allowance must certainly be made for the different beliefs current in Christian as well as Jewish circles in the days when the gospel narratives were taking form. Among these, the more widespread and powerful was the expectation of the speedy supernatural appearance of the Messiah and the miraculous establishment of his rule. The best basis for answering these difficult questions is furnished by the large body of Jesus' ethical teachings, de-rived from the earliest collections of his sayings (Q) and from the original narrative of Mark.

Jesus illustrated the characteristics of the kingdom of God by a wealth of figures and parables. To no subject did he devote greater attention. He evidently recognized the necessity of a clear and mi-nute description, for it was a subject regarding which there was much confusion and misunderstanding. In several instances he adopted the question method, endeavoring thereby to formulate the problem definitely in the minds of his disciples. The parables of the mustard seed, the leaven, and the seed that silently germinates, each illustrated certain characteristics of the kingdom. By these figures he taught that the growth of God's kingdom was natural, slow, and silent, yet pervasive and transforming; that it was due not merely to the work of man in planting the seed, but to God, who constantly nurtured and fostered it. The parable of the wheat and the tares deals with the problem of evil which so deeply stirred the soul of the author of Job. Possibly it reflects an earlier struggle in the thinking of Jesus; but the words indicate that he had reached the calm of a higher vantage-point. He fully appreciated the fact that the good could thrive side by side with the evil, and that to attempt to root out the evil by force was to injure even the good. Thereby he inculcated that broad toler-ance which characterizes all his teachings. The explanation in Mat-thew 13[36-43] reflects the later Jewish-Christian eschatological point of view that frequently appears in the quotations which that gospel takes from its independent sources. It also lacks Jesus' positive note. From verse [43], as well as from the parallel in Luke, it is clear that in the original not the Son of man but God himself was declared to be the one who would ultimately separate the tares from the good seed. This conclusion is confirmed by the corresponding figure of the net (in [47-50]) which contains no suggestion of the presence of the Son of man.

The parable of the tares stands in the same relative position in Mat-thew as that of the man "who sowed seed on the ground, and then slept and rose day and night until it sprang up and grew, he knew not how," in Mark 4[26-29]. The many points of similarity between the two parables suggest that they go back to a common original. The sim-pler form is found in Mark. It describes the gradual growth of the kingdom in the present. Mark's version is also closely parallel to the parables of the mustard seed and of the loaves, which are found in Luke. The Gospel of Matthew, however, in 13[36-43], interprets the parable of the good grain and of the tares as a prediction of the future appearance of the Son of man at the final judgment. It is significant that this interpretation does not follow immediately after the parable, but is found in the midst of a section that is apparently from the editor. This passage is of value because it illustrates the tendency to interpret Jesus' original teaching in the light of the problems that later came to the Christian community and to read into them the popular hope of his second coming with his angels to judge the world. It is, therefore, one of the many signs which indicate that sometimes we must go back of the synoptic gospels in our quest for the real Jesus and his original teachings. The parable of the net filled with fishes is a variant of that of the tares. The one was adapted to an audience consisting of farmers, the other to the fishermen's point of view.

The crowning feature in Jesus' description of the characteristics of the kingdom of God is found in Luke 17[20, 21]. The words were evidently taken from an earlier source—possibly the Greek version of Matthew's sayings of Jesus. They were introduced by the ever-recurring question of the Pharisees as to when the kingdom of God would come. It reflected their belief that it was to be something sudden, catastrophic, and revolutionary, instituted by God without man's co-operation. With this popular expectation Jesus took direct issue. He declared that the kingdom of God does not come in a form to be seen with the human eye. When it comes, no one can say, "See, here it is," or, "There it is." In giving his reason for this conclusion, Jesus made the most illuminating statement found in all the gospels regarding his conception of the kingdom. Unfortunately, the Greek idiom admits of two possible interpretations. The one interpretation, "For the kingdom of God is in your midst," is supported by the common meaning of the phrase in classical Greek. If this be the correct translation, it means that the kingdom of God is not to be looked for merely in the future but is already in the process of being established. In the light of Jesus' teaching and ministry it can refer to nothing else than the evidence furnished by Jesus' work, for God's spirit was not only transforming and controlling the minds and bodies of certain men, but they were also willingly and joyfully acknowledging his rule as supreme in their lives. If this translation be adopted, the passage emphasizes the moral and spiritual character of the kingdom of God rather than the external and material elements which were prominent in the popular hope.

The meaning of the phrase, however, in the Greek translation of the Old Testament, in such passages as Psalms 39³ 103¹ 109²² Isaiah 16¹¹ and Daniel 10¹⁶, supports the current rendering, "Behold the kingdom of God is within you." This testimony is exceedingly strong, for the gospel writers were more powerfully influenced by the Greek version of the Old Testament, which they constantly quoted, than by the classical Greek usage. If, as seems reasonably certain, this translation represents the thought in the mind of Jesus, it indicates that he definitely rejected the popular nationalistic conception of the kingdom of God, and taught that it was individual and spiritual, something within the heart of man. This interpretation is also in accord with his teachings regarding God and man and the strong emphasis which he always placed upon that which was personal, inner, and spiritual, rather than upon that which was national, external, and material.

It is not impossible that Jesus shared to a certain extent the belief that God would ultimately interpose in a supernatural way to establish his universal rule on earth. Jesus' chief concern, however, was with the present. "Of the future no man knows" expressed his attitude toward the vague hopes that stirred so many of his countrymen. Not until he faced the practical certainty that the period of his activity on earth was nearly ended did he apparently begin to meditate on what the distant future held in store. Then his calm faith in the justice and goodness of the Father, the God of the ever-living, failed him not. He declared in words, perhaps suggested by the current apocalyptic hopes, his absolute conviction that he would speedily be vindicated, that the rule of God would surely be established, and that he, as well as his disciples, would have a prominent place in it.

III. **Conditions of Entrance into the Kingdom.** Jesus' teachings are equally explicit regarding entrance into the kingdom. While at the beginning of his ministry he echoed the words of John the Baptist, "Repent, for the kingdom of Heaven is at hand," and he never ceased to recognize the fundamental importance of repentance, in his later teaching he added the positive note, "Believe." Thus, in Matthew 18³, he declared: "Except you turn and become as little children, it is impossible for you to enter the kingdom of Heaven." He taught that what was required for entrance into the kingdom was not merely a renunciation of a man's past life, ideals, and acts, but that childlike attitude of receptivity which was absolutely essential if God's divine rule was to be established in the mind and life of man. All personal barriers, therefore, that kept men from placing their will completely under the control of the divine will must be torn down. This teaching

Jesus put in his usual concrete, dramatic form. If a man's hand or foot or eye, his most treasured and necessary possessions, constituted such a barrier, he must cut them out and cast them away, for they are of insignificant value compared with membership in God's kingdom. In the parables of the treasure hidden in the field and of the pearl of great price he emphasizes the necessity of giving up, if need be, every material possession in order to attain the larger good. In the same connection he pointed out that the entrance into the kingdom of God depended upon the voluntary and decisive action of each individual. Like all the great issues of life, it is a choice between the greater and lesser good.

IV. **Riches a Barrier to Entrance into the Kingdom of God.** Jesus' teaching regarding riches is vividly illustrated by the story of the man who came to him with the question as to what he should do in order to attain that larger and unending life which the great Teacher proclaimed was alone possible to those who were members of the kingdom. The narrative is taken from Mark and is modified slightly by Luke and Matthew. Matthew, for example, changes Jesus' original words (preserved both in Mark and Luke), "Why callest thou me good; none is good except one, even God," into the statement: "Why askest thou me concerning what is good. One there is who is good." The real question, however, is, What is the import of Jesus' original words? The first and most natural inference is that he did not claim for himself absolute perfection any more than he did for the man who stood before him; but his words are by no means a confession of sin. They simply indicate that God himself represented the absolute ideal of perfection which Jesus, as well as his disciples, was striving to attain. They were evidently intended to encourage the man who knelt before him in the attitude of an earnest seeker for truth. They also aimed to prepare the man's mind for the great sacrifice that he was asked to make that he, as a true disciple of Jesus, might be perfect, even as his heavenly Father was perfect.

The story also illustrates the way in which Jesus built on the older law and teachings of his race. He passed over the commands regarding external worship to which the man, as a disciple of Judaism, had hitherto given the first place. Instead, he emphasized simply those commands which inculcate positive moral and social virtues and define man's duty to his fellow-men. When the man replied that he had kept these from his youth, Jesus was profoundly impressed by his spirit and character. Not in rebuke, but with growing enthusiasm at having found one whom he might at once admit into the ranks of his immediate followers, Jesus answered his question in the sense in which he had asked it. He proposed a definite act which would at once commit the man to the exalted ideals which Jesus proclaimed: "Go and transform your wealth into treasure current for all time, and follow me, poor and homeless, yet the happiest of men." But the pride of possession and the habits of a lifetime held the man back from entering the great door of opportunity that was thus flung open to him.

Only rarely in the ancient East were great riches justly amassed. The taint of money was far more universal than to-day; yet the psychological principles illustrated by the incident are equally true at all times. Recognizing these, Jesus turned to his disciples and uttered one of those broad generalizations which voice universal human experience: "How difficult it is for those who possess riches to enter the kingdom of God." Noting the amazement of the disciples on hearing this statement, so diametrically opposed to the popular estimate of riches, Jesus analyzed the problem still more deeply: "The reason is because, like this rich man, they trust to their riches and therefore do not feel that hunger and thirst which participation in the kingdom of God alone will satisfy." In his graphic, concrete, hyperbolic way, Jesus declared that it was almost impossible for a rich man to attain this higher good. Yet he added, in response to the astonished questions of his disciples, that which, from the point of view of psychology and experience, seems impossible to man is nevertheless possible to God, for he is working to save the rich as well as the poor.

The incident, among other things, reveals Jesus' superlative breadth and sanity. It also corrects the impression, made by certain passages in Luke, that he was alone interested in the poor and the outcast. It does, however, emphasize the fact that he who, by inheritance or by virtue of his own achievement, possesses more than ordinary wealth is thereby often handicapped in his quest for the highest things which life can offer. He is limited, not because God is unwilling to give them, but because he himself lacks the motive and the passionate, single-minded desire to acquire them. In his teachings regarding wealth Jesus did not declare that its possession was a crime. He only sought to set forth plainly its effect upon the motives and ideals of its possessors. His conviction regarding material possessions, implied in the familiar prayer, "Give us each day our bread for the coming day," was probably expressed in the petition of the ancient sage (Prov. 30$^{7-9}$):

Two things I ask of thee;
Deny them me not before I die:
Deceit and lying put far from me,
Poverty and riches give me not;
Provide me with the food I need,
Lest I be full and deny thee,
And say, "Who is Jehovah?"
Or be needy and steal,
And profane the name of my God.

V. The Place and Meaning of the Kingdom in Jesus' Teach= ings. The term, kingdom of God, or its equivalent, kingdom of Heaven, occurs over eighty times in the gospels. The author of the First Gospel prefers the form, kingdom of Heaven. In later Jewish writings, as, for example, I Maccabees, Heaven was constantly employed as a synonym for God. Both forms of the term appear to have been used in the early teaching source (Q). Why does Jesus give so great prominence to the kingdom of God in his teachings? One, and possibly the chief reason is because it was uppermost in the minds of all the different classes with which he came into contact. It was undoubtedly prominent in the atmosphere in which he was reared. It was a watchword in the preaching of the courageous John the Baptist. The term was constantly on the lips of the scribes. His followers frequently raised questions regarding it. It furnished, therefore, to a wise teacher like Jesus, the most natural and effective point of contact with his hearers. Its nationalistic interpretation was the will-o'-the-wisp luring the Jewish nation into disastrous rebellion against Rome. Its apocalyptic interpretation dulled the sense of personal and moral responsibility; but the use of the term in the Psalms had prepared the minds of the more thoughtful students of the older scriptures for that individual, ethical, and at the same time universal interpretation that Jesus gave to it.

It is significant that Jesus never attempted to define the term, kingdom of God. The vast number of cumbersome definitions with which scholars have attempted to describe it confirm his wisdom. In its real meaning—the dominion or rule of God—is found the simplest and best definition. It is God's rule not only in nature and in human history, but, above all, in the minds and hearts and wills of men. It is man's acknowledgment of God's sovereignty in every thought and act. It is not the arbitrary rule of a despotic Deity, but is based upon man's voluntary submission of his will to that of God. It is a divine gift, and yet is something to be achieved through human volition and effort. In its origin it is individual and spiritual, within, not without, the mind of man. But in its ultimate development God's kingdom or rule is destined to transform society, for devotion and loyalty to the divine King, the common Father of all mankind, is the strongest and only universal bond that can bind all men together. Hence, in their final realization, Jesus' teachings regarding the kingdom of God have a large social as well as individual significance, for they contemplate a universal brotherhood or democracy in which all men are united in the common desire to do the will of God.

§ CXXXIII. THE OBLIGATIONS OF CITIZENSHIP IN THE KINGDOM OF GOD

Store up no treasures for yourself on earth,
Where moth and rust consume,
And where thieves break through and steal;
But store up for yourselves treasures in heaven,
Where neither moth nor rust consume,
And where thieves do not break through or steal.
For where thy treasure is,
There shall thine heart be also.

1. The necessity of a right motive in all human effort (Matt. 6[19-21], cf. Luke 12[33, 34])

The lamp of the body is the eye;
If thine eye then be perfect,
Thy whole body shall be lighted up.
But if thine eye be useless,
Thy whole body shall be darkened.
If the light in thee is darkness,
How great is that darkness!

2. Of the generous spirit and the open mind (Matt. 6[22, 23], cf. Luke 11[34-36])

No man can serve two masters;
For either he will hate the one and love the other,
Or else he will hold to one and despise the other.
You cannot serve God and mammon.

3. Of single-minded loyalty to God (Matt. 6[24], cf. Luke 16[13])

And a man out of the crowd said to him, Teacher, tell my brother to share the inheritance with me. But he said to

4. The folly and danger of greed (Luke 12¹³⁻¹⁵) him, Man, who made me a judge or an arbiter over you? And he said to them, Take heed and keep yourselves from every kind of covetousness, for a man's life consists not in having more possessions than he needs.

5. The attitude of selfish materialism (16-19) And he spoke a parable to them, saying, The ground of a certain rich man bore large crops. And he argued with himself, saying, 'What shall I do, for I have no room to store my crops?' And he said, 'This will I do: I will pull down my barns and build larger ones; and there I will store all my grain and my goods. And I will say to myself, "Now you have many goods laid up for many years; take your ease, eat, drink, and be merry."'

6. Its tragic consequences (²⁰, ²¹) But God said to him, 'Foolish man! this very night thy life is demanded of thee. And the things which thou hast prepared—whose shall they be?' So is the man who stores up treasure for himself instead of being rich toward God.

7. An illustration of the use of wealth to obtain the approval of God and men (Luke 16¹⁻⁹) And he also said to his disciples, There was a certain rich man, who had a steward, and this steward was accused to him of squandering his goods. So he called to him and said to him, What is this I hear about thee? Render the account of thy stewardship, for thou canst be steward no longer. Now the steward said to himself, 'What am I to do, seeing that my master is taking the stewardship from me. I have no strength; to beg I am ashamed. I know what I will do, so that when I am put out of the stewardship, people may receive me into their houses.' Then calling to him every one of his master's debtors, he proceeded to say to the first, 'How much dost thou owe my master?' And the man said, 'A hundred barrels of oil.' And the steward said to him, 'Take thy bond; sit down at once and write fifty.' Then he said to another, 'And how much dost thou owe?' And the man said, 'A hundred measures of wheat.' The steward said to him, 'Take thy bond and write eighty.' And his master commended the dishonest steward, because he had acted shrewdly; for the sons of this world are more shrewd in dealing with their own generation than are the sons of the light. And I tell you:

Make friends for yourself with the mammon of dishonesty;
So that when it fails, they may admit you to the eternal tents.

He who is faithful in what is least is faithful also in much;
And he who is dishonest in what is least is dishonest also in
much.
If then, you have not proved faithful in the dishonest mammon,
Who will trust you with the true?
And if you have not proved faithful in what is another's,
Who will give you what is your own?

8. Fidelity in the use of wealth an evidence of character (10-12)

Now the Pharisees, who were lovers of money, were listening to all this and sneering at Jesus. So he said to them, You are they who justify themselves in the sight of men, but God knoweth your hearts; for what is exalted among men is an abomination in the sight of God.

9. Rebuke of the greedy Pharisees (14, 15)

Now there was a certain rich man, and he was clothed in purple and fine linen and living sumptuously from day to day. And a poor man named Lazarus lay at his gateway, covered with sores, and desired to fill himself with what fell from the rich man's table; yes, even the dogs used to come and lick his sores. Now it came to pass that the poor man died and was carried away by the angels into Abraham's bosom. The rich man also died and was buried. In Hades, he lifted up his eyes, tormented as he was, and saw Abraham afar off and Lazarus in his bosom. And he cried aloud and said, 'Father Abraham, have mercy on me, and send Lazarus to dip the tip of his finger in water and cool my tongue; for I am in anguish in this flame.' But Abraham said, 'My son, remember that thou didst get thy good things in thy lifetime and Lazarus likewise his evil things. Now here he is comforted, but thou art in anguish. And besides all this, between us and you a great gulf is fixed, that those who would pass from here to you may not be able, nor may any cross from there to us.' And the rich man said, 'Then I pray thee, father, send him to my father's house—for I have five brothers—that he may bear testimony to them, so that they may not also come to this place of torment.' But Abraham said, 'They have Moses and the prophets; let them listen to them.' But he said, 'Nay, Father Abraham, but if some one were to go to them from the dead they would repent.' But Abraham said to him, 'If they do not listen to Moses and the prophets, they

10. An illustration of the fatal folly of ignoring the responsibilities of wealth (19-31)

will not be persuaded, not even if one were to rise from the dead.'

11. The faithful use of individual talents (Matt. 25¹⁴⁻²⁸, cf. Luke 19¹¹⁻²⁶)

The kingdom of Heaven is like a man going abroad; so he called his servants and put his possessions into their charge. And he gave to one five talents, to another two, to another one; to each according to his individual ability. Then he went on his journey. Immediately the servant who had received the five talents went and traded with them and gained five other talents. In the same way he who had received the two, gained two more. But he who had received the one went away and dug a hole in the ground, and hid his master's money. Now after a long time the master of those servants comes and settles his account with them. And he who had received the five talents came forward and brought five more talents, saying, 'Master, you delivered to me five talents. Look, I have gained five more talents.' His master said to him, 'Well done, good and faithful servant! You have been faithful over a few things, I will set you over many things. Enter into the joy of thy lord.' And he who had received the two talents also came forward and said, 'Master, you delivered to me two talents. Look, I have gained two talents more.' His master said to him, 'Well done, good and faithful servant! You have been faithful over a few things, I will set you over many things. Enter into the joy of thy lord.' And he who had received the one talent also came forward, and said, 'Master, I knew that you were a hard man, reaping where you did not sow, and gathering where you did not winnow. So I was afraid and went and hid your talent in the ground. Look, you have what is yours.' But the master answered and said to him, 'You wicked and slothful servant! You know that I reap where I have not sown, and gather where I have not winnowed. You ought, therefore, to have placed my money with the bankers, and at my coming I should have received my own with interest. Take away the talent from him, therefore, and give it to him who has the ten talents.'

12. The best gifts only for the worthy (Matt. 25²⁹, cf. Mark 4²⁵, Luke 19²⁶)

For to every one who has shall be given, and he shall have abundance;

But from him who has not shall be taken even that which he has.

SINGLE–MINDED LOYALTY TO GOD

I. Single-Minded Loyalty to God. Jesus did not promulgate a system of morals or philosophy; but there is perfect consistency in the principles that underlie his teachings. It is also important to note that these principles are in full accord with the established conclusions of modern science, for both rest on the same ultimate basis of fact and experience. Jesus taught that the motive dominant in the mind of the individual determined his character as well as his acts. He had no fear that the individual acts would be wrong if the motive that prompted them was right. It was for this practical reason that he placed the strongest possible emphasis on the absolute necessity of single-minded loyalty to God. Human effort he thoroughly approved. He himself was a tireless worker; but he laid down as a first condition for membership in God's kingdom the axiomatic truth that "no man can serve two masters." He admitted no neutral ground. The strong, hyperbolic terms that he employed—"love and hate"—indicate how intense was his conviction. The old heathen gods had long ceased to have any attraction for the men of his race. More subtle temptations assailed them. Already the Jew was an important factor in the commercial life of the Roman world. Galilee itself was the home of an active, prosperous people. In the simple life of Capernaum, Zebedee and his sons were probably regarded as wealthy. Not to the rabble of the streets, but to the men of ability, from whose ranks Jesus drew his disciples, came the promptings of innate greed. This was the god whom Jesus described by the Aramaic word, *mammon*. The term means riches and material possessions of every kind.

In the story of the man who pulled down his barns to build larger, Jesus analyzed, with absolute fidelity to human experience, the insidious character of that innate selfishness which debars men from true fellowship with God and man. The desire for the material possessions, which represent ease and luxury and a certain type of pleasure, is what keeps men from their highest good. It is a result of the natural impulse which man shares with the beast and inherits from his childhood. To be rich and to have what wealth can buy was the ambition of at least three out of every four of the men and women whom Jesus met in Capernaum. It is still the chief motive with the majority of the human race. This was the master whom Jesus taught his disciples to hate and despise.

Jesus urged four reasons for the acceptance of his revolutionary principle. Two were calculated to appeal to the intelligence of the most superficial: (1) No man can be assured that his life will be pro-

171

longed even for an hour to enjoy material possessions. God alone has man's life in his keeping and may take it at any moment. Hence he is the only master whom a man's self-interest, if nothing more, should prompt him to serve. (2) Material possessions are but perishable and, therefore, do not reward the effort and sacrifice. The same teaching is expressed in the Testament of Levi (13⁵): "Do righteousness, my sons, on earth that you may have treasure in heaven."

The other two reasons are psychological and more fundamental. Man cannot have two chief centres of interest. In Jewish thought, the heart was the seat of thought and intelligence. If a man's mind is intent on storing up treasures on earth, he can have no other higher centre of interest. It is, therefore, impossible for him to focus his attention on the establishment of God's rule within himself or in others. Finally, if a man's motives are selfish and niggardly, he thereby blinds his eyes to all visions of truth and gropes in darkness. Jesus' use of the metaphor of the eye was familiar to his Jewish readers. In the Old Testament an evil eye represented avarice and greed, and a good eye, generosity (Deut. 15⁹ Prov. 23⁶ 28²²). Ben Sira is very explicit: "An evil eye is grudging of bread" (14¹⁰). In these teachings Jesus went to the heart of the human problem and suggested its only solution. His message to men striving and toiling for those things which only brought passing pleasure, if won, and discontent, if lost, was: "Look up. Set a goal before you that is worth while. Let the one passion of your life be loyalty to God. Then your joys will be wholesome and permanent, and you shall walk in the light, not in darkness."

II. The Right Use of Wealth. Certain teachings of Jesus interpreted by themselves convey the impression that he regarded riches as altogether evil. He told the rich young ruler to sell all his possession and give to the poor; he commanded his disciples to take no money with them on their journeys; he himself possessed neither home nor wealth; he taught his followers to hate mammon; and yet these represent but one side of his teachings. His words regarding his own poverty are not the utterance of an ascetic, but reveal, instead, the sacrifice which he was making for the larger life of service upon which he had entered. His commands to the rich ruler and to his disciples were given to exceptional men called to a unique task. In his daily work Jesus constantly associated with the rich and shared their hospitality without protest. By his harsh critics he was called "a glutton and a wine-drinker." The fact that the tax-collector Zaccheus retained half of his possessions did not weaken Jesus' approval of his action. It was not wealth in itself, but the slavish pursuit and the wrong use of it that Jesus sternly condemned, and he did so simply because of the baneful effect upon the individual. This aspect of the problem of wealth was ordinarily overlooked and hence was most strongly emphasized by him.

Luke, who was inclined to regard all wealth as evil, has preserved a unique, although easily misunderstood parable which clearly illustrates Jesus' teachings regarding the use of wealth. The story of the unjust steward was evidently told, not to the crowd, but to Jesus' disciples, and was intended to illustrate simply one main point. It is a discussion, not of personal honesty, but of the way in which riches may be rightly and effectively used. Jesus commends, not the methods, but the practical wisdom and foresight of the steward, who he plainly states is dishonest. There is a gentle irony in his comparison between the readiness of unprincipled " sons of the world " and the failure of " the sons of the light" to work for their best interests; but this contrast brings out the teaching of the parable. The phrase "mammon of dishonesty" is probably due to Luke's extreme attitude toward wealth. The logic of the context strongly suggests that Jesus simply said, "Make friends by means of mammon" (wealth); that is, make it your slave rather than your master. This conclusion is supported by the broad statement that follows:

He who is faithful in what is least is faithful also in much;
And he who is dishonest in what is least is dishonest also in much.

Either this verse does not belong here or else the dishonesty that is condemned is the failure to put the intrusted wealth to a wise use. In either case the teaching is the same: wealth is a sacred trust; when acquired and used with a single-minded loyalty to the divine King, it can be made not a curse but a blessing to its possessor. Jesus' teachings, therefore, are very clear: the acquisition and possession of wealth as an end in itself means slavery and moral blindness for the individual, injustice to society, and disloyalty to God. Regarded as a trust and used faithfully for the service of God and man, riches have their important place in the kingdom of God.

III. **The Improving of Present Opportunities.** The parable of the rich man and Lazarus raises many questions. In its present form the only sin of the rich man is his riches; the only virtue of Lazarus is his poverty and suffering, which are so extreme that the unclean, oriental dogs lick his sores, like vultures anticipating the feast that awaits them. It is a dramatic illustration of Luke's version of the beatitudes: "Happy are you poor, for yours is the kingdom of God," and "Happy are you who hunger now, for you shall be filled." The popular Jewish conception of life after death is the background of the story. As in Enoch 61^{12} and 70^3, the righteous go immediately to Paradise. There is no suggestion here of a temporary place of abode or of a future judgment or resurrection.

In the latter part of the parable the later apostolic point of view is assumed. The words of Abraham are a condemnation of the Jews who refused to accept the testimony either of Moses and the prophets regarding the Messiah or the evidence furnished by Jesus' resurrection. It is also the only parable in which the name of one of the characters is given. Lazarus is the Latinized form of the Hebrew name Eleazer. In the Fourth Gospel it is the name of the man whom Jesus raised from the dead (11^1-12^{11}). It is possible that there is a connection between the two stories. Certain scholars have even urged that the closing line of the parable, "If one rise from the dead," suggested the miraculous story found in the Fourth Gospel.

We have every reason to believe that back of the narrative in Luke lies an original parable of Jesus. The intuitions of the Christian church have also found in it the broad principle which he wished to teach, even though Luke, because of his extreme interest in the poor and oppressed, has obscured it. It teaches that wealth and position are unimportant in themselves. The one essential is whether or not each man improves his present opportunities and fully meets the responsibilities entailed by his position in life. The implication is that the rich man's guilt was due to no definite crime except his failure to recognize his stewardship and help the man who lay at his door. If he had been awake to his responsibility, the scene portrayed in the beginning of the parable would have been impossible. The presence of the needy beggar was an opportunity and a challenge. The rich man, intent on his own selfish interests, lost his great opportunity. The application of the principle is universal. As long as want and suffering exist, the citizens of the kingdom of God are under obligation to do all in their power to relieve them. The greater their resources and influence the greater is their responsibility.

IV. **The Use of Natural Gifts.** The familiar parable of the talents comes from the older teaching source (Q). The oldest version is apparently found in Matthew. It is introduced by the words: "For like a man going abroad." Evidently it was given to illustrate certain characteristics of the kingdom of God. Luke prefaces it with the words: "He spoke a parable because they supposed that the kingdom of God was to appear at once." Luke departs at many points from the version in Matthew. Instead of five talents to one, two to another, and one to another servant, a pound is given to each of ten servants. The master is also a nobleman journeying to a distant country to secure a kingdom. The historical example is probably Archelaus, who at the beginning of his reign went to Rome to lay before Augustus his claim to a part of the kingdom of his father Herod (Jos., *Ant.*, XVII, 112). Even though it obscures the original parable, the fact that the Jews sent an embassy to Rome to protest against the rule of Archelaus is here introduced. The reason for so doing is probably because it suggested to the later church the rejection of Jesus by the Jews. Luke has also adjusted the parable to the setting which he gives it, so that it is a prediction that at Jesus' second coming the Jews who rejected him would receive the judgment that they deserved, while his true servants would receive their due reward. The author of Matthew has also added a verse which carries in part the same implication: "Cast out the unprofitable servant into the outer darkness; there shall be weeping and gnashing of teeth." The reference is to the punishment that is to follow the final judgment. It introduces a figure foreign to the original parable, unless the phrase "joy of thy lord," in $^{21, 23}$, refers to the bliss of those who were to share in the return of the Christ.

In its original form the parable was not limited in its application, but evidently illustrated the principle that in the kingdom of God each man must have courage and faith, and that he will be rewarded according to his fidelity. A talent was equivalent to about one thousand dollars, and possessed twice the purchasing power of the same sum to-day. The rewards did not depend upon the amount earned but upon the spirit and fidelity shown. They consisted not of money, but of larger responsibility and opportunity for service. Failure to use the one talent meant that the one to whom it had been intrusted would lose the opportunity and the ability to serve. The principle is true in the natural as in the spiritual world.

As usual Jesus emphasizes not the external rewards but the effect of the attitude and the action upon each individual. Two become ever more efficient and able to undertake the larger trusts. One is paralyzed by the insidious fear of failure or mediocrity, and so not only forfeits the confidence of his master, but also loses the power to achieve. This principle is further illustrated by the command to take from the cowardly, self-conscious servant, who distrusted his own ability and the master's judgment, the one talent and to intrust it to the one who had demonstrated his fitness to administer the ten talents. In conclusion Jesus puts this teaching in the form of a paradoxical general statement. The "one who has" is he who has proved his ability to use his talents efficiently; the "one who has not" is the man who through cowardice or false pride has forfeited his opportunity and therefore failed to develop efficiency.

The obligations of citizenship in the kingdom of God, as defined by Jesus, are simple but insistent. They require that a man be ready to give all to God: possessions, talents, his complete loyalty and love. Every thought and act are to be prompted by loyalty to his sovereign King. He is God's slave, but voluntarily so; his steward, intent solely upon guarding his master's interests. His obligations do not necessarily require him to leave the world or to reject possessions or to lose one of the real joys of life. Complete acknowledgment of the rule of God in a man's economic, social, intellectual, moral, and religious life gives him a right conception of wealth and its use, a proper social consciousness, a normal relation to the universe, true ethical standards, and, above all, the knowledge that he has the approval of his divine King and Father.

§CXXXIV. MAN'S DUTIES TO HIS NEIGHBOR AND TO HIMSELF

1. The crime of cherishing anger against another (Matt. 5²¹, ²²) You have heard that it was said by the men of old, Thou shalt not kill, and whoever kills shall be liable to the local court, But I tell you,

Everyone who is angry with his brother shall be liable to the local court;
And whoever says to his brother, 'Ignoramus!' shall be liable to the Sanhedrin.
And whoever says to his brother, 'Fool!' shall be liable to the Gehenna of fire.

So if thou art offering thy gift at the altar and rememberest there that thy brother has something against thee, leave thy gift there before the altar. Go, first be reconciled to thy brother, then come and offer thy gift. Come quickly to terms with thine adversary while thou art still with him on the road; lest the adversary deliver thee up to the judge and the judge to the officer, and thou be thrown into prison. I tell you truly, Thou shalt not leave that place until thou hast paid the last penny.

2. The duty and wisdom of reconciliation (23-26)

You have heard that it was said, Thou shalt not commit adultery. But I tell you, Every man who looks at a woman for lust has committed adultery with her already in his heart.

3. The crime of impure thought (27, 28)

Now if thy brother sin,
Go show him his fault between thee and him alone;
If he listen to thee, thou hast won over thy brother.
And if he sins against thee seven times in the day,
And turns back to thee seven times, saying, 'I repent,'
Thou shalt forgive him.

4. Treatment of a wrong-doer (Matt. 18¹⁵ Luke 17⁴, cf. Luke 17³)

Then Peter came and said to him, Lord, how often is my brother to sin against me and I to forgive him, seven times? Jesus said to him, I say not to thee, Seven times, but seventy times seven.

5. Obligation to forgive indefinitely (Matt. 18²¹, ²²)

Therefore the kingdom of Heaven may be compared to a certain king, who wished to settle his accounts with his servants. And when he had begun to settle them, one was brought to him who owed him ten thousand talents (about $10,000,000), but as he was unable to pay, the master commanded him to be sold, together with his wife and children and all that he had, and payment to be made. The servant, therefore, fell on his knees and prostrated himself before him, saying, 'Master, have patience with me, and I will pay you everything.' Then the master having pity on that servant, released him and forgave him the debt. But on going out, that servant found one of his fellow servants who owed him a hundred denarii (about $20). And he laid hold on him, and took him by the throat, saying, 'Pay what thou owest.' His fellow servant then fell down and kept begging him, saying, 'Have patience with me and I will pay thee.' And he would not, but went and had him cast into prison, until he should pay what was due. So when his

6. The reason why a man should forgive his brother (23-35)

fellow servants saw what had been done, they were exceedingly sorry; they came and told their master all that had taken place. Then the master called him, and said to him, 'Thou wicked servant, I forgave thee all that debt, because thou didst beg me. Oughtest not thou also to have had mercy on thy fellow servant even as I also had mercy on thee.' And his master in anger delivered him to the tormentors, until he should pay all that was due. So also shall my heavenly Father do to you, unless each of you sincerely forgives his brother.

7. The obligation to make fair and charitable judgments (Matt. 7¹⁻⁵, cf. Luke 6³⁷⁻⁴²)

Judge not,
That you may not be judged;
For with what judgment you judge,
You shall be judged,
And with what measure you measure,
It shall be measured to you.
Why look at the splinter in thy brother's eye,
And consider not the beam in thine own eye?
Or how wilt thou say to thy brother,
Come, let me pull the splinter out of thine eye,
When behold the beam is in thine own eye?
Hypocrite! first pull the beam out of thine own eye,
Then thou shalt see clearly to pull the splinter out of thy
brother's eye.

8. The attitude of non-resistance (Matt. 5³⁸⁻⁴², cf. Luke ⁶²⁹, ³⁰)

You have heard that it was said, An eye for an eye and a tooth for a tooth. But I tell you:

Resist not the evil man;
But whoever smites thee on the right cheek,
Turn the other to him also.
If any one wishes to sue thee for the possession of thy coat,
Let him have thy cloak also.
Whoever shall force thee to go one mile,
Go two with him.

9. Love for enemies (Matt. 5⁴³⁻⁴⁷, cf. Luke 5²⁷, ³²⁻³⁵)

Give to him who asks thee,
Turn not away from him who would borrow of thee.

You have heard that it was said, Thou shalt love thy neighbor and hate thine enemy. But I tell you:

Love your enemies and pray for those who persecute you,
That you may become sons of your Father who is in heaven;
For he makes his sun rise upon evil and good,
And sends rain upon just and unjust.
For if you love those who love you, what reward have you?
Do not even the tax-collectors do the same?
And if you salute your brothers only, what are you doing
   beyond others?
Do not even the Gentiles do the same?

You are to be perfect then,
As your heavenly Father is perfect.

All things, therefore, that you would have men do to you,
So do you also to them; for this is the law and the prophets.

And there was a certain lawyer, who stood up to make
trial of Jesus, saying, Teacher, what shall I do to inherit
eternal life? He said to him, What is written in the law?
How readest thou? He replied, Thou shalt love the Lord
thy God with all thy heart, with all thy soul, with all thy
strength, and with all thy mind; also thy neighbor as thyself.
And Jesus said to him, Thou hast answered correctly; do
this and thou shalt live.

But as he wished to show that he was right, he said to
Jesus, And who is my neighbor? Jesus answered and
said, A certain man was going down from Jerusalem to
Jericho; and he fell in with robbers, who even stripped him
and after beating him, went off, leaving him half dead.
Now it happened that a certain priest was going down by
that road; but when he saw him, he went past on the opposite side. And in the same way, a Levite, when he came to
the place and saw him, went past on the opposite side.
But a certain Samaritan, travelling, came to where he was.
And on seeing him, he was filled with pity. And going to
him, he bound up his wounds, pouring on them oil and wine.
And putting him on his own beast, he brought him to an inn,
and took care of him. And on the following day, he took out
two denarii and gave them to the innkeeper, saying, Take

10. The ideal (Matt. 5⁴⁸, cf. Luke 6³⁶)
11. The golden rule (Matt. 7¹², cf. Luke 6³¹)
12. Man's first duty (Luke 10²⁵⁻²⁸, cf. Mark 12²⁸⁻³¹ Matt. 22³⁵⁻⁴⁰)
13. An example of true love to God and man (Luke 10²⁹⁻³⁷)

179

care of him and whatever more you spend, I will repay you when I return. Which of these three thinkest thou proved himself the neighbor to him who fell in with the robbers? He said, The man who dealt mercifully with him. Jesus said to him, Go thou, and do likewise.

14. The religion of the heart and life (Mark 12³²⁻³⁴) And the scribe said to him, Of a truth, Teacher, thou hast rightly said that he is one, and beside him there is no other. Also to love him with all the heart, with all the understanding, and with all the strength, and to love one's neighbor as one's self is much more than all whole burnt-offerings and sacrifices. And Jesus seeing that he answered intelligently, said to him, Thou art not far from the kingdom of God. And after that no one dared question him.

I. The Fatal Crime of Wrong Thinking. Jesus recognized that a man's duties to himself and to his fellow-men were indissolubly connected. He taught that, if a man was true to his own highest interests, he could not fail to discharge his obligations to his neighbors. Conversely he taught that, if a man was faithful to the interests of his fellow-men, he could not be faithless to his own. Hence, in dealing with the relations of a man to his fellow-men, Jesus was chiefly concerned with the thought and motive in the mind of the individual. No teacher emphasized more strongly than he the truth that "as a man thinks in his heart, so he is." With him the deadly sins were, not neglect of the ritual nor even crimes punishable by the laws of all civilized nations, but wrong ideas, motives, and feelings. Even in his teaching regarding a man's duty to his neighbor, he decried the fatal effects of hatred and jealousy in the mind of the individual more vehemently than he did the acts that hate and jealousy prompt. Modern physiology, psychology, and criminology signally confirm the practical wisdom of his teaching. These evil passions destroy a man's physical vigor and efficiency. They pervert his mental perceptions and render him incapable of resisting the temptation to commit acts of violence. They undermine his moral health. By insidious stages they transform the man who cherishes them into a criminal. On the other hand, if they are banished, and wholesome, kindly thoughts and emotions take their place, the man is incapable of crime. Right thoughts and feelings, if persistently kept in the forefront, inevitably lead to right acts. "A good tree bears good fruit, an evil tree, evil fruit," lies at the foundation of Jesus' ethical teachings. His whole effort was to make the tree good, for when that end was achieved, the good qualities of the fruit were assured.

II. **Reverence and Regard for the Person of Another.** The principle underlying Jesus' teachings regarding man's duty toward his neighbor is well illustrated by his treatment of the ancient laws concerning murder and adultery. The laws of society in the past, as to-day, punished simply the act. Jesus did not for a moment question the justice of so doing; but with that vehemence and emphasis which showed how intense was his conviction and how important he regarded the teaching, he declared that the feeling of anger or revenge, which prompted murder, were as reprehensible as the crime itself. He condemned not so much the angry word, *raca*, which means *empty* and is equivalent to our modern word, *stupid!* or *ignoramus!* as the unbrotherly spirit which it revealed and the fuel which the expression added to the flame of anger. The word translated, "fool," is stronger than ignoramus, for, as in the Psalms and Proverbs, it implies impiety, as well as lack of sense. These are the concrete terms by which Jesus portrayed uncontrolled anger. The manner in which he described the guilt of entertaining, even for a moment, anger against a fellow-man is equally concrete and dramatic. Anger unrestrained, like murder, deserves to be punished, he declared, before the local courts. Anger that leads a man even mildly to condemn his brother is a crime that might well be tried before the supreme court of the nation. Hot passion that impels a man to strike a revengeful blow at his brother's reputation is a crime that must be judged before God's judgment throne. As a matter of fact, none of the three crimes were recognized as such by Jewish law. Passion that flamed only in the heart could not be punished by the state. It was not a law but a principle that Jesus proclaimed: the supreme crime against one's self and against society is to cherish anger, even for an instant; much more to intensify it by giving the slightest expression to the feeling of hatred toward another.

Jesus' revolutionary treatment of the law regarding adultery is precisely similar. The impure thought, he declares, is the primary sin. If this is banished from the mind, it is impossible for a man to commit that heinous social crime. The great Chinese teacher, Laotsze, proclaims the same truth: "Not contemplating what kindles desire keeps the heart unconfused."

Jesus' incisive utterances also teach that deep reverence for the person of another which is one of the chief correctives of the passions that lead to murder and adultery. In his eyes, the personality of every man and woman is sacred because of its divine origin and possibilities. There is a remarkable reserve and delicacy in his treatment of the intimate relations between the sexes. No teacher ever held up a higher ideal of social purity. For him there was no double standard. The primary responsibility was thrown upon the man; but the principle was equally applicable to both sexes. Having laid down the principle, Jesus did not spend his time denouncing current immorality, as did many another earnest prophet. Rather he set about healing social sores. The penitent outcasts always found in him a friend. When the religious teachers of the day condemned and hunted them to death, he reached out to them the helping hand. But his method of dealing with the major crimes that afflicted mankind was primarily preventive and, therefore, fundamental. In the place of hatred and lust he sought to inspire in his disciples deep reverence and strong brotherly love, and thereby to save the neighbor by first saving the individual.

III. **Forgiveness.** Jesus taught that forgiveness was a duty not only to the offender but also to the one wronged. Prolonged resentment, like hot anger, is a deadly menace to a man's physical, mental, and spiritual health. It injures him who cherishes it far more than its object. Jesus placed reconciliation before the formal acts of worship. He declared that resentment or the sense of injustice done or received made true worship impossible. He also taught that the direct personal method was the only right way to express forgiveness and to effect reconciliation. "Go to thy brother," was his reiterated counsel. He recognized that resentment fed on suspicion and often grew fastest when secretly repressed.

To Jesus' brief teachings regarding forgiveness, which were quoted by both Matthew and Luke from the early teaching source (Q), the author of the First Gospel has added certain detailed regulations that were observed in the apostolic church: "If thy brother does not listen to thee, take one or two others along with thee, so that by the testimony of two or three witnesses every case may be decided. But if he will not heed them, tell the church, and if he will not heed even the church, treat him as a Gentile or a tax-collector" (18[16, 17]). The last regulation means that when all else had failed, the case was to be referred to the public courts. These wise rules doubtless governed the early Christian communities at Jerusalem and elsewhere, and represent the beginning of that huge body of ecclesiastical laws which grew up after the death of Jesus. Of the same origin and tenor is the regulation (found only in Matthew): "I tell you truly whatever you shall prohibit on earth shall be prohibited in heaven, and whatever you shall permit on earth shall be permitted in heaven" (18[18]). In Matthew 16[19] this power is given especially to Peter. Each of these passages record the tendency in the church to make its action final and to assume an authority corresponding to that claimed by the Jewish hierarchy. The extreme claims of the Holy Catholic Church represent the culmination of this tendency. In the same context in Matthew the noble thought of the Jewish proverb, "Where two sit at the same table and talk about the law, the glory of God lets itself down upon them," is expressed in its Christian form: "Where two or three are gathered together in my name there am I in the midst of them" (20).

The logical sequel of Jesus' teaching regarding forgiveness in Matthew 18[15] is found in [21-35]. In reply to Peter's question he declared that there is no limit to the number of times a man should forgive his brother. This was the implication of the complete number seven, which Jesus used in the command that Luke has quoted. That there might be no shadow of doubt regarding this important question, Jesus told one of his dramatic stories in which the numbers were purposely exaggerated. The debt of the unforgiving servant amounted to more than ten million dollars, while the debt of his fellow-servant, which he refused to overlook, was only about twenty dollars. The amazing contrast recalls Jesus' other hyperbolic figure of a beam and a splinter. By this means he drove home the truth that reconciliation and that intimate union with the heavenly Father, which is the source of all peace and strength, is impossible unless a man feels only reverence and love for his fellow-men. Forgiveness, therefore, is the essential foundation of a normal relationship with God, as well as with men.

IV. **Charitable Judgment.** The same principles are illustrated in Jesus' teachings regarding the almost universal tendency to condemn another man's character and acts. Luke has apparently expanded the saying, taken from the older teaching source (Q), in order to interpret it:

> Judge not and you shall not be judged;
> Condemn not, and you shall not be condemned;
> Release and you shall be released;
> Forgive and it shall be forgiven you.

While Luke gives a more natural setting for the Jewish proverb, which reappears in the Mishna (*Sota*, I, 7), "With the measure with which man measures it shall be measured to him," Matthew has the simpler, more consistent version. The teaching is universally true: a man is judged according as he judges others. Luke is right in paraphrasing Jesus' "judge not" by "condemn not." It is the spirit and attitude toward others that the great Teacher emphasizes. His words leave no doubt that he expects his followers to form their own estimates of others. His command that they first correct their own glaring faults and then help their brothers to correct theirs implies a moral judgment. He is aiming to give each man a true perspective for judging and overcoming his own faults, and to substitute for harsh and sympathetic censure a zeal to help another remove the obstacles that prevent his clear-seeing. The psychological basis of the command is the fact that harsh censure of others destroys the mental and spiritual health. Like greed and anger it is the foe of the normal religious life, and is a thousand times more baneful to the man who indulges in it than to the object of his condemnation, for, even if it does not arouse within him resentment and anger, it drives out love and sympathy.

V. Jesus' Law of Love. Again Jesus took issue with the prevailing Jewish attitude toward law and, like a true prophet, went back to the foundations of all legislation. He sought a principle so simple and so broad that every man might find the higher law of God in his own heart and so be freed from the detailed precepts and casuistry of the scribes. This comprehensive principle was love. He did not define it, but, as was his wont, showed by a series of dramatic illustrations what it was in essence and in practice. These illustrations come straight from the older teaching source (Q). Matthew and Luke have reported them in almost identical form. The chief difference is that Luke introduces the vigorous injunction to offer no resistance to unjust demands in order to illustrate the duty of love to enemies. Matthew's more general setting is probably original.

Jesus was strenuously opposing the ancient law of revenge. In the Code of Hammurabi (about 1900 B.C.) this cruel, elemental principle is the basis of fifteen laws. Thus, for example: "If a man has knocked out the eye of a patrician, his eye shall be knocked out." Exodus 21[22-25] also taught: "Thou shalt give life for life, eye for eye, tooth for tooth, hand for hand, foot for foot, branding for branding, wound for wound, stripe for stripe" (*cf.* also Lev. 24[19]). Revenge and retaliation are instinctive in the child and in the undisciplined man, as they were among primitive peoples. Even in civilized states the *lex talionis* was a corner-stone of both civil and criminal law. The more enlightened leaders of Judaism, however, had begun to break away from this grim principle. In Tobit 4[15] is found the injunction, "What thou thyself hatest, do to no man." Hillel, when asked for a summary of the whole law, echoed this noble teaching, but still expressed it in negative form. Jesus built upon these older Jewish foundations, but far more gloriously. He not only taught the duty of refraining from doing hateful things, but enjoined love and unstinted service even toward an enemy. Thus, again, he did not destroy but fulfilled the ancient law.

To understand Jesus' paradoxical words it is important to note that he is laying down principles not specific regulations, and that for the moment he is concerned more with the individuals whom he addresses than he is with their neighbors and enemies. He is not, however, as has sometimes been falsely urged, presenting an ideal for a favored few or for merely the men of his own generation. He is striving to show how each and every man, subject to the ordinary human passions, may "be perfect as his heavenly Father is perfect." To men enmeshed in wrong prejudices and beliefs, he was struggling to tell how he had found in the midst of the turmoil and contentions of ordinary existence perfect life in God. Modern science and a deeper study of society and of the mind of man are enabling us to understand more clearly the universal truth that he proclaimed. Anger and hate are the deadly foes of the normal life. The physical act that expresses forgiveness and deliberate non-resistance aids immeasurably in developing those divine qualities. The angry countenance and the clinched fist add fuel to the flames of anger and hate in the heart of the man who does not control them, as well as in the heart of his foe. "Turning the other cheek" is simply Jesus' dramatic way of showing that the injured man feels no resentment but only forgiveness and love. Experience abundantly proves the benign effect of non-resistance even upon unprincipled and barbarous enemies. Although the immediate effect sometimes seems disastrous, its ultimate results are well illustrated by Jesus' own experience. He did not resist, even though he was the victim of a nefarious plot and of cruel injustice. The immeasurable impression that he made upon human history is the final proof of the practical wisdom of the principle that he proclaimed. The attitude of non-resistance is the evidence and at the same time the preservative of that love toward an enemy which Jesus declared was an essential characteristic of every true son of God.

The Old Testament teachers had already in part enunciated this crowning principle of Jesus' doctrine regarding man's duty to his neighbor and to himself. Leviticus 19[17, 18, 34] contains the command: "Thou shalt not hate thy fellow countryman in thy heart. Thou shalt not take vengeance nor bear a grudge against the members of thy race; but thou shalt love thy neighbor as thyself." Deuteronomy 10[19] went still further: "Love the resident alien, for you were once resident aliens in the land of Egypt." Jesus spiritualizes, universalizes, and at the same time personalizes these commands. The motive that he urges is loyalty and gratitude to the heavenly Father. Love is to overleap all racial barriers, for the ideal is the perfect man. Here most scholars are inclined to follow Luke's version: "Be merciful even as your father is merciful." But this does not fit the context, for the question under discussion is not mercy toward others, but a man's attitude toward his enemies. Matthew's version probably gives the original reason which Jesus urged:

> You are to be perfect then,
> As your heavenly Father is perfect.

This absolute standard Jesus repeatedly presented in the recurring exhortation, "become sons of your Father who is in heaven," for the Semitic phrase, "son of," expressed kinship and likeness. Godlike love, not cold, but warm, not impersonal, but tender and strong, expressed in look and act toward friend and foe alike, is the mark of membership in the divine brotherhood that Jesus sought to establish.

VI. **The Expression of Love toward a Neighbor.** In its social application the law of non-resistance presents certain difficult problems. Offering the other cheek to a bully may encourage him in his cowardice and cruelty. Giving a cloak to a thief, who seeks to steal a tunic, makes vice easy. Indiscriminate giving pauperizes the objects of charity. Evidently nothing was further from Jesus' purpose. No man ever resisted intrenched graft more sternly than did Jesus when he rebuked the corrupt rulers of the temple. No stronger denunciations are found in all literature than those which he uttered against the Pharisees (§ CXXXVII, CXL). In his law of love he was not legislating for a state or for organized society. His primary object was to develop right motives and emotions in the individual. Yet in the generalization, which both Matthew and Luke have quoted from the older teaching source (Q) in practically identical form:

> All things that you would have men do to you,
> So do you also to them.

Jesus guards the best interests of the neighbor as well as of the individual. The "doing to others as you would have them do to you" does not mean that the neighbor's unreasonable demand will be granted nor that the disciple will be governed by his own selfish desires. "The golden rule" teaches plainly that in the treatment of others each man is to be guided by his enlightened sense of what is best for his neighbor and, therefore, for society. To pauperize himself for others and to countenance theft or social injustice are foreign to its intent. And yet its demands are revolutionary. Jesus declared that in the divine brotherhood each man must give the interests of others absolutely equal consideration with his own; that in the character and lives of others he should ever strive to realize his highest ideals; that thus in losing his life he might find it; that as servant of all he should be greatest of all.

The classic illustration of the love which Jesus described is found in the story of the good Samaritan. The lawyer of Luke 10$^{25-37}$ and the scribe of Mark 12$^{28-34}$ are probably identical. Matthew quotes Mark, but calls the questioner a lawyer, as in Luke. The summary of man's whole duty is based on Deuteronomy 6$^{4, 5}$ and Leviticus 19^{18}. The passage reveals the central place that the law of love held in Jesus' teaching. Paul echoes the same in his declaration that "he who loves another has fulfilled the law. To love then is to fulfil the law" (Rom. 13$^{8-11}$). Mark 12^{32} implies that Jesus, in his reply to the scribe, also quoted the opening words of the familiar Jewish confession of faith, "He [God] is one and beside him there is no other." Jesus' answer was undoubtedly acceptable to the more liberal leaders of Judaism, like Hillel, but not to the narrow legalists, for, as interpreted by the great Teacher, it placed the whole emphasis on feeling, attitude, and service, and said not a word regarding ceremonial obligations.

The story recorded by Luke is a definition not only of man's duty to his neighbor but also of true worship. It is a concrete example rather than a parable, and was apparently told during the closing days at Jerusalem. The scene is the rocky, uninhabited wilderness through which the pilgrims found their way from the Jordan Valley to Jerusalem. Josephus, in his *Jewish War*, IV, 81^2, vividly portrays the dangers of the way. The priest and Levite represent the ceremonial type of religion and its barren fruits. The Samaritans in Jewish eyes were counted with the tax-collectors and Gentiles. In the face of all this prejudice Jesus chose a Samaritan as the example of true piety. The Samaritan's spontaneous, friendly act to a member of a hostile people is the great Teacher's concrete definition of brotherly love. The love which he sought to call forth finds its source in every heart uncorrupted by prejudice and false doctrine. It is the Godlike gift that enables man worthily to worship and love him who is infinite love. It is the invincible power which alone is capable of overcoming anger and resentment and of enabling each man to love and serve his neighbor as himself. It is the divine flame which Jesus kindled and which, as it burns on through the ages, is fusing all mankind into a common brotherhood in which God is recognized as the Father of all.

§ CXXXV. MAN'S RESPONSIBILITY TO SOCIETY

1. Marriage indissoluble because a divinely established institution (Mark 10²⁻⁹, cf. Matt. 19³⁻⁸)

Now certain Pharisees came to Jesus and asked him in order to test him, Is it lawful for a man to divorce his wife? And he answered and said to them, What did Moses command you? And they said, Moses gave permission to write a bill of divorce, and so divorce her. But Jesus said to them, Because of the hardness of your heart he wrote you this commandment. But from the beginning of the creation male and female he made them. For this cause a man shall leave his father and mother, and the two shall become one flesh. What, therefore, God hath joined together, let no man put asunder.

2. Divorce for remarriage equivalent to adultery (Mark 10¹⁰⁻¹², cf. Matt. 5³¹, ³² 19⁹ Luke 16¹⁸)

And in the house, his disciples asked him again in regard to this matter. And he said to them:

Whoever shall divorce his wife and marry another commits adultery against her;
And if she divorces her husband and marries another, she commits adultery.

3. Some called to voluntary celibacy in the service of the kingdom (Matt. 19¹⁰⁻¹²)

The disciples say to him, If that is the status between a man and his wife, it is not expedient to marry. But he said to them,

All men cannot comprehend this saying, but those to whom it is given.
For there are eunuchs who are born thus from their mothers' womb,
And there are eunuchs who are made eunuchs by men,
And there are eunuchs who made themselves eunuchs for the sake of the kingdom of Heaven.
He who is able to comprehend it, let him comprehend it.

Now when they came to Capernaum, those who collected the temple tax came to Peter and said, Does your teacher not pay the temple tax? Yes, he said. And when he came into the house, Jesus spoke first to him, saying, What thinkest thou, Simon? From whom do the kings of the earth collect customs or taxes, from their own sons or from strangers? And he said, From strangers. And when he said, Strangers, Jesus said to him, Therefore, the sons are free. But that we may give them no offence, go to the sea, cast in the hook, and take the first fish that comes up. Open its mouth and thou shalt find a stater. Take that and give it to them for me and for thyself.

4. Jesus' attitude toward the temple tax (Matt. 17²⁴⁻²⁷)

Then the high priest sent to Jesus certain of the Pharisees and Herodians, to catch him in his talk. And when they came, they said, Teacher, we know that thou art truthful, and carest not for anyone; for thou dost not regard the person of any man, but teachest in truth the way of God. Is it right to pay taxes to Cæsar or not? Should we pay, or should we not pay?

5. Question regarding Roman taxes (Mark 12^{13-15a}, cf. Matt. 22¹⁵⁻¹⁷ Luke 20²⁰⁻²²)

But he, knowing their hypocrisy, said to them, Why do you make trial of me? Bring me a denarius, that I may see it. And they brought it. And he said to them, Whose likeness and inscription is this? They said to him, Cæsar's. And Jesus said to them, Render to Cæsar the things that are Cæsar's and to God the things that are God's. And they were filled with wonder at him.

6. Pay to rulers their due (Mark 12^{15b-17}, cf. Matt. 22¹⁸⁻²² Luke 20²³⁻²⁶)

Now all the people went to their own homes, but Jesus went to the Mount of Olives. But early in the morning he came again to the temple, and all the people came to him, and he sat down, and began to teach them. Then the scribes and the Pharisees bring a woman caught in adultery. And after they had placed her in the midst of the company, they say to him, Teacher, this woman has been caught in the very act of adultery. Now in the law Moses commanded us to stone such women. What then do you say? And they said this to test him, that they might have something of which they might accuse him. But Jesus stooped down and began to write with his finger on the ground. And when they kept on asking him, he stood up, and said to them, Let him who is sinless among you fling the first stone at her. And

7. The treatment of the criminal (John 7⁵³-8¹¹)

again he stooped down and went on writing with his finger on the ground. Now when they heard this, they went out, one by one, beginning with the oldest; and Jesus was left alone with the woman. Then he stood up and said to her, Woman, where are they? Did no one condemn thee? And she said, No one, Master. And Jesus said, Neither do I condemn thee. Go thy way. Henceforth sin no more. And he said to his disciples:

8. Of tempting the ignorant and the weak (Luke 17¹, ², cf. Mark 9⁴², Matt. 18⁶, ⁷)

It is inevitable that temptations should come,
But woe to him through whom they come!
It were better for him if a millstone were fastened about his neck and that he were thrown into the sea,
Rather than that he should be a source of temptation to one of these little ones!

9. Of despising them (Matt. 18¹⁰)

See that you do not despise one of these little ones;
For I tell you that their angels in heaven look ever on the face of my Father who is in heaven.

I. Jesus' Method as a Social Teacher. Jesus was not primarily a social reformer. Though keenly alive to the social injustice and evils of the system under which he lived, he persistently refused to be drawn into class and party strife. Though himself a manual laborer, penniless, the friend of outcasts, and in the end rejected by the rich and powerful of his nation, he set his face against every attempt to proclaim him the popular Messiah, the champion of the oppressed who was expected to overthrow existing evils and to institute a rule of justice and equality. Even when a private grievance was referred to him, he protested, "Who made me an arbiter?" (Luke 12¹³, ¹⁴). This silence and deliberate inaction was certainly not due to a lack of knowledge or of interest in social questions. A partial explanation, often urged, is that the political and social conditions of his day were exceptional. Largely through the folly of their former rulers, the Jews were helpless in the hands of Rome. To stir their patriotism would be but to precipitate a suicidal rebellion. Moreover, the social consciousness, as in most oriental lands to-day, was still undeveloped. Hence, it is urged, there were no social ideals or social sense to which to appeal. There is truth in these assertions; yet in his denunciation of the greed of the temple rulers and the cruel hypocrisy of the scribes and Pharisees,

JESUS' METHOD AS A SOCIAL TEACHER

Jesus' burning words vividly recall the social sermons of Amos and Isaiah. In his mind there was certainly a keen social consciousness and his woes against the blind, corrupt guides of the nation must also have awakened a strong response among those who were in spirit disciples of the earlier prophets.

Diametrically opposite conclusions have been drawn from the facts presented by the gospel records. Many, since the days of the brilliant French scholar Renan, have found in Jesus a social agitator, the forerunner of all socialistic propagandists. Others have declared with equal insistence and conviction that he had no social message or programme for his own or for the present age. Each of these extreme statements is false, and each is in a sense true. Jesus was not a socialistic agitator and did not present a programme of social reorganization; and yet no one was ever more intent upon bettering social conditions or has done more for the evolution of society than he. What is the explanation of this seeming paradox? It is found in the character of both his method and his message. He sought to perfect society, not by popular agitation or by reorganization, but by perfecting the individual. He recognized the fatal fallacy in the dream of those who hoped to make a perfect state out of imperfect individuals. The ideal social state, which he described as the kingdom of God, was a commonwealth in which all men were united and governed by a commanding love both for God and for their neighbors. Jesus was a prophet, not an organizer. Hence his social teachings are not detailed or systematic. In a sense they are only incidental, and yet they are of inestimable present-day value. He sets forth not programmes but principles. He alleviates evil social conditions by putting the right ideals into the minds of the men whose duty it is to correct them. He instituted an ideal social order because he freed the minds of his true followers from greed and hate and implanted within them a self-giving love for all mankind. In its demands the social message of Jesus is far more radical and revolutionary than that of the most advanced modern socialism. It makes the possession of wealth and position a heavy responsibility rather than a privilege. It declares that each man is "the keeper," not only of the members of his party or class or race, but of all with whom he comes into contact directly or indirectly. It demands equal love for friend or foe. Jesus' social message, instead of being antiquated, is the lone star that inspires hope in men depressed by the social injustice of our modern civilization and by the failure of cherished plans for social betterment, and guides them onward toward that perfect state in which love shall be the supreme controlling principle.

II. His Teachings Regarding the Family. On one point at least Jesus took absolute issue with modern anarchistic socialism, as well as with powerful tendencies in the Roman and Jewish world of his day. He declared that the marriage relation was of divine origin and that under no conditions should its claims be set aside. Here for once he departed from his usual method and laid down a definite law. This fact indicates how important was the place that he attributed to the family in the development of the individual and of society. Back of his teaching lay centuries of human experience. The wisdom of his conclusions is confirmed by modern sociology, which recognizes in the family the historical and actual basis of all stable society. To-day the prevailing disregard of the rights and duties of the family is demonstrating anew their supreme importance. Leaders in modern thought are beginning to see clearly that the only final solution of our gravest political, social, and economic problems must come through the faithful and efficient training of the individual in the home. The shame of our divorce courts and of our modern social system is slowly but surely preparing the present generation to listen attentively to Jesus' strenuous teaching regarding marriage.

Jesus' decisive declaration is recorded both in the early teaching source (Q) and in Mark: "What God hath joined together, let no man put asunder." Matthew alone adds that fornication is a sufficient reason for divorce and remarriage. This clause destroys the logical and literary unity of the passage. The fact that it is lacking both in Mark and in Luke's quotation from the early teaching source (16^{18}) indicates that it was probably not found in the original record of Jesus' words. Adultery under the Jewish law was punishable by the death of the culprit, so that divorce was unnecessary and there was no occasion for Jesus to discuss this question.

Mark has given the historical setting of Jesus' teaching regarding divorce. Like many of his profoundest utterances, it was incidental. The Pharisees, seeking to entrap him, came with the much-debated question, "Is it ever lawful for a man to divorce his wife?" Jesus' answer left no doubt in their minds. Here he again took direct issue with the Mosaic law. The regulation in Deuteronomy 24^3 was originally intended to relieve the injustice of a Semitic custom which made the divorce of a wife easy and possible whenever the husband desired it. This law, in providing that the husband must state in writing the charges against his wife, simply made the divorce more difficult but did not prevent it. This compromise Jesus set aside and reaffirmed the deeper principle laid down by the early prophetic writer in Genesis $2^{24, 25}$. He appealed in reality from the traditional law of Moses to the unchanging law of God. He declared that the marriage bond is sacred because it rests upon the innate characteristics and needs of man and woman and, therefore, of society. It is no more to be set aside than the relation between parent and child. It is, indeed, more divinely sacred and inviolable than that close natural bond.

In response to the question of his disciples, he embodied the broad principle in a plain, unqualified statement: "Whoever shall divorce his wife and marry another commits adultery against her." Again it was the motive even more than the act that he emphasized. He said nothing against separation or even divorce for sufficient reasons. He dealt directly with the motive: "He who divorces his wife in order to remarry commits the vilest of crimes." He brands it as the most unsocial of acts, for it is a menace to the welfare not only of the individuals involved but also to that of the family and of society. Mark, writing for the larger Roman audience, which, unlike the Jewish, were acquainted with laws which made it possible for a woman to divorce her husband, applies the same principle to the woman. Even if this second injunction is not original, it is true to the intent of Jesus' teachings.

Matthew alone has preserved the conversation in which this theme was further developed by Jesus and his disciples. The high ideal of marriage which Jesus set forth prompted them to exclaim: "If this is the status between a man and his wife, it is not expedient to marry." It is the protest that is urged to-day with increasing insistence and fortified with strong arguments and a grim array of facts. Jesus, however, offered no qualifications or modifications to the law that he had laid down. Instead, he acknowledged its rigorousness and the fact that many would be unable to comprehend its full significance and apply it.

To this statement he added a saying that may well reflect his own feeling and experience. "Some men," he declared, "are born incapable of marriage; others are rendered so by their fellow-men; but there are others who deny themselves the joys of marriage that they may give their time and strength wholly to the service of the kingdom of Heaven." Whatever be the exact meaning of this difficult saying, it certainly does not teach the superiority of celibacy to marriage, for that would be but a denial of Jesus' assertion that marriage was divinely ordained. Neither does it teach that all of Jesus' disciples should refrain from marriage. The teaching of I Timothy 3², "A bishop must be unblamable, the husband of one wife," and the usage in the early church are decisive on this point. If original, as they probably are, these words of Jesus mean that he, like Jeremiah, regarded the renunciation of the joys of married life as a great but voluntary sacrifice which he and certain of his followers were called to make that they might devote themselves uninterruptedly to doing the will of God in the fields, already white for the harvest, that opened before them. Paul and others in the later history of the church have demonstrated the eminent wisdom of this saying of Jesus, which is an observation rather than a command.

The insistent question still remains and will doubtless be hotly debated in the future as in the past, "Is not Jesus' absolute prohibition of divorce with a view to remarriage cruelly unjust?" Thousands of examples may be cited in which the wife or husband is the innocent victim of deception or infidelity. Shall they be denied the joy of a happy remarriage? Jesus, who was pre-eminently the champion of the rights and liberty of the individual, here replies, "For the sake of society they shall." The justice of this seemingly harsh law can be rightly apprehended only in its social bearing and in the light of Jesus' teachings as a whole. Statistics and scientific observation have demonstrated beyond a doubt that lax divorce laws are not the solution of social evils. Where divorce is easy, the duties of marriage are hastily assumed and lightly esteemed. The modern innocent victims of unhappy marriages are largely the result of a wrong conception of that most sacred of all human relations. Jesus was not seeking to place an intolerable burden upon their shoulders, but to save the countless millions who would share their fate unless the sanctity of marriage was thus absolutely safeguarded. This law was in harmony with the preventive measures that he always advocated. Furthermore, it did not stand alone but was a part of that absolute and yet pre-eminently sane and practical ideal that he placed before the individual and society. When he asserted the inviolability of marriage, he proclaimed at the same time the dethronement of greed, lust, hate, worry, and all the brood of selfish, cowardly motives that destroy the peace of the family life and result in the heart-rending tragedies that deeply appeal to our sympathy and lead us at times even to question the wisdom of Jesus' law.

HIS TEACHINGS REGARDING THE FAMILY

HIS TEACHINGS REGARDING THE FAMILY

Earlier teachers, "because of the hardness of men's hearts," had compromised their ideals. Not so the great Teacher. He knew that only the absolute truth and strict adherence to it would make men wholly free. His sympathy with suffering, whether innocent or sinful, was boundless; but he never attempted to relieve it by compromise. To the innocent victims of wrong social ideals he calls, asking them to share with him the God-given task of saving society by voluntary, patient renunciation and by thus losing their life to find it.

III. **Obligations of the Individual to the State.** Political conditions in the Palestine of Jesus' day gave him little opportunity to declare his attitude toward the state. Two incidents are recorded which are intended to illustrate his teachings on this subject. Matthew alone contains the account of his payment of the temple tax. This tax consisted of a half-shekel of the sanctuary and was equivalent to two drachmæ (about 33 cents). The stater was equal to four drachmæ, and therefore represented the annual tax for both Jesus and Peter. This poll-tax was paid by all faithful Jews for the support of the temple. Like many of the independent narratives in Matthew, the story was apparently told in order to establish a precedent for the guidance of the Christian community in Palestine. The sons of the divine King are the followers of Jesus. He had taught them that they owed direct allegiance to God and that the formal ritual of the Jewish temple was no longer essential. Hence it became an insistent question whether or not they should continue, out of their limited resources, to pay the temple tax. The answer suggested by the story probably reflects Jesus' own practice, as well as that of the early Christian community in Palestine. He aimed never to give offence unless a principle was at stake. Jesus may have instructed Peter to return for a time to his old occupation of fishing in order to secure the needed money. The value of the narrative lies not in its suggestion that Jesus' ordinary wants were supplied in a miraculous manner, for this is contrary to the teaching of the story of his temptation, but in the belief of his early followers that he, by his example, encouraged them to support the organized religious agencies of their race. The temple tax also represented the support of the state, as well as the church, for the high priests retained the surviving vestiges of the political power once held by Israel's kings.

Jesus' answer to the captious question of the Pharisees and Herodians, as to whether or not it was right for faithful Jews to pay a poll-tax to Cæsar, is recorded in each of the synoptic gospels. The incident belongs to the closing days of his ministry when the opposition was bitter. The question was a burning one in Judea. The Pharisees contended that to pay tribute to a heathen king was disloyalty to their divine King. Refusal to pay it was equivalent to rebellion against Rome. The flattery with which the cunning question was introduced reveals the eagerness of the Jews to entrap him. Either "yes" or "no" was certain to crystallize opposition. His answer is one of the many illustrations of his mental alertness and his broad outlook. He sympathized neither with the narrow Jewish piety nor with the popular hatred of Rome. His attitude was that of a prophet who refused to be involved in the contentions of the hour. With a touch of humor he unmasked their hypocrisy: "You are glad to be able to carry about the coins of Cæsar: therefore pay to him, whom you thus acknowledge, the money that is his due. But be sure that you do not fail to give also to your divine King fitting proofs of your loyalty."

Jesus' epigrammatic words are variously interpreted. Certainly they do not proclaim the divine right of kings. A clear distinction is drawn between the material things which are Cæsar's and the divine things which are God's. Jesus' primary interest was in the things that are God's; but his absolute sense of justice demanded that Rome be paid for whatever service she rendered. It was inevitable that he should speak contemptuously of such rulers as Herod Antipas, Caiaphas, Annas, Pilate, and Tiberius. Their pride, their greed for power, and their selfishness were all patent to him (Mark 10⁴²). Jesus' patriotic spirit is shown by the boldness with which he denounced the blind guides who, like wolves in sheep's clothing, were perverting their office and preying upon the helpless people. The intensity of his invectives (§ CXL¹¹⁻¹⁹) shows how deeply he was interested in pure government and how eager he was to uphold just authority. He has also left a priceless example of courageous citizenship to his followers. He accepted the political principles which had already been proclaimed by Israel's earlier prophets; but the one supreme standard which he set forth was that of service. His was the most democratic political principle ever enunciated. Hereditary authority, power attained by intrigue or violence, the pride and pomp of office all go down before it. "Whoever would be first among you, let him be your servant." While Jesus' teachings regarding the state were revolutionary, they were not iconoclastic. He proposed no sudden or forcible overthrow of existing conditions. His method, as always, was to work from within rather than from without. Moreover, he did not aim to level all distinctions.

He fully recognized the differences in ability and, therefore, the different degrees of individual attainment and honor; but for the prevailing incidental and superficial standards he substituted the one absolute standard, that of social efficiency. His ideal was that of a social organization in which every man would have the joyous consciousness of laboring and striving, not for himself, but for the welfare of his fellowmen, and where the highest rewards and honors would go simply to those who were able to contribute the most to society.

IV. Treatment of the Criminal. Jesus' quiet but commanding note of authority led both friends and foes to refer difficult questions to him for a decision. In the closing days of his work at Jerusalem the Pharisees repeatedly attempted to induce him to commit himself to a position that might be used as the basis of a charge of treason against the law of Moses or of Rome. In the third-century texts of the Fourth Gospel there is found a remarkable illustration of Jesus' attitude toward the criminal. The account of the woman taken in adultery has no connection with the context in John and is not found in the early Greek texts; yet it shares all the characteristics of the oldest synoptic narratives. It was probably taken from an early written source and attached to the Fourth Gospel at the close of the seventh chapter. In some manuscripts it stands after the thirtieth verse, in others after the forty-fourth, but in the majority at the end of that chapter and at the beginning of the eighth.

Its contents attest its historical character. The incident took place on the Mount of Olives, to which, according to the synoptic record, Jesus frequently retired during the last perilous days at Jerusalem. According to the Jewish law of Leviticus 20^{10} and Deuteronomy 22^{22}, a married or betrothed woman, convicted of adultery, was to be stoned, and the witnesses were to fling the first stones. The fact that Jesus' foes brought the woman to him suggests that her case presented certain features that they believed would appeal to his sympathies. Their act was probably inspired by their knowledge of his reputation as a friend of sinners. If so, it was an implied insult: "Here is one of your friends; what will you do for her?" With his usual tact Jesus reserved his answer until his foes had departed and he was alone with the woman. His appeal was from the harsh Jewish law, which was concerned simply with protecting society from an insidious peril, to the higher moral law, that considered the welfare of the individual, as well as that of society. He also rebuked the unjust double standard that visited the heaviest penalties for social crimes upon the helpless weaker sex. Paul undoubtedly had good authority for asserting that Jesus made no distinction between male and female (Gal. 3²⁸). The incident is one of the most dramatic and significant in the gospels. One after another the woman's accusers went out self-accused. The lesson best calculated to save society from the social evil had been taught. The problem that remained was individual. It was not to shield the guilty woman from the inevitable consequences of her crime, but to redeem her. Stoning certainly would not save her. Counsel, sympathy, and an opportunity to redeem herself might. Those Jesus gave her. More he could not give, for her shame and suffering were essential to her redemption.

Jesus' action illustrates those higher Christian principles that are to-day beginning to govern the attitude not only of the individual but also of society toward the criminal. Remedial methods are rightly taking the place of mere punishment. The individual criminal is being considered as well as outraged society. Prison reforms, indeterminate sentences, and the humane, scientific treatment of criminals are being substituted for cruel, simply punitive methods. The result is that criminals are being redeemed instead of being confirmed in their hostile attitude toward society. Society in turn is not only being delivered from the menace of the individual criminal, but is beginning to profit by his restoration to the ranks of its productive citizens.

V. Care of the Poor. Jesus sprang from a race that has always been pre-eminently considerate and faithful in its care of the poor. The Old Testament laws, and especially the code of Deuteronomy, abound in regulations and injunctions concerning liberality and charity to the needy and dependent classes. In all Semitic countries giving alms is regarded as an essential virtue. Responsibility for the unfortunate and dependent was a survival of the tribal and communal stage in Semitic civilization. It was strengthened by the strong Jewish sense of racial unity. It was even extended to the resident aliens who identified themselves with the race and local community. This philanthropic virtue evidently met with Jesus' full approval. It has passed as a heritage to the Christian church and has inspired many of the noblest achievements in human history.

In view of these facts it is surprising that the gospels record no instance in which Jesus was appealed to for alms or gave them. Aside from the command to the rich man who came to him, he appears to have given no direct command to his followers to distribute to the poor (Luke 18²² Matt. 19²¹). In the few cases in which he advocated charity, it was more for the sake of the giver than the recipient. His conviction is clearly expressed in the beatitude: "It makes a man happier to give than to receive." Jesus' teaching that wealth was to be held in stewardship meant not only its faithful administration but also its wise and efficient distribution. Although the later practice of the Christian church has often created a wrong impression, Jesus never taught indiscriminate giving either by word or example. When he saw that his work of healing was creating a wrong impression and distracting the people from his more vital message, he at once left the multitudes. All his recorded giving was individual rather than general. He gave as opportunity offered in connection with his daily task. He adapted his gifts to the needs of each recipient. His giving was doubly valuable, for he gave himself, his intelligent sympathy, and his love and inspiration.

What Jesus taught his followers by his example he also embodied in the parable of the good Samaritan, who is the most perfect type of the ideal giver in all literature and life. He was a busy traveller intent on reaching his destination. The motive which prompted him to give was absolutely free from the blight of ostentation. It was a spontaneous brotherly sympathy so strong that it conquered all self-interest. He first investigated carefully the needs of the unfortunate man who had fallen among robbers. Then he supplied them in the most direct and practical way. He gave what the unfortunate man's wants required, but not so as to demean or tempt him. Thus Jesus taught his followers to give not thoughtlessly nor unsystematically, but sanely, practically, personally, as opportunity offered and as their trained intelligence and feelings prompted. Practical sociology and philanthropy are daily making clearer the wisdom of his counsel. In such wise, considerate stewardship of wealth lies the solution of our most difficult social and industrial problems, for it transforms but does not destroy society and ennobles both the giver and the one helped.

VI. Protection of the Weak and Ignorant. Jesus' knightly spirit is revealed not only in his heroic acts but also in his advice to his followers regarding the weak and ignorant. From the context of Luke and Mark it is clear that the term "little ones" included not only the children but the weak and helpless, the lost sheep of the house of Israel who commanded Jesus' first attention. Pity and contempt are mingled in the strong words with which he denounced those who tempted or misled these "little ones." The millstone was the heavy circular stone used for grinding grain in every Palestinian home. The words of Jesus are so familiar that they have lost for us their original vigor. "Better that a man be deliberately drowned in the sea than that he put an obstacle in the way of the weak that may cause them to stumble either in faith or act." This is the teaching that Paul nobly expands in the fourteenth and fifteenth chapters of his letter to the Romans: "It is an excellent plan to abstain from flesh and wine or anything at which thy brother stumbles. We who are strong ought to bear the infirmities of the weak instead of pleasing ourselves. Let each of us please our neighbor to do him good, to bind him up; for Christ also did not please himself." Jerome also reports what is possibly an original utterance of Jesus: "He commits a great crime who makes sad the spirit of his brother." By such teachings as these Jesus sought to call forth the courageous, militant qualities inherent in all men, and to teach the strong not to crush and mislead but to deliver and guide the weak and helpless classes. The principle laid down is the condemnation of the disastrous industrial and military systems that are the bane and disgrace of modern civilization. At the same time it solves the deeper problems that underlie these systems. Jesus' chivalrous ideal offers to the bold and strong tasks worthy of their courage and strength. It develops heroism and self-sacrifice without the horrors of war and cruel, competitive industrialism. The "little ones" of to-day are the underfed, overworked, ignorant, often vicious masses who even in the time of peace bear the burdens of war and of our unjust industrial system, and who are the victims not only of their own vices but also of those of the ruling classes. "Despise not one of these little ones," is Jesus' exhortation, "for they are especial objects of God's care and love." Paul's familiar words express Jesus' challenge to the men of strength: "You who are strong ought to bear the burdens of the weak." The great Teacher appealed to the natural spirit of competition implanted within every normal man; but the goal he set was not personal honor or possessions but the glory of the heroic, self-sacrificing, efficient service for those who need the help of the strong.

VI. **The Application of Jesus' Principles to Society.** Jesus began with the individual, but the influence of his work and teachings touch and transform all social relationships. He provides a remedy for every social evil, for he commands the motives that control the men who collectively constitute society. His cure, for example, for murder and violence, class strife, war, and social immorality is the banishment of angry, revengeful, selfish, impure thoughts from the minds of men. His corrective of poverty is to develop a sense of social responsibility so strong that on the one hand the possession of wealth and authority become a heavy burden rather than a privilege. On the other hand, his principles of living, when they are practically applied, eliminate the crime and shiftlessness which are the chief causes of poverty. In the place of self-interest and class interest and narrow national patriotism, he inspires interest in human society as a whole. Above all, it is an interest kindled by love for a common Father and expressed in intelligent, devoted service for one's neighbor—the man who, like him who fell among robbers, needs a helping hand.

Jesus' conception of an ideal society must be inferred from his incidental utterances and from the way they were interpreted by the primitive church. His ironical references to the prevailing social and political order indicate that he was keenly aware of its vanity and imperfections. He regarded no existing institution as final. Each must be tested by its fruits. With him society was but a means to an end and that end was the perfecting of the individual. For one whose eyes were fixed with love and adoration upon a divine King whose rule knew no bounds or limitations, the pretences and contentions of the rulers who lorded it over their fellows seemed trivial and petty. Jesus, like certain of Israel's earlier prophets, had in mind a universal kingdom in which the principles of justice and mercy should guide all men in their relations to one another, in which organized society would not merely protect the interests of each member, but also give him ample opportunity to express himself in largest measure. He sought to lay the foundations for a society in which the chief ambition of each citizen should be not to be ministered unto but to minister.

The family, with its close interrelationships, with its ample demands and opportunities for service under loving, parental guidance, according to his conviction, furnished the natural basis for such a social structure. This undoubtedly was the fundamental reason why he guarded the sanctity of the family with such strenuous zeal. The second stage in the social structure which Jesus apparently contemplated may be designated as the communal unit. It is implied in his tragic lament over the cities of Chorazin, Bethsaida, and Capernaum, the towns on the northern shores of the Sea of Galilee where he had sought to realize this phase of his social ideal. It included all who by proximity or residence in the same community were bound together by common economic, social, and religious interests. It corresponded to that wonderful brotherhood of disciples that he rallied about him. In certain aspects the primitive church at Jerusalem appears to have realized this ideal. The third and final social unit was intended to include all men. It was the ultimate, concrete expression of Jesus' ideal of the kingdom of God. The realization of this ideal was the inspiration of all of Jesus' work and of that of his disciples throughout the succeeding ages. The Holy Catholic Church and the Holy Roman Empire were intended to be the embodiment of this ideal; but in their thirst for power the leaders in this great world movement forgot the fundamental principles laid down by Jesus, so that their work in the end became a mere mockery rather than the fulfilment of the plan of the Master Builder who inspired them. Jesus' social ideal, therefore, remains a goal which humanity has yet to attain. The watchwords of to-day, efficiency, democracy, fraternity, world-unity, and, in certain of its aspects, socialism, are the heralds of that divine social order, seen from afar by Hebrew prophets but proclaimed by Jesus so clearly that it is still the inspiration of every man of faith and courage who is ready to acknowledge as Master the heroic Son of God and the peerless Lover of men.

§ CXXXVI. THE REWARDS OF THE CHRISTIAN LIFE

1. True honor comes only to those who conquer self-seeking and pride (Luke 14¹, ⁷⁻¹¹)

Now it came to pass that when Jesus went into the house of one of the rulers of the Pharisees, to take a meal on the sabbath day, they watched him closely. And he spoke a parable to those who had been invited, when he observed how they selected the chief seats. He said to them, When thou art invited by anyone to a marriage feast, do not recline on the chief seat, lest perhaps the host has invited some one of a higher rank than thyself. Then he who invited you both shall come and say to thee, Give up your place to this man and then thou shalt begin with shame to take the lowest place. But when thou art invited, go and recline in the lowest place, that when he who has invited thee comes, he may say to thee, Friend, come up higher. Then thou shalt have honor in the presence of thy fellow-guests.

For everyone who exalts himself shall be humbled,
And he who humbles himself shall be exalted.

He also said to the man who had invited him, When thou givest a dinner or a supper, do not call in thy friends or thy brothers or thy kinsmen or rich neighbors; lest perhaps they too invite thee in return and so thou be repaid. Rather when thou givest a feast, invite the poor, the cripples, the lame, the blind. Then thou shalt be happy; for they have nothing with which to repay thee; for thou shalt be repaid at the resurrection of the just.

2. Unselfish service for those who need it alone of lasting value (12-14)

For the kingdom of Heaven is like a householder, who went out early in the morning to hire laborers for his vineyard. And after agreeing with the laborers for a denarius a day, he sent them into his vineyard. And on going out at about nine o'clock, he saw other men in the market place standing idle. And he said to them, 'Go also into the vineyard and I will pay you whatever is right.' So they went. Again on going out again at twelve o'clock and three o'clock in the afternoon, he did the same thing. And on going out about five o'clock in the afternoon, he found other men standing. And he said to them, 'Why stand here all the day idle?' They said to him, 'Because no one has hired us.' He said to them, 'You go also into the vineyard.' Now when evening came, the owner of the vineyard said to his steward, 'Call the laborers and pay their wages, beginning from the last up to the first.' And when those who had been hired about five o'clock in the afternoon came, they each received a denarius. And when the first men came, they supposed that they would receive more. Yet they too received a denarius each. So on receiving it, they began to murmur against the householder, saying, 'These last worked but a single hour, yet thou hast made them equal to us, who bore the burden of the day and the scorching heat!' But he answered and said to one of them, 'Friend, I am doing thee no wrong. Didst thou not agree with me for a denarius? Take what is thine and go. I wish to pay this last man what I pay thee. Is it not lawful for me to do what I wish with what is mine own? Or dost thou look on with envious eyes, because I am generous.' So shall the last be first and the first last.

3. Rewards dependent upon the quality and spirit of service (Matt. 20¹⁻¹⁶)

4. The simple doing of duty not a basis for special rewards (Luke 17¹ᵃ, 7-10)

And he said to his disciples, Which of you is there who has a servant plowing or guarding the sheep and will say to him when he comes from the field, 'Come forward at once; lie down and eat.' Will he not rather say to him, 'Get something ready for my supper. Gird thyself and wait upon me, until I have eaten and drunk. Then after that, thou shalt eat and drink thyself?' Does he give thanks to the servant for doing as he was instructed? So too of yourselves, when you have done all things as you are instructed, say, 'We are useless servants. We have only done that which it was our duty to do.'

Peter began to say to him, Behold, we have left all and followed thee. Jesus said, I tell you truly, there is no man who has left house, or brothers, or sisters, or mother or father or children or lands for my sake and for the sake of the gospel, without receiving a hundred-fold now in this time: houses, brothers, sisters, mothers, children and lands, with persecutions, and in the age to come eternal life. But many who are first shall be last and the last first.

Happy the poor in spirit!
For theirs is the kingdom of Heaven.
Happy the meek!
For they shall inherit the earth.
Happy they who mourn!
For they shall be comforted.
Happy they who hunger and thirst for righteousness!
For they shall be satisfied.

Happy the merciful!
For they shall obtain mercy.
Happy the pure in heart!
For they shall see God.
Happy the peacemakers!
For they shall be called sons of God.

Happy they who have been persecuted on account of righteousness!
For theirs is the kingdom of Heaven.
Happy are you when men shall denounce you and persecute you,
Speaking falsely on account of me, and say all manner of evil against you!
Rejoice and exult! For great is your reward in heaven;
For so they persecuted the prophets who were before you.

5. The inestimable rewards of self-sacrifice (Mark 10²⁸⁻³¹, cf. Matt. 19²⁷⁻²⁹ Luke 18²⁸⁻³⁰)
6. Superlative happiness of those eager for God's rule in their lives (Matt. 5³⁻⁶, cf. Luke 6²⁰, ²¹)
7. Of those who are devoted to the welfare of others (Matt. 5⁷⁻⁹)
8. Who endure persecution because of Jesus and his teachings (Matt. 5¹⁰⁻¹²,cf. Luke 6²², ²³)

204

Happier they who give than they who receive!
[For their Father in heaven shall recompense them.]

9. Who
freely
give
(Acts
20³⁵ᵇ)

I. Jesus and the Jewish Doctrine of Rewards. In all early religions rewards are made the important, if not the chief incentives for right conduct. In the Jewish religion of Jesus' day the fear of punishment and the hope of present good fortune and of future blessedness were the leading motives that influenced the individual. The new-born belief in personal immortality spiritualized the ancient doctrine of rewards; but it did not eliminate the mercenary element. The motive for right-doing was still largely selfish. According to the prevailing pharisaic teaching, a title to blessed immortality was assured only when a man's righteous deeds exceeded his evil acts. This type of religion made God a mere book-keeper and judge. It developed the selfish and egoistic rather than the altruistic and social impulses in men. It encouraged the invention of superficial devices, such as long prayers, alms-giving, fasting, and different types of ceremonial sacrifice, whereby men thought that they might add to their credit with God and to their claims upon his favor. This selfish, mercenary conception of religion has always proved the worst foe of vital personal faith. Even in the gospel records of Jesus' teachings there are traces of its baneful influence. Thus, for example, in the important utterance preserved by Luke (14¹²⁻¹⁴), in which Jesus emphasized the importance of an unselfish motive in doing deeds of kindness, the pharisaic phrase, "Thou shalt be repaid at the resurrection of the just," appears. The next verse states that "on hearing this, one of his fellow-guests said to him, 'Happy the man who eats bread in the kingdom of God,'" indicating that the original words probably referred to participation in the responsibilities as well as the joys of God's kingdom. Jesus was contending against the false doctrine of rewards. "Invite those who cannot repay you," was his exhortation to his disciples. "The poor, the cripples, the lame, and the blind present to you a rare opportunity, for they have nothing with which to repay you." In Jesus' teachings rewards are regarded not as the motives but as the results of unselfish action. Herein lies a vital distinction between the Christianity of Jesus and all other religions. "When thou hast entertained those who are unable to repay you, thou shalt be happy and hast indeed entered into the kingdom of God," was Jesus' conclusion. The motive as well as the act must be unselfish. Then and only then happiness comes as a result, even as effect follows cause.

THE REWARDS OF THE CHRISTIAN LIFE

Jesus was also well aware that he who pushes himself forward thereby arouses the antagonism and rivalry of his fellows, and that he who claims less than his due thereby makes all men his champions. In the quieter, conventional life of the ancient East this truth was more often illustrated than in the rushing modern world. The illustration in Luke 14[7-11] is drawn from the oriental banquet in which all the guests reclined and where great attention was given to the order of precedence. It is the adaptation of the figure already developed in Proverbs 25[6, 7]. It is one of several graphic illustrations of Jesus' epigrammatic teaching:

> Every one who exalts himself shall be humbled,
> And he who humbles himself shall be exalted.

In Luke 18[9-14] Jesus applies the same principle to man's relations to God and illustrates it by the story of the Pharisee and the tax-collector who went up to the temple to pray. In this parable Jesus emphasizes the sharp contrast between his own teaching regarding rewards and that of the Pharisees. The Pharisee, confident of divine favor because of his good deeds, entered boldly into the divine presence and began to recount them. He returned to his home unblessed; but the poor tax-collector, who was conscious of no deserts and expected no rewards, gained the divine blessing that he sought.

In the new divine order that Jesus proclaimed, the law of the family, not of the market-place, prevails. The spirit and the quality of service, not the quantity, are essential. This principle is illustrated by the parable of the laborers in the vineyard. According to the law of rewards, the claim of the men who had labored longest, that they deserved the larger compensation, was entirely valid. Their complaint was akin to that of the older brother in the parable of the prodigal son. It is noteworthy that Jesus did not deny God's favor to these jealous protestants. The heavenly Father's goodness was boundless enough to overlook their faults and to reward their worthy acts. But to those who had labored one hour he gave the same gifts. In any case those gifts so far exceeded their deserts that none had cause to complain. This fact Jesus illustrated by the story of the servant (literally, slave) who did simply the task assigned to him. The thought is: "We all belong to God, as slaves to their master. Even if our conduct is perfect, it gives us no claim to special rewards." The word "useless" is not found in the old Syriac version and is possibly a later addition. Even if the original read, "We are servants; we have done that which it was our duty to do," the meaning of the passage is the same.

II. **The Rewards of Faithful Service.** Although Jesus rejected the mercenary doctrine of rewards, he knew well that if a man is to do his best he must have a worthy goal for which to strive. The more attractive that goal the more effective his effort. The way in which Jesus attracted and held his disciples was by appealing to their nobler ambitions. "Leave your fishing and I will teach you a far nobler craft: I will make you fishers of men," were the words with which he drew four of his disciples to him. There is no reference to material or personal rewards; but the request of James and John on their last journey with Jesus to Jerusalem (§ CXXXIX[9]) shows how selfish their ambitions were. The statement of Peter, recorded in Mark 10[28], "Behold we have left all and followed thee," throws further light upon their motives. Peter's words suggest a natural, universal human question, "What are the advantages to be gained by leaving all and following Jesus' way of thinking and living?" The answer that the Christian church has frequently given in the past is but a reassertion of the Jewish doctrine of rewards: "You shall have a sure title to blessedness in the future life."

Jesus declared that this was one of the results of membership in God's kingdom; but its attainment was by no means the chief goal that he set before his disciples. References to future blessedness are as rare in the earliest records of Jesus' teachings as they are prominent in the later ecclesiastical versions of his utterances. The cruel persecutions which decimated the ranks of the Christians during the second half of the first century led them to contemplate with increasing desire the prospect of rewards beyond the grave. Monasticism and the many forms of asceticism that crept into the church also turned men's attention from society to themselves, from this life to that beyond. Jesus' distinction between things earthly, that is, material, and things heavenly, that is, spiritual, was also transformed into a sharp contrast between the interests of the present life and those after death. Jesus himself recognized no such contrast. He taught that the kingdom of God was both present and future. God is "God not of the dead but of the living." Eternal life begins here and now. Death simply marks a transition, not the end of life. The goal, therefore, which he sets before men was the attainment of full life with God in the present, not merely in a distant future. That life itself is the supreme reward of man's self-denial and effort. It is what he described as entering the kingdom of God. It is on the one side a complete acknowledgment of God's mastery; on the other it is the enjoyment of the multiple gifts which the heavenly Father can and will bestow.

When Peter came to him with the implied question, "What are the rewards for our self-denial and fidelity?" the apostle apparently had in mind material honors and possessions. Jesus' answer, as recorded in Luke 18[29, 30], was: "No man who leaves house or wife or brothers or parents or children for the sake of the kingdom of God without receiving in this time manifold more and in the age to come life eternal." Instead of "for the sake of the kingdom of God," Mark has "for my sake and for the sake of the gospel." He also adds a list of the possessions that come to those who give up all for Jesus' sake. "Brothers and sisters and mothers and children" are, as in Romans 16[14] and I Peter 5[13], the kinsmen in Christ, the members of the larger Christian family. "The houses and fields" are the common possessions which the earlier followers of Jesus shared with each other (Acts 2[44] 4[32]). Possibly the promise of eternal life in the age to come is a later addition to Jesus' original saying. Matthew here vividly illustrates how strong was the influence of the current apocalyptic hopes even upon the evangelists. In the Matthean version of Jesus' reply to Peter the promise of eternal life is expanded into an elaborate apocalyptic prediction:

At the restoration, when the Son of man shall sit on the throne of his glory,
You who have followed me shall also sit on twelve thrones, judging the twelve tribes of Israel.

Back of these later interpretations of Jesus' words lies his bold, paradoxical statement of eternal principles: "He who seems to lose his life shall find it"; he who gives up all through loyalty and love for his divine King shall receive infinitely more. Often in practical experience these manifold things include material possessions and the honors that men confer. Many a man finds that when he ceases to strive selfishly for something, it suddenly comes to him. But Jesus' teachings as a whole, as well as Christian experience, reveal the nature of the manifold things which come to those who adopt his way of living and thinking. They are the permanent, the only altogether satisfactory possessions that man can acquire: the peace and confidence and the perfect physical, mental, and spiritual health which are possible only as a man stands in an honest, trustful, helpful relation to God and his fellow-men. The goal which Jesus set before his followers was emancipation from greed, anger, jealousy, fear, and worry, and the complete and normal development of their divine powers through right thinking and unselfish, efficient service. Not things nor mere rewards, but perfected, divine manhood, with its resulting happiness, is that for which he bids men strive. All nature and history testify that this is the object for which God himself is striving. Jesus, therefore, urges men to become co-workers with God and in the perfecting of themselves and of their fellow-men to find their supreme reward.

III. **The Place of Happiness in Jesus' Teaching.** Too often in its history Christianity has been interpreted as a harsh, gloomy religion. The followers of Jesus have sometimes forgotten that "happy" or "blessed" was one of the words most frequently on his lips. The true happiness of men was the chief aim for which he labored. The author of Matthew emphasizes this fact by placing the beatitudes at the beginning of his major collection of Jesus' teachings. They correspond in certain respects to the decalogue in the Old Testament legal system. In the briefest possible statement they indicate the conditions of real happiness. Their broad significance lies in the fact that they give happiness the central place in his teachings. Like all beatitudes, they are axiomatic. They state not that the gentle and merciful and the peace-maker will ultimately be rewarded by attaining happiness, but that they are already happy. Happiness is the inevitable result of the possession of these qualities. Each beatitude also states the reason why.

Unfortunately, happiness to-day suggests to many minds something selfish and trivial. Puritanism dethroned happiness from the high place Jesus assigned it and gave it largely over to the devil. The result is that the son of the Puritan to-day experiences certain twinges of conscience whenever he is thoroughly happy and unconsciously expects that he will soon be the victim of a corresponding calamity. Jesus taught that to make personal happiness the chief goal of one's endeavor was selfish and suicidal. Also he pointed out the barrenness of many things that are popularly supposed to be sources of happiness. With the vulgar, superficial conceptions of happiness he had no sympathy. The happiness of which he spoke is the fruit of whole-hearted self-denial, sacrifice, and service. It is freedom from the fears, the jealousies, the unsatisfied ambitions that are the foes of happiness.

It is the exuberance that comes from abounding mental, moral, and spiritual health. It is the joy that springs from the sense of perfect adjustment with one's environment, from love and loyalty to God, and from good-will toward men. Jesus was, indeed, "a man of sorrows and acquainted with grief," and yet he maintained and demonstrated in his own life that happiness was the rightful possession of every son of God. Though persecuted and cruelly wronged, he remained the most dauntless optimist the world has ever seen, for he taught men how poverty, hunger, persecution, men's hate, and all the pains of life might be made the stepping-stones on which they might mount to the serene heights of perfect peace and happiness.

IV. **The Original Form of the Beatitudes.** The peculiarities of Matthew and Luke explain the wide variations of the beatitudes and of the four corresponding woes. The first three are:

> Happy you who are poor now!
> For yours is the kingdom of God.
> Happy you who are hungry now!
> For you shall be filled.
> Happy you who are weeping now!
> For you shall laugh.

The mechanical form of the woes indicates that they were probably added by Luke, who had in mind the contrast between the righteous and the wicked in the beatitude which stands as an introduction to the Psalter (*cf.* also Secrets of Enoch 5²). Contrary to Jesus' teaching elsewhere, they condemn unqualifiedly the possession of wealth:

> Woe to you who are rich!
> For you are getting your comfort.
> Woe to you who are satisfied now!
> For you shall hunger.
> Woe to you who laugh now!
> For you shall mourn and weep.

The fourth beatitude in Luke is practically identical with that which the author of Matthew appends to the beatitude:

Happy are they who have been persecuted on account of righteousness!
For theirs is the kingdom of Heaven.

THE ORIGINAL FORM OF THE BEATITUDES

This beatitude is peculiar to Matthew and has the characteristic phrase, "on account of righteousness," which strongly suggests that it is from the author of that gospel. The beatitudes in Luke are all in the second person and were evidently addressed to Jesus' immediate followers. In Matthew they are in the third person and more impersonal. The only exception is the last beatitude, in which the second person appears. The simplicity and directness of Luke's version suggests that in this respect it stands nearer the original. Probably Jesus spoke in the second person; but Luke's version reveals the evangelist's peculiar ideas regarding riches and wealth. The beatitudes in Luke refer to a condition in life, while those in Matthew emphasize, in general, character and acts. The difference, however, is not so great as first appears. The term "the poor" was evidently used by Jesus, as by the psalmists (e. g., Ps. 9¹² 34⁶), not in an economic but in a social sense. They were those of whom the Pharisees say in John 7⁴⁹, "As for this mob, with its ignorance of the law—it is accursed!" They were not necessarily poor in material possessions, but had no social or religious standing in the Jewish community. They were represented by the tax-collector, who went up to the temple with the self-righteous Pharisee. That familiar parable is the best commentary on the meaning of Jesus' paradoxical words. For modern readers Matthew, therefore, gives the truer interpretation of the original intent of these beatitudes.

The other beatitudes peculiar to Matthew are probably from an independent source. Their contents are sufficient proof of their authenticity. The only possible exception is the beatitude which stands third in most texts, but second in others:

> Happy are the meek!
> For they shall inherit the earth.

It is an adaptation of the thought in Psalm 37¹¹:

> The meek shall inherit the earth,
> And shall delight themselves in the abundance of peace.

It is also closely parallel to the first beatitude which it logically follows.

In Matthew the beatitudes are arranged in three groups. The first four refer especially to the character and spirit; the next three to a man's attitude toward society; the last two, which are duplicates, are intended to comfort and encourage Jesus' followers amidst the bitter persecutions that came to them in the years following his death.

Many other beatitudes are found in the gospels (Matt. 11[6] 13[16] 16[17] 24[46] Luke 11[28] 12[37] John 20[29]). Strangely enough, one of the most important has escaped the evangelists. It is recorded in Acts 20[35] in the form: "It makes a man happier to give than to receive" (R. V., "It is more blessed to give than to receive"). According to the analogies in the gospels, the original form of the beatitude was: "Happier they (or you) who give than they (or you) who receive." In the light of Jesus' teachings recorded in Matthew 6[4] we may conjecturally supply the missing member:

> Happier they who give than they who receive!
> For their Father in heaven shall recompense them.

V. The Conditions of True Happiness. The beatitudes are not the beginning but the crown of Jesus' teachings. They also present a marvellous portrait of the great Teacher. They reveal the individual traits which, blended, produced that divine serenity which shone from his face and are reflected in all his words and acts. They are the simple principles by which every son of God may attain the same divine peace and happiness. They involve no mystery except the supreme mystery of God's incarnation in man. They present the goal which mankind is endeavoring to reach by the longer, more tortuous path of scientific investigation and experimentation. They teach that the ultimate sources of happiness are not things nor even achievements, but thoughts and emotions. They assume that it is God's purpose that all men should be perfectly happy and that he has provided the means and the conditions necessary for their happiness. Jesus' message is not for an ideal or impossible world, but for humanity and society as they actually are. Although he spared no effort to banish sorrow and pain, he demonstrated that they were not necessarily hostile to individual happiness.

Each beatitude describes not a distinct class of men, but the essential qualities which must be combined in the same individual to insure perfect happiness. In these eight or nine paradoxes Jesus analyzes the essentials of man's mental and spiritual well-being. The first beatitude emphasizes the receptive attitude. The "poor" stood in contrast to the proud and self-satisfied. The poor in spirit alone possessed the childlike trust and the sense of need that were essential to admission to God's kingdom. They were happy because they enjoyed the privileges of the kingdom. This beatitude was, perhaps, suggested to Jesus by Isaiah 61[1]: "Jehovah hath anointed me to preach good tidings to the poor." The meek and gentle are the unresisting and submissive who, like the poor, figure prominently in the Psalter. The two terms describe slightly different characteristics of the same class. In the original passage (Ps. 37[11]) the meek are those who are submissive to God's will. In the thought of the psalmist, the earth or the land which the meek were to inhabit was probably Palestine, the land of their fathers; but in Jesus' teaching their heritage, as in the first beatitude, was citizenship in God's spiritual kingdom. As in the first beatitude, the happiness of those who mourn was, perhaps, suggested by Isaiah 61. The second and third verses of that immortal chapter state that the supreme task of Jehovah's faithful servant was

> To comfort all who mourn,
> To give them a head-dress instead of ashes,
> Oil of joy instead of a garment of mourning,
> A song of joy instead of a crushed spirit.

The II Isaiah had in mind those who were mourning over their nation's humiliation and guilt. Paul uses the same Greek word to describe those who were mourning over their own sins or the guilt of their fellow-Christians (cf. Rom. 7[24] I Cor. 5[2] II Cor. 12[21]). In the beatitude the mourners are those who are filled with a divine discontent with their own spiritual attainments, as well as with that of their race. When God's rule is fully established in their lives and in the lives of men, they shall be comforted. Luke's version is even stronger: "You shall laugh."

The thought of the fourth beatitude is similar. Luke limits it to physical hunger; but the Matthean form evidently expresses Jesus' thought. It is akin to that of Psalm 107[9]:

> For [Jehovah] satisfieth the longing soul,
> And the hungry soul he filleth with good.

The righteousness of which Jesus speaks is not merely that which comes through conformity to the law, but the personal consciousness of God's approval (cf. also Ps. 37[5, 6]). As in the parable of the tax-collector and the Pharisee praying in the temple, it is the intense longing for God's forgiveness and approval that is essential to happiness. In each of these first four beatitudes Jesus emphasizes the extreme importance of the open, receptive attitude toward God and of that spirit which says "thy will be done," and yet is insistent in the quest for the highest spiritual blessings.

The next three beatitudes describe in concrete terms that loving attitude toward his fellow-men which is essential to the happiness of the individual. "Merciful" includes more than mere forgiveness of others. It means kindliness expressed in helpful acts, as illustrated by the parable of the good Samaritan. Jesus teaches that it is not only a source of joy to the one who has it, but essential, if God is to show mercy to men. Again, while using the popular language, Jesus avoids the mercenary doctrine of rewards: God's merciful attitude is not a reward but an inevitable result.

The same principle is illustrated in the next beatitude. Its setting strongly suggests that when Jesus used the term "pure in heart" he had in mind Psalm 24[3-5]:

> Who shall go up to the hill of Jehovah?
> Who shall stand in his holy place?
> He who has clean hands and a pure heart;
> Who has not lifted up his soul to falsehood,
> And has not sworn deceitfully;
> He shall receive a blessing from Jehovah,
> And righteousness from the God of his salvation.

The purity absolutely essential to happiness is purity of thought, purpose, and act. The sixth beatitude, therefore, has both a religious and a social significance, and embodies a foundation principle in Jesus' teaching. To lead men to "see God face to face" (I Cor. 13[12]), "to see him as he is" (I John 3[2] Rev. 22[4]), was the primary aim in the great Teacher's work. His ethical teachings all have this larger end in view; for greed or anger or an impure thought or motive weakens or destroys the power of spiritual vision. "If thine eye is useless how great is that darkness!"

In the seventh beatitude Jesus reveals his method and the incontestable basis of his own claim to be the Son of God. Both the Greek and the Aramaic word, translated "peace," has a far larger meaning than we ordinarily attribute to it. The corresponding Hebrew word, suggested by such titles as "the Prince of Peace" (Isa. 9[6]), comes from a root which means, to be well, to be whole or complete. The peace-makers are not cowards, who avoid the difficult issues of life, but the whole-makers and the harmony-makers. They are not passive but aggressive and efficient champions of health, wholesomeness, and perfection in all the varied relations of life. Their dominant aim is to bring peace and harmony and completeness into their own life, into that of the family, into the economic world, and into all departments of organized society. Their aims and methods, therefore, are the same as those of God himself. In striving to do the will of God they show their kinship with him, and so win the divine title that Jesus gave them—"the sons of God."

The last beatitude in Matthew, which appears in two versions (Matt. 5[10] and [11, 12]), constitutes a fitting conclusion, for it sets forth that quality of heroic endurance, prompted by loyalty to God, which through the ages has been the crowning mark of Christian knighthood. It is the incontrovertible evidence of citizenship in the kingdom of God. It reveals that Christ-like fearlessness and that complete devotion to the service of God and man which, like the other divine qualities emphasized in the beatitudes, are essential to perfect happiness.

The Christian martyrs throughout the ages have also proved the truth of the all-comprehending beatitude:

Happier they who give than they who receive!

In the laboratory of human experience men are demonstrating by innumerable experiments the absolute truth of this fundamental principle, directly opposed though it is to their ordinary impulses and practices. It is the superlative paradox and yet the logical conclusion of Jesus' revolutionary teachings. Not only does he counsel men to exchange all their material possessions for those things which are spiritual and eternal, but he declares that they shall find real happiness in so doing. Other philosophies and systems of ethics seem superficial and petty beside the teachings of Jesus. Their full acceptance and application represent the narrow way that alone leads to life. He who, with mind open to God's revelation and guidance, lives in accordance with the divine will, eternally craves for himself and others the highest spiritual blessings, heroically and unreservedly labors for the peace and well-being of society and the establishment of God's rule on earth, will not only find for himself real happiness, but will need no other proof that the great Teacher of Nazareth was divine and his message eternally true.

THE CULMINATING EVENTS OF JESUS' LIFE

§ CXXXVII. THE CRISIS IN GALILEE

The
popu-
lar es-
timate
of
Jesus
Luke
9⁷⁻⁹, cf.
Matt.
14¹, 21
Mark
6¹⁴⁻¹⁶)
2. The
feeding
of the
multi-
tude
Mark
6³²⁻⁴⁴,
cf.
Matt.
14¹³⁻²¹
Luke
10ᵇ⁻¹⁷
Mark
3¹⁻¹⁰
Matt.
5²⁹⁻³⁹)

Now when Herod the tetrarch heard of all that was taking place, he was greatly perplexed; for some said, John has risen from the dead, some, Elijah has appeared, and others, One of the old prophets has risen again. Herod said, John I beheaded; but who is this of whom I hear such things? So he sought to see him.

And Jesus and his disciples went off by themselves in a boat to an uninhabited place. But many people saw and recognized them as they were going. And running together on foot from all the cities, they arrived before them. So when Jesus disembarked, he saw a large crowd. And moved with pity for them, because they were like sheep without a shepherd, he began to teach them many things. And as the day was now far advanced, his disciples came to him and said, It is a desert place and it is now late in the day. Send the people away that they may go to the neighboring farms and villages, and buy themselves something to eat. But he answered and said to them, You give them something to eat. And they said to him, Shall we go and spend two hundred denarii upon bread and give them to eat? And he said to them, How many loaves have you? Go and see. And when they knew, they said, Five, and two fishes. Then he commanded them to recline in groups on the green grass. So they lay down in companies, by hundreds and by fifties. And he took the five loaves and the two fishes, and, looking up to heaven, he blessed and broke the loaves in pieces. And he went on giving them to the disciples to set before them. He also divided the two fishes among them all. And they all ate and were satisfied. Also they took up twelve baskets full of fragments of the bread and of the fish. And those who ate the loaves were five thousand men.

Then he immediately made his disciples enter into the boat and go before him to the other side, to Bethsaida, while he himself sent the crowd away. And after taking leave of them, he departed into a mountain to pray. And when evening came the ship was in the midst of the sea, while he was on the land alone. When he saw them distressed as they rowed, for the wind was against them, he came to them about the fourth watch of the night walking in the sea. And he would have passed them. But when they saw him walking in the sea, they imagined that it was an apparition, and cried out. For they all saw him and were troubled. But he immediately spoke with them and said to them, Be of good cheer; it is I, be not afraid. And he went up to them in the boat, and the wind ceased. And they were greatly amazed within themselves.

3. Jesus' meeting with his disciples after a night of danger (Mark 6⁴⁶⁻⁵¹, cf. Matt. 14²²⁻³³)

Now there gathered to Jesus the Pharisees and certain of the scribes, who had come from Jerusalem. And they had observed that some of his disciples ate their food with unclean (that is, with unwashed) hands. For the Pharisees and all the Jews do not eat without washing their hands very thoroughly. Also after coming from the market place they do not eat before taking a bath; and there are many other things which they have been taught that they hold to, such as the washing of cups and pots and brass vessels. And the Pharisees and the scribes asked him, Why do not your disciples do as the early teachers taught, instead of eating their food with unclean hands?

4. The captious question of the Pharisees (Mark 7¹⁻⁵, cf. Luke 11³⁷, ³⁸ Matt. 15¹, ²)

And he said to them, Well did Isaiah prophesy about you hypocrites, as it is written:

5. Jesus' condemnation of their hypocrisy (Mark 7⁶⁻¹³, cf. Matt. 15³⁻⁹ Luke 11³⁹⁻⁴¹)

> This people honoreth me with their lips;
> But their heart is far from me;
> Yet in vain do they worship me,
> Teaching doctrines which are only precepts of men.

Disregarding the command of God, you hold to man's tradition. And he went on to say to them: A fine thing it is for you to set aside God's command, that you may keep your own tradition! For Moses said, 'Honor thy father and thy mother,' and, 'He who speaks evil of father or mother, let him surely die.' But you say, 'If a man says to his father or his mother, "What I might have used to help thee is Korban"' (*i. e.*, given to God), you no longer allow him to do anything for his father or his mother. Thus you set aside the word of God by your tradition, which you have handed down. And you do many such things.

6. The only source of uncleanness (Mark 7¹⁴⁻²³, cf. Matt. 15¹⁰⁻²⁰)

Then calling the crowd to him again, he said to them, Hear me, all of you, and understand:

Nothing can make a man unclean by entering him from outside;
But it is what comes out of a man that makes him unclean.

And when he had gone into the house away from the crowd, his disciples began to question him about the parable. And he said to them, Are you, too, so ignorant? Do you not understand that whatever from outside goes into a man cannot make him unclean? For it goes not into his heart, but into his belly and passes out into the drain. (He thus made all foods clean.) And he said, What issues from man is what makes a man unclean, for out of the heart of man within issue evil thoughts, fornications, thefts, murders, adulteries, coveting, wicked acts, deceit, sensuality, enviousness, slander, pride, foolishness: all these wicked things issue from within and make a man unclean.

7. Jesus' refutation of the charges of the Pharisees (Luke 11¹⁴⁻²⁶, cf. Matt. 12²²⁻³⁰, ⁴³⁻⁴⁵ Mark 3²²⁻²⁷)

And he was casting out a dumb demon. And it came to pass when the demon had gone out, that the dumb man spoke, and the crowds marvelled. But certain of them said, It is with the help of Beelzebub, the ruler of the demons, that he casts out demons. But others, to test him, asked of him a sign from heaven. But he, knowing their thoughts, said to them, Every kingdom divided against itself becomes desolate, and house falls upon house. If Satan is also divided against himself, how shall his kingdom stand? Because you say, 'By Beelzebub I cast out demons.' But if I cast out demons by Beelzebub, by whom do your sons cast them out? Therefore, they themselves shall be your judges. If I, by the finger of God, cast out demons, then the kingdom of God has already reached you. When a mighty man, clad in full armor, guards his own dwelling, his possessions are undisturbed. But when a stronger man comes against him and conquers him, he seizes his full armor, upon which he trusted, and divides his spoils. He who is not with me is against me. And he who gathers not with me, scatters. Whenever the unclean spirit leaves a man, it passes through waterless places in search of rest, and not finding it says, 'I will return to my house, which I left.' And on coming, it finds it swept and in order. Then it goes and takes seven other spirits, more harmful than itself, and entering, there they dwell. And the last state of that man is worse than the first.

Meantime, while the crowd was gathering in thousands, so that they were trampling on one another, he began to say to his disciples, first of all:

8. Words of warning and encouragement to the disciples (Luke 12^{1, 2} Matt. 10²⁷⁻³³, cf. Matt. 10²⁴⁻²⁶ Luke 12³⁻⁹)

Beware of the leaven of the Pharisees, which is hypocrisy.
Nothing is covered up, which shall not be revealed,
Or hidden, which shall not be made known.
What I tell you in the darkness, speak forth in the light;
And what you hear in the ear, proclaim on the housetops.
Then fear not those who kill the body, but are not able to kill the soul;
Rather fear him who is able to destroy both body and soul in Gehenna.
Are not two sparrows sold for a penny?
And yet not one of them shall fall to the ground without your Father.
Yea, and as for you, the hairs of your head are all numbered.
Fear not, then, you are worth more than many sparrows.
Everyone, therefore, who shall confess me before men,
I will also confess him before my Father in heaven;
But whoever shall disown me before men,
I will disown him before my Father who is in heaven.

Everyone, also, who speaks a word against the Son of man shall be forgiven;
But whoever shall speak a word against the Holy Spirit, it shall not be forgiven him.

9. Blasphemy against the Holy Spirit (Luke 12¹⁰), cf Matt. 12^{31, 32}

Then he began to reproach the cities in which most of his mighty deeds had been performed, because they did not

219

10. Lament over the cities that had failed to heed Jesus' words /(Matt. 11 20-24, cf. Luke 10 12-15)

repent: Woe to thee, Chorazin! Woe to thee, Bethsaida! for had the mighty deeds that have been performed in thee been performed in Tyre and Sidon, they would have repented long ago in sackcloth and ashes. Yet I tell you, Tyre and Sidon shall find it more bearable on the day of judgment than you. And thou, Capernaum, shalt thou be exalted to the sky? Thou shalt go down to Hades! For had the mighty deeds performed in thee, been performed in Sodom, it would have remained until this day. Yet I tell you the land of Sodom shall find it more bearable on the day of judgment than thou.

I. The Attitude of Herod Antipas toward Jesus. Jesus' teachings reveal the motives and principles that governed him in the great crisis which came to him during the closing days of his activity. At points his acts and words during these last weeks may have been partially obscured by the later traditions which gathered about them; but the gospels contain certain vivid pictures which make it possible to trace, not only the external course of events, but also Jesus' inner thoughts and purposes.

According to the implications of the context in Mark and Luke, the immediate cause of the suspicion of Herod Antipas was the return of Jesus' disciples from their successful healing and teaching mission. Matthew connects it with Jesus' visit to Nazareth; but Mark 6[14] indicates that it was probably due to the report of Jesus' acts of healing. The passage records the impression his teachings and personality made on the various classes in Galilee and their conceptions of his character and work. The impression that he was the prophet Elijah returned to life was doubtless due to the boldness of his teaching and his fearless attitude toward the leaders of the nation. Others, who knew his spirit and teachings better and interpreted them more truly, compared him with such prophets as Isaiah and Jeremiah. Herod's guilty conscience identified him with that bold herald of righteousness and of the coming kingdom of God, John the Baptist, whom he had beheaded. The passage stands detached in Mark; yet it is plainly intended to explain the radical change in Jesus' field and method of work that now took place. Herod's eager desire to see Jesus was doubtless prompted by more than mere curiosity. His new capital, Tiberias, was but five miles from Capernaum, along the level Roman road that encircled the western side of the Sea of Galilee. He who had imprisoned and beheaded that popular champion of the people, John the Baptist, was a sinister foe. Jesus' later allusion to him as "that fox" indicates that he was well aware of the crafty, treacherous nature of this unprincipled son of Herod the Great. John's work had been done in a remote border of Herod's kingdom; but Jesus, as John's successor, had rallied about him great multitudes in the most populous centres of Galilee. Not only was Herod watching Jesus, but Jesus was doubtless aware of the significance of that surveillance. The news that John had been beheaded was to Jesus the unmistakable sign that the days of his activity in Galilee were limited. Mark 3[6], probably referring to this period, states plainly that the Pharisees, with the Herodians, were planning how they might destroy Jesus. The Herodians were the unprincipled spies and sympathizers connected with the court of Herod Antipas. The situation was perilous, not only for Jesus, but also for his cause. The two strongest forces in Palestine were allied against him. Both were inspired with the jealous fear that his growing authority with the masses would endanger their own. Herod possessed the power, and when he struck, the blow would be sudden, secret, and deadly. There is also reason to believe that the imprisonment or death of Jesus at this stage would have endangered the permanent results of his work. The truth had been scattered broadcast, but it had not yet had time to germinate and bear fruit in loyal, intelligent, efficient discipleship.

II. **The Culmination of Jesus' Popularity.** Two stories are associated with this crisis. Each suggests an important side of Jesus' activity. The first is the account of the feeding of the needy multitudes. It marks the culmination and close of Jesus' work in Galilee, for suddenly the crowds lost their enthusiasm. He himself a little later spoke of his work at Chorazin, Bethsaida, and Capernaum as though it had proved an almost complete failure. A reasonable explanation of this sudden loss of popularity is that the crowds, intent chiefly on physical health and miraculous signs, were dissatisfied with the ethical and spiritual food that he gave. The four gospels have preserved six slightly variant versions of the story. Mark 6 states that the disciples found in the crowd five loaves and two fishes. Mark 8 speaks of seven loaves and a few small fishes. According to Mark 6, the crowds had been with Jesus one day; but Mark 8 states that they had been with him three days. According to Mark 6, five thousand were fed and twelve baskets full of food were gathered after the feast; Mark 8 records that four thousand were present and seven baskets full were collected. The two versions can scarcely refer to distinct events, for

the words of the disciples in Mark 8⁴, "Where can men get bread to satisfy these men here in a deserted place?" indicate that they were ignorant of any previous miraculous feeding of the multitudes. Mark 8¹⁴⁻²¹ (Matt. 16⁶) contains an illustration of the way in which even Jesus' disciples interpreted with misleading literalness one of the many luminous figures of speech which he so often employed in his teachings. When Jesus told them to beware of the leaven of the Pharisees and Herod, they understood him to be speaking of material bread. Jesus' words in Matthew 16¹¹ may throw light on the popular accounts of his feeding of the multitudes: "How is it you do not understand? I did not speak to you about bread." In connection with its account of the feeding of the crowds, the Fourth Gospel has possibly preserved an echo of the words of Jesus which lie at the basis of the familiar story: "Work not for the food which perishes, but for the food which abides until eternal life, which the Son of man will give you. I am the bread of life; he who comes to me shall not hunger" (John 6²⁷, ³⁵ᵃ).

To this critical period also belongs the vivid description of the disciples' heroic all-night struggle against the head winds and waves. It reveals not only Jesus' love, but his constant solicitude for them. It is not entirely clear what facts underlie the variant accounts of this incident. The simplest explanation of the later versions is that the Greek translators transcribed the original Aramaic preposition, which meant either *in* or *on* (*cf.*, *e. g*, Dan. 3¹, ²⁵, ²⁷, where it has both meanings), so that an original account of how Jesus, in the blackness of the night, waded out to meet his disciples has been unintentionally clothed with a miraculous splendor. The Fourth Gospel adds the definite statement that just as Jesus met his disciples they reached the land. In any case it records an important incident in the experience of that heroic brotherhood which Jesus built up about him. Mark may have introduced the story here because of its deeper significance. For Jesus, as well as for his disciples, this was a period of seemingly hopeless struggle against overwhelming opposition. Doubts and fears were beginning to sweep over them. These fears assailed Jesus; but his absolute trust in the wisdom and goodness of God brought peace to them, as well as to him, for his words, "Be of good cheer. It is I; be not afraid," gave them confidence even in the wildest storm.

III. **The Grounds on Which Jesus Condemned the Scribes and Pharisees.** During his early work in Galilee Jesus carefully avoided a breach with the Pharisees and the scribal interpreters of the Jewish law. As a youth, he undoubtedly shared the popular respect and veneration for them. His references to them in his early parables, as, for example, the father's words to the elder brother in the parable of the prodigal son, were always courteous and conciliatory. He recognized that there was much that was good in their character and work. But the radical nature of his teachings and the success of his work in Galilee had, in time, transformed their critical attitude into active opposition. It is not clear whether or not "the Pharisees and certain of the scribes who had come from Jerusalem," mentioned in Mark 6³¹, had been officially sent by the sanhedrin to investigate the teachings of this new and famous rabbi. It is probable that they had, although their presence may have been due to some other cause. It is evident from the incidental references in the gospels that Jesus' activity had already made a deep impression upon the people of Palestine. In the palace at Tiberias, as well as in the humblest homes of Galilee, his deeds were the common subjects of report and discussion. The question which the pharisaic scribes propounded to him suggests that they came as inquisitors. It raised at once the main issue between them and the new teacher. It was more than a question; it was a charge against him: "Why do not your disciples do as the earlier teachers taught, instead of eating their food with their hands ceremonially unclean?" Jesus met the issue squarely, and yet he appears to have reserved for the closing days of his activity his final scathing denunciation of these "blind leaders of the blind" (*cf.* § CXLⱽ). According to Mark, Jesus at this time first applied to them the word hypocrite. In its earlier usage the word did not have its modern malign meaning. In the classical Greek it means (1) an interpreter, or expounder, and (2) one who plays a part. Its secondary meaning is dissembler, or pretender. By the use of this word, as well as those which follow, Jesus transferred the attack from himself to the Pharisees. In substance he declared: "These detailed ceremonial laws, which you regard as all-important, are not the essential teachings of the older scriptures. They are but the precepts and traditions of the later scribes; yet you place the chief emphasis upon them. In so doing you disregard the spirit and intent of the older law. Moses, for example, made the obligation of the child to the parent of primary importance; yet you teach your disciples that it is more important to bring gifts to the temple than to give to their parents that assistance which is their due." The principle involved had been discussed for ages by prophet and priest. It concerned the relative importance of deeds and character on the one hand, and of ceremonial worship on the other. Jesus allied himself unequivocally with the prophets. He knew how important was the issue and how difficult it was to make a permanent impression upon the minds of the scribes and Pharisees in his audience. Therefore, he appealed to the crowd in the hope that they, less blinded, would see the truth. The words with which he addressed them recall also the voice of the ancient prophets: "Hear me, all of you, and understand" (cf., e. g., Micah 1²). In conclusion he gathered up the entire discussion in one of the broad generalizations which characterize his teachings:

Nothing can make a man unclean by entering him from outside;
But it is what comes out of a man that makes him unclean.

In answer to the questions of his disciples, he made clear the meaning of this principle which, with one stroke, swept away that vast, cumbersome body of laws which represented, to a great extent, contemporary pharisaic Judaism. "The food," he explained, "which a man takes into his mouth, and which affects only the physical side of his nature, has no moral or religious significance. It does not touch the heart. The thoughts in a man's mind and the acts prompted by them are the only things that can make him unclean."

Mark, in the dislocated passage 3²²⁻³⁰, and Matthew, in 12²⁴, place the charge that Jesus cast out demons by the help of Beelzebub in the mouth of the pharisaic scribes, but Luke attributes them to certain men who spoke for the crowd. The name Beelzebub was a popular and contemptuous designation of Satan. The original form, Baalzebul (literally, master of the dwelling, that is, of heaven, the dwelling of the gods), had been transformed by a slight change into the vulgar epithet, "Master of the dung-heap." The logic of Jesus' reply was incontrovertible. In essence he declared, "The character of my deeds shows which Lord I serve." The standard by which he proposed they test his theology was not theoretical but pragmatic.

IV. Jesus' Warnings to His Disciples. The open attacks of the pharisaic scribes evidently made a deep impression upon the crowds that hitherto had gathered about Jesus. Luke 12¹ implies that the people still followed him in even greater numbers; but there were indications that their enthusiasm was changing to suspicion. The logic and authority of the scribes appealed to their life-long training and to their deep veneration for the traditions of their race. Independence of thought and action are far more unusual among orientals

than among occidentals. The earlier prophets had rarely carried their
audiences with them. Jesus turned, henceforth, from the masses to his
disciples, and appealed to their reason, to their courage, to their personal
devotion to him, and, above all, to that unfaltering faith in the divine
Father which he had endeavored to inculcate. His words regarding
the "leaven of the Pharisees" are those of a shepherd defending his
sheep from wolves disguised as shepherds. The figure of leaven was
well chosen. It was hidden, pervasive, contagious, and transforming.
It suggests the shrug of the shoulder, the sarcastic question, the poi-
sonous libel whereby these now sworn foes of Jesus endeavored to destroy the effect of his work with the people.

Jesus' words to his disciples, as recorded in Matthew 10$^{26-33}$, contain
echoes of much that he had taught them before. They suggest the
struggles and the victory of faith in his own soul. They represent
the principles which he had earlier proclaimed in process of practical
demonstration. Luke has transformed Jesus' glorious promise that,

> Every one who shall confess me before men,
> I will also confess him before my Father which is in heaven,

into a form more in keeping with the thought and expectations of the
later church:

> Every one who shall confess me before men,
> Him shall the Son of man also confess before the angels of God.

Luke is probably right, however, in introducing here the words regarding blasphemy against the Holy Spirit which have proved a fertile
source of discussion in the Christian church. They are significant because they reveal Jesus' natural humility and his inclination to place
his own personality in the background. At the same time they testify
to his profound appreciation of the importance and divine authority
of his teachings. He appears to have had in mind primarily the hypocritical Pharisees and the pernicious leaven which they were dissem-
inating. Their unjust attacks against him were forgivable, but their
defiant and persistent refusal to listen to the spirit of God, the Holy
One, speaking through Jesus and revealed in the deeds which he was
performing, was unforgivable. The malicious libel, "He has Beelzebub," revealed to Jesus their attitude and called forth his warning
protest. It was directly contrary to his most profound and sacred
conviction that his power and message were not his own but had been
given him from above. Nothing was so well calculated to stir his

deepest and holiest indignation as the assertion that the power which worked in him was not divine but devilish. These words also revealed the perilous tendency in the minds of the Pharisees to stifle their deeper convictions and to close their ears to truth. The misuse of their spiritual organs meant that they would be gradually atrophied so that they were in danger of becoming incapable of seeking or of receiving that forgiveness which God is ever ready to give to every truly penitent sinner. Jesus nowhere specifies any who had committed the unpardonable sin, but, being a profound and sympathetic student of human character, he saw the danger that, as in the case of the Pharisees, deliberate and repeated rejection of the truth would crystallize into a habitual attitude of mind which would render a man incapable of true repentance and destroy his ability to ask or receive God's forgiveness.

V. The Influence of This Crisis upon Jesus' Method of Work. In many ways this crisis in Jesus' work in Galilee was the greatest tragedy in his life. At the moment of apparent success he was compelled suddenly to give up his work and to flee for his life beyond the bounds of Galilee. Luke 13[31] states one, possibly the chief, reason for Jesus' departure. It was because Herod intended to kill him. He departed, therefore, not merely to save his own life, but also his cause. His departure at this time proves that he was no blind enthusiast who courted death, as some have interpreted him, but that each of his acts was determined by a deliberate purpose. The other reason for his departure was the changed attitude of the people. Jesus' words concerning the cities of Chorazin, Bethsaida, and Capernaum, the scenes of his chief activity, reveal the bitter sense of disappointment and failure that came to him at this time. In Matthew his words stand detached from their context. Luke, because of the mention of Sodom, connects them with Jesus' reference to the Sodomites in his charge to his disciples. These words come from the earliest teaching source (Q). They were, perhaps, uttered by Jesus as he set out with his disciples along the northern road which led from Capernaum through Chorazin to the territory of Tyre and Sidon on the north. The heights near the inland town of Chorazin commanded a view of the rocky glen that led southward to Capernaum, two miles away. Over the hills to the southeast was Bethsaida, and beyond were the quiet uplands where he had frequently taken refuge with his disciples. Before him on the south lay the blue waters of the Sea of Galilee, and to the southwest the hills where he had often gone for quiet prayer and meditation. Even to-day, in its utter loneliness, it is one of the most beautiful scenes in all Galilee. The hush that has fallen upon this region vividly recalls the sad woes pronounced upon those populous cities which are now but deserted ruins. So complete is their desolation that their identification until the present has been a matter of much dispute.

Before him as his objective lay the territory of Tyre and Sidon. These typical heathen cities probably suggested to him the comparison which he drew between them and the three strongly Jewish cities which for months had witnessed his acts of healing and listened to the simple, life-giving truths which he had proclaimed. It was not a curse which Jesus pronounced upon these scenes of his activity; it was rather a statement of fact put in the characteristic oriental form of a lament. A great opportunity had come to their citizens, but most of them had rejected it. Jesus had longed and labored to lay in these favored centres the corner-stone of God's kingdom on earth. He had sought to banish from their streets all pain and ignorance and sin. He had yearned to teach young and old alike how they might find that peace and joy and fulness of life which he knew would be theirs if they would but turn from their sins and follies and learn to love and serve their heavenly Father with all their powers and their neighbors as themselves. Here he had hoped to found a perfect community. Jesus' words reveal the intensity of his desire to realize this ideal and his tragic sense of failure.

Apparently only once, and possibly only for a few hours, did he return to Capernaum. His task from this time on was to perfect the training and the faith of the few who were loyal to him. In accomplishing this task, private conversation takes the place of public address. Deliberate choice, as well as necessity, led him to seek for this new work a quiet field beyond the authority of Herod Antipas where the leaven of the Pharisees could not permeate. This place of temporary refuge was found among the lofty hills of upper Galilee, in closest touch with the land and people whom Jesus loved, but out of reach of his foes.

§ CXXXVIII. JESUS IN RETIREMENT WITH HIS DISCIPLES

Then Jesus arose and went away into the territory of Tyre. And going into a house, he wished no one to know of it. Yet he could not escape notice. But at once a woman, whose little daughter had an unclean spirit, when she heard of him, came and fell down at his feet. Now the woman was a Greek by faith and a Syro-phœnician by race. And she

1.
Jesus and the Syro-Phœnician woman
(Mark 7[24-30]
cf. Mt. 15[21-28])

227

begged him to cast the demon out of her daughter. But he kept saying to her, Let the children be satisfied first, for it is not fair to take the children's bread and throw it to the dogs. But she answered and said to him, True, sir, yet the little dogs under the table eat the children's crumbs. And he said to her, For this saying go thy way. The demon has gone out of your daughter. And on returning home she found the child lying on the bed and the demon gone from her.

2. Healing of a blind man (Mark 7³¹ 8²²⁻²⁶, cf. 7³²⁻³⁷)

Then once more he left the territory of Tyre and went through Sidon to the Sea of Galilee, through the middle of the district of Decapolis. And he with his disciples came to Bethsaida. And the people bring him a blind man and beseech Jesus to touch him. And he took hold of the blind man's hand and brought him out of the village. And after spitting upon his eyes and laying his hands upon them, he asked him, Dost thou see anything? And he looked up and said, I behold people. I see them walking like trees. Then Jesus laid his hands once more upon the man's eyes, and he looked intently and was restored, and began to distinguish everything clearly. And he sent him away to his home, saying, Do not even enter the village.

3. Peter's declaration (Mark 8²⁷⁻³⁰, cf. Matt. 16¹³⁻²⁰ Luke 9¹⁸⁻²⁰)

Then Jesus went away with his disciples to the village of Cæsarea Philippi. And on the way he asked his disciples, saying to them, Who do people say that I am? And they told him, 'John the Baptist'; others say, 'Elijah,' but others, 'One of the prophets.' And he asked them, But you—who do you say that I am? Peter answering, said to him, Thou art the Christ. And he kept charging them to tell no one about him.

4. Jesus' first intimation of the danger that he faced (Mark 8³¹⁻³³, cf. Matt. 16²¹⁻²² Luke 9²¹, ²²)

And he began to teach them that the Son of man must suffer many things, and be rejected by the elders, and the high priests, and the scribes, and be killed, and after three days rise again. And he made the statement openly. Then Peter took him and began to rebuke him. But Jesus turned and on seeing his disciples, he rebuked Peter, saying, Get thou behind me, Satan, for thou art not thinking the thoughts of God, but of men.

Then he called the crowd to him with his disciples, and said to them:

If any man will come after me,
Let him deny himself, take up the cross, and follow me.
For whoever would save his life shall lose it;
And whoever shall lose his life for my sake and the gospel's
shall save it.
For what use is it for a man to gain the whole world and
forfeit his life?
For what could a man give in exchange for his life?
For whoever is ashamed of me and my words in this adul-
terous and sinful generation,
The Son of man shall also be ashamed of him, when he
comes in the glory of his Father with the holy angels.

And he said to them, I tell you truly, There are some of those
standing here who shall not taste death until they see the
coming of the kingdom of God with power.

Now after six days Jesus took Peter and James and John
apart and brought them up to a high mountain privately,
alone. And he was transformed before them; and his garments glistened with an exceeding whiteness, as no fuller
on earth can whiten them. And Elijah, together with Moses,
appeared to them, and they were talking with Jesus. Then
Peter, interrupting, said to Jesus, Rabbi, it is well for us to
be here. Now let us make three booths, one for thee, and
one for Moses, and one for Elijah. For he did not know
what to say; for they were greatly frightened. And a cloud
came overshadowing him and there was a voice from the
cloud, This is my son, the beloved; hear him. And suddenly, on looking round, they no longer saw anyone, except
Jesus alone with themselves.

And as they were coming down from the mountain, he
charged them not to tell anyone what they had seen until
after the Son of man should have arisen from the dead.
And they kept the saying, discussing among themselves
what the arising from the dead meant. And they went on
to question him, saying, How is it that the scribes say,
'Elijah must first come.' And he said to them, Elijah indeed comes first and restores all things. And yet how is it
written regarding the Son of man, that he is to suffer much
and be despised? But I tell you, Elijah has really come

5. The cost and reward of fidelity to him (Mark 8³⁴⁻⁹¹, cf. Matt. 16²⁴⁻²⁸ Luke 9²³⁻²⁷)

6. The transfiguration (Mark 9²⁻⁸, cf Matt. 17¹⁻⁷ Luke 9²⁸⁻³⁶)

7. Relation of Jesus' work to earlier prophecy (Mark 9⁹⁻¹³, cf. Matt. 17⁹⁻¹³)

229

and they have done to him even as they pleased, even as it is written of him.

8. Healing of an epileptic boy by Jesus (Mark 9¹⁴⁻²⁹, cf. Matt. 17¹⁴⁻²⁰ Luke 9³⁷⁻⁴³ᵃ)

And when they came to the disciples, they saw a large crowd about them and the scribes discussing with them. And on seeing him, all the crowd were immediately astounded, and running to him, saluted him. And he asked them, What are you discussing with them? And one of the crowd answered him, Teacher, I have brought thee my son, who has a dumb spirit. And whenever it seizes him, it hurls him down and he foams and grinds his teeth. And he is pining away. And I told thy disciples to cast it out, but they were not able. Then Jesus answered them and said, O unbelieving generation! How long shall I be with you? How long shall I bear with you? Bring him to me. And they brought him to him. But on seeing him, the spirit at once threw him into convulsions, and throwing him to the ground, he rolled about, foaming. And Jesus asked the father, How long is it since this has come upon him? And he said, From childhood; and many a time it has thrown him both into fire and into water, to destroy him. But if thou canst do anything, have pity on us and help us. And Jesus said to him, 'If thou canst!' All things are possible for him who believes. Immediately the father of the child cried out and said, I do believe; help mine unbelief! Now when Jesus saw that the crowd came running together, he rebuked the unclean spirit, saying to it, Thou dumb and deaf spirit, I command thee, leave him and never enter him again. Then after crying and throwing him into a great convulsion, it came out. And the boy became as a corpse, so that many said, He is dead. But Jesus took him by the hand and raised him. And he arose. And when Jesus went into the house, his disciples began to question him in private, How is it that we could not cast it out? And he said to them, This kind can come out by nothing except prayer.

9. Second intimation of his death (Mark 9³⁰⁻³², cf. Matt. 17²², ²³ Luke 9⁴³ᵇ ⁴⁵)

Then they departed from there and passed through Galilee. Yet he wished no one to know it, for he was teaching his disciples, and telling them, The Son of man will be delivered up into the hands of men and they shall kill him, but when he is killed he shall rise again, after three days.

230

But they did not understand the saying and they were afraid to question him.

I. The Request of the Syro=Phœnician Woman.

Jesus always avoided the large Gentile cities. There is no evidence that in his quest for a place of refuge and quiet with his disciples he even approached the cities of Tyre and Sidon. According to Josephus (*Jew. War*, 3^{38}), the territory of Tyre extended eastward across the foot-hills of the Lebanons, so that it constituted the northern boundary of Galilee. Mark distinctly states that Jesus passed over this northern border into the territory of Tyre. Here, among the elevated plateaus that lead up to the Lebanons, he was still in the midst of a largely Jewish population. At the same time he here came into closer contact with the Gentile world than in any other period in his activity. Mark, followed by Matthew, has at this point recorded an exceedingly significant incident in the life of Jesus. Once before (as recorded in Matt. 8^{5-10}) a centurion, representing that outer world, had come to Jesus with a request that had been readily granted. Now Jesus was again met with a similar request. According to Mark 3^8, news of Jesus' power to heal had, at an earlier period, penetrated the Galilean hills, so that people, even from the territory of Tyre and Sidon, had come to be healed by him. His reputation as a healer now brought to him a woman of that mixed race and faith which had resulted from the conquests of Alexander the Great and of the Greek culture which he brought with him. Matthew describes her as a Canaanite, and undoubtedly the blood of the ancient Canaanites ran in her veins. By faith she was a Greek, probably worshipping the old Semitic gods under their Greek names. She represented, therefore, that type of heathen which was most hateful and repulsive to the Jew. There was ample grounds for this feeling, for that gross immorality which had characterized the Canaanite race and religion from its earlier days had only been intensified by its contact with the degenerate Greek civilization.

Matthew's version of the incident emphasizes the woman's faith; Mark's purpose is to illustrate Jesus' attitude toward the heathen. In Matthew Jesus replies to the woman, "I was only sent to the lost sheep of the house of Israel." While this may possibly be the original form of the statement, it is probably due to the tendency of the author of the First Gospel to emphasize the fact that at first Jesus' mission was solely to the Jews. It is parallel to the command, found only in Matthew, that the disciples on their mission were to go simply to the house of Israel and were to avoid the cities of the Gentiles. The same thought, however, underlies Jesus' words in the Marcan version. As they stand they seem harsh and repellent; and yet, as the narrative indicates, there must have been something in Jesus' tone or face that encouraged the woman to persist in her request. His words may reflect the painful experiences, still fresh in his memory, of his rejection by his own people. It is possible that he here formulates the narrow Jewish attitude toward all foreigners because he himself is beginning to question its validity. Mark is probably right in interpreting this incident as another important turning-point in Jesus' life. Should he give the food which the children had rejected to the heathen dogs? The Greek has probably reproduced the original word, which gave the woman a basis for hope and which she used effectively in attaining the end which she desired. The ordinary dog of Palestine is simply a scavenger, an outcast without an owner. The term which Jesus used, however, in describing the woman and her class means puppies or lapdogs, which enjoyed very much the same care and attention as do pet dogs to-day. They were not only tolerated at banquets, but were frequently fed with dainties. It was this privilege, therefore, which she claimed. Jesus evidently granted her request, not merely because of her quickness of wit, but because he was prompted to do so both by his sympathy and judgment. In so doing he set an example to his disciples which at first they were slow to follow, but which has become in time the inspiration of that missionary movement which is Christianizing the world.

There was evidently great uncertainty in the minds of the evangelists regarding the order and nature of events during Jesus' period of retirement. Mark has introduced, immediately after the story of the Syro-Phœnician woman, an account of the healing of the deaf mute. It is apparently a duplicate of an equally detailed account of the healing of the blind man at Bethsaida, found in Mark 8$^{22-26}$. The language of these sections differs from the ordinary New Testament Greek and is very similar to that used in the Septuagint. There is strong evidence that Mark had in mind such passages as that in Isaiah 29^{18}, "In that day shall the deaf hear the words of the book, and the eyes of the blind shall see out of obscurity and out of darkness." Certain scholars hold that both narratives are but variants of Matthew 12^{22}: "Then they brought to him a man with a demon, who was both blind and dumb, and he healed him so that the dumb man both spoke and saw." Of the two narratives, that in Mark 8$^{22-26}$ is the more detailed. The scene is

Bethsaida, east of the Jordan. The setting to which Mark has assigned it implies that Jesus had returned from the territory of Tyre. He probably passed down the eastern side of the Jordan, where he would still be outside the territory of Herod Antipas, to Bethsaida, the home of certain of his disciples. Possibly the account of the healing of the blind man is simply symbolic and represents the blind Pharisees to whom Jesus frequently refers. The details, however, strongly suggest a definite incident in Jesus' healing work. Certain simple therapeutic methods, which he employed to aid the man's faith, are also described. The story also indicates that certain of Jesus' cures were gradual rather than immediate.

II. Peter's Confession. By far the most important incident that occurred during Jesus' period of retirement is the confession which he drew from his disciples. It is told so simply and briefly in Mark that its import is easily overlooked. Matthew has transformed and expanded it in accordance with the experiences and beliefs of the later church. In the original narrative, Peter is condemned by Jesus because of his failure to appreciate the spiritual character of the Messiah's work, but in Matthew's account he is unqualifiedly commended. He is the rock upon which Jesus is to build his church, against which the gates of Hades shall not prevail. To him are given the keys of the kingdom of Heaven, which in Luke are intrusted to the disciples as a whole. Luke, like Mark, knows nothing of the later expansion of the Petrine tradition, and the oldest gospel leaves no place for it. A comparison of these variants well illustrates one of the marked tendencies of the Gospel of Matthew.

Jesus' question to his disciples was the culmination of a long period of training. The experiences of the preceding weeks had prepared them for it. The crisis in Galilee had brought to the front certain traits in his character and in his interpretation of his mission which it was essential that they should know before they could fully appreciate his ideals. Hitherto they had known him only as the personal friend, the popular hero, and the faithful teacher. Now he was a fugitive, discredited by the religious leaders of the nation and rejected by a majority of the people. Now they knew him, too, undaunted by failure. Their loyalty to him was demonstrated by the fact that they followed him in his retreat. What men said about him was of interest to Jesus; but far more important was their answer to the intimate question: "Who do you say that I am?" Interpreted in its historical setting, Peter's reply in behalf of the disciples possessed a far greater significance than it would have had in the prosperous days in Galilee.

It is difficult to determine exactly what Peter's words, "Thou art the Messiah," meant to him. Doubtless Peter himself would have had difficulty in interpreting them. At least it did mean, "We regard you as the fulfilment of Israel's highest hopes." Peter, in common with the other disciples, still retained many of the ideas that entered into the popular expectation regarding the Messiah. The later requests of James and John indicate that they hoped soon to see Jesus seated on a heavenly throne, if not on the restored throne of David at Jerusalem. Having associated closely with Jesus and having listened to his teachings, they were not wholly oblivious to the spiritual elements in their master's conception of the task of the Messiah; and yet it was only through hard and painful experiences that they could be led to appreciate and accept it fully. Hence, the reason is obvious why Jesus enjoined upon them the same silence regarding his messianic character that he himself had hitherto so strictly observed.

III. **Jesus' First Prediction of His Passion.** Did Jesus, at this period, definitely predict the fate that awaited him at Jerusalem, or are the repeated predictions found in the gospels simply due to the tendency to read back later history into this earlier setting? This question has been answered both "yes" and "no." A third alternative is possible. Did he, during these days of retirement, interpret to his disciples the unmistakable meaning of the crisis which confronted him, and intimate to them that he was considering a course of action which would, according to all probability, lead to a practically inevitable result? The latter seems to be the intent of the earliest gospel records. Jesus never claimed to be a seer (*e. g.*, Mark 13³²). He declared plainly that "no one knows the future except God alone." At the same time the meaning of the situation which had developed was clear. To continue his work in Galilee was impossible, for it meant the increased opposition of the Pharisees and probably imprisonment and death at the hands of Herod. To seek permanent refuge in a foreign land meant inevitable failure and disgrace, for it was equivalent to abandoning his ideals and followers. His temporary retirement was that he might meditate upon the situation and prepare his disciples for the greater crisis that impended. To perform his mission he must face Israel's leaders, declare himself at Jerusalem, and, if need be, die for the truth which he proclaimed. Gradually these facts had forced themselves upon the mind of Jesus. His lament over Chorazin, Bethsaida, and Capernaum, and, later, over Jerusalem, leave no doubt that he had ardently hoped that the outcome would be different. His prayer in Gethsemane shows beyond doubt that he at times prayed that he might not be obliged to drink the bitter cup of suffering and seeming failure; but as a careful student of the II Isaiah and of the larger book of life, he recognized that the way in which the servant of Jehovah was to perform his task was the way of seeming shame and of patient suffering and of complete self-sacrifice. It is clear, therefore, that his question to his disciples was intended to precipitate their opinions and prepare them for the probable fate which awaited him. In their original form the words which followed may have been but an assertion that if the Son of man goes up to Jerusalem he must suffer many things. The details of the prediction now found in the gospels are, without reasonable doubt, due to the evangelists, who were familiar with the subsequent events, for that familiarity could not fail to color their narratives.

The statement that Peter took Jesus aside and began to rebuke him is consistent with the situation. The intensity of Jesus' feeling is shown by his quick response to Peter. In the reproaches of his most enthusiastic followers Jesus recognized a temptation similar to that which came to him when he earlier decided the nature and methods of his mission. The exact words of Jesus at this critical moment were probably impressed upon the mind of Peter, so that they are reproduced verbatim in Mark's realistic record, "Get thee behind me, Satan, for thou art not thinking the thoughts of God, but of men." These words still further reveal Jesus' interpretation of the task of the Messiah. He was fully aware of the sharp antithesis between the thoughts and expectations of men and those of God. The words which follow have the poetic form (rare in Mark) in which Jesus usually expressed his fundamental teachings. They vividly recall the ideal of the II Isaiah and embody the essence of Jesus' teaching. It is only by losing his life to proclaim the good tidings that a man can make his life count for the most. This revolutionary truth, so far removed from ordinary human practice, was evidently at this time uppermost in Jesus' mind. It guided him in the great crisis which confronted him, and as he meditated on the way in which he could in the trying circumstances serve God most effectively. His chief solicitude was for his disciples. If he could but bring them to his point of view and lead them fully to accept his ideals, no seeming shame nor calamity could prevent the realization of his divine mission. His absolute faith in God left no doubt in his mind regarding the ultimate results of his work. As a keen student of history and of men, he knew that the more violent and unjust the opposition, the sooner and more inevitable the reaction.

His sure conviction that God would soon vindicate the right is clearly the basis of the promise, also attested by Paul's words in I Thessalonians 4[17] and Philippians 3[21]: "Some of those standing here shall not taste death until they see the kingdom of God coming with power." In this, the oldest form of the saying, Jesus did not speak of his own coming, but of the establishment of God's rule. His followers, however, soon transformed it, as they did many other of his teachings regarding the coming of the kingdom, into a prediction that the Son of man would himself come again to establish by supernatural means his reign upon earth. Another illustration of this tendency is found in the preceding verse in Matthew, where Jesus' original utterance, already quoted:

> Whoever shall disown me before men,
> I will disown him before my Father which is in heaven,

is transformed into the apocalyptic statement:

> Whoever is ashamed of me and my words in this adulterous and sinful
>   generation,
> The Son of man shall also be ashamed of him, when he comes in the
>   glory of his Father with the holy angels.

In the complete overthrow of the temple, the central stronghold of Judaism, in the heroic loyalty of Jesus' followers, and in the marvellous growth of the early church many who listened to Jesus' words, indeed, saw the "coming of the kingdom of God with power."

IV. **The Story of the Transfiguration.** No narrative in the gospel is beset with more difficulties and more differently interpreted than the story of the transfiguration. Some interpreters regard it as simply another version of the preceding account of Peter's confession. Others find in it only a creation of the faith of the later church. In the recently discovered fragments of the Revelation of Peter it apparently followed the account of Jesus' resurrection. If it is the oft-mentioned but otherwise lost account of Jesus' resurrection appearance to Peter, the interpretation of the story in its present form in Mark would be simplified, for students have long recognized the difficulty of reconciling a revelation, in its present form and setting so marvellous and unmistakable, with the misunderstanding and infidelity of the disciples recorded in the succeeding chapters. Emotional and changeable though Peter was, it is almost incredible that he could have openly denied

THE STORY OF THE TRANSFIGURATION

Jesus only a few days later if he had, with his physical eyes, seen him walking with Moses and Elias and heard with his ears the voice of God proclaiming Jesus' divine sonship and authority. Scholars have also noted the many analogies with the earlier account of the revelation to Moses at Sinai. As the skin of Moses' face shone as he came down from the sacred mount, so, according to Mark, Jesus' garments appeared to be glistening white. As at Sinai, a cloud overshadowed the mountain. According to the Syriac version, which has probably preserved the Marcan original, this cloud rested not upon the disciples, but upon Jesus. As at Sinai, God was represented as speaking audibly.

Luke gives certain important details which suggest his own interpretation of the story. He states that it was while Jesus was praying that the appearance of his face was changed; also that Peter and the other two disciples, who were with Jesus, were overpowered with sleep. This fact is implied by Peter's confused words recorded in the Marcan version. The gospel narratives all indicate that Peter, and probably the two other disciples, failed at the time to understand the full import of the transfiguration. Apparently they, as well as the evangelists, attempted to interpret it, as was natural, by the aid of older analogies and in the light of Jesus' resurrection and of their own maturer thought and experiences.

Like the baptism and the temptation, Jesus' transfiguration was primarily of significance to himself. Its background is his rejection by the multitudes in Galilee, the malignant attacks of the Pharisees, and the ominous suspicions of Herod. In the foreground is his proposed journey to Jerusalem and the perils and probably death which he could see there awaited him. The intensity of the struggle in his mind was revealed by his tense question addressed to the disciples and his almost passionate reply to Peter's protest, which tempted him to turn aside from the path that led to practically inevitable martyrdom. The transfiguration was the visible evidence of the crowning victory won on the quiet mountain height. Apparently the necessity for the supreme act of self-sacrifice had gradually dawned on Jesus' consciousness. It would seem that while the conflict still raged within him he endeavored to present the problem to his disciples; but they proved of little help. Out of the larger group he singled the three who stood closest to him that they might be with him; but the ultimate decision rested with him alone.

Luke, with his usual keen insight, indicates that prayer was the immediate setting of Jesus' transfiguration. The radiance which filled his face was not merely the peace and joy of victory won, but the reflection of the very face of God himself and the visible evidence of his approval. It was the same divine radiance that so illumined and transformed the face of Moses that to those who looked upon him his very skin seemed to shine. Sometimes, in lesser measure, at moments of great decision and victory, even to-day the light of God's presence shines through the faces of Jesus' followers and discloses the divine radiance that transfigures them. Even the obtuse disciples could not but at once vaguely realize that they stood in the presence of God. Their later experience and meditation also aided them greatly in interpreting the truer and larger significance of that which they at first had only dimly understood. Jesus' decision, like the revelation to Moses at Sinai and through Elijah to the people on Mount Carmel, was one of the great focal points in human history when, through the heart of his willing child, the eternal Father revealed in large measure his gracious purpose for mankind. Henceforth, Jesus quietly, unflinchingly faced danger, public shame, and death, for from his soul there never faded the radiance of the transfiguration.

Luke omits the conversation between Jesus and his disciples regarding the second coming of Elijah. This current Jewish hope was based on the prediction in Malachi 4⁴. While Jesus practically assented to the conclusion that John, through his reformatory work, had fulfilled the spirit of that early prediction, he turned the attention of his disciples to the more significant prediction in Isaiah 53 that the true Messiah must suffer and be despised. It is evident that his disciples only partially realized the meaning of Jesus' significant words during these days of quiet training. His purpose is obvious. With all his skill as a teacher, he was endeavoring to adjust his followers to the new situation and to give them a true appreciation of the real task of the Messiah and of the way in which that task must be accomplished.

V. The Healing of an Epileptic. The three synoptic gospels agree in assigning the story of the healing of an epileptic to a place immediately after the account of the transfiguration, although the content of the narrative suggests a Galilean environment. It is difficult, however, to see why Mark has placed it here, unless for historical reasons. He also binds it closely to the story of the transfiguration, for he states that, as Jesus drew near to the crowds, they were impressed by that divine radiance which still shone from his countenance. Jesus' words to his disciples and to the multitude ([19]) implied that his work was nearly ended.

The symptoms of epilepsy are described with unusual detail in Mark. In Matthew and Luke the story is greatly abridged. The act of healing corresponds to many recorded in the Galilean ministry. In Jesus' presence the child was seized with a paroxysm and then fell in a swoon from which Jesus revived him. The incident was introduced to emphasize the importance of faith and prayer in performing acts of healing, and therefore was of peculiar interest to the early church, where similar cures were of common occurrence.

The record of the days spent by Jesus with his disciples in retirement concludes with a second prediction of his coming death at Jerusalem. The vagueness of this second prediction suggests that the first was far more general than the gospel record implies. Luke, in his version of the second prediction, seeks to reconcile it with the disciples' surprise at its fulfilment. He is certainly right in affirming that they failed to grasp the full meaning of Jesus' words. The statement that he would "rise after three days" may possibly have been suggested by Hosea 6², "After two days he will revive us, and on the third day we shall rise up and live before him," or else it may be a later addition to the narrative. Pathetic, yet heroic and majestic, is the picture which the gospels give of Jesus during these days of readjustment. Wandering amid strange environment, almost overwhelmed with a deep sense of disappointment, apprehensive regarding the loyalty of even his immediate followers, facing death and the shame of seeming failure, he prepared not only himself but his disciples for the supreme sacrifice which they were called to make.

§ CXXXIX. INCIDENTS OF THE LAST JOURNEY TO JERUSALEM

And Jesus and his disciples came to Capernaum. And when he was in the house he questioned them, What were you discussing on the way? And they kept silence, for they had been disputing with one another on the way about who was the greatest. Then he sat down, called the Twelve and said to them, If anyone would be first he shall be last of all and servant of all. And taking a little child, he set him in their midst. And putting his arms around him, he said to them:

1. The basis of precedence among Jesus' followers (Mark 9³³⁻³⁷,⁶¹ cf. Matt. 18¹⁻⁵ Luke 9⁴⁶⁻⁴⁸)

Whoever shall receive a little child like this in my name,
    receives me;
And whoever receives me, receives not only me but him
    who sent me;

For whoever shall give you a cup of water to drink because
you are Christ's,
I tell you truly, he shall not lose his reward.

2. The inhospitality of the Samaritans (Luke 9⁵¹⁻⁵⁶)

Now it came to pass, when the days for him to be taken
up were nearly come, Jesus set his face steadfastly to go
to Jerusalem. And he sent messengers before him. And
as they went, they entered a village of the Samaritans in
order to make ready for him. But the people would not
receive him, because his face was turned toward Jerusalem.
And when his disciples, James and John, saw it, they said,
Lord, wilt thou not have us bid fire come from heaven and
consume them? But he turned and rebuked them. And
they went on to another village.

3. The journey (Mark 10¹ Luke 13²², cf. Matt. 19¹, ²)

And rising up he went from there into the territory of
Judea, and across the Jordan. And crowds again gathered
to him; and again he taught them, as was his custom. And
he passed through the cities and villages, one after another,
teaching as he journeyed on to Jerusalem.

4. The narrow way of life (Luke 13²³ Matt. 7¹³, ¹⁴)

And a certain man said to him, Lord, are they few who
are saved? And he said to them:

Enter in by the narrow gate;
For wide is the gate and broad is the way that leads to
destruction,
And those who are entering in by it are many;
For narrow is the gate, and strait the way that leads to
life,
And those who are finding it are few.

5. The danger of not finding it (Luke 13²⁴⁻³⁰, cf. Matt. 7²¹⁻²³ 8¹¹, ¹²)

Strive hard to enter by the narrow gate;
For many, I tell you, shall seek to enter, but will not be able.
When once the master of the house has risen up and shut
fast the door,
And you begin to stand outside and knock at the door, say-
ing, 'Open to us, Lord!'
He shall answer and say to you, 'I know not whence you
come.'
Then you shall begin to say, 'We ate and drank in thy pres-
ence,
And thou hast taught in our streets.'

240

And he shall say, 'I tell you, I know not whence you come;
Depart from me, all you workers of iniquity.'
There shall be weeping and gnashing of teeth,
When you see Abraham, Isaac, and Jacob, and all the
    prophets in the kingdom of God,
But you yourselves thrown out.
Yea, they shall come from east and west and north and south,
And they shall recline in the kingdom of God.
And behold! there are last which shall be first,
And there are first that shall be last.

At that very hour, certain Pharisees came and said to him, 6.
Go forth, leave this place, for Herod wishes to kill thee. Jesus'
But he said to them, Go and tell that fox, 'Behold I cast out to
demons and perform miracles to-day and to-morrow, and warn-
on the third day I am finished! But to-day and to-morrow against
and on the following day I must go on my way, for it cannot Herod
be that a prophet perish outside Jerusalem!' (Luke 13³¹⁻³³)

Oh, Jerusalem, Jerusalem! that killeth the prophets and 7. La-
    stoneth them who are sent to her! ment
How often would I have gathered thy children together, over
Even as a fowl her brood under her wing and you would not! Jerusa-
Behold, your house is left desolate to you! lem
I tell you, you shall not see me until you say, (Luke 13³⁴, ³⁵,
'Blessed is he who comes in the name of the Lord.' cf.
Matt. 23³⁷⁻³⁹)

Now they were on the way going up to Jerusalem, and 8. The
Jesus was going before them. And they were in dismay. third
And they who followed were afraid. And he once more dec-
took the Twelve aside, and began to tell them what things lara-
were to happen to him, saying, Behold, we are going up to regard-
Jerusalem; and the Son of man shall be delivered to the ing his
high priests and scribes, and they shall condemn him to fate
death, and deliver him to the Gentiles. And they shall (Mark 10³²⁻³⁴,
mock him, and spit on him, and scourge him, and kill him; cf.
yet after three days he shall rise again. Matt. 20¹⁷⁻¹⁹
Luke 18³¹⁻³⁴)
And James and John, the sons of Zebedee, came to him,
and said to him, Teacher, we want thee to do for us whatever we shall ask. And he said to them, What do you want

8.
Reply
to the
request
of
James
and
John
(Mark
10³⁵⁻⁴⁰,
cf.
Matt.
20²⁰⁻²³)

me to do for you. And they said to him, Grant that we may
sit, one on thy right hand and one on thy left hand, in thy
glory. But Jesus said to them, You do not know what you
are asking. Are you able to drink the cup that I drink, or
to be baptized with the baptism with which I am baptized?
And they said to him, We are able. And Jesus said to them:

The cup that I drink, shall you drink;
And with the baptism with which I am baptized, shall you
    be baptized;
But to sit on my right hand and on my left is not mine to
    grant.
It is only for those for whom it has been prepared.

9.
The
true
stand-
ard of
great-
ness
(Mark
10⁴¹⁻⁴⁴
Luke
22²⁷ᵇ,
cf.
Matt.
20²⁴⁻²⁸
Mark
10⁴⁵
Luke
22²⁴⁻²⁷ᵃ)

And on hearing this request, the ten disciples began to be
indignant at James and John. But Jesus calling them to
him, said to them:

You know that they who are regarded as leaders of the
        Gentiles lord it over them,
And their great men exercise authority over them.
But it is not so among you;
Nay, whoever would become great among you, must be
        your servant,
And whoever would be first among you, must be servant
        or all.
And I am in your midst as one who serves.

11.
Jesus'
re-
quest
of Zac-
cheus
(Luke
19¹⁻⁶)

And he entered and was passing through Jericho. And
there was a man by the name of Zaccheus; and he was the
head of the tax-collectors, and was rich. And he tried to
see who Jesus was, but could not for the crowd, because he
was short in stature. So he ran on ahead and climbed up
into a sycamore tree to see Jesus, for he was to pass that way.
And when Jesus came to the place, he looked up, and said
to him, Zaccheus, come down; for to-day I must stay at thy
house. Then Zaccheus made haste to come down, and received him with joy.

But on seeing it, everyone began to complain, saying, He
has gone in to eat with a man who is a sinner. But Zaccheus

stood up and said to the Lord, Behold, Lord, the half of my goods I will give to the poor. And if I have taken anything from any man wrongfully, I will give it back fourfold. Then Jesus said to him, To-day has salvation come to this house, for he is also a son of Abraham. For the Son of man came to seek and to save what has been lost.

12. The saving of Zaccheus (7-10)

And as he was leaving Jericho with his disciples and a considerable crowd, a blind beggar, Bartimaus (the son of Timaus), sat beside the way. And when he heard that it was Jesus of Nazareth, he began crying out and saying, Jesus, thou son of David, have mercy on me! And many people reproved him, that he might keep silence. But he cried out all the more, Son of David, have mercy on me! Then Jesus stood still and said, Call him. So they called the blind man, saying to him, Be of good cheer; rise, he is calling thee. Throwing away his garments he sprang up and came to Jesus. And Jesus, addressing him, said, What wilt thou have me do to thee? The blind man said to him, Rabbuni, let me regain my sight. And Jesus said to him, Go thy way, thy faith has made thee whole. And immediately he regained his sight and proceeded to follow him on the way.

13. Healing the blind beggar at Jericho (Mark 10⁴⁶ᵇ⁻⁵², cf. Luke 18³⁶⁻⁴³ Matt. 20²⁹⁻³⁴)

I. **Jesus Facing Jerusalem.** Ever since the great crisis in Galilee, Jesus' face had been set toward Jerusalem. Apparently he was waiting, before going thither, until he could be sure that the training of his disciples was reasonably complete. His choice of the Passover season was probably not an accident, but a result of his deliberate plan. At this, the greatest of the annual Jewish festivals, he could be sure that the crowds from Galilee, as well as the leaders of the people, would be assembled at Jerusalem. Then, if ever, he could appeal successfully to the better conscience of the nation. Whatever the outcome, it would be sure to make a deep impression upon his race.

There is no evidence in the gospel narratives that Jesus was conscious of following a preordained programme. On the contrary, they testify that even to the last he cherished the hope that Jerusalem would not maintain its evil reputation of killing its prophets. Like a mother bird, he longed to gather her children together and protect them from the fate that he saw was inevitable if his nation continued to follow its false ambition. But Jesus knew well the forces with which he had to deal, and the evidence is cumulative that he went up to Jerusalem in the spirit of a martyr, fully aware of the dangers which confronted him.

Luke has introduced, in 9^{51}–18^{14}, a large group of narratives and teachings peculiar to his gospel. These have sometimes been regarded as the records of a Perean ministry, concerning which the other gospels are silent; but it is evident that Luke has here grouped in an artificial manner narratives that belong in part to the Galilean ministry, so that the order is editorial rather than historical. Jesus did, however, pass through Perea. As he set out with his disciples from Capernaum, he doubtless avoided the more direct road along the western side of the Sea of Galilee, for it ran through Herod's capital, Tiberias. He either passed along the east side of the lake or more probably went by boat. At the southern end of the Sea of Galilee he appears to have taken the west-Jordan road, skirting the territory of Galilee and Samaria. From the vicinity of Scythopolis he probably sent certain of his disciples to ascertain whether the direct road, which ran through the ancient Tirzah and the heart of Samaria to Jerusalem, was open to the Jewish pilgrims. As was frequently the case, they found the Samaritans unfriendly and so reported to Jesus. The request of James and John that Jesus command them to call down fire from heaven on these inhospitable Samaritans is in keeping with their reputation as sons of thunder. Jesus' rebuke to his disciples suggests that pity which he ever felt toward this despised race.

To this same geographical and historical setting Luke has assigned the healing of ten lepers, of whom one only, a Samaritan, returned to give thanks to Jesus. Luke's story, however, is probably an expanded duplicate of the narrative of the healing of the leper recorded in Mark 1^{40-45} and Luke 5^{12-16}. The numbers differ, but otherwise the details are strikingly similar. In each case the malady appears to have been not the incurable disease which we know as leprosy, but the so-called leprosy which was recognized as curable by the ancient Levitical law.

Finding the direct road barred, Jesus crossed the Jordan into Perea. Here he was again in the territory of Herod Antipas, but this change in his itinerary was so sudden and his sojourn east of the Jordan was so brief that there was little danger of pursuit. It was here, however, that certain Pharisees came to Jesus, told him of Herod's desire to kill him, and advised that he leave at once. Luke has again preserved one of those rare passages which reveal Jesus' heroic spirit and incidentally supplement the evidence that he was fully convinced that the days of his public activity were numbered. His words are concrete and yet figurative: "To-day and to-morrow I continue to do my work, but on the third day (that is, in a few days more) it shall be finished. Not at the hands of Herod, but like a prophet, at Jerusalem, at the hands of my ungrateful countrymen, shall I meet a martyr's fate."

II. The Narrow Way of Salvation. In Perea Jesus was largely beyond the influence of the leaven of the Pharisees. Here he was among the people who had responded most readily to the earlier preaching of John. Again the crowds gathered about him and he taught them, as was his custom. Leisurely he appears to have journeyed from village to village, for he had ample time before the feast of the Passover. According to Luke, a group of his priceless sayings were precipitated by the question of a certain unknown hearer, "Lord, are they few who are saved?" Matthew has retained what is clearly the older form of this teaching, but has included it in the so-called, "Sermon on the Mount." These sayings and the application which follows belong most naturally in the setting to which Luke has assigned them, for they share the characteristics of the farewell messages which come from this period. Their background is the refusal of the majority of the Jews to enter the narrow gate and to walk the strait path of life which Jesus had pointed out. These sayings were taken by Luke and the author of Matthew from their older teaching source (Q). They are among the most significant utterances of Jesus. They show the effect which the rejection of his teachings by the Jews and his recent contact with the Gentiles had upon his own thinking. Too late and with bitter laments would the sons of Abraham realize the meaning of their refusal to enter the kingdom of God. From the east and from the west, from the north and from the south, and from the lands of the heathen should come those who would share the privileges of the kingdom which the Jews themselves had disdained. Thus those who felt that they had the first claim to divine favor should be the last to enjoy it. And those who were despised as heathen dogs and outcasts should receive it in fullest measure.

The figure of the narrow gate and the straitened way was doubtless suggested to the mind of Jesus by the narrow gateways that led out from the Palestinian cities, and by the rocky paths, often only wide enough for a single foot-passenger or beast, that ran from village to village. The other figure, that of the great feast, was a familiar one in Jewish thought. Thus, in the *Sayings of the Fathers* 3:20 is found the saying, "Everything is prepared for the banquet." It was also suggested by the lavish oriental hospitality with which Jesus was received at the different villages which he visited. The dominant note in these sayings, as in all the utterances which come from this period, is the necessity of self-denial, steadfastness, and loyalty to the will of the divine Father. Out of the depths of his own trying experience Jesus taught the multitudes and his disciples the one lesson, which it was absolutely essential for them to learn, if there were to be efficient citizens in the commonwealth of God.

The synoptic gospels, following Mark, agree in recording at this point a third prediction by Jesus of the fate that awaited him at Jerusalem. The language and content of the prediction is practically identical with those preceding, except that it adds certain details. Like the preceding predictions, it is probably colored by the evangelist's knowledge of later events. Luke, as before, recognizes the psychological difficulty and endeavors to explain the disciples' obtuseness in apprehending that which, in the present form of the narrative, is a detailed reference to the closing events of Jesus' life. The passage is significant because it emphasizes the fact that the chief aim of Jesus during this period was to lead his disciples to see that he would not and could not fulfil the popular hopes which they associated with the magic word Messiah, but that through self-renunciation and suffering he was to accomplish his mission.

III. **The Request of James and John.** To this same period probably belongs the request of James and John, recorded in Mark 10$^{35-45}$ and quoted in abridged form by Matthew (20$^{20-28}$). Luke introduces his account of the contention among the disciples as to who was greatest, recorded in Mark 9$^{33-36}$, and Jesus' statement regarding the only valid standard of preferment immediately after the drinking of the cup at the last supper; but Mark's order (followed by Matthew) is evidently the original. The incident is significant because it reveals the complete failure of the disciples, even at this time, to understand the real meaning of Jesus' teachings. The narrative is colored throughout by the point of view of the age in which Mark lived. According to Acts 12^2, James was put to death by Herod Agrippa in 44 A.D. As has already been noted (p. 32), John, his brother, had probably met a martyr's death before the destruction of Jerusalem in 70 A.D. Both of these events were, therefore, fresh in Mark's mind when he wrote. Underlying the narrative is the historical fact that the disciples still hoped that Jesus would set up a temporal kingdom at Jerusalem. It was also natural that the two favorite disciples should request for themselves a pre-eminent position in it. In Matthew their request appears less selfish because it is presented by their mother. The figure of the cup which Jesus was to drink, which recurs in his prayer at Gethsemane, was common in the later prophets and Psalms, as, for example, in Isaiah 51[17] (*cf.* Jer. 25[15] Ps. 16[5]):

> Jerusalem, who hast drunk at Jehovah's hand the cup of his wrath,
> The bowl of reeling thou hast drunken, thou hast drained.

Jesus' conception of political conditions throughout the heathen world is that of the Jews of his day. His whole emphasis is placed upon the importance of the spirit of service. In the spiritual kingdom which he founded, conquest and rule by force had no place. In these words to James and John he entirely repudiates the Jewish ambition to conquer and rule the heathen world.

The logical and probably original conclusion of Jesus' reply to his disciples is found in the parallel passage in Luke 22[27b]: "And I am in your midst as one who serves." For this Mark has a teaching which reflects the influence of Paul and of the age in which the evangelist wrote: "For the son of man also came not to be ministered to, but to minister, and to give his life a ransom for many." It assumes that Jesus had already come and completed his mission. It is the result of that mature meditation on the deeper and broader meaning of his life-work which is presented still more fully in the Fourth Gospel. It introduces the Jewish idea of substitution, which is not found elsewhere in the teachings of Jesus or even in the synoptic gospels. It is a doctrine which may be traced in Isaiah 53, but it is most clearly expressed in IV Maccabees 6[28, 29] (*cf.* 17[22]): "Be propitious to thy people. Let the punishment suffice thee, that we have borne in its behalf. Let my blood be a purification for them and accept my life as a substitute for their life." The words in Mark do not state in what sense the ransom was effective, nor to whom it was given, whether to God or to Satan. These questions belong to the refinements of later theology. Possibly Mark had in mind Paul's teaching in Galatians 4[8]: "But at that time, since you did not know God, you were in servitude to gods that by nature were no gods" (*cf.*, also, I Cor. 12[2]). According to the oldest gospel records, it was by Jesus' work as Friend and Brother and Teacher that he delivered men, not from an angry God, but from servitude to false ideas and wrong habits. He saved them, not by magic or by a miracle, but by teaching them how to find their heavenly

Father and their true life, as Jesus himself had found it, in the service of God and men. Narrow is the gate and strait is the way which he pointed out, and each man must decide for himself whether he will walk in it or not. But it leads to life, as Jesus himself fully demonstrated.

IV. **The Blind Man and the Tax-Collector at Jericho.** All east-Jordan highways converge at Jericho. In the days of Jesus, next to Jerusalem, Jericho was the most important city in Judea. It lay on the western side of the Jordan Valley, which at this point is fourteen miles in width. The plain is naturally dry and barren, but when irrigated becomes a fertile garden. Herod the Great and Archelaus had conducted the waters of the Wady Kelt, which come down from the western hills, out across the plain, so that a large area was brought under cultivation. The Roman city of Jericho extended almost to the Jordan and far up and down the valley. Its climate was hot but equable. Here the fruits of the tropics flourished luxuriantly. Jericho was important as the eastern commercial outpost of Judea and commanded the northern trade routes which ran on either side of the Jordan, or directly across Gilead to Damascus and the Far East. From Jericho traders set out for Petra and the more distant Arabia. Highway and boundary customs were here levied on all merchandise, so that at this point the office of chief tax-collector was important. In this corrupt, half-heathen city the temptations to extortion and excess were especially strong. Luke alone has retained the account of the impression which Jesus made upon the rich, corrupt tax-collector of Jericho. The incident illustrates the great Teacher's tactful method in dealing with men of all classes. Denunciation would have only confirmed Zaccheus in his wrong manner of life. Hospitality was his pride and one virtue. Through this open door Jesus entered his life. What Paul declared of himself, "I am all things to all men," was equally true of Jesus. Jesus' act naturally called down the disapproval of all orthodox Jews in Jericho, as it had in Galilee. Zaccheus, however, justified Jesus' method. His quick repentance took form, not in words only, but in acts. Zaccheus, the prosperous, unprincipled grafter, was an excellent example of "the lost" which Jesus came to seek and to save. Contact with the great Teacher enabled him to see his former acts in their true significance, led him to repudiate the evil and to devote himself and his possessions to a life of service. Truly did Jesus declare, "To-day has salvation come to this house."

Another incident at Jericho is recorded by each of the synoptic gospels, and indicates that even in his hour of disappointment and distress Jesus neglected no opportunity to help those who appealed to him. Mark has retained the earliest record of the incident, and Luke has reproduced the Marcan narrative practically verbatim. Matthew tells of two blind men instead of one, but otherwise the details of the narrative are practically identical. The independent narrative in Matthew 9²⁷⁻³¹ is apparently only a variant of this same story. Beside the road which led from Jericho up over the hill to Jerusalem sat a blind Jewish beggar. He was one of the hundreds that the traveller finds in Palestine to-day, as in the past, some of them wholly blind, many partially blinded through the effects of the hot sun and the filthy dust, which are disastrous to the eyesight. In his journeys between Nazareth and Jerusalem, Jesus had often gone through Jericho. He may have also been known to the citizens of that town through his association with John the Baptist. The report that Jesus the Nazarene was passing by put hope in the heart of the dirty beggar. His case was like that of scores of the needy whom Jesus helped or healed. But the term, Son of David, with which Bartimaus addressed him, struck a new note, for, as he used it, it was a messianic title. Did he employ this term, prompted by oriental politeness, or was he voicing a popular hope which was still strong in Jericho, where false messiahs before and after met with a ready reception? Or was it because Jesus' disciples had communicated their expectations to the multitude and these had been caught up by the keen-eared son of the streets? The narrative gives no answer to these questions. Mark evidently introduces the incident here as a prelude to his account of Jesus' triumphal entry into Jerusalem. Jesus quietly ignored the messianic title. With the simplicity and directness that marked all his activities, he requested that the beggar be brought to him; then he relieved his malady. As so often in connection with the acts of healing recorded during this period, Jesus assured the man that it was his own faith that had made him well. These two accounts of the healing of men morally and physically blind furnish a fitting conclusion to the record of Jesus' activity outside of Jerusalem. They proclaim far more clearly than abstract words that his greatness consisted in his unbounded capacity to serve and that he was godlike because, like God himself, he saw the possibilities in even the lowliest, and was able to awake the divine qualities latent in every man.

§ CXL. THE RENEWAL OF JESUS' PUBLIC ACTIVITY IN JERUSALEM

1. Jesus' entrance into Jerusalem (Mark 11¹⁻¹⁰, cf. Matt. 21¹⁻¹¹ Luke 19²⁹⁻⁴⁴)

When Jesus and those who were with him drew near to Jerusalem, to Bethphage at the Mount of Olives, he sent two of his disciples and said to them, Go into the village yonder, in front of you; and as soon as you enter it, you will find a colt tied, on which no one has ever yet sat. Untie it and bring it. And if any one says to you, 'Why are you doing this?' say, 'The Master needs it, and he will send it back here at once.' And they went away and found a colt tied at the door outside in the open street, and they untied it. And certain men who were standing there said to them, Why are you untying the colt? And the disciples spoke to them just as Jesus had told them, and the men let them go. And they brought the colt to Jesus, and they cast their garments on it; and Jesus sat on it. And many spread their garments on the road, and others green branches that they had cut from the fields. And those in front, and those who followed kept shouting:

Hosanna!
Blessed is he who comes in the name of the Lord!
Blessed is the kingdom to come, the kingdom of our father David!
Hosanna in the highest!

2. At the temple (Mark 11¹¹)

3. The parable of the barren fig tree (Luke 13⁶⁻⁹, cf. Mark 11¹²⁻¹⁴, ²⁰, ²¹ Matt. 21¹⁸⁻²²)

And he entered Jerusalem and went into the temple; and after looking around at everything, as it was already late in the day, he went out to Bethany with the Twelve.

And on the next day after they left Bethany, they came to Jerusalem. And Jesus spoke this parable: A certain man had a fig tree planted in his vineyard; and he came seeking fruit on it, but found none. So he said to the vinedresser, 'Here, three years I have come in search of fruit on this fig tree and found none! Cut it down. Why should it still cumber the ground?' And he said in reply to him, 'Sir, leave it alone this year also, until I dig around it and enrich it. If it bears fruit henceforth, well! but if not, thou shalt cut it down.'

Then Jesus entered the temple, and began to drive out those who sold and those who bought in the temple; and overturned the tables of the money-changers, and the seats of those who sold doves; and he would not allow any man to carry a vessel through the temple. And he taught and said to them, Is it not written, 'My house shall be called a house of prayer for all the nations? But you have made it a den of robbers!' And the chief priests and scribes heard it, and tried how they could destroy him; for they feared him, since all the crowd was astonished at his teaching. But whenever it was evening, they went outside the city.

4. Purifying the temple (Mark 11 15b-19, cf. Matt. 21 12-17 Luke 19 45-48)

And they came again to Jerusalem. And as he was walking in the temple, the high priests, the scribes, and the elders came to him; and they said to him, By what authority art thou doing these things? Or who gave thee this authority to do these things? And Jesus said to them, I will ask of you one question; answer me, and I will tell you by what authority I do these things. Was the baptism of John from heaven or from men? Answer me. And they argued among themselves, saying, If we say, 'From heaven'; he will say, 'Why then did you not believe him?' But should we say, 'From men'—they feared the people, for all believed that John was truly a prophet. So they said, in reply to Jesus, We do not know. Then Jesus said to them, Neither do I tell you by what authority I do these things.

5. Jesus' defence of his God-given authority (Mark 11 27-33, cf. Matt. 21 23-27 Luke 20 1-8)

What do you think? A man had two sons; and going to the first, said, 'Son, go, work to-day in the vineyard.' And he answered, 'I will not'; but afterward he changed his mind and went. And going to the second, he spoke in the same way. And he answered, 'I will go, sir'; but he did not go. Which of the two did what his father wished? They say, The first. Jesus said to them, I tell you truly, the tax-collectors and sinners shall enter the kingdom of God before you. For John came to you in the way of righteousness, yet you did not believe him. But the tax-collectors and harlots believed him. And when you saw it, you did not even change your minds afterward, that you might believe him.

6. Parable of the two sons (Matt. 21 28-32)

Hear another parable: A man who was a householder planted a vineyard; he set a hedge about it and dug a pit for the wine press and built a tower. Then he leased it to vinedressers and went abroad. And at the season he sent

7. Of the wicked vinedressers (Matt. 21³³⁻⁴², ⁴⁶ᵃ Luke 20¹⁹ᵇ, cf. Mark 12¹⁻¹² Luke 20⁹⁻¹⁷, ¹⁹ᵃ)

a servant to the vinedressers, that he might receive from the vinedressers the fruits of the vineyard. But they took and flogged him and sent him away empty-handed. Then again he sent to them another servant; and this one they wounded on the head and insulted. Then he sent another. And this one they killed and many others, flogging some and killing some. He had yet one, his beloved son. Him he sent last of all to them, saying, 'They will reverence my son.' But those vinedressers said to themselves, 'This is the heir. Come, let us kill him and the inheritance will be ours.' So they took and killed him, and threw him outside the vineyard. What will the owner of the vineyard do? He will come and destroy the vinedressers and give the vineyard to others. Have you not even read this scripture:

The stone which the builders rejected,
This has been made the head of the corner:
This is the Lord's doing,
And it is marvellous in our eyes.

Then they sought to seize him, but they feared the crowd; for they knew that he spoke the parable against them.

8. Rejection of the popular interpretation of calamity (Luke 13¹⁻⁵)

Now at that time there were some people present who told him about the Galileans, whose blood Pilate had mixed with their sacrifices. And he said in reply to them, Do you think those Galileans were greater sinners than all the Galileans, because they suffered thus? Not so, I tell you. But unless you repent, you shall all likewise perish. Or those eighteen men whom the Tower of Siloam fell upon and killed? Do you think that they were greater offenders than all the men dwelling in Jerusalem? Not so, I tell you. But unless you repent, you shall all likewise perish.

9. The future life of the individual (Mark 12¹⁸⁻²⁷, cf. Matt. 22²³⁻³³ Luke 20²⁷⁻⁴⁰)

And Sadducees came to him (men who say there is no resurrection) and they asked him, saying, Moses wrote for us that, 'If a man's brother die and leave a wife and leave no child, his brother is to take his widow and raise up offspring for his brother.' There were seven brothers. And the first took a wife, and dying, left no offspring. Then the second took her and died, leaving no offspring. And the third likewise. And the seven left no offspring. Last of all the woman died also. At the resurrection whose wife shall she be, for the seven had her as wife? Jesus said to them, Is it not for this cause that you err, because you are ignorant of God's scriptures and of the power of God? For when people rise from the dead, they neither marry nor give in marriage, but are like angels in heaven. But in regard to the raising of the dead, have you not read in the book of Moses, in the place of the Bush that God spoke to him, saying, 'I am the God of Abraham, and the God of Isaac, and the God of Jacob?' He is not the God of the dead but of the living. You greatly err.

And as Jesus taught in the temple, he would ask, How is it that the scribes say that the Christ is the son of David? David himself said in the Holy Spirit, 'The Lord said to my Lord:

> Sit at my right hand,
> Until I make thine enemies a footstool for thy feet.'

David himself calls him, Lord. How then is he his son?

And the common people listened to him gladly. And in his teaching he said, Beware of the scribes, who are fond of walking in long robes, and of receiving salutations in the market-places, and the chief seats in the synagogues, and the first places at feasts; these men, who devour widow's properties and make long prayers for a pretext shall receive the greater condemnation.

Woe to you, [scribes and Pharisees, hypocrites]!
For you bind up heavy burdens and lay them on men's shoulders,
But you yourselves will not move them with your finger.

Woe to you, scribes and Pharisees, hypocrites!
For you shut the kingdom of Heaven in men's faces,
And you enter not yourselves and you will not let those enter who are entering.

Woe to you, scribes and Pharisees, hypocrites!
For you tithe mint and dill and cummin,
But you have left undone the weightier matters of the law: justice, mercy, and faithfulness.

10. The Davidic descent of the Messiah (Mark 12³⁵⁻³⁷, cf. Matt. 22⁴¹⁻⁴⁵ Luke 20⁴¹⁻⁴⁴)

11. Warnings against the scribes (Mark 12³⁸⁻⁴⁰, cf. Matt. 23¹⁻³,⁵⁻⁷ Luke 20⁴⁵⁻⁴⁷)

12. Their cruel exactions (Luke 11⁴⁶, cf. Matt. 23⁴)

13. Rejection of Jesus (Matt. 23¹³, cf. Luke 11⁵²)

14. Their wrong emphasis (²³ᵃ)

15.
Their
greed
(26)

Woe to you, scribes and Pharisees, hypocrites!
For you cleanse the outside of the cup and plate,
But inside you are filled with extortion and indulgence.

16.
Their
hypoc-
risy
(27)

Woe to you, scribes and Pharisees, hypocrites!
For you are like white-washed sepulchres,
Which outwardly appear beautiful,
But inwardly are filled with dead men's bones and all un-
cleanness.

17.
Rev-
erence
for
mar-
tyrs
and
mur-
derous
hate
toward
living
proph-
ets
(Matt.
23²⁹⁻³²,
cf.
Luke
11⁴⁷, ⁴⁸)
18. Re-
sponsi-
ble for
the
slaugh-
ter
of the
proph-
ets
(Luke
11⁴⁹⁻⁵¹,
cf.
Matt.
23³⁴⁻³⁶)

Woe to you, scribes and Pharisees, hypocrites!
For you build the sepulchres of the prophets and adorn the
tombs of the righteous,
And you say, 'If we had been living in the days of our
fathers,
We would not have shared with them in the blood of the
prophets,'
So you witness against yourselves that you are the sons of
those who slew the prophets.
Fill up then for yourselves the measure of your fathers!

Therefore the wisdom of God also said,
I send to you prophets and wise men and scribes;
Some of them you will slay and persecute,
That upon you may come the blood of all the prophets which
has been shed since the foundation of the world,
From the blood of Abel to the blood of Zachariah, whom you
slew between the temple and the altar.
I tell you truly, these things shall all come upon this gen-
eration.

19.
The
true
piety
of the
poor
widow
(Mark
12⁴¹⁻⁴⁴,
cf.
Luke
21¹⁻⁴)

And as Jesus was sitting down opposite the treasury he
beheld how the crowd cast money into the treasury. Many
who were rich cast in much. And a poor widow also came
and cast in two lepta (which is about half a cent). Then
calling his disciples to him, he said, I tell you truly, this
poor widow has cast in more than all those who are casting
their money into the treasury. For they all cast in out of
their abundance, but she out of her want has cast in all that
she possessed, the whole of her living.

254

THE TRIUMPHAL ENTRY INTO JERUSALEM

I. The Triumphal Entry into Jerusalem. After a circuitous journey Jesus at last reached the city of sacred yet tragic memories. The Marcan narrative (*cf.* 10[46]) indicates that he was accompanied, at least from Jericho, by many besides his twelve disciples. His following included women as well as men. The majority were probably, like Bartimaus, bound to Jesus by the bonds of personal obligation and gratitude. Mingled expectation and apprehension filled their minds as they made the steep ascent toward Jerusalem from the barren wilderness of Judea. The manner of Jesus' entrance into Jerusalem made a deep impression upon the minds of the disciples. The Fourth Gospel (John 12[16]) states plainly that "the disciples did not at first understand these things," that is, the meaning of the events connected with his triumphal entrance. The interpretation given to them by the early evangelists, therefore, represents the results of the later meditations of his followers.

The real question is, What was Jesus' purpose in entering Jerusalem as he did? Was it to incite the people to proclaim him then and there Israel's promised Messiah, or to inaugurate publicly his work in Jerusalem and to test his strength with the people? Or was there originally nothing intentionally symbolic in the way in which he entered Jerusalem, and did he send for an ass simply because he was tired after his long and arduous journey from Jericho? The first explanation may be dismissed at once. Mark 11[11], as well as his acts and utterances elsewhere, indicates beyond all doubt that he did not for a moment encourage the people in the hope that he was the Messiah of popular expectation. If he had given the least public encouragement to that hope, the fact would certainly have been cited against him in his trial later before the Jewish authorities.

On the other hand, the authors of the synoptic gospels evidently regarded the manner of Jesus' entrance into Jerusalem as a fulfilment of the predictions which they found in Zechariah 9[9] and 14[4]. Both passages were interpreted by the Jews of the day as messianic. The one described a humble, unassuming, peasant deliverer.

> Rejoice greatly, O daughter of Zion!
> Shout aloud, O daughter of Jerusalem!
> Behold, thy king will come to thee;
> Vindicated and victorious is he,
> Humble, and riding upon an ass,
> Upon the foal of an ass.

The other passage was interpreted to mean that the kingdom of the Messiah would be proclaimed on the Mount of Olives. It was there, according to Josephus (*Jewish Ant.*, XX, 8⁶), that the Egyptian false Messiah raised his standard, which attracted thousands of fanatical followers. The words sung by Jesus' followers and the pilgrims whom they met also suggested more than a commonplace incident. They are taken from Psalm 118²⁵, ²⁶, and were regularly recited at the feast of Tabernacles. Mark has probably preserved the more nearly original form of the popular song. Luke adds, "Peace in heaven and glory in the highest," a refrain from the angels' song found in his account of Jesus' birth. The words of the multitude suggest a sudden revival of their hope that, after all, Jesus, as the Messiah, would fulfil the promises given to David and his house. If ever this faith was to find expression, the moment was opportune. The narrative, in the form in which Mark has told it, does not necessarily imply anything miraculous or purposely symbolic on the part of Jesus. He was already acquainted with Jerusalem and evidently had intimate friends living somewhere on the Mount of Olives. He probably did not anticipate that sudden burst of popular enthusiasm which greeted his appearance. It was induced by the occasion and prompted by a personal devotion and by the heroism revealed in his faith and actions. It was a sudden flame to which he added no fuel, and as a result it quickly died down. But for the events which followed, the incident would probably not have been recorded.

Yet, in connection with Jesus' subsequent acts, it is exceedingly probable that the evangelist and the Christian church are right in attributing to it a more than ordinary significance. It illustrates Jesus' method during the last few days of his public activity. No longer does he enjoin silence upon his followers, but rather he courts publicity, for this was his chief safeguard in the perilous situation which he now faced. Hitherto he had borne the insults of the Jewish leaders almost in silence, but now he proceeded to arraign them at the centre of their power and in terms that are merciless in their severity. In the public way in which he entered Jerusalem, Jesus proclaimed his presence to all and at the same time rallied his followers about him. It was the prelude to that challenge which he made to his nation to choose between him, the champion of the neglected masses, and their corrupt, self-seeking leaders. Possibly in the mind of Jesus were the words of the unknown prophet who speaks in Zechariah 9⁹, for they emphasized those qualities of gentleness, humility, and simplicity which were most prominent in his conception of the Messiah's character and methods of work. His unassuming action, however, on reaching the temple, while absolutely consistent with his own character, forever disproved the conclusion still held by many that he hoped at this time to establish himself on the throne of David as Israel's long-awaited messianic king.

Jesus' quiet withdrawal to Bethany, as evening came on, is one of the many indications, found in the records of this period, that he was fully aware of the danger that lurked everywhere in Jerusalem. This point is exceedingly important in understanding and estimating Jesus' character and purpose. For his followers and for his cause he deliberately faced what he knew to be the probability, almost the certainty, of ultimate death; but he did not court it. Jerusalem, with its narrow streets and its narrower religious ideas, must have oppressed the Master Builder of Nazareth, accustomed as he was to the hill-tops, the open fields, and large vistas of nature, as well as of God's truth. It was as natural as it was significant that he should retire, whenever it was possible, to the Mount of Olives, with its larger outlook, and to Bethany, which was near Jerusalem and yet out of sight of the city with its clamor and its bickerings. At Bethany, amidst the fig trees and the olive orchards, he was again in touch with nature. There he was no longer shut in by the narrow, rocky Judean hills, but could look far out over the wilderness of Judea toward the Jordan Valley and the heights of Gilead and Moab beyond.

II. **The Story and Parable of the Fig Tree.** Mark, followed by Matthew, has preserved a narrative which is exceedingly suggestive, for it shows how readily, even in the days when the gospel narratives were taking form, a miracle story could come into existence. Mark relates that on the day following his triumphal entry, as Jesus and his disciples were returning from Bethany, he was hungry. Seeing a fig tree in the distance, with leaves, he went to it in the hope that he might find fruit on it. Finding nothing (for, as Mark states, it was not the season for figs), Jesus addressed the tree, saying: "May man never eat fruit from thee after this." The next morning, as they passed by, they found the fig tree withered to its roots, and Peter called Jesus' attention to it with the words, "Rabbi, look! The fig tree thou didst curse is withered." Matthew, in his version, heightens the contranatural element by stating that the fig tree immediately withered away and that the disciples were amazed, saying: "How was it that the fig tree immediately withered away," and that Jesus replied to their question, "I tell you truly, if you have faith and doubt not, you shall not only do what has been done to the fig tree, but even if you say to this mountain, 'Be thou taken up, and cast into the sea,' it shall be done."

The difficulties involved even in the simpler Marcan version of the story have long been recognized. It is exceedingly improbable that a man of the fields, like Jesus, would make the mistake of expecting to find fruit on a fig tree in March, when that fruit does not ripen at the earliest until June. The cursing of a tree because it had no fruit is equally inconsistent with his methods and spirit. To address a tree personally has the flavor of popular story or fable rather than of an historical record.

Fortunately, Luke has preserved the older version of the incident, and this at once explains these difficulties. What was originally a parable, later tradition interpreted as a miracle. Possibly the parable was suggested by a fig tree near Bethany, which had the reputation of bearing no fruit or else was withered and dying. The teaching of the parable of the fig tree is suggested by Isaiah's parable of the unfruitful vineyard (Is. 5¹⁻⁷), and its teaching is similar to that of the parable of the vineyard leased to the vine-dressers, which Jesus used at this time with a similar application. He clearly had in mind the Jewish nation, and especially its pharisaic leaders, whose life and works sadly belied their promise of fruitfulness. In this marvellously tactful way, Jesus arraigned the nation. The method was that of the ancient prophets. The parable also reveals Jesus' process of thinking. Gradually the tragic conviction had been borne in upon him that the race whose rich memories he cherished, the temple with its sacred associations, and even the high priests and pharisaic scribes were but dying, fruitless trees undeserving of God's continued favor, and doomed, in accordance with an unchanging law of the universe, to destruction.

III. The Public Rebuke of the Temple Authorities. Why did he, who taught and supremely exemplified the principles of gentleness and non-resistance, suddenly seize a scourge and attack the peaceful merchants who plied their trade with the full permission of the temple authorities. It seems at first thought almost like the deed of a fanatical Zealot. Was it due to the hot indignation of the moment or to deliberate purpose? These are questions which the gospel narratives leave unanswered except by implication. The author of the Fourth Gospel, in transferring the cleansing of the temple to the beginning of Jesus' ministry, has simply lost sight of the historical perspective

and offers no solution to the problem. Three acts mark the culmination of the growing opposition between Jesus and the leaders of the
nation. The one is his cleansing of the temple, the second the "woes"
pronounced upon the scribes, and the third, his crucifixion at the
hands of his foes. Considered from the point of view of Jesus' personal interest, his rebuke of the temple authorities was disastrous, for
his death was the direct result. The reasons for his earlier premoni-
tions regarding his death become evident when we recognize that to
protest against the crimes of the high priests and the hypocrisy of the
Pharisees was probably the chief reason why he came to Jerusalem
at this time. Here Jesus approaches more closely to the rôle of the
ancient Hebrew prophets than at any other time in his ministry. Suddenly the teacher became a social and national reformer. Most of
his parables of this period deal not so much with private as with social
and national questions. When Jesus for a brief moment assumed virtual control of the temple, he spoke thereby not to individuals or to a
class, but to his race as a whole. His authority was the same as that
of Jeremiah and of the II Isaiah, whose words he significantly quotes
(Jer. 7:11 Is. 56:7). He spoke in the name of justice and of Jehovah,
whose temple he was attempting to reclaim from the hands of the
robbers who had seized it. For the moment even the robbers themselves bowed before that authority. He rose as the champion of the
helpless people, who were a prey to the greed and rapacity of their
high priests.

It was no exaggeration when Jesus declared that the nation's house
of prayer had become a den of robbers. The high priests of the period
were famous for their avarice and unscrupulous methods. Several of
them had won their place by assassination. As a result of their shame-
less intrigues with Rome, the people were victimized. Annas, the
ex-high priest and father-in-law of Caiaphas, the reigning high priest,
maintained a bazaar of doves, probably in the precincts of the temple
itself. Here the poor people purchased, undoubtedly at exorbitant
prices, the wherewithal to make their offerings. The greed of Annas
and his class completely thwarted the aim of the ancient law, which
was to relieve the burdens of the needy. The presence of the money-
changers in the temple is explained by the fact that the current Roman
coins, most of which bore the inscription of the emperor, would not
be accepted in payment of the temple tax. Hence, it was necessary
to exchange them for the temple currency. These were a few of the
most obvious ways in which the high priests, through their agents,

robbed the people by fraud and extortion. The crime which Jesus attacked was all the more odious because it was practised under the guise and authority of religion. It robbed the temple service of the spirit of worship and made it a scene of contention and injustice.

The incident illustrates a trait in Jesus' character often overlooked but not inconsistent with those qualities which are elsewhere prominent in his ministry. His courage was of the unquestioning type begotten by a complete forgetfulness of self and an enthusiastic devotion to a just cause. His act was prompted by a hot indignation, not over a personal affront, but over a wrong to the helpless. It was not, however, the result of momentary passion but of a carefully developed plan. It also reveals superlative tact. The occasion, as well as the method, was carefully chosen. The presence of the crowds that partially sympathized with Jesus was necessary to save him from the fury of the high priests. On the other hand, equally dangerous was the wild enthusiasm of the multitudes, who might hail him as the Messiah and bring him at once into a clash with the Roman authorities. So successfully did Jesus carry through his plan that the sense of guilt and shame prevented his enemies from making the slightest mention in his trial of this act, which the Roman authorities might well have regarded as an index of lawlessness and of revolutionary ambitions. Although it ultimately cost him his life, Jesus' first public appeal to the conscience of his nation succeeded. The assembled crowds appear to have listened to his teachings as never before, and the high priests and their followers were held back in impotent rage, cowed by their fear of the masses.

IV. Public Discussions with the Leaders of Judaism. The period which followed the cleansing of the temple appears to have been for Jesus one of intense activity. A recent writer (Wellhausen, *Evangelium Marci*, 88) raises the question whether or not all the recorded events could have been crowded into a short week, and suggests that the Jerusalem ministry extended for a longer period. While this suggestion is possible, it seems more probable that we have here simply a detailed record of an exceedingly active week in Jesus' life. Also the events took place in Jerusalem, the home of Mark, who is the chief source of information regarding them, so that it is not strange that the narrative suddenly becomes more detailed. Each of these incidents reveal the galling fire to which Jesus was subjected and the valiant fight which he made for the rights of the people. As he was walking in the temple, the scribes and elders, the leading members of the sanhedrin, approached him with the tense question: "By what and whose authority are you doing these things?" The question was an inevitable one, and Jesus answered it in a manner far from acceptable to those who asked it. He answered it, as he had many captious questions, by another more incisive: "Was John's call to repentance and a life of purity, sealed by the rite of baptism, of divine authority, or by the authority of men?" The dilemma which Jesus' question presented to these corrupt traducers of the people was obvious, for they hated John and feared the people. Hence, they lamely confessed their unwillingness to answer. "Neither do I tell you by what authority I do these things," was Jesus' quick reply. Yet by his question he had answered theirs: "My authority, like that of John and every God-sent prophet, is not from men, but from above."

Matthew is doubtless right in assigning to this setting the parable of the two sons, with its clear-cut application to the situation. The despised tax-collectors and outcasts, with no professions of righteousness, had accepted the principles and the way of life which Jesus had presented to them; but the high priests and Pharisees, with their sacred titles and loud protestations of righteousness, were rejecting Jesus as they had the teaching of John. Even now, when they saw the truth, they lacked the courage to confess their error and accept the revolutionary principles that these prophets proclaimed.

The more elaborate parable of the vineyard, which Mark introduces at this point, teaches the same lesson. It is Isaiah's parable of the vineyard, found in Isaiah 5[1-7], which has been adapted to the new situation. It has evidently been worked over from the later Christian point of view until it resembles in many respects the allegories found in the Fourth Gospel. Its points of view and teachings resemble closely those found in the sermons of the earlier apostles recorded in the book of Acts. It is also based upon the words of Psalm 118[22, 23]. God is the owner of the vineyard, the Jews are the vine-dressers to whom he intrusts it, the prophets are the servants whom the owner sends, and Jesus is the "beloved son," the "stone which the builders rejected," who, though slain, "has been made the head of the corner." The others to whom the vineyard was to be intrusted were probably, in the original parable, the lowly classes, who listened to the teachings of the kingdom. In the parable, as it stands, they can be none other than the Gentiles, who, by the end of the sixth decade of the first century, constituted a very large proportion of the Christian church. Matthew, in his parallel version, develops this thought still further, and declares that the "kingdom of God shall be taken away from the Jews and given to a nation that brings forth the fruits of the kingdom."

In an isolated passage found only in Luke, Jesus aligns himself with the author of the poetic sections of the book of Job and takes issue with the popular doctrine that calamity was always an index of guilt on the part of its victims. Contemporary history does not record Pilate's mixing the blood of the Galileans with their sacrifices. The act, however, is in general keeping with the character of that cruel, tactless Roman procurator. The event was probably too insignificant to attract the attention of the secular historians. Jesus simply employs this incident and the fall of the tower of Siloam to illustrate his familiar teaching that the essential thing in a man's life is not what befalls him, but rather his attitude toward God and his own acts. Incidentally, the narrative illustrates Jesus' intimate familiarity with current events.

The Sadducees also approached him with one of their much-mooted questions and endeavored to entrap him by their casuistry. Jesus at once took the question out of the field of mere dialectics, and on the basis of the ancient Torah or law, which they claimed to be alone authoritative, endeavored to lead them to an acceptance of his own conception of God and of the individual. "God is the God of the living, not of the dead." On this assertion he based his absolute conviction that he who loves and cares for his children in this life will continue to do so in the life to come. The logic is not of the schools, but of the heart. In his teachings Jesus said little about the future life of the individual. The reason is because he took it for granted, as he did the sunshine and the flowers. Evidently he did not wish to discuss with the Sadducees whether or not the resurrection of the individual was to be, as the Jews believed, a bodily resurrection. By his declaration that when people rise from the dead they neither marry nor give in marriage, but are like the angels in heaven, he probably intended to imply that the resurrection was to be spiritual, not bodily. Paul's teaching supports this conclusion.

Mark gives, in 12³⁵⁻³⁷, an isolated and difficult teaching which, if original with Jesus, doubtless comes from this period of conflict and discussion. The present Greek form implies that it was a question frequently raised by Jesus: "How is it that the scribes say that the Christ is the son of David, when David [Ps. 110⁵] called him Lord?" There is every reason to believe that the psalm was originally addressed to Simon, the Maccabean leader. It is, therefore, to be dated long after the time of David; but in common with the majority of the psalms in the Psalter, it was attributed by Jesus' contemporaries to David; and this tradition regarding its authorship is the basis of the argument here presented. The method of reasoning is that of the rabbis. The meaning of this utterance is obscure, but the most natural interpretation is that it was intended to prove that the Messiah was not necessarily to be of Davidic descent. Its isolation, its obscurity, its peculiar logic, and the fact that Jesus otherwise always avoided public discussion of the question of his messiahship lend a certain weight to the contention of some modern scholars that it is not an original utterance of Jesus, but an argument used by his early followers and akin to many found in the book of Acts. To Jesus the question of human descent was certainly unimportant compared with that of doing the will of his heavenly Father.

V. **The Arraignment of the Scribes and Pharisees.** The First and Second Gospels agree in the statement that during this strenuous period in Jesus' activity he publicly arraigned, not only the high priests, who led the party of the Sadducees, but also the scribes and Pharisees. Luke seems inclined to assign the incident to the earlier crisis in Galilee, and possibly may be right in so doing; but the synoptic gospels as a whole convey the impression that Jesus spared no effort to conciliate the Pharisees until, during the last week at Jerusalem, it became evident that reconciliation was impossible.

By the gospel writers the terms, scribe and Pharisee, are used almost interchangeably. The great majority of the scribes, or learned interpreters of the law, belonged to the party of the Pharisees. There were many in the pharisaic party, however, who were not scribes by profession. In Mark this class is spoken of under the general designation, scribes. In Luke's version of Jesus' woes the Pharisees are first denounced and then the lawyers or interpreters of the law. Matthew, in the corresponding passage, uses the inclusive term, scribes and Pharisees. It is possible that in his original utterances Jesus used only the one word, Pharisees. Mark's narrative simply gives a brief epitome of the characteristics of these proud, self-satisfied, hypocritical leaders of the people. Matthew and Luke have fuller versions of Jesus' arraignment, which they evidently derived from their common teaching source (Q). Luke has abbreviated his material, leaving out that which would be distasteful or meaningless to his Gentile readers. Matthew, however, has expanded, drawing a part of his description of the sins of the Pharisees from the Marcan narrative. Matthew's version also shows the influence of the bitter contest which raged between Jew and Christian during the latter part of the first Christian century. Such passages as, "Neither be called masters, for one is your master, even Christ," recall the exhortations of Paul and the early apostles rather than the original utterances of Jesus. The denunciation of the pharisaic inclination "to encompass sea and land to make one proselyte, and when he is become so, you make him twofold more a son of Hades than yourself," suggests as its background the apostolic age rather than the days of Jesus' ministry.

With the aid of Matthew and Luke it is possible to recover with reasonable assurance the original seven "woes." In the first woe the scribes and Pharisees are denounced because, through their minute laws, they imposed intolerable burdens upon the people, while they themselves showed no inclination to relieve them. In this way the pharisaic scribes constantly enriched the priesthood at the expense of the common people. The second charge is that they not only refused to enter the true kingdom of Heaven, but also deterred others from doing so, as they had constantly during Jesus' Galilean ministry. The third charge is that they insist upon the minutest demands of the ceremonial law, but neglect the far more important questions of justice, kindness, and personal integrity. The next two woes, as recorded in Matthew, are directed against the hypocrisy of the Pharisees, who insist upon ceremonial cleanliness and the appearance of morality, but in reality are given to extortion, indulgence, and immorality. The last charge is that they pay great homage to the martyred prophets, while their attitude toward the living prophets is that of their fathers. The last theme is developed in a quotation from an unknown source. Luke has preserved what appears, on the whole, to be the older form. Upon the Pharisees and the race and generation which they represent will inevitably come the punishment for the cumulative guilt of their nation.

While this arraignment did not apply to all the Pharisees or to all the scribes, yet at this period in Israel's history it laid bare with marvellous insight and justice the faults of the men who, by training and inheritance, were called to interpret truly to the people the ideals of the kingdom of God, but had largely failed. In their inner consciousness, they appreciated far more clearly than did the sordid high priests and Sadducees, the real significance of Jesus' message. If they had accepted it, Israel's fate and the course of human history would doubtless have been far different. They could have carried the majority of the Jewish nation with them and made it possible for Jesus to have realized his ideal and to "have gathered its children together, even as a fowl her brood under her wing."

In dramatic contrast to the malice and greed of the high priests, to the materialism and sophistry of the Sadducees, and to the hypocrisy and moral obliquity of the Pharisees is the picture of the simple piety of the poor widow, who out of her poverty was willing to cast her all into the temple treasury. It was indignation aroused by the sight of greed preying on helplessness and piety of this type that impelled Jesus to espouse so strenuously the cause of the common people, and in so doing to give his life for the sheep.

§ CXLI. JESUS' PREPARATIONS FOR HIS DEATH

Now as Jesus was going out of the temple, one of his disciples said to him, Teacher, see what splendid stones and buildings! And Jesus said to him, Seest thou these great buildings? Not one stone shall be left upon another, that shall not be thrown down. But in three days another shall rise without hands.

1. Prediction of temple's destruction (Mark 13¹,², cf. Matt. 24¹, ² Luke 21⁵, ⁶)

And as he was sitting on the Mount of Olives opposite the temple, Peter and James and John and Andrew ask him privately, Tell us, when shall these things be? And Jesus said to them, No one knows of that day or hour, not even the angels in heaven, nor the Son, only the Father.

2. His reply to the disciples' question (Mark 13³, ⁴ᵃ, ³², cf. Matt. 24³,⁴ᵃ,³⁶ Luke 21⁷)

Then shall the kingdom of Heaven be like ten maidens, who took their lamps and went out to meet the bridegroom. Five of them were foolish and five were wise. For the foolish ones, when they took their lamps, took no oil with them. But the wise took oil in their vessels with their lamps. Now while the bridegroom was delayed, they all slumbered and slept. But at midnight a cry was raised, Here is the bridegroom! Come out to meet him! And all those maidens arose and trimmed their lamps. And the foolish ones said to the wise, 'Give us some of your oil, for our lamps are going out.' But the wise answered, 'Perhaps there may not be enough for us and for you. Go rather to those who sell and buy for yourselves.' Now while they went away to buy, the bridegroom came, and those who were ready went in with him to the marriage feast. And the door was shut. Afterwards the other maidens came also

3. Parable of the wise and foolish virgins (Matt. 25¹⁻¹²)

and said, 'Lord, Lord, open to us.' But he said in reply, 'I tell you truly, I do not know you.' Watch, therefore, for you know not the day nor the hour.

4. The coming of the Son of man (Matt. 24⁴⁷⁻⁵¹, cf. Mark 13¹ᵇ⁻²¹, ³⁶⁻³⁷ Luke 12³⁵⁻⁴⁸ 17²²⁻³⁷ 21³⁴⁻³⁶)

For as were the days of Noah, so shall be the coming of the Son of man. For as in the days before the flood they were eating and drinking and marrying and giving in marriage, until the day when Noah entered the ark, and knew nothing until the flood came and took them away, so shall be the coming of the Son of man. There shall be two men in the field. One is taken and one is left; two women shall be grinding at the millstone; one is taken and one is left. Watch then, for you know not on what day your lord is coming. But know this, Had the master of the house known the hour in which the thief was coming, he would have been on his guard and would not have allowed his house to be broken into. Therefore, be you also ready, for at an hour that you think not the Son of man is coming. Who then is the faithful and wise servant whom his master has appointed over his household, to give them their food in due season? Happy that servant, whom his master shall find so doing when he comes. I tell you truly, he will appoint him over all that he has. But if that evil servant says in his heart, My master is delaying, and shall begin to beat his fellow-servants, and to eat and drink with drunkards, the master of that servant shall come in a day when he does not expect him and in an hour which he does not know and shall cut him in two and appoint his portion with the hypocrites. There shall the weeping be, and the gnashing of teeth.

5. Plot of the high priests (Mark 14¹,², cf. Matt. 26³⁻⁵ Luke 22¹,²)

Now after two days it was the Passover and the feast of unleavened bread. And the high priests and scribes were seeking how they could seize Jesus by craft and kill him, for they said, Not during the feast, lest possibly there be a tumult among the people.

6. Jesus' anointing at the home of Simon (Mark 14³⁻⁹, cf. Matt. 26⁶⁻¹³)

And while Jesus was reclining at dinner in the house of Simon the leper at Bethany, a woman came with an alabaster flask of pure nard, perfume, most costly. And breaking the flask, she kept pouring it over his head. Some were indignant, saying to themselves, Why this waste of perfume? For this perfume might have been sold for more than three hundred denarii and given to the poor. And they kept finding fault with her. But Jesus said, Let her alone. Why do you trouble her? She has done for me a beautiful deed. For the poor you have always with you, and whenever you wish, you can do them good. But me you do not always have. She has done what she could. She has anointed my body beforehand for burial. And I tell you truly, wherever the gospel shall be preached throughout the whole world, what this woman has done shall also be told in memory of her.

Now during the day, Jesus used to teach in the temple, but at night he went out and passed the night on the hill, which was called the Olive Orchard. And early in the morning all the people used to come to him in the temple to hear him. *7. His daily program (Luke 21³⁷, ³⁸)*

Then Judas of Kerioth, who was one of the Twelve, went off to the high priests, to betray him to them. And when they heard it they were glad and promised to pay him money. And he kept trying how he could betray him at a favorable moment. *8. Judas' bargain (Mark 14¹⁰, ¹¹, cf. Matt. 26¹⁴⁻¹⁶ Luke 22³⁻⁶)*

And on the first day of unleavened bread, when people sacrificed the paschal lamb, his disciples said to him, Where wilt thou have us go and make ready for thee to eat the paschal lamb. And he sent two of his disciples and said to them, Go over into the city. A man will meet you carrying a pitcher of water. Follow him, and wherever he shall enter, say to the master of the house, The Teacher says, 'Where is my guest chamber, where I may eat the paschal lamb with my disciples?' And he himself will show you a large upper room, made ready, and furnished. There make ready for us. And the disciples departed and went to the city and found it just as he had told them. And they made ready the Passover. *9. Preparations for the last supper (Mark 14¹²⁻¹⁶, cf. Matt. 26¹⁷⁻¹⁹ Luke 22⁷⁻¹³)*

And when it was evening Jesus came with the Twelve. And he said, I tell you truly, One of you shall betray me, even one who is eating with me. They began to be sorrowful and say to him, one by one, It is not I, is it? But he said to them, It is one of the Twelve, one who is dipping in the dish with me. For the Son of man departs even as it is written of him. But woe to that man through whom the Son of man is betrayed. It were better for that man had he never been born. *10. Jesus' prediction of his betrayal (Mark 14¹⁷⁻²¹, cf. Matt. 26²⁰⁻²⁵ Luke 22²¹⁻²³)*

11.
The
last
supper
(I Cor.
11²³⁻²⁵
Mark
14²⁶, cf.
Mark
14²²⁻²⁵
Matt.
22²⁶⁻³⁰
Luke
22¹⁴⁻
²⁰, ³⁹)

12.
Jesus'
pre-
diction
of his
denial
(Mark
14²⁷⁻³¹,
cf.
Matt.
26³¹⁻³⁵
Luke
22³¹⁻³⁸)

Jesus on the night in which he was betrayed broke bread, and when he had given thanks, he broke it and said, This is my body, which is for you; do this in remembrance of me. In like manner also the cup after supper, saying, This cup is the new covenant in my blood. This do in remembrance of me. Then, after singing a hymn, they went out to the Mount of Olives.

And Jesus said to them, All of you shall be led to fall away, for it is written: 'I will smite the shepherd and the sheep shall be scattered abroad.' But after I rise I will go before you into Galilee. But Peter said to him, Though all should be led to fall away, yet I will not. Then Jesus said to him: I tell you truly: to-day, this very night, before the cock crows twice, thou shalt deny me three times. But Peter said the more vehemently, Though I have to die with thee, I will not deny thee. And all of them said the same thing.

I. The Prediction of the Temple's Destruction. In the beginning of the thirteenth chapter of his gospel, Mark recounts a commonplace incident which had a far-reaching result. As Jesus was leaving the temple court with his disciples, one of them, impressed by the magnitude of the stones and the beauty of the structures which crowned it, commented upon them. To Galilean peasants the vast temple reared by Herod was, indeed, an impressive sight. Josephus states that some of the stones in the temple were twenty-five cubits long, twelve broad, and eight high. At certain places in the foundation the modern traveller may see huge stones twenty-five to thirty feet in length. Memory of his recent conflict with the high priests and a recognition of the hollowness and hypocrisy of the national religion which it represented caused Jesus to reply that the time should come when this vast structure would lie a shapeless mass of ruins. The variants in certain Western texts add the words, "But in three days another shall rise without hands." These words are implied by the charges that are later brought against Jesus (cf. Mark 14⁵⁸ and 15²⁹). The Fourth Gospel (2¹⁹) introduces them in the conversation between Jesus and the high priests; but they were probably addressed to Jesus' disciples as they were commenting on the Herodian temple. The Western variants may be right in restoring them to the text of Mark. In these paradoxical words Jesus drew the contrast between the temple of stone, with its empty ceremonialism, and the spiritual temple, not to be seen with the eyes, but eternal.

The temple of Herod, with its elaborate rites and traditions and creeds, stood in the way of that divine temple, in which alone God could be truly worshipped. In the vivid, concrete language which Jesus used, three days represented a brief period. The words reveal his absolute conviction that ere long the true and spiritual temple would take the place of that structure and type of worship which Israel's faith and needs had long since outgrown. As has truly been said, Jesus, in uttering these words in public, where spies were dogging his footsteps, eager to catch up any suspicious word, "put a sword in the hands of his foes." To the minds of the Jews a word spoken against the temple was blasphemy. The same had been true in the days of Jeremiah, for a similar prediction nearly cost the life of that great prophet of the earlier days (Jer. 7 and 26).

The thirteenth chapter of Mark presents many problems to the careful student of the gospels. A long discourse, filled with words and phrases peculiar to the Jewish apocalypses, suddenly takes the place of the simple narrative. The natural query of the four disciples, as to when the temple would be destroyed, is answered by a series of predictions which seem to bear no real relation to the questions raised. Recognizing this fact, the author of Matthew, in quoting Mark, has altered the question in order to adapt it to the answer given, so that it reads: "What shall be the sign of thy coming and of the end of the world?" In Mark 13$^{30-32}$ two answers are given to the question raised by the disciples. The one answer (^{30}) is very definite: "I tell you truly, this generation shall not pass away until all these things be accomplished." The second (^{32}) is entirely different and practically irreconcilable with the first: "No one knows of that day or hour, not even the angels in the heavens, nor the son, only the Father." The latter is probably the answer which Jesus gave to the question of the disciples. He saw with prophetic insight the germs of decay that meant the ultimate destruction of his nation. Like earlier prophets he boldly proclaimed his conviction; but with equal frankness declared that God only knew when that destruction would come.

II. Jesus' Warnings to His Disciples. Into the heart of the thirteenth chapter Mark or a later author has inserted a composite Jewish-Christian apocalypse. Three distinct divisions may be recognized. The first ($^{5-8}$) was intended to warn the Christians against being led astray by the many false messiahs who came in the years succeeding Jesus' death. An additional aim was to prevent them from interpreting wars and natural calamities as proofs that the end of the world was at hand. It contains apparent allusions to the Parthian wars between 51 and 62 A.D., the great famine in Palestine in 46 and 47, and the earthquakes in Asia in 61 or 63. The second apocalypse ([14-23]) refers to the destruction of Jerusalem and alludes in detail to the escape of the Christians. The point of view is that of the later church, as is well illustrated by [20]: "Unless the Lord had shortened the days no flesh would have been saved, but for the sake of his elect he did shorten the days." The third division, in the language of such Old Testament apocalyptic passages as Isaiah 13[10] 24[4, 21, 23] and Daniel 7[13], describes the coming of the Son of man "in the clouds with great power and glory and the gathering of his elect from the four quarters of the heavens." The ideas, as well as the expressions of this passage, are as far removed from the simple, direct, ethical teachings of Jesus as the book of Daniel is from the teachings of Amos. Evidently the aim of this apocalyptic prophecy as a whole, like that of Paul in II Thessalonians, was to curb the fanatical beliefs of the early Christians that Jesus' second coming was imminent. The prominence of these beliefs among the early Christians is revealed by many passages in the epistles, as well as in the gospels (cf. I Cor. 15[51, 52] I Thess. 4[16, 17] 5[3-5]).

The synoptic gospels are by no means in agreement regarding the time of that coming. In Matthew 10[23] the promise is put in the words of Jesus that it will be before the disciples had completed their preaching and teaching tour in the cities of Palestine. According to Matthew 16[27, 28] and Mark 8[38] 9[1], it was to be while some of the disciples were still living. In the apocalypse of Mark 13[26] and its parallels the implication is that it was to be immediately after the destruction of Jerusalem; while in Mark 13[32] it is clearly stated that no man knows the day or the hour. Apparently no authoritative and generally accepted statement regarding the coming of the Son of man was known to the evangelists.

The more fundamental question is, Did Jesus predict his second coming or is this widespread belief in the early church simply the read-justment of the contemporary Jewish apocalyptic hope to the point of view of the early Christian community? Paul himself is a striking illustration of how many Jewish ideas were still retained even by a broad-minded follower of Jesus. The atmosphere in which the early Christian community developed was surcharged with these apocalyptic hopes. The synoptic gospels are full of proof that the evangelists themselves were dominated by them. Repeatedly, as in Matthew's quotation of the Marcan original, where Jesus spoke of the destruction of Jerusalem or of the establishment of the kingdom of God, the later evangelists, in transcribing, substituted the coming of the Son of man. It is also significant that these apocalyptic passages are almost completely lacking in the Fourth Gospel. In view of these established facts, many scholars think it doubtful if Jesus ever referred to his second coming. Certainly he never gave it the prominent place in his teachings that it has in the synoptic gospels. Furthermore, it seems to be contrary to his conception of the kingdom or rule of God. With him the kingdom of God was present, not merely future. Its growth was gradual, not sudden and catastrophic. It was to be instituted, not through a miracle, but through the voluntary co-operation of men. History has demonstrated both the absolute truth of his teaching regarding the kingdom and the vanity of these apocalyptic hopes. The belief in the second coming of the Son of man has been a fetter rather than an aid in the development of Christianity. The question still remains, Did Jesus give any basis for this belief so widely held by his followers? It is found embedded in the earliest teaching source (Q). Paul's testimony indicates that it also reached its height about the middle of the first Christian century. Jesus, in his conception of nature, in his apparent belief in a personal devil, and in his acceptance of the Jewish tradition regarding the origin and authorship of the Jewish scriptures, showed himself in many respects a son of his age and race. It would not have been strange if, to a certain extent, he had also shared its apocalyptic hopes. Many, perhaps a majority, of modern New Testament students hold that he did. But if so, this belief evidently exerted little influence upon his thought and teaching. His robust spiritual nature felt no need of these doctrines which were the consolation of the persecuted and despairing. They were too indefinite and lacking in ethical and religious content to appeal to him strongly.

It is significant that the oldest gospel records do not reveal a single apocalyptic note in those teachings of Jesus which belong to the period of the Galilean activity. The apocalyptic predictions first appear among the utterances that come from the closing days of his work at Jerusalem, when he found himself abandoned by the masses and confronting martyrdom at the hands of the leaders of his nation. With the Jewish prophets who penned the later apocalypses he shared the undying conviction, even in the face of persecution and calamity and death, that God was in his world and that the right would surely triumph in the end. This is the great principle that underlies all the apocalyptic promises attributed to him. It is also noteworthy that in the parables and passages, which come from the oldest teaching source (Q) and which imply the second coming of Jesus, the emphasis is not placed on the miraculous element involved in that coming, but on the personal responsibility of his disciples. "Watch and be faithful" is the distinctive note in the parable of the wise and foolish maidens and of the faithful and wise servant.

The original basis, therefore, of these teachings, which appear to have been recast and greatly elaborated under the influence of current Jewish ideas, are predictions regarding (1) the calamity that was richly deserved and sure to come upon the Jewish temple and nation, (2) the trials and persecutions that would befall his faithful disciples, even as they had their master, (3) definite assurance that if his disciples proved faithful, they would ultimately be rewarded, and (4) that God in his gracious and all-wise way would surely realize his purpose in the world and that the truths which Jesus had proclaimed would ultimately prevail and conquer.

III. **The Anointing at Bethany.** The temper of the high priests had been clearly revealed to Jesus. Knowledge of their desire to seize him by craft and kill him had probably already been brought to him by some of his sympathizers. The record of his activity at this time makes it clear that he was constantly on the alert to thwart their purpose. By day in the temple and amidst the multitudes he was safe from the high-priestly authorities, for they feared nothing more than a tumult, which would give Pilate and his barbarous soldiery an excuse for bloody intervention. Evidently Jesus spent his nights sometimes at one place and sometimes at another, but always outside Jerusalem.

Mark has given one of his clear-cut pictures of the scene at the house of a certain Simon in Bethany. The fact that he is called a leper implies that, like many in Palestine at this time, he had been afflicted with a disease popularly classified as leprosy, but curable. Even had he been the victim of real leprosy, in a little village like Bethany, his wealth and influence may have enabled him to disregard Jewish law. Jesus had repeatedly shown that he had no hesitation in associating with this class. The Fourth Gospel has possibly retained a fact overlooked by Mark, namely, that the woman who showed her deep devotion to Jesus was Mary the sister of Martha. The exact character of the perfume with which she anointed Jesus' head is unknown. It may have been an aromatic oil made from pistachio nuts. Its value, about seventy-five dollars, suggests that she was a woman of comparative wealth. Her act was one of deepest devotion, but to her and to

Jesus, and probably to the assembled guests, it possessed a deeper symbolic meaning. Since the days when Samuel had anointed Saul as king, the public pouring of oil upon the head possessed in Palestine a unique significance. The word Messiah itself means "the anointed." Jesus' words to her show deepest appreciation and tenderness, but they recall what he said to Peter when that disciple first hailed him as Messiah. He assured her and the assembled guests that the anointing was not that he might sit upon a throne, but for his burial. Thus at every point, even in the ranks of his most devoted disciples, Jesus was assailed by the same temptation that confronted him when he left John beside the banks of the Jordan. With the same firmness and calm faith, he turned from the dream of material glory to the ideal of the Messiah, who should do the will of God by humble, tireless service, even though the path of service led to the cross.

IV. Judas's Bargain with the High Priests. The gospel narratives imply that Jesus, by his care and foresight, had succeeded in circumventing for the time being his high-priestly foes. Luke states that each night he went across the Kidron Valley to the Mount of Olives and there spent the night in seclusion at a certain olive orchard, probably at the home of some friend. Fear of the people led the high priests to at least postpone action until after the sacred Passover festival. Knowledge of this situation and of the opportunity personally to profit by it proved too great a temptation for Judas of Kerioth. The fact that he was probably a native of one of the suburbs of Jerusalem may explain why he was eager to win the favor of the Jewish authorities even at the cost of treachery. The historical narratives furnish little basis for the elaborate attempts that have been made to palliate Judas's crime. It is incredible that he should be so obtuse as to think it possible by such action to force Jesus to proclaim himself a temporal Messiah.

The reasons which actuated Judas were probably simpler and more mercenary. He, like the other disciples, had felt the charm of Jesus' personality, had noted his influence with the multitudes, and had probably joined with enthusiasm that brotherhood which had shared the privations and the triumphs of the Galilean teacher. But now he lacked the courage to bear disappointment and to face ostracism and personal danger. Possibly he felt personally aggrieved because Jesus persistently refused to realize the selfish ambitions of his disciples. The Fourth Gospel (John 12[6]) declares that he was a thief, and that he was the one who protested against the waste of the ointment in the house of the leper, "because he pilfered what was put into the purse, of which he had charge." If this statement is historical, Judas's deterioration had been gradual and the prospect of receiving a rich reward for his treachery was not the least of the temptations that lured him on to commit the crime. The cold-blooded way in which he later betrayed Jesus by a kiss indicates that his character had become thoroughly depraved. His was evidently the case of a man of ability, capable of responding to an exalted ideal, but who, even in the presence of the supreme incarnation of that ideal, yielded to his naturally selfish ambition and innate covetousness. Even membership in the wonderful brotherhood which Jesus gathered about him did not save Judas from the faults which he secretly cherished. His act was base and utterly inexcusable, and yet he was not the most arrant criminal of history. He was a type of the thousands who listened to Jesus and then failed to find their lives because they were not willing to lose them for his sake and for the sake of the truth which he proclaimed. It was only because he was intimately associated with Jesus that later tradition pictured his character so darkly.

Jesus' words to his disciples during this crisis indicate that he suspected treachery of this type. With his intimate knowledge of human nature and his personal acquaintance with his disciples, his suspicions probably pointed to Judas. This knowledge is evidently the basis of his words, recorded in Mark, on the eve of his last supper with his disciples. The countenance and bearing of Judas doubtless confirmed this suspicion, but there is no evidence in the oldest records that Jesus indicated upon which one of his disciples it rested. The Fourth Gospel has heightened the dramatic element by representing Jesus as saying to Judas, "What thou doest, do quickly"; after which the traitor quickly departed to consummate his crime. According to Mark, Jesus' words of warning were intended to make clear to Judas the enormity of his act and, if possible, to deter him. Like many of the incidents in the Marcan record, the predictive element has possibly here been heightened, since the account was written in the light of the event, but Jesus was keenly sensitive to the men and forces with which he had to deal, and he here reveals that knowledge of men which characterized his entire ministry.

V. Jesus' Last Supper with His Disciples. Jesus' intuitive feeling that Judas was plotting with the high priests explains his eagerness to eat once more with his disciples in Jerusalem. The synoptic gospels, following Mark, state definitely that this supper was on the

JESUS' LAST SUPPER WITH HIS DISCIPLES

fourteenth of Nisan, the Friday evening on which the Passover was inaugurated by the slaying of the paschal lamb. Here many hold that the Marcan account has been influenced by the later tendency which grew into the custom of commemorating this event at the same time as the Jewish Passover. This close association of the Lord's supper and the Passover was of great practical value to the early church, for many Jewish Christians were still inclined to observe the Jewish festival. The Fourth Gospel is, beyond reasonable doubt, right in stating that Jesus' last supper with his disciples was observed on the Thursday before the Passover feast (so John 13[1, 29] 18[23] 19[14, 31]). Even the Marcan narrative records the fact that the Jewish high priests, unprincipled though they were, would not countenance a crucifixion on the Passover day.

The detailed directions and the secrecy which Jesus observed in regard to the place where he was to eat the last supper with his disciples was in perfect keeping with the caution which he had constantly observed since his arrival at Jerusalem. Apparently he did not reveal the place, even to his most intimate disciples, until the last moment. Christian tradition, perhaps rightly, associates it with the home of Mary, the mother of John Mark. If so, this fact explains the unusually detailed character of the narrative at this point. Judas was among the Twelve, and Jesus may well have hoped that his presence there and the later words of warning might possibly deter him from his treacherous purpose.

Paul, in his first letter to the Corinthians (11[23-25]) has given the oldest account of this last supper. He doubtless tells it as he heard it from the lips of the apostles. The details correspond to the Kiddush, or Ritual of Prayer, that was observed by the pious Jewish families on the night preceding the Passover. It included a preliminary prayer, followed by the formal breaking of the bread, and the blessing and distribution of a cup of wine by the head of the household. In the early church the breaking of the bread and the pouring out of wine were more significant than eating the bread or drinking the wine. In Paul's early record the memorial element is the most prominent. As has been truly said, it was "not a sacrament, but an example and parable." It stood for all that Jesus was and taught: his friendship, his teachings, his deeds of healing, his ideals, and his self-sacrifice. His purpose was to keep these vividly before the minds of his disciples. It illustrates the methods of the great Teacher. There is no clear evidence that he intended it to be observed, as it later fittingly was by the church.

as an institution. In fact, Jesus purposely avoided establishing institutions or laying down laws that might prevent the natural adaptation and application of the principles which he set forth. Bread and wine were the two most common articles of food with the people of Palestine. Necessity compelled them to partake of them each day. By this constantly recurring act Jesus sought to keep ever vividly before the minds of his followers their fellowship with him and all that it meant to them. It was also the reminder of the covenant, which bound them together closer than the bonds of blood-kinship and of that new personal relation which Jesus had sought to establish between each of his followers and their common Father. The figure of the new covenant in the heart of the individual was probably drawn from the memorable words of Jeremiah (31^{31-34}):

Behold the days are coming, is Jehovah's oracle,
That I will make a new covenant with the house of Israel.
Not like the covenant which I made with their fathers,
In the days that I took them by the hand to bring them out of the land of Egypt—
My covenant which they themselves broke, and I was displeased with them,
But this is the covenant which I will make with the house of Israel:
After those days, is the oracle of Jehovah,
I will put my teaching on their breast, and on their heart will I write it;
And I will be to them a God, and they shall be to me a people.
And they shall not teach any more, every man his neighbor,
And every man his brother, saying, 'Know Jehovah,'
For they shall all know me, from the least of them to the greatest;
For I will forgive their iniquities and remember their sins no more.

It well describes the work of the great Teacher, who, as the result of his life and teaching, set aside the old, imperfect covenant between Jehovah and the nation by proclaiming the possibilities and the conditions of that new covenant between God and every human child, whatever be his race and position in life. In its historical content, therefore, the institution of the Lord's supper suggests, not defeat and gloom, but heroic, self-sacrificing friendship and a joyous, complete faith in God which human injustice and sin could not daunt.

VI. **Jesus' Farewell Words to His Disciples.** Mark, who appears to have heightened the predictive element in Jesus' discourses during these closing days, records the prediction that not only Peter would deny him, but that the other disciples would fall away (lit., would cause to stumble). Their defection was regarded as a fulfilment of the prophecy of Zechariah 13⁷: "I will smite the shepherd and the sheep shall be scattered abroad." Mark also adds the promise, "After I arise, I will go before you into Galilee," which anticipates the resurrection appearances beside the Sea of Galilee.

The corresponding passage in Luke 22²⁸⁻³⁸ evidently represents an independent source. Luke is followed by the Fourth Gospel. Matthew holds to the Marcan version of Jesus' farewell words, which are uttered during the walk across the Kidron Valley rather than during the last supper, as in Luke and John. The Lucan version seeks to palliate Peter's sin of desertion, and says nothing about that of the other disciples; but it reveals the depth of affection which bound Jesus to them and that divine enthusiasm and humanity which drew men to him: "You are the men who have remained with me throughout my trials." The promise that they should "sit upon twelve thrones, governing the twelve tribes of Israel," voices the hope and belief of the later church.

The words, which on their surface seem to contain the command that henceforth they should resort to the sword, may well be original, for this is the simplest explanation of why they have been preserved. If so, they must be interpreted figuratively, not literally. It was Jesus' dramatic, hyperbolic way of announcing to his disciples the peril and stress that were imminent. The reference to the ideal of the suffering servant in Isaiah 53¹², "He was reckoned among the wicked," is equally significant, for it again suggests how prominent at this time in the mind of the Master was this noblest and divinest of the Old Testament messianic ideals. With these marvellous proofs of Jesus' solicitude for his disciples and of his complete devotion to the task intrusted to him, he and the eleven went forth to their usual place of concealment on the Mount of Olives, while Judas apparently slipped away in the darkness to give the fatal signal to the high priest.

§ CXLII. JESUS' ARREST AND TRIAL

1. The struggle and victory in Gethsemane (Mark 14³²⁻³⁶, cf. Matt. 26³⁶⁻³⁹, Luke 22³⁹⁻⁴²)

And Jesus and his disciples come to a place called **Gethsemane**. And he says to his disciples, Sit here while I pray. And he takes with him Peter and James and John. And he began to be appalled and greatly troubled. And he says to them, My soul is very sorrowful, even to death; stay here and watch. Then going forward a little, he fell on the ground and prayed that, if it were possible, the hour might pass away from him. And he kept saying, Abba Father! All things are possible to thee; remove this cup from me. Yet not what I will, but what thou wilt.

2. The agonized Master and his sleeping disciples (Mark 14³⁷⁻⁴², cf. Matt. 26⁴⁰⁻⁴⁶, Luke 22⁴³⁻⁴⁶)

Then he comes and finds them sleeping. And he says to Peter, Simon, art thou asleep? Hadst thou not strength to watch one hour? Watch and pray, lest you enter into temptation. The spirit indeed is eager, but the flesh is weak. Then he went away again and prayed, saying the same words. And once again he came and found them sleeping, for their eyes were very heavy; and they did not know how to answer him. And he comes the third time and says to them, Sleep on now and rest! It is enough. The hour has come; behold, the Son of man is betrayed into the hands of sinners. Arise, let us be going. Behold, the betrayer is near.

3. Jesus' arrest (Mark 14⁴³⁻⁵², cf. Matt. 26⁴⁷⁻⁵⁶, Luke 22⁴⁷⁻⁵³)

And immediately, while he was still speaking, Judas, one of the Twelve, came, together with a crowd, with swords and clubs, from the high priests and the scribes and the elders. Now the betrayer had given them a signal, saying, Him whom I kiss, that is he. Seize him and lead him away safely. So on coming, he immediately goes and says to him, Rabbi, and kissed him. And they laid hands on him and seized him. But one of those who stood by drew his sword and struck the servant of the high priest and cut off his ear. And Jesus spoke up and said to them, Did you come out as against a robber, with swords and clubs to arrest me? I was daily in the temple with you, teaching, and you did not seize me. But it is in order that the scriptures may be fulfilled. Then they all left him alone and fled. But a certain young man accompanied him, with a linen cloth thrown

278

around him, over his naked body. And they seized him; but leaving the linen cloth, he fled naked.

Now after arresting Jesus, they took him and brought him to the house of the high priest. But Peter followed at a distance. And when they had kindled a fire in the middle of the court yard and had sat down together, Peter sat down among them. Now a certain maid servant seeing him seated by the firelight, looked steadily at him and said, This man also was with him. But he denied, saying, Woman, I do not know him. Then shortly after, another person saw him and said, You also are one of them. But Peter said, Man, I am not. After about an hour had passed, another man confidently declared, Certainly this man also was with him. And it must be so, for he is a Galilean. But Peter said, Man, I do not know what you are talking about. Then instantly, while he was still speaking, the cock crowed. And the Lord turned and looked upon Peter. Then Peter remembered the statement, how he had said to him, Before the cock crows this day, thou shalt deny me three times. And he went out and wept bitterly.

4. Peter's denial of his Master (Luke 22⁵⁴⁻⁶², cf. Mark 14⁵³ᵃ, ⁶⁶⁻⁷² Matt. 26⁵⁷ᵃ, ⁶⁹⁻⁷⁵)

And all the men who kept guard over Jesus kept mocking him and beating him. And after blindfolding him, they kept asking him questions. Prophesy, who is it that struck thee? And many other insulting things they said to him.

5. The insults of the guards (Luke 22⁶³⁻⁶⁵, cf. Mark 14⁶⁵ Matt. 26⁶⁷, ⁶⁸)

As soon as it was day, the assembly of the elders of the people was gathered together, both high priests and scribes, and they led him away to their council, saying, If thou art the Christ, tell us. He said to them, You will not believe, if I tell you, nor will you answer, if I ask. But from this time the Son of man shall be seated at the right hand of God's power. And they all said to him, Art thou then the Son of God? And he said to them, You say that I am. So they said, But what further need have we of evidence? For we have heard it ourselves from his own lips.

6. Examination before the high priests (Luke 22⁶⁹⁻⁷¹, cf. Mark 14⁵³ᵇ⁻⁶⁴ Matt. 26⁵⁷ᵇ⁻⁶⁶)

Then the whole company of them rose up and led him to Pilate. And they began to accuse him, saying, We found this man perverting our nation, forbidding people to give tribute to Cæsar and saying that he himself is Christ the king. But Pilate asked him, saying, Art thou the King of the Jews? And he said to him in reply, Thou sayest. So

7. His acquittal by Pilate (Luke 23¹⁻⁷, cf. Mark 15¹⁻⁵ Matt. 27¹, ², ¹¹⁻¹⁴)

Pilate said to the high priests and the crowds, I find nothing criminal in this man. But they were the more insistent, saying, He stirs up the people, teaching throughout all of Judea, beginning from Galilee and coming even here. Hearing this, Pilate asked, Is the man a Galilean? And when he learned that he belonged to Herod's jurisdiction he sent him to Herod, as he too was at Jerusalem during these days.

8. Jesus before Herod Antipas (Luke 23:8-12) Now when Herod saw Jesus, he was greatly delighted, for he had long wished to see him on account of what he had heard of him. And he also hoped to see some sign performed by him. So he questioned him with many words, but he did not answer him at all. And after Herod, together with his soldiers, had scoffed at him and mocked him, arraying him in gorgeous raiment, he sent him back to Pilate. On that day Herod and Pilate became friends with one another, for previously they had been at enmity with each other.

9. Pilate's sentence (Luke 23:13-25, cf. Mark 15:6-15 Matt. 27:15-26) Now after Pilate had called together the high priests and the rulers and the people he said to them, You brought this man to me as a seducer of the people. Yet, behold, I have examined him before you and have found nothing criminal in him of those things of which you accuse him; no, nor even has Herod, for he sent him back to us. And behold he has done nothing worthy of death. I will therefore chastise him and release him. But they all cried out together, Away with him! Release for us Barabbas! (a man who had been cast into prison, because of a riot which had taken place in the city and on account of murder). But Pilate, wishing to release Jesus, again addressed them. But they kept shouting, Crucify him! Crucify him! But he, for the third time, said to them, Why, what evil has this man done? I have found nothing worthy of death in him. I will therefore chastise him and release him. But they were insistent, loudly demanding that he might be crucified. And their voices prevailed. And Pilate gave sentence that their request should be granted, and he loosed the man as they requested, who had been cast into prison for riot and murder. But Jesus he delivered up according to their wish.

THE STRUGGLE IN GETHSEMANE

Ⅰ. The Struggle in Gethsemane. The Fourth Gospel states that Judas left the group of the Twelve before the close of their final supper together. The earlier records imply, however, that he remained with them until the close of the supper; but from his countenance and manner it was easy for Jesus to see that his general words of warning had made no impression upon him. Probably Judas accompanied the disciples far enough to ascertain that they were bound for the place on the Mount of Olives where they had hitherto found refuge at night. His absence, when discovered, was the unmistakable signal to Jesus that the tragic hour had arrived. Distances are so short in Jerusalem that Judas could have given the signal to the agents of the high priests even while Jesus and his disciples were crossing the Kidron Valley. Luke has abbreviated and at the same time transformed Mark's account of the scene in the Garden of Gethsemane by excusing the failure of the disciples to remain awake during the brief period of Jesus' prayer and inner struggle. The statement that "an angel appeared to him from heaven, strengthening him," and that "his sweat became, as it were, great drops of blood falling upon the ground," is lacking, not only in the other gospels, but in the best texts of Luke. The reference to the angel corresponds to the similar allusion in the apocryphal passage in John 5⁴.

The exact site of the Garden of Gethsemane is probably to be found nearer the top of the Mount of Olives than the spot, far down the Kidron Valley and only a short distance from the temple walls, which is pointed out to-day as the scene of Jesus' agony and arrest. In a quiet, rock-strewn garden, shaded by gnarled olive trees and surrounded by a rough stone wall, Jesus faced his last great temptation. At the beginning of his ministry he had met the temptations peculiar to manhood and to one consecrated to a great mission. At the transfiguration he decided to brave the dangers that lurked in Jerusalem and to give himself, if need be, for his cause. Now at this third supreme crisis of his life he was face to face with death, clothed in the hideous garb of treachery, hate, greed, injustice, and intrenched graft. In the darkness, lighted only by the stars, without the consoling friendship of his disciples, who had fallen asleep, overcome by the wearying anxiety of the strenuous days and the night vigils that had preceded, Jesus resisted the natural temptation to seek refuge in flight. He also conquered the deadlier temptation to yield to doubt and despair. He learned then, as he had before, the truth of the words which he spoke to his disciples, "The spirit indeed is eager, but the flesh is weak." He learned it not through defeat, but through victory. The words of his prayer, which must have fallen upon the half-awake ears of one of his disciples, admit of only one interpretation. Jesus still longed, even though with slight hope, that the impending crisis might be averted. The words are exceedingly important to a true interpretation of his character. As in Mark 10[39], the cup stands as a symbol of shame and martyrdom. It was not death that he feared, although he instinctively shrank from it, as does every normal man, and for him life and friendship and achievement were supremely attractive. The "cup" was rather the sense of failure and apprehension for his cause. To him had come the clear vision of the most glorious, and yet the most practical, social order ever seen by man. During his early Galilean activity he had seemed on the eve of realizing it. Now, repudiated by the Pharisees, regarded with suspicion by the people, hated with a murderous hate by the heads of the Jewish hierarchy, betrayed by one of his disciples, and followed hesitatingly by the others, he was confronted by the most cruel death that human barbarity could devise. Yet Jesus' faith in God was such that he was able to pray, "Not what I will, but what thou wilt." In so doing he proved himself forever, not only the Teacher, but the Master and Saviour of men.

II. **The Arrest of Jesus.** Luke, as usually in his narrative, minimizes and Mark magnifies the predictive element. Probably Jesus' lone vigil had not continued long before the torches of the rabble could be seen across the Kidron Valley and the sound of their footsteps could be heard in the still night. Mark is undoubtedly right in stating that the rabble consisted simply of the menials and dependents of the high priests and their temple associates. This conclusion is confirmed by circumstantial evidence, for the one whose ear was cut off in the attempt to deliver Jesus from this mob was a servant of the high priest. Jesus' own words indicate that a disorganized mob with swords and sticks and clubs came out to seize him, the unresisting Galilean teacher. The statement of the Fourth Gospel that Jesus was arrested by a cohort of soldiers, numbering many hundreds, and that they at first fell to the ground at the sight of Jesus, has all the characteristics of later tradition. The same characteristic is illustrated by the statement of Luke that Jesus miraculously healed the wound inflicted by one of his followers. These later elements are not found in the detailed narrative of Mark. Luke places the attempt of one of his unknown followers to defend Jesus before his arrest, but Mark after. From all the records it is perfectly clear that Jesus made no attempt to resist. His simple words of protest undoubtedly reveal his attitude. Mark has recorded an incident so personal that the other evangelists have omitted it. This reference to the youth who fled is probably due to the vivid memory of either Peter or Mark, and therefore is psychologically of great value in testing the historical accuracy of the record as a whole. Alone, unresisting, deserted by his disciples, Jesus was dragged away in the midnight darkness to the palace of his relentless persecutor.

III. **Jesus' Examination Before the High Priests.** Beginning with the fifty-fourth verse of the twenty-second chapter, Luke introduces an account of Jesus' trial and crucifixion which at many points departs widely from the Marcan record. It presents a far simpler and more consistent picture of the events than does Mark. The only satisfactory explanation of why Luke followed this narrative rather than that in Mark, which in many ways appealed to him most strongly, is that he recognized its superior historical value. He may have found it in the early teaching source (Q). If so, the author of Matthew did not quote it because he preferred to follow Mark. Certain inconsistencies in Mark's record at this point have been noted (*cf.* Bacon, *Begs. of Gospel Story*, 210–11). Mark's aim was apparently (1) to establish Jesus' messiahship and (2) to fix the responsibility for Jesus' death on the entire Jewish nation. The superior Lucan narrative leaves no doubt that Jesus at this time, as on all other occasions, gave no encouragement to the popular, kingly, messianic hope. Furthermore, the chief aim of Annas and his fellow-conspirators was to relieve themselves, as well as their nation, of public responsibility for Jesus' death, and this aim they nominally realized. Mark's account conveys the definite impression that there was a midnight session of the sanhedrin at which Jesus was formally placed on trial and condemned. The unconstitutionality of such procedure, if not its absolute impossibility, has long been recognized. Luke's account, on the contrary, is remarkably simple, consistent, and in keeping with the situation. It states that Jesus was held a prisoner until morning in the court of the high priest. Luke does not give the name of the arch-conspirator. The author of Matthew, recalling the fact that Caiaphas was the ruling high priest, states that Jesus was examined at his house. Here, however, the Fourth Gospel is probably right in asserting that Jesus was first led to the house of Annas, the ex-high priest and father-in-law of Caiaphas. Annas appears to have still been the ruling spirit in the Jewish hierarchy and to have been chiefly responsible for that extortionate policy which Jesus publicly condemned. There is little doubt that he was the one who, inspired by personal spite, planned and carried through the conspiracy which resulted in Jesus' death.

Mark introduces the account of Peter's denial after the account of Jesus' midnight trial before the sanhedrin. Peter's disloyalty is represented as an exact fulfilment of the detailed prediction found in Mark. Luke makes the far more probable statement that Peter's denial came while Jesus was still under guard in the court of Annas awaiting the early morning examination. Luke's description is exceedingly vivid and circumstantial. As Peter and the menials of the high priest crowded about the flickering light of a fire, he was repeatedly asked if he was not a follower of the Galilean teacher. His garb, his appearance, and his peculiar pronunciation all unmistakably proclaimed his northern origin. In his fright and confusion, Peter yielded to the great temptation, until the crowing of the cock proclaimed the approach of morning and recalled Jesus' warning. Luke has tempered the words of Peter and omits Mark's statement that in his fright the impulsive disciple "began to curse and to swear, 'I know not this man of whom you speak.'" Luke, however, has retained a touching incident in the story which is consistent with his record of the event. He states that Jesus' reproachful yet loving look, directed toward Peter, revealed to him his weakness and transformed him into the disciple who caught the first true vision of the risen Lord and became the stalwart leader of the early church.

Luke is also undoubtedly right in stating that Jesus was shamefully treated by the rude servants of the high priest in the early morning hours before the private examination rather than by the dignified members of the sanhedrin after that event. According to Luke the examination was not held until after sunrise. His account, which is probably here influenced by that of Mark, implies that it was an assembly of the sanhedrin; he describes it as "an assembly of the elders of the people." The variations in the accounts of this examination are doubtless due to the fact that Jesus' disciples had already fled. In any case, they would not be admitted to this secret conclave. It is probable that at this early hour few besides Annas and Caiaphas and their fellow-sympathizers and conspirators were present. It was the morning following the strenuous day on which every faithful Jew had been busily occupied, together with the members of his family, in purifying his house of all traces of leaven that might pollute the sacred Passover feast which began at sunset of the day on which Jesus was crucified. Luke's testimony is very explicit: Jesus was led before the high priests, not for trial, for in their minds he was already condemned, but that they might gain evidence to aid them in forcing Pilate to put him to death.

Mark states that they first tried to prove by witnesses that Jesus had blasphemed against the temple in declaring, "I will destroy this temple that is made with hands and in three days I will build another, made without hands." This statement, misunderstood and misinterpreted, undoubtedly added flames to their wrath; but a charge of this kind, if proved, would have little weight with Pilate. If they could prove, as they later attempted, that Jesus had proclaimed himself the Messiah or Christ, Pilate might thereby be led to recognize him as a dangerous conspirator against Rome and, therefore, best put to death. According to Luke's account, this was the question that they put at once to Jesus. His cautious answer is in keeping with his answers to his persecutors at other times. Indeed, in the circumstances, it was the only answer which he could truthfully make. To have asserted definitely that he was the Christ (as Mark, with less historical insight, records) would, in the light of the popular interpretation of that term, have been as misleading as to have asserted that he was not the Messiah. Jesus' words reveal the dilemma which confronted him. With his usual tact he replied: "If I tell you, you will not believe, and if I ask you, you will not answer." The gulf fixed between their conception of the Messiah and his own was impassable; and yet Luke adds that Jesus could not refrain, at this supreme moment of his life, from asserting that they would soon see the evidence of his divine calling. These words reveal the profound conviction in the mind of Jesus that God in his own good way would quickly vindicate him. His reply prompted the natural question, "Art thou the Son of God?" Again Jesus gave a qualified answer: "You say that I am." These words were neither a denial nor an absolute assertion. It was a question which only his life and teachings as a whole could answer. For his accusers, however, it sufficed. It gave them the basis which they were seeking for their charge before Pilate that Jesus claimed to be the Messiah.

IV. **Jesus' Trial Before Pilate.** Luke states that Jesus' high-priestly accusers led him at once before Pilate, the Roman governor. Pilate's residence at Jerusalem, when he came to guard the city on the occasion of the great annual festivals, was either in the Tower of Antonia, immediately northwest of the temple area, or at the palace of Herod. The site of this palace appears to have been near the western wall of Jerusalem, just south of the present Joppa Gate. The Fourth Gospel adds that the scrupulous high priests and elders would not enter the palace of their heathen governor. In accordance with the Roman policy, Pilate yielded to their prejudices and held court in front of his palace. The hour was early in the morning, some time between six and eight o'clock, for Roman judges were accustomed to hold their court early in the day (Seneca, *De Ira*, 2⁷; Macrob., *Sat.*, 1³). The Marcan account places Pilate's question, "Art thou the King of the Jews," before the formal accusation of the high priests had been presented. Many think that this is due to Mark's purpose to demonstrate that Jesus was, indeed, the King of the Jews, and that it reflects those early controversies between Jew and Christian which are still more prominent in the Fourth Gospel.

Luke preserves the logical order of events and his account again bears all the marks of superior historical accuracy. The Jewish leaders prefer a threefold charge against Jesus: (1) that he had perverted their nation, (2) that he had given command not to pay tribute to Cæsar, and (3) that he claimed that he was the Messiah, a king. The first charge is that which is made against Jesus in the Talmud, namely, that he was a seducer. It is equivalent to the modern term, heretic. Viewed from the point of view of narrow Jewish ceremonialism, there was truth in the charge; but with the Roman governor it had little weight. The second charge was a deliberate perversion of the facts, for Jesus had taken direct issue with the extremists of his nation in teaching the duty of giving to Cæsar his due (§ CXXXViii). The charge was well calculated to rouse the suspicions of Pilate, whose chief duty was to see that the rebellious Jews paid their regular tribute to Rome. The last was evidently the chief charge, as is indicated by Pilate's question. Again Jesus' answer was carefully qualified. To have answered "No" might have resulted in his acquittal, but he could not do so and remain true to his convictions. To have answered "Yes" would have been equally misleading. In the mind of Pilate, Jesus' answer was apparently equivalent to saying, "Judge for yourself." The Roman governor's decision, "I find no fault in this man," was doubtless based on the impression made upon him by the accused and by his knowledge of the character and reputation of his accusers.

With this decision Pilate regarded the case as closed, but he soon found that he had to deal with the pertinacity and devilish ingenuity of the high priests. Ordinarily the Roman governors were quite content to leave the punishment of Jewish criminals to the native tribunal. If the sanhedrin in full session had regularly condemned Jesus to death and thus assumed the responsibility, it is more than probable that

Pilate would have at once acquiesced in their decision. It is doubtful, however, whether the high priests, even with their influence and the popular prejudice against Jesus, could have carried their point. At least this would have been impossible, if the laws governing the sanhedrin that are recorded in the Mishna were then in force. For no criminal could be tried on the day immediately preceding the Sabbath, or a sacred feast, or condemned at the same session as that at which his case was tried. The object of the crafty conspirators was plainly to throw the responsibility on Pilate and thus to be able to say to the world: "Even the Roman rulers found the Galilean seducer a criminal worthy of death." Accordingly, Jesus' accusers went on to reiterate and expand their charge. Pilate, perceiving their purpose, endeavored to shift the responsibility to Herod. Even though Luke alone recounts this incident, the grounds on which its historicity has been questioned are insufficient. In the light of Pilate's statement to the high priests in Luke 23[15], that Herod sent Jesus back to them, it appears that verse [10], which states that they pled their case before Herod, is an interpolation from Mark 15[3]. Otherwise the narrative is thoroughly consistent with the situation. Herod's curiosity was natural. Jesus' silence in the presence of "that fox" was equally so. The circumstantial statement that Pilate's act established a friendship between himself and Herod confirms the reliability of the narrative. It is also significant that the Lucan narrative states that Jesus was mocked and arrayed in royal garments, not by the soldiers of Pilate, but by those of Herod.

Pilate's policy at this time reveals that vacillation, combined with selfish cruelty, which marked his career. He was entirely willing to cruelly scourge him whom he pronounced innocent; but his innate Roman sense of justice made him eager to release Jesus. The crafty high priests knew the weakness of the man, and played upon it. In his extremity he apparently appealed to the crowd, in the hope that the sympathizers with Jesus would support him in refusing the demands of the leaders of the nation. The attempt, however, was futile. The high priests had taken good care that their agents and supporters should be present in goodly numbers, and their cry, "Crucify him! Crucify him!" decided the issue. Jesus was condemned and Barabbas, the insurrectionist and murderer, was released. Only Matthew tells of Pilate's public washing of his hands. Many question this, for it is doubtful if a Roman official like Pilate would have resorted to such a measure to vindicate his execution of a humble Jewish prisoner. The story may, perhaps, be the beginning of the tradition which was later expanded in the apocryphal *Acts of Pilate*. It is, however, a symbolic interpretation of what Pilate was trying to do throughout the trial.

Of similar origin was probably Matthew's account of the dream of Pilate's wife. In the broad perspective of history we need no official or miraculous confirmation of Jesus' innocence. His condemnation was the result of the murderous hate of a group of unprincipled men and of a gross disregard of the Roman traditions of justice. In justice, however, it must be said that it was not the act of the Jewish nation as a whole, nor, in all probability, of its best representatives. It is equally important to note that Jesus courted death no more than he feared it. Amidst the passionate scenes of that early morning he alone was serenely confident, assured that God would surely overrule the crimes of men and establish his divine reign.

§ CXLIII. JESUS' DEATH AND BURIAL

1. The mocking by the soldiers
(Mark 15¹⁶⁻²⁰ᵃ, *cf.* Matt. 27²⁷⁻³¹ᵃ)

Now the soldiers led Jesus away within the court, that is, the Prætorium. Then calling together the whole cohort, they clothe him in purple, and after plaiting a crown of thorns, they put it on him. And they began to salute him, Hail, King of the Jews! And they smote his head with a reed and they spat on him, and bending the knee they did homage to him. And when they had mocked him, they stripped off the purple and put his own garments upon him.

2. The crucifixion
(Mark 15²⁰ᵇ⁻²² Matt. 27³¹ᵇ⁻⁴⁴ Luke 23²⁶⁻⁴³)

And they lead him out to crucify him, and compel a passerby to carry his cross, a certain Simon of Cyrene, who was coming from the country (the father of Alexander and Rufus). And they bring him to the place, Golgotha, which translated means, "the place of a skull." Then they offered him wine flavored with myrrh; but he would not take it. And they crucify him and divide his garments among them, by casting lots over them as to what each man should take. And it was the third hour when they crucified him. The superscription stating his crime was inscribed, THE KING OF THE JEWS. And with him, they crucify two robbers, one on his right hand, and one on his left. And those who passed by reviled him, wagging their heads and saying, Ha! thou who wouldst destroy the temple and rebuild it in three days, save thyself and come down from the cross! Likewise the high priests also mocked him among themselves with the scribes, saying, Others he saved; himself he cannot save. Let the Christ, the King of Israel, come down now from the cross, that we may see and believe! And they who were crucified with him kept reproaching him.

And when the sixth hour came, darkness was over the whole earth until the ninth hour. At the ninth hour Jesus cried with a loud voice, Eloi, Eloi, lama sabachthani (which translated, means, My God, my God, why hast thou forsaken me?). And on hearing it, some of those who stood by, said, See, he is calling Elijah! Then one ran and, filling the sponge full of vinegar, put it on a reed and gave it him to drink, saying, Hold, let us see if Elijah does come to take him down! But Jesus, after uttering a loud cry, expired. And the veil of the temple was torn in two from top to bottom. Now when the centurion, who stood opposite him, saw that he thus expired, he said, Truly this man was a Son of God.

3. Jesus' death (Mark 15{33-39}, cf. Matt. 27{45-54} Luke 23{44-47})

Now there were also women, looking on from afar. Among them was Mary Magdalene, Mary the mother of James the younger and of Joses, and also Salome, women who had followed him in Galilee, and had ministered to him; and many other women who had come up with him to Jerusalem.

4. The attendant women (Mark 15{40, 41}, cf. Matt. 27{55, 56} Luke 23{48, 49})

And now when evening came, because it was the Preparation, that is, the day before the sabbath, Joseph of Arimathæa, a councillor of honorable position, who was also himself looking for the kingdom of God, took courage and went into Pilate and asked for the body of Jesus. And Pilate marvelled that he was already dead. And, calling the centurion, he asked him if he had been dead for a long time. Learning the facts from the centurion, he granted the corpse to Joseph. And he bought a linen cloth, took him down, wrapped him in the linen cloth, and laid him in a tomb, which had been hewn out of a rock. Then he rolled a stone against the entrance of the tomb. And Mary Magdalene and Mary the mother of Joses were looking on to see where he was laid.

5. Jesus' burial (Mark 15{42-47}, cf. Matt. 27{57-60} Luke 23{50-56})

I. **The Record of Jesus' Crucifixion.** Few are the facts regarding Jesus' last hours. This was almost inevitable, for the disciples had fled. Apparently the only sympathizers to witness the crucifixion were the ministering women who followed Jesus from Galilee and who looked on from afar.

Mark's narrative is the basis of the account of the crucifixion found in the other gospels. The author of Matthew follows it closely, expanding it at certain points. Thus, for example, he adds to Mark's statement that the veil of the temple was rent in two from top to bottom: "The earth quaked and the rocks were torn apart, and many bodies of the saints who had fallen asleep were raised and, coming forth from the tombs after Jesus' resurrection, entered into the Holy City and appeared to many." This expansion of the story may be due to the popular belief that the death of great persons was marked by marvellous portents. Vergil, in his *Georgics* (1⁴⁶⁶), states that "at the death of Cæsar there was an eclipse from the fourth to the ninth hour." Mark's statement that "when the sixth hour came a darkness covered the whole earth until the ninth hour," is believed by many to be based on the prediction of Amos 8⁹:

> And it shall come to pass in that day
> Is the oracle of the Lord Jehovah,
> That I will make the sun set at noon,
> And darken the earth in broad day.

Similarly the statement that the veil of the temple was torn apart may be the concrete interpretation of the prediction in Amos 9¹ that Jehovah would rend the temple from top to bottom. At certain points in the description of Jesus' crucifixion it would seem that, not being eyewitnesses and lacking exact historical data, the evangelists turned to the Old Testament prophecies for help in completing the picture.

II. His Last Words. Apparently the women who heard from afar the loud cry which Jesus uttered just before he died were unable to distinguish the detailed words. Each of the gospel writers has endeavored to supply them as best he could. Mark found them in the words of the suffering martyr who speaks in Psalm 22. The singularly appropriate words of this wonderful psalm may have been in the mind of Jesus and on his lips during his last hours; but from the evidence that we possess, it is doubtful if the initial line:

> My God, my God, why hast thou forsaken me?

expressed his dominant thought. Evidently this conviction was shared by Luke and the author of the Fourth Gospel, for their silence indicates that they were either unacquainted with this part of the Marcan narrative or else deliberately rejected it. With true intuition Luke interprets the last loud cry of Jesus in the spirit of his prayer in Gethsemane, "Father, into thy hands I commend my spirit." The author of the Fourth Gospel, in keeping with his belief that Jesus came down from heaven to accomplish a preordained task, interprets the dying Saviour's last cry with the words, "It is finished." As interpretations of the different aspects of the crucifixion, the gospel narratives, widely variant though they are, each conveys a great truth. Far more significant than words, however, is the act itself, and the spirit in which Jesus endured the disappointment and the cruel injustice of which he was the victim.

III. **The Place and Manner of the Crucifixion.** The established historical facts regarding Jesus' crucifixion, which have been preserved, may be briefly formulated. The mocking by the Roman soldiers in the Prætorium is paralleled by a somewhat similar incident recorded by Philo (*Flaccum*, 6). It reflected the scorn with which the Roman world regarded the Jews. The reference to Simon of Cyrene is one of the vivid historical details with which Mark frequently illuminates his narrative. The earlier or present home of Simon was evidently the city of Cyrene, in northern Africa, which at that time was a strong Jewish centre (*cf.* Acts 6⁹). The expression, "on his way from the country," is obscure, but if it implies, as seems probable, that he was coming from labor in the fields, the fact establishes beyond all doubt the implication of the Fourth Gospel that Jesus' crucifixion was on Friday rather than on Saturday, the day of the Passover, when all work was absolutely forbidden. Mark's narrative implies strongly that Simon's sons, Alexander and Rufus, were living when he wrote, and personally known to many of his readers. Their Græco-Roman names confirm the statement that their father was a Jew of the dispersion. Mark is very explicit in his description of the scene of the crucifixion, but unfortunately the data required to identify it absolutely have long since been lost. Mark states that the place was called "The Skull." Whether this was because of its appearance or because it had been used as a place of burial is not certain. The Jewish law of Leviticus 24¹⁴ and of Numbers 15³⁵, ³⁶ commanded that all public executions should be outside the city. Roman custom also provided that crucifixions should take place at a prominent site, usually beside an important highway; for the object was to impress all possible malefactors with the fate that would overtake them if they committed similar crimes. The identification of the place of the crucifixion depends largely upon whether the northern wall of Jerusalem in the days of Jesus followed in general the line of the present city wall or ran farther south, so that the traditional site of the crucifixion, now marked by the Church of the Holy Sepulchre, lay outside the walls. The probabilities are that the present wall marks the northern bounds of the Roman city. If so, the deserted height just outside the wall, north of the temple area, was, without much doubt, the place of "The Skull."

It was probably at that time separated from the city by the quarries from which Herod had taken many of the stones with which he rebuilt the ancient city. Later excavations have extended these quarries still farther to the north. As travellers have frequently noted, the remaining rock front above the so-called grotto of Jeremiah, viewed from certain angles, still presents a resemblance to the form of a skull. The heights above were probably, in the past as to-day, covered with shallow tombs, for the Jews, as well as the modern Moslems, believed that the final judgment scene was to be in the adjacent Kidron Valley. Hence they were eager that their bodies might be laid here in order that they might be among the first to arise when the final trump should be blown announcing the beginning of the messianic era. Hebrews 13[12] describes the place where Jesus suffered as "without the gates." The details of the Fourth Gospel's account of the crucifixion imply that it took place close to the city. Of all possible sites about Jerusalem, that north of the temple area, just outside the present Damascus Gate and within sight of the great highway that led northward, best satisfies the biblical data. If this conclusion be true, the excavations of the sixteenth century have probably quarried away the rock on which the cross stood, so that it is embedded somewhere in the present walls of Jerusalem, and the actual site of Golgotha is somewhere in the air, twenty or twenty-five feet above the rocky floor of the present quarry. While this conclusion does not wholly satisfy that narrow type of faith which glories in sacred sites, it turns our eyes from that which is material and temporal to the spiritual and eternal significance of Jesus' death on the cross.

According to the Roman custom, the soldiers sent out to execute a criminal were responsible for his death. They therefore remained until the end. The clothes of those condemned also, according to the prevailing custom, belonged to them. To mitigate the intolerable sufferings of the crucified, wine mingled with myrrh was frequently offered to the victims. Its object was to dull the senses of the one crucified. Possibly a similar usage is the background for the strange injunction in Proverbs 31⁶: "Give strong drink to him who is about to perish." Jesus' refusal of this kindly offer reveals his dauntless spirit and his desire to retain full consciousness to the last. According to Mark's chronology, the crucifixion took place about nine o'clock in the morning and Jesus' death came at three o'clock in the afternoon. Contemporary writers assert that those who were crucified often survived two or three days. Jesus' early death testifies to the tense nervous, as well as physical agony which he endured, and his sudden end, marked by a loud cry, implies that death did not come to him, as to ordinary criminals, through gradual loss of strength, but as the result of a sudden heart failure or kindred cause.

Roman usage also prescribed that the one crucified should wear on his way to the crucifixion, hung from his neck, a tablet indicating the cause for which he was condemned. It was this title which, in the case of Jesus, was placed over the cross. While each of the evangelists has a different version of this title, its simplest form, the King of the Jews, as given by Mark, is, without reasonable doubt, the original. To make the shame complete, and possibly at the instigation of the malicious high priests, two criminals were crucified beside Jesus. Luke alone, interpreting with marvellous insight and skill Jesus' attitude at all times toward the lowly and outcast, tells the story of the penitent thief.

A fitting conclusion to the story of the crucifixion is the testimony of the Roman centurion. Jesus' manner, his unflinching endurance, and, above all, the loud cry that proclaimed a physical and spiritual strength that defied death, apparently so impressed this heathen soldier that he declared involuntarily, "Truly this man was a Son of God"—or as probably expressed, from his heathen point of view, "a son of the gods."

IV. Jesus' Burial. Two acts of loving friendship illuminate the shadows that surround the close of Jesus' mortal life. The one was the devotion of the women, who had accompanied him from Galilee, and who, showing greater courage than the twelve disciples, watched the crucifixion from afar and probably remained until his body was laid away in the tomb. The other act was the boldness of Joseph of Arimathæa, who dared avow himself a friend of Jesus and offer what was probably his own family tomb as a temporary resting-place for the body of the crucified one. Arimathæa is usually identified with Ramathaim, near Lydda, on the Philistine Plain. The town is mentioned in I Maccabees 11⁴. History records only this incident regarding Joseph. Mark's description of him suggests that he was at the time a member of the sanhedrin; at least he was a man of wealth and influence in the Jewish state. He is a type of that doubtless large group of sympathizers whose names do not appear in the early, comparatively meagre gospel records which deal chiefly with Jesus' work in Galilee. The author of the Fourth Gospel is probably right in implying, as he does in 19³⁸, that Jesus had many secret followers. The rapid growth of the early Jerusalem church strengthens this inference. The swiftness and secrecy with which the high-priestly conspirators carried through their plot suggest strongly that they feared a popular opposition which did not have time to crystallize and to which there is no direct reference in the gospel narratives.

Ordinarily the bodies of those who were crucified were publicly exposed long after their death and then thrown away as common refuse. The imminence of the Passover feast made it necessary to remove Jesus' body at once; therefore Joseph's offer was most opportune. That the interment was but temporary, until the Passover was past, is implied by the situation. The exact site of this tomb will, of course, never be known, for no inscription would be placed upon it. The recently discovered, so-called Gordon's tomb, near Jeremiah's Grotto, a few steps from the quarries (which represent the most probable site of the crucifixion) possesses a peculiar interest. Even though it may not be the tomb of Joseph, it is a splendid example of a tomb of the period. A small door which could be readily closed by a large stone, leads into a rock-cut room lighted by a small opening in the front. Two spaces are cut in the rock for the bodies of the dead. In western terms, it would be called a vault rather than a tomb. In some such place as this, as the sun was beginning to set over the Western hills and the Jews were completing their preparations for the approaching Passover meal, the body of Jesus was temporarily laid to rest.

V. The Date of Jesus' Death. The chronology of Jesus' life is shrouded with uncertainty for the reason that the earliest gospel writers were interested primarily in his teachings and not in dates. The one definite chronological datum in the gospels is found in Luke 3¹⁻³. It states that John the Baptist began his ministry in the fifteenth year of Tiberius. Even here there is a slight element of uncertainty, for it is held by some writers that this should be reckoned from 12 A.D., when Tiberius became co-regent, rather than from 14 A.D., when he actually became emperor. There is no reason, however, for interpreting Luke's words other than in their natural meaning. The fifteenth year of the reign of Tiberius extended from August nineteenth of the year 28 to August nineteenth, 29 A.D. This date is supported in general by the statement in John 2²⁰, that Herod's temple, which was begun in 19 B.C., had been forty-six years in building. Allowing a year or two for the necesssary preparations for the building, it would establish the date of the beginning of Jesus' work about 28 or 29 A.D. The date of Jesus' death turns upon the duration of John's public ministry and later imprisonment, for Jesus' active work in Galilee appears to have begun at the time of John's imprisonment and to have ended soon after the news came of John's death. The radical nature of the teachings of both John and Jesus suggests that the period of their activity was comparatively brief. If John began his public preaching in the latter part of 28 or in the early part of 29 A.D. it is probable that it lasted only a few months. Furthermore, it is doubtful if John was imprisoned more than a year. If so, Jesus' public work, probably begun early in 29, ended at the Passover in March or April of 30 A.D. The testimony of the synoptic gospels, on the whole, favors a ministry of a year or a year and a half. It is difficult, however, to believe that Jesus could have accomplished all that he did in so brief a period. Possibly the days spent in retirement with his disciples extended to many weeks and months. The testimony of the Fourth Gospel is usually cited in support of a longer ministry. The evidence turns on John 6⁴, which suggests that there was a Passover in the middle of Jesus' ministry that is not mentioned in the synoptic gospels. This passage in the Fourth Gospel was apparently unknown to the Church Fathers. The Christian writers of the second century are unanimous in the belief that Jesus' ministry was limited to one year. The same belief is shared by many of the Church Fathers of the third century. The impression given by the gospels of the strenuousness of Jesus' work and the intensity of the opposition which it aroused, on the whole, tends to confirm the weighty testimony of these earliest Church Fathers. If these data be accepted, the death of Jesus took place in March or April of A.D. 30. Certainly it was after the year 26, when Pilate entered upon his procuratorship, and before 33, when Caiaphas ceased to be high priest.

VI. The Meaning of Jesus' Death. No event in history has been more differently interpreted than the death of Jesus. For Jesus, his death on the cross meant suffering, shame, and cruel injustice, from which he naturally, inevitably shrank; but these were only passing incidents, repulsive and unutterably painful though they were. For him, as his final words to his disciples indicate, his death meant the triumphant completion of his life-work and the realization of his exalted ideal. Leonard, in his *The Poet of Galilee* has truly said, "One pain at least was spared Jesus: he had not to suffer the pain of mocking his own visions by any disloyalty or weakness in himself." Having put his hand to the plough, he had not turned back, but quietly and consistently had given his all, even his life-blood for those whom he loved and the Father whom he served. The giving of his life was, in one sense, his supreme gift to his fellow-men. It was also the highest expression of his loyalty to God's will as revealed to his inner consciousness and by the course of events. In the light of all that he believed and taught, it is also clear that for Jesus his death was the open door to a still larger fellowship with God.

The "shame of the cross," which in reality was the glory of the cross, marked a great transformation in the character and ideals of Jesus' disciples and of the early church which followed their leadership. It forever tore away from their eyes the veil of the popular, national, materialistic type of messianic hope, which had hitherto beclouded their vision of the ideal which Jesus had sought with all his marvellous skill as a teacher of men to set clearly before them. It confirmed, as no other event could, all that he had taught them regarding himself and his mission. His departure also threw upon them the responsibility of carrying on his work. As so often in human history, great responsibility developed strong men, and in time transformed the self-seeking, fearful Galilean peasants into effective preachers and teachers who did not flinch when they faced a martyr's death. Above all, Jesus' death revealed to them, far more clearly than his previous teachings, the way in which they must perform the task which he left them. Henceforth they trod unhesitatingly the way of the cross and even gloried in its pain and shame, for they recognized that this was the way their Master had trod and that in following it they were assured of his approval.

For the Jewish nation the death of Jesus meant the rejection through its leaders of God's highest revelation to them. It was also a tragic demonstration of the fatal fallacy inherent in the prevailing legalistic religion. In the eyes of the high priests who hunted him to death Jesus was, indeed, a dangerous iconoclast. In refusing to observe the explicit demands of the ritual, in casting aside the bonds of the Sabbath legislation, and in declaring that God's forgiveness could be secured entirely apart from sacrifice and formal expiation, he had transgressed the canons of Jewish law which they held to be most binding. Strictly speaking, Jesus was put to death in accordance with Jewish law as then interpreted; but by that act the law itself stood condemned.

The public rejection of Jesus' teachings, so tragically expressed in his death, marked the beginning of the destruction of the Jewish nation, for the only thing that would have saved it was a full acceptance and application of the principles which he advocated. If Judaism had faithfully rendered to "Cæsar that which was Cæsar's and to God that which was God's," the historian would not have been called to record the calamities of the year 70 A.D.

For the human race the death of Jesus was the transfiguration of all that he was and taught. This fact is expressed by the profound words, recorded in the Fourth Gospel: "I, if I be lifted up, will draw all men to me." It was the challenge to his race, to his generation, to the whole world to halt and to heed. History presents many illustrations of this principle. The tragic death of Lincoln, at the height of his power and usefulness, transfigured and ennobled the simplicity and beauty of his character and the greatness of his service for humanity. Jesus' death was the supreme demonstration that the one unfailing way in which sinners may be saved is the way of love and complete self-sacrifice. His death was the final, incontrovertible proof of his love and willingness to give himself for them and for all who needed his help. In an equally true and concrete sense it was the noblest expression of God's love for man. Thus Jesus' death transformed the friend of the disciples, and the shepherd of the lost sheep of Israel, into the Saviour of the world, and expressed the purpose and meaning of his life in terms intelligible to all ages and races.

§ CXLIV. THE LIVING CHRIST.

Now I make known to you, brothers, that gospel which I preached to you, which also you received, in which also you stand, by which also you are being saved, if you hold fast the word which I preached to you, unless you believed in vain. For I passed on to you first of all, that which I also received; that Christ died for our sins according to the scriptures, and that he was buried; and that he had been raised on the third day, according to the scriptures and that he appeared to Cephas, then to the Twelve. Then he appeared to upward of five hundred Christian brothers at one time, of whom the greater number are still alive, though some are asleep; then he appeared to James; then to all the apostles; and last of all, as to the child untimely born, he appeared to me also.

1. Paul's account of Jesus' appearances to his disciples (1 Cor 15¹⁻⁸, cf. Mk. 16 Mt. 28 Luke 23⁵⁶–24⁵³ Acts 1¹⁻¹¹)

THE LIVING CHRIST

I. The Immediate Effect of Jesus' Crucifixion upon His Disciples. The direct evidence that the tomb could not hold Jesus is threefold: (1) the marvellous transformation in the spirit and work of his disciples; (2) the direct testimony of the earliest New Testament writer, Paul, and (3) the practically universal belief of the early church, recorded not only in the variant accounts of the resurrection found in the canonical and extra-canonical gospels, but also in its life and activity through the succeeding centuries. This evidence rests not merely upon historical documents but is written in the life of the great civilized nations during the intervening centuries. Unfortunately the earliest gospel source, the collection of the sayings of Jesus, appears to have been silent regarding his resurrection. Even the direct testimony of Peter ceases with his tragic denial of Jesus. In the light of the situation, and of occasional references that have survived in the synoptic gospels, it is possible, however, to picture the immediate effects of Jesus' death upon his disciples. At first they seem to have been not only terrified, but stunned. The suggestion that Jesus was to face death at Jerusalem had at an earlier memorable occasion aroused Peter's protest. Evidently he voiced the feelings of the other disciples. At last, suddenly, that which Jesus' followers had thought might be only the product of his imagination, although, as we can see, a natural anticipation, had become an awful reality. The blow was all the more crushing because it had been struck by the recognized religious leaders of their nation and with the full authority of Rome. According to the oldest record, no supernatural portents had recorded the divine disapproval of the act. The temple still stood and pilgrims by thousands were busily engaged on that memorable Passover evening in preparing for the great national festival. The foes of Jesus, the crafty, unscrupulous high priests ruled the Jewish nation as they had before, and stood as the official representatives of Jehovah's power on earth. Rome, the cruel oppressor of the Jews, was still regnant. The sun, as on preceding days, descended in the western sky. Darkness that penetrated their very souls closed in upon them. They who had been so dependent upon their Master were left leaderless. More than that, suspicion, begotten by the old popular Semitic dogma that found in all calamity and suffering a sinister significance, crept into their minds and threatened for the moment not only to crush all hope, but even to shake their faith in Jesus' goodness and sincerity. Gloom impenetrable and woe unutterable took possession of them. And with the darkness came fear. Like hunted animals they fled, as the oldest account implies, back to their old haunts in Galilee. There, apparently for a brief time,

298

they resumed their former occupations (*cf.* testimony of Gospel of Peter and a possible variant, Luke 5⁵⁻⁹). For the moment they must have seemed to themselves like men who had followed a glorious star over hills and valleys and through trackless wastes, until suddenly it had vanished and they were left in darkness.

II. **Their Sudden Recovery of Faith and Courage.** Of the many marvellous facts recorded in the gospel history none is more astonishing than the transformation in the character and ideals of the disciples that came apparently within a few days after the death of Jesus. What is the explanation of these well-authenticated historical facts? May the new energy and activity of the disciples be explained as a result of their quiet but intense meditation on what Jesus had taught them and of a return of their old love and loyalty to him? Was it because in the light of the event they now understood the meaning of his warnings that the way of the true Messiah would be the way of the cross? Was it also because they reinterpreted the Jewish scriptures in the light of "the shame of the cross" and saw that what at first had stunned them was but the fulfilment of those ancient writings? Certainly this method of interpreting the crucifixion occupied a prominent place in the thought of the early apostles. Thus in I Corinthians 15³, ⁴ Paul declares that "Christ died for our sins according to the scriptures" and "that he was buried and that he rose on the third day according to the scriptures." In the speech attributed to Peter in Acts 2²⁴⁻³² he found in the Psalms predictions of Jesus' crucifixion and resurrection (*cf.* also Acts 13³⁴⁻³⁷ based on Isa. 55³ and Ps. 16¹⁰). Similarly Luke and the author of the Fourth Gospel interpreted Jesus' resurrection as the fulfilment of the scriptures (Luke 24⁴⁶ and John 20⁹). Did their interpretation of these ancient predictions and Jesus' own words regarding his death and future relations to them and the associations suggested by the return to scenes which recalled at every point his personality and teachings create in their minds an impression of their Master so definite that it was transmitted by suggestion and contagion from disciple to disciple until that sense of his immediate presence became the commanding force in all that they thought, said, and did? Modern psychology is able to produce analogies that are in many ways exceedingly close. Meditation amidst familiar environment on a departed friend sometimes results in a vision of the departed which is as vivid and realistic as an ordinary daily experience. These visions not infrequently come to men and women whose sanity cannot be questioned. It is not strange, therefore, that there are many modern New Testament scholars, as well as scientists, who are inclined thus to interpret the resurrection stories.

It is important to note in passing that this view, far removed as it is from the current doctrines of the church, does not undermine the historical foundations of Christianity. The essential elements in the gospel narratives, after all, are what Jesus was and taught; and these corner-stones stand quite independent of the resurrection stories. In any case, it was the influence of Jesus' personality and words that remained with his disciples and encouraged and inspired them to heroic actions. Likewise, belief in individual immortality does not primarily depend upon whether or not Jesus communicated with his disciples after his death, although the establishment of the fact that he did would furnish in many ways the strongest support to that hope. God in any case remains the God of the living, not of the dead, and the evidences of his fatherly training and provision for the future life of his children abide, even though none come back from the grave to attest these basal truths.

The question, however, remains, Does this naturalistic interpretation satisfactorily explain all the facts and the evidence of the earliest biblical records?

III. **Paul's Testimony.** The Christian church in the past has turned almost exclusively to the gospel narratives for the record of the resurrection. This tendency was perfectly natural, for they furnish the logical conclusion to the gospel story. They do not, however, represent the earliest and most direct testimony. That is found in I Corinthians, one of the earliest and most unquestioned epistles of Paul. It was written within the first quarter-century after the death of Jesus and after the great apostle to the Gentiles had had ample opportunity, as he states in Galatians 1^{19}, to learn from Peter and James, the brother of Jesus, the details regarding the events immediately following the death of Jesus. The subject was of keenest interest to Paul and is central in all his teachings. His testimony is that of a man famous for his sanity in action and for his fidelity to his convictions—no matter where they led him. It embodies not only that regarding which he was well informed through converse with others, but also his own personal experience. It is all the more significant because it is entirely independent and in many respects at variance with the accounts found in the gospels. It speaks of six appearances to various disciples or groups of disciples of whom Paul himself is the last. Its exact designations of time and order imply that it records all the appearances known

300

at the period when he wrote. Of these six appearances a definite reference is found in the gospels to only one—that to Peter—to which simply an allusion is made in Luke 24³⁴. Paul's reference to the appearance to the Twelve is so brief that it is not clear which of the gospel accounts of the appearance to the disciples records this event. The James mentioned by Paul is clearly the brother of Jesus, who later became the head of the Jerusalem church.

It is significant that Paul describes Jesus' appearances to the other disciples in precisely the same terms as he does the Lord's appearance to him on the way to Damascus. Herein is found the key to the interpretation of the essential facts underlying the variant narratives of the resurrection appearances. In order, however, to understand the variations between the testimony of Paul and that of the gospels it is essential to note the diverse beliefs regarding the resurrection of the dead that were current in Paul's day.

IV. A Comparison between the Current Conceptions of the Resurrection of the Dead and That of Paul. Three forms of belief regarding the life beyond the grave were current in Paul's day. The Sadducees rejected the comparatively recent belief in individual resurrection and held with the author of Job 3 that the life after death was a passionless, joyless existence. With Ben Sira, they believed that "thanksgiving perishes from the dead as from one who is not." The majority of the Jewish people, however, accepted the teaching of the Pharisees that the dead would be again restored to life and inhabit their former bodies. This belief is clearly expressed in Daniel 12²: "And many of those who sleep in the dust of the earth shall awake; some to everlasting life and some to shame and everlasting contempt." This firmly established hope is repeatedly expressed in contemporary Jewish writings (II Mac. 7⁸, ¹⁰, ¹¹, ²³ 14⁴⁶; II Esd. 7³²⁻³⁵, Jos., *Antiq.*, XVIII, 1³, *Jew. War*, III, 8⁵). The same hope was held by the early Christians (Acts 4³ Rev. 20¹³). The chief characteristic of this expectation was the belief that the dead would be restored again to life on earth, there to participate with the saints who survived in Jehovah's eternal kingdom. The conception of individual immortality apart from the body was foreign to orthodox Jewish thinking. Hence the Jewish Christians naturally thought of Jesus as reappearing in bodily form. Tradition taught that Moses and Elijah came back in visible form to converse with Jesus and that at his death the saints arose from the dead and appeared to many. Herod believed that Jesus was John the Baptist returned to life. To the common people of Palestine, from whom came the first and second generations of Christians, the rising from the dead was no more marvellous than an eclipse.

About the beginning of the Christian era, through the Jews of the dispersion, the Platonic idea of spiritual resurrection was beginning to touch certain Jewish minds. While the orthodox Jewish belief is reasserted in certain parts of the Wisdom of Solomon, this new type of hope is also reflected, as, for example, in such statements as "God created man for incorruption" and "the souls of the righteous are in his hand." A slightly variant type of this belief, very similar to that held by the Stoics, is expressed in the first century writing, known as IV Maccabees. The same teaching appears also in the Palestinian Book of Jubilees, in 23[11, 12]: "The bones of the righteous will rest in the earth, and their spirits will have much joy."

In Paul's discussion of the resurrection, in I Corinthians 15[42-50], he shows the influence of the pharisaic doctrine of bodily resurrection in which he had been instructed from his earliest days. It is evident, however, that his own experience had demonstrated to him its insufficiency. Repeatedly and unequivocally he rejects it. He declares that "flesh and blood cannot inherit the kingdom of God," nor does the "corruptible inherit incorruption." In the last statement he echoes the teaching of the Wisdom of Solomon, already quoted. Furthermore, he adds that "the dead shall be raised incorruptible." Like the Jews of his day, however, he looked forward to a great judgment scene, in the twinkling of an eye at the last trumpet, the dead should be raised incorruptible, and this mortal should put on immortality. From II Corinthians 5[1-9] it appears that he believed that each individual soul would after death be clothed with a heavenly body prepared by God for his own. Paul, therefore, represents the transition from the material Jewish belief in the bodily resurrection to that purely spiritual conception of individual immortality which was the great contribution of the wisest thinkers of Greece. It is this peculiar Pauline conception of the resurrection that has determined the form of many of the familiar narratives in the closing chapters of the gospels. Indeed, in these narratives each of the different conceptions of the resurrection current in the first Christian century are reflected.

During the second half of the first Christian century, when the gospels were written, the leaders of the church were also powerfully influenced by the Gnostic controversy. The Gnostics believed that the flesh is inherently evil. Hence they refused to believe in a real incarnation of God in the human Jesus, but taught that the divine Logos only appeared to take the form of man. Therefore they were sometimes called Docetists—the name being derived from the Greek word meaning *to appear*. The tradition of a spiritual resurrection seemed to support the contention of these Docetists, who were trying to spiritualize the entire life of Jesus so as to make it a mere appearance. Hence Ignatius insists, not only that Jesus was "truly crucified and truly died," but also that he was "truly raised from the dead" (*Tral.*, IX; see also *Smyrneans*, III). "For I know that after his resurrection also, he was still possessed of flesh. . . . And after his resurrection he did eat and drink with them as being possessed of flesh." It is probable that this fear of Gnosticism and similar heresies was one of the chief reasons why Jesus' physical resurrection is so strongly emphasized in the narratives of Luke and John.

V. A Comparison of the Different Gospel Records of the Resurrection. Nowhere do the gospel narratives present wider variations than in their accounts of the resurrection. The stories, however, fall into two general groups: (1) those which place the different revelations to the disciples in Galilee, and (2) those which gather about Jerusalem. Unfortunately the original ending of the Gospel of Mark has been lost; but the fragment which remains indicates that the lost ending recorded a revelation to the disciples in Galilee. According to Mark 14[28], Jesus promised his disciples, even before his death, that after he was raised up he would go before them into Galilee. According to Mark, the command given to the women at the empty tomb was to tell his disciples and Peter: "He goeth before you into Galilee. There shall ye see him as he said to you." The fragment of the early Mark narrative records the visit of the three women, Mary Magdalene, Mary the mother of James, and Salome, to the tomb on the first day of the week after sunrise. They find the stone rolled away and a young man clad in a white robe sitting within. He tells them that Jesus is risen and calls their attention to the empty tomb. After receiving the promise just quoted, that Jesus will appear in Galilee, the women fled, but "said nothing to anyone, for they were afraid." Here the original version of the Gospel of Mark ends abruptly.

The Gospel of Matthew quotes the Marcan fragment with certain additions, as, for example, the statement that there was a great earthquake and that an angel descended from heaven and rolled away the stone. It also repeats the commands to the disciples to go to Galilee where they should see the risen Jesus. It states, however, that the women, instead of saying nothing to any one, ran and told the disciples, and that on the way Jesus met them, and that they took hold of his feet and worshipped him. Then Jesus himself gave the command: "Go tell my brothers that they depart into Galilee and there shall they see me." The first gospel concludes with a brief account of his appearance to the eleven disciples in Galilee "on the mountain which Jesus had appointed them."

The recently discovered Gospel of Peter apparently also confirms this older group of narratives, which place the appearances of Jesus to his disciples in Galilee. Unfortunately the conclusion of the decisive paragraph is lost. The first part reads: "But I, Simon Peter and Andrew my brother, took our nets and went out on the sea. And with us was Levi, the son of Alpheus, whom the Lord . . ." From the context it may be inferred with great probability that the original described an appearance of Jesus to Peter. It may have been that first appearance to which Paul refers in I Corinthians 15. The twenty-first chapter of John, which is probably a later addition to the original, also gives a detailed account of an appearance to the disciples beside the Sea of Galilee in which Simon Peter is the central figure. Thus the oldest and some of the later accounts are agreed in stating that Jesus' appearances to his disciples were in Galilee, amidst the familiar scenes of his work with them. Luke's account of Jesus' meeting with Peter and the other disciples beside the Sea of Galilee (5¹⁻¹¹) is also regarded by some scholars as a variant of the same narrative. Peter's words, "Depart from me, for I am a sinful man, O Lord," are more appropriate in this setting than before his denial of his Master.

While Paul says nothing regarding the place, the appearances which he records find their most natural setting in Galilee. There five hundred of his followers might be found gathered together soon after his death, but not in Jerusalem. The revelation of the risen Lord probably came to James, the brother of Jesus, somewhere in Galilee, either at Capernaum or Nazareth, for not until he saw the real significance of Jesus' character and work would he join his followers at Jerusalem.

The resurrection stories in Luke depart widely from those in Mark. Their setting throughout is at Jerusalem and Judea; Luke is absolutely silent regarding the appearances in Galilee. Even the details regarding the initial appearance to the women differ at almost every point from those recorded in Mark and Matthew. Not after sunrise, but at early dawn, they go to the tomb, which they at first find empty. Then not one, but two men, in shining clothing, stand before them, and tell them that Jesus is not dead but risen. The promise that he will appear to his disciples in Galilee here reappears in very different form: "Remember how he spoke to you when he was yet in Galilee." The number of women who visited the tomb is also greatly increased. While there is no evidence in the other gospels that the disciples were then in Jerusalem, in Luke they are still present, and Peter, on being informed, rushes at once to the tomb. Luke alone gives an account of the journey of the two followers of Jesus to Emmaus. In Luke also the original narrative has undergone a fundamental transformation apparently under the influence of the popular Jewish belief that the spirits of the dead came back and took possession of the physical body. In these narratives Jesus is represented as walking, eating, and as inviting his disciples to touch his body that they might be assured that he was before them clothed in flesh and blood. This element in the story is strongly emphasized in the subsequent account of his appearance to his disciples, in which he declares: "Handle me and see; for a spirit has not flesh and bones as you behold me having." In conclusion Jesus is represented as having led them out in the direction of Bethany and after blessing them to have been carried up into heaven. The Lucan version excludes the appearances in Galilee, for its account of his disappearance in the heavens is at the close of the day on which he rose from the tomb, and the narrative ends with the statement that, "after they had worshipped" their departed master, "the disciples were continually in the temple blessing God." Acts 1¹⁴ also leaves no place for the appearances in Galilee, although it states that Jesus continued to appear to his disciples for forty days.

The Fourth Gospel, following its usual method when there are widely differing variants in the earlier gospels, combines both the Galilean and Jerusalem cycles of stories, but gives the Lucan version the precedence. The evidence, however, is reasonably conclusive that the Galilean group is the older. The Jerusalem cycle of narratives recorded in Luke apparently grew up about the empty tomb and the scene of Jesus' crucifixion, and under the influence of the fact that Jerusalem soon became the centre of the life of the early Christian community. The two elements which the gospel stories all share in common is the account of the empty tomb and the certainty that Jesus in some form or other appeared repeatedly to his disciples. Of these two elements only one is confirmed by Paul. If he had known of the empty tomb, it is difficult to see why he did not refer to it. The statement in the older Marcan version, that the women "said nothing of it to anyone," may perhaps be intended to explain why this was unknown to the Christian community in the days of Paul. If it is but a later tradition that gathered about some tomb near the scene of the crucifixion, the problem which it presents needs no explanation. Assuming that the empty tomb figured in the earliest narratives, many hold that the body was removed some time between the close of the Jewish Sabbath and sunrise of the first day of the week, at the command of Joseph, who, under the pressure of preparing for the Passover feast, had offered the tomb as a temporary resting-place for the body of him whom he secretly respected or revered. Naturally, Joseph would wish to reserve the tomb for the use of his own family, and the Saturday night following the Passover feast offered ample time in which to remove the body of Jesus. In any case the problem of what became of it was of significance chiefly to those who shared the current Jewish belief in a bodily resurrection. The fact that Paul had in part rejected this belief and the influence of his own personal vision of Jesus may explain why the story of the empty tomb finds no place in his record.

To summarize the facts: The earliest account of the appearances of Jesus to his disciples was given by Paul. These appearances, Paul indicates, were not physical, but in the form of visions. Paul makes no mention of the empty tomb. The oldest gospel narratives, Mark and Matthew, speak of it; but Matthew implies that Jesus' revelations to his disciples were not through the physical senses, but through the inner spiritual consciousness. Suggestions of physical resurrection are found only in Luke and John. They all centre about Jerusalem, not only ignore but also exclude the older Galilean group of narratives, and apparently represent a later development of the belief in Jesus' resurrection.

VI. **The Naturalistic Interpretations of the Resurrection Stories.** To-day three distinct types of interpretation are offered to explain the resurrection stories. The first may be called the naturalistic, the second the supernatural, and the third the spiritual. The first type assumes two widely different forms. One that at certain periods has commanded wide acceptance and is being constantly revived assumes that Jesus did not really die, but fainted on the cross, and that, in the haste of the preparation for the Passover, he was placed in the tomb before death had really overtaken him. In the quiet of the night he revived. That marvellous power over physical forces which he had so often used in the healing of others asserted itself, and he not only revived, but gathered such accessions of strength that he was able himself to roll away the stone which guarded the entrance to the tomb. In the dusk of the morning he met the devoted women, as they came to embalm this body, and told them that he would join his disciples in Galilee. Amidst the familiar scenes about the Sea of Galilee he repeatedly appeared to his disciples, until at last the cruel wounds which he had received proved fatal, and he bade his disciples a last farewell. Then he breathed out his spirit on the lone hill-top where he took leave of them.

Others, with more fervent imagination, claim that he survived and went away to live in retirement far from the scenes of his earlier activity. To some minds this explanation is alluring, for it satisfies the implications of a bodily presence that are found in certain of the stories and especially in those in Luke. But it does not satisfy historical students, for it finds its support simply in the later stratum of the narrative. It also fails to explain Paul's testimony and that of the older gospel narratives. It is fundamentally at variance with Jesus' character and purpose as revealed in the gospels. Furthermore, it furnishes no satisfactory explanation of the later activity of the disciples, nor does it meet the spiritual demands of the Christian world to-day any more than it would those of the primitive church.

Another view is that Peter, the emotional, living in an age and circle characterized by the prominence of ecstasy and similar abnormal mental states, under the influence of an hallucination, believed that he actually saw Jesus. It is urged that in this highly wrought state he so influenced the other disciples that they had similar hallucinations and believed that they likewise saw the form and heard the words of the Master, who had been with them only a few days before and whose crucifixion, death, and burial they themselves had not witnessed. But there are many obvious difficulties in accepting this explanation. Why did these hallucinations not continue indefinitely? The older narratives give no support to the theory of a self-generated hallucination. Above all, this explanation does not satisfactorily explain the triumphant faith of the apostles and the marvellous conquests of early Christianity.

VII. The Supernatural Explanations. On the surface Paul's account in I Corinthians 15 and the earliest narratives in the gospels seem to imply that Jesus, clothed in a glorified body, appeared repeatedly to the disciples, and last of all to Paul. This explanation accords with Paul's peculiar theory of the resurrection. It furnishes an explanation of how Jesus could be seen by five hundred of his followers at once. It is in some respect similar to that which is claimed regarding their departed friends by modern spiritualists. It postulates phenomena hitherto entirely uncorrelated by modern science. To the present age, therefore, as well as to the past, it was a miracle. In support of this explanation it is strongly urged that, if ever in the world's history conditions called for a miracle, it was in the days following the death of Jesus, and that a supernatural appearance alone explains the faith and the achievements of those who went forth assured that they had seen the risen Christ. Throughout the intervening centuries this has been the conception that has prevailed in the Christian church. To-day it appeals, as does no other explanation, to all who crave a supernatural attestation of Jesus' authority. And yet in this connection one cannot but recall Jesus' words in the parable of Dives and Lazarus in which he asserted that even though the dead should return to life men would not believe their words. Throughout his entire ministry he sternly refused to win men to the truth by external signs. Either this prevailing explanation is the true one, or else it was the popular early Christian as well as the Old Testament way of recording a deeper spiritual experience.

VIII. **The Spiritual Interpretation.** In determining the real nature of the historical fact that underlies the stories of the resurrection, Paul remains the one contemporary witness. His experience on the way to Damascus is the natural key by which to interpret its true historical meaning. Unfortunately, he has not given in any of his epistles a complete or detailed account of that experience. The three accounts found in the book of Acts are valuable, even though they vary in detail; but they represent second-hand testimony. Acts 9^2 states that his companions heard the voice but saw no man. Acts 22^9 says that they saw the light but did not hear the voice. In Galatians $1^{12,\ 15}$ Paul declares: "I did not receive the gospel from man, nor was it taught me. Rather I had it by revelation of Jesus Christ. When it was the good pleasure of him who set me apart from my mother's womb, and called me through grace to reveal his son in me, that I might preach him among the Gentiles, I did not immediately communicate with flesh and blood nor go up to Jerusalem to those who were apostles before me." These words of Paul imply that the revelation thus given him was internal and subjective, not external and objective. He also traces his inner vision to God, who was thus speaking to and through him, and thereby preparing him to preach Jesus among the Gentiles. His more detailed description of the same or a similar experience which he gives in II Corinthians 12^{1-4} likewise suggests an inner vision: "I must needs glory, though it is not expedient, but I will come to visions and revelations of the Lord. I know a man in Christ fourteen years ago (whether in the body I know not or whether out of the body I know not. God knoweth) that one was caught up into the third heaven, and I know that man (whether in the body or apart from the body, I know not, God knoweth) that he was caught up into Paradise, and heard unspeakable words, which it is not lawful for a man to utter." Certainly these words of Paul do not indicate that he saw a bodily presence or an apparition, but rather that his vision was subjective, and that what he saw was under the influence of a divine power that took possession of him. Paul's vagueness does not indicate that he was the victim of an illusion or hallucination, but simply illustrates the difficulty that confronts every man who attempts to describe a profound spiritual experience in concrete terms. For his early readers his bare testimony was sufficient, for it was amply substantiated by his character and work. It was, in fact, the only explanation of his sudden transformation from a bitter persecutor into an ardent apostle.

On the basis of this definite testimony of Paul regarding the way in which Jesus appeared to him, it is possible by analogy to analyze the similar experiences which came to Peter and the other disciples. The chief guides are (1) our knowledge of the situation and of the thoughts and hopes in their minds and (2) the analogous experiences of the Old Testament prophets. In picturing the process by which "God revealed his son in him," Paul used in part the very words employed by Jeremiah in describing his own initial call (cf. Gal. 1^{15} and Jer. 1^5). Although Paul's statement that Jesus "was raised on the third day according to the scriptures," was probably based on the passage in Hosea 6^2, it may also record an important historical detail. The sturdy fishermen, pursued by fear and anxiety, would easily reach the Sea of Galilee on the third day from Jerusalem. That the familiar environment, forever associated with the words and presence of Jesus, were important precursors of Peter's vision cannot be doubted. If Isaiah, the devoted patriot, had not gone up to the temple to worship at the hour when the news came that Uzziah, the great king, was dead, his mind might never have received the memorable vision of Jehovah's holiness and the divine call to service recorded in the sixth chapter of his prophecies. Peter, the impulsive and emotional, to whom later came another vivid vision, recorded in Acts 10, had been prepared by the great Teacher himself for the epoch-making revelation which came to him as he returned to the memory-haunted scenes about the Sea of Galilee. Possibly the apocryphal Gospel of Peter has preserved the true setting of his vision. It may have been while he and Andrew his brother were casting their nets into the sea that the vision came which transformed the vacillating disciple into the courageous apostle and martyr. From the gospel narratives it may be inferred that, even as Isaiah in his vision saw Jehovah sitting on his throne, so Peter saw clearly, with the eye of faith, the Friend and Master, whose spirit and words filled his mind, directing him to the mission that lay before him. If the early church had been less interested in signs and wonders and had been able to preserve more accurately the memory of inner spiritual experiences, we should have fuller knowledge of the exact nature of the visions of Christ which came to those other disciples to whom God spoke, even as he did to Peter and Paul.

One fact stands in clear relief: Peter and the other disciples saw Jesus. Paul likewise saw Jesus. The exact form of those revelations is not so essential as the effects traceable throughout the entire history of the primitive church. In the early Christian centuries they became the great dynamic that carried the apostles of Jesus to the ends of the world. It was, indeed, the consciousness of the living Christ that alone explains the spirit of the early Christians, their simple unflinching heroism, and the triumphant power of the message which they proclaimed. Death had no terrors for them, for they knew that their Master had conquered it. Whether they gained that knowledge through a series of unprecedented miracles, through visions, or through the still small voice of God within their souls, one fact is certain: the Heavenly Father, through Jesus, had spoken to them, as he had to his earlier messengers, the prophets, calling them to their divine task and giving them their message and the power to deliver it. To-day also, as in the past, it is the vivid consciousness of "the Christ who abides" that gives vital power and efficiency to Christianity.

§ CXLV. JESUS THE SAVIOUR OF MANKIND

1. The mission of the Son of man to save mankind (John 3 14-17)

As Moses lifted up the serpent in the wilderness,
So must the Son of man be lifted up,
That everyone who believes in him may have eternal life.
For God so loved the world that he gave his only Son,
That everyone who believes in him might not perish but
     have eternal life.
For God sent not his son into the world to judge the world,
But that the world might be saved through him.

He who believes on him is not condemned;
He who believes not is condemned already,
Because he has not believed on the name of the only Son of
    God.
And this is the condemnation, that the light has come into
    the world,
Yet men have loved the darkness rather than the light,
For their deeds were evil.
For everyone who does wrong hates the light and comes not
    to the light,
Lest his works should be exposed.
But he who does the truth comes to the light,
That his works may be manifest, that they have been
    wrought in God.

2. Reason why those who do not believe in him are condemned (18-21)

The hour is coming and now is,
When the true worshippers shall worship the Father in
    spirit and truth;
For such the Father seeketh to be his worshippers.
God is a Spirit,
And those who worship him, must worship in spirit and truth.

3. True worship spiritual not formal (4²³, ²⁴)

Work not for the food that perishes,
But for the food that lasts until eternal life,
Which the Son of man shall give to you.
For him the Father, even God, hath authorized.
For the bread of God is what comes down out of heaven,
And gives life to the world.
Jesus said, I am the bread of life;
He who comes to me shall never hunger,
And he who believes on me shall never thirst any more.

4. Jesus the bread of life from above (6²⁷, ³³, ³⁵)

I am the light of the world;
He who follows me shall not walk in the darkness,
But he shall have the light of life.

5. The light of the world (8¹²b-d)

If you remain in my word,
You are truly my disciples;
And you shall know the truth,
And the truth shall make you free.

6. Who by the truth frees his disciples (³¹b-d, ³²)

311

7. And
releases
from
the
bond-
age of
sin
(34b-36)

Everyone who commits sins is the slave of sin;
And the slave remains not in the house forever;
The Son remains forever.
If therefore the Son shall make you free,
You shall be free indeed.

8.
Jesus
the
shep-
herd
of all
man-
kind
(10¹⁴⁻
¹⁶)

I am the good shepherd,
And I know my own and my own know me,
Even as the Father knoweth me and I know the Father;
And I lay down my life for the sheep.
And other sheep I have which are not of this fold;
Those I must also bring,
And they shall hear my voice;
And there shall come to be one flock, one shepherd.

9. The
source
of eter-
nal life
(11²⁵ᵇ⁻
²⁶ᵃ)

I am the resurrection and the life;
He who believes on me, though he die, shall live;
And whoever lives and believes on me shall never die at all.

10. Be-
cause
he re-
veals
the
char-
acter
and
will
of the
Father
(12⁴⁴ᵇ⁻
⁵⁰)

He who believes on me,
Believes not on me, but on him who sent me.
And he who beholds me,
Beholds him who sent me.
I have come into the world as a light,
That whoever believes on me may not remain in the dark-
    ness.
And if anyone hears my sayings and keeps them not, I do
    not judge him;
For I came not to judge the world, but to save the world,
He who rejects me and receives not my sayings has one to
    judge him;
The word that I have spoken, that will judge him on the last
    day.
For I have not spoken of myself,
But the Father, who sent me,
He hath commanded me what I should say and what I should
    speak.
And I know that his commandment is life eternal.
What therefore I speak, I speak even as the Father hath
    told me.

You call me Teacher, and Lord,
And you say rightly, for so I am.
If I then, Lord and Teacher, have washed your feet,
You also ought to wash one another's feet.
For I have given you an example,
That you also should do even as I have done to you.
Indeed, I tell you truly,
A servant is not greater than his master,
Or one who is sent greater than he who sent him.

11.
Jesus'
example of
loving
service
(13^{12-16})

A new commandment I give you, to love one another,
Even as I have loved you that you also love one another.
By this shall all men know that you are my disciples,
If you have love one for another.

12.
His
law of
love
(34, 35)

I am the way, the truth, and the life;
No one comes to the Father except through me.
If you had known me, you would have known my Father also;
Henceforth you know him and have seen him.

13.
Jesus
the
way
to the
Father
(14^{6b-7})

Believest thou not that I am in the Father and the Father
    in me?
The words that I speak to you, I speak not from myself;
But the Father who abides in me doeth his works.
Believe me, I am in the Father and the Father in me;
Or else believe me on account of the works themselves.

14.
His
words
and
works
reveal
the
Father
(10, 11)

Indeed I tell you truly,
He who believes on me, he also shall do the works that I do;
And greater works than these shall he do, because I am going
    to the Father.

15.
His followers
to do
greater
works
(12)

And whatever you shall ask in my name, I will do it,
That the Father may be glorified in the Son.
If you ask for anything in my name I will do it.
If you love me you will keep my commandments.

16.
Their
prayers
to be
granted
(13-15)

And I will pray the Father, and he shall give you another
    Comforter,
That it may be with you forever, even the Spirit of truth,
Which the world cannot receive, for the world neither be-
    holds it nor knows it;
But you know it, because it remains with you and is in you.

17.
The
Spirit
of
truth
to be
within
them
(16, 17)

18.
Reward of the faithful (21)

He who holds fast my commands and keeps them,
He it is who loves me;
And he who loves me shall be loved by my Father,
And I will love him and will manifest myself to him.

19.
Jesus' prayer for his disciples (17[11c]-[12a], [15-19])

Holy Father, keep them in thy name which thou hast given me,
That they may be one, even as we are one.
While I was with them, I kept in thy name those whom thou hast given me;
I pray not that thou wouldst take them out of the world,
But that thou wouldst keep them from the evil one.
They are not of the world,
Even as I am not of the world.
Consecrate them by the truth:
Thy word is truth.
As thou hast sent me into the world,
So I have sent them into the world.
And for their sakes I consecrate myself,
That they may also be consecrated in truth.

20.
For all who believe in him and his teachings (20-[26])

Not for these only do I pray,
But for those also who, through their words, believe in me;
That they may all be one,
Even as thou, Father, art in me and I in thee,
That they may also be in us;
That the world may believe that thou hast sent me.
And the glory thou hast given me I have given them;
That they may be one even as we are one,
I in them, and thou in me,
That they may be perfected in one,
That the world may know that thou hast sent me,
And hast loved them even as thou hast loved me.
Father I would that they, whom thou hast given me, may be with me where I am,
That they may behold my glory which thou hast given me;
For thou hast loved me from the foundation of the world.
O righteous Father, while the world knoweth thee not, I know thee,
And these know that thou hast sent me;

314

And I have made known and will make known thy name to
    them,
That the love wherewith thou hast loved me may be in them,
And I in them.

I. The Fourth Gospel's Conception of Jesus as Teacher and
Saviour. The Fourth Gospel is in accord with the synoptic gospels in
describing Jesus primarily as a teacher. He was the Saviour because
he was the Teacher of men. Knowing God, he led men to God. Having found peace, he was able to lead men in the way of peace. Having
learned the value of service, he taught men how to find their life by
losing it in behalf of their fellow-men. The synoptic gospels simply
record Jesus' work as the Teacher and Saviour of a limited group. The
Fourth Gospel aims to interpret the larger significance of his work.
Its underlying doctrine of the pre-existence of Jesus and that he was
the incarnation of the divine Logos naturally pervades all its teachings,
and imparts to them that universal note which is largely lacking in the
synoptic gospels. Yet in its detailed interpretation of Jesus as the
Saviour of mankind it develops motives already found in the synoptic
gospels. His work is described by means of a variety of powerful
figures. As a teacher, he is the light which reveals the character and
will of God. He not only guides men in the way of truth, but their
attitude toward him and his teachings is the supreme test of character.
His teaching is the life-giving bread which gives life to the world.
The figure is drawn from the Old Testament account of the miraculous
provision of manna in the wilderness. The earlier story had already
been allegorized by Philo. The figure of eating the bread was, perhaps,
suggested by Ezekiel's declaration that he ate the roll on which the
divine message which he was to deliver was inscribed. It suggested a
complete assimilation of the truth. The figure of the good shepherd
was frequently used by the earlier prophets in describing Jehovah as
the restorer and guide of his people. The reference to the "other
sheep, not of this fold," points to the period when Christianity had
broken its Jewish bonds and had entered upon its world-wide conquest.
Nowhere is the Fourth Gospel's conception of Jesus as the universal
Saviour of mankind more clearly and beautifully expressed than in the
words:

> Those I must also bring,
> And they shall hear my voice;
> And there shall come to be one flock, one shepherd.

The Fourth Gospel insists that belief in Jesus is essential to salvation; but belief in Jesus is defined as belief in the God who sent him and whose will he interpreted. That belief is not something abstract, but must be experienced and expressed by obeying the commands of Jesus and by living in accordance with his teachings. Jesus' work, therefore, as the Saviour of men, according to the Fourth Gospel, consisted (1) in giving men a true conception of God, (2) in teaching them how to attain a larger, freer life, and (3) in leading them into such a harmonious, loving relationship with the Father that he might manifest himself through each individual, even as he did through Jesus. This is the chief thought in the wonderful prayer in the seventeenth chapter of John, which interprets the purpose and meaning of Jesus' work as no other passage in the gospels. It expresses with marvellous effectiveness and dramatic power the heroism and the universal significance of Jesus' patient training of his disciples. The setting of these concluding words of comfort, counsel, exhortation, and prayer, found in John 14–17, is the great crisis at Jerusalem and the shadow of Judas's treachery. Never was a theology presented more dramatically or taught more effectively. Sayings, possibly remembered by the disciples as they fell from the lips of Jesus, have here been joined with the words which he doubtless would have uttered had he clearly before his vision the church which later rose to carry on his message and work. Although they are but a later postscript to the gospels, they furnish an appropriate conclusion without which the records would be incomplete.

II. **Jesus' Self=Designation.** Direct light is thrown upon Jesus' own conception of his character and mission by the designation which he constantly applied to himself. The term Son of man occurs eighty-one times in the synoptic gospels and almost always in the reported sayings of Jesus. Allowing for duplications in parallel passages and for cases where a later editor has substituted the term for an original I, a score of passages remain in which there is little doubt that Jesus applied this title to himself. Inasmuch as the later Christian writers ceased to use it, its presence in the gospels is in all probability due to the great Teacher himself. Barring a few possible exceptions (Mark 2[10] Matt. 9[6]), the term does not appear to have been used by him until the latter part of his ministry. In one or two cases (e. g., Mark 2[28]) it was clearly employed by him as an equivalent to mankind, for the famous saying, "The son of man is master of the sabbath," cannot from its context refer to Jesus, but rather to mankind, whose rights he was defending. It is possible, therefore, that Jesus used the term, even as did the prophet Ezekiel, to emphasize simply his humanity and sense of dependence upon God, as well as his close kinship with the men whom he was endeavoring to reach and teach.

In the Aramaic, the common language of Palestine at the beginning of the Christian era, the term son of man was simply the equivalent of the word man. Its meaning, however, to the Jew of the first Christian century was closely associated with its use in Daniel 7[13]. In that oft-quoted verse Daniel declared that he beheld in a vision "One like the son of man" coming on the clouds of heaven. While in the original passage the son of man refers either to the saints, who were to participate in the divine kingdom about to be established, or else to Israel's patron angel Michael, it appears to have been regarded by later Judaism as a messianic title. Thus in the forty-sixth chapter of the Similitudes of Enoch (about 80 B.C.), in response to the question of the seer as to who was the Son of man, the angel replied: "This is the Son of man who has righteousness, with whom dwells righteousness, and who reveals all the treasures of that which is hidden, because the Lord of Spirits hath chosen him, and his lot before the Lord of Spirits has surpassed everything in uprightness forever. And this Son of man whom thou hast seen will arouse the kings and the mighty ones from their couches and the strong from their thrones, and will loosen the reins of the strong and grind to powder the teeth of the sinners" [3, 4]. In certain Jewish circles, therefore, the term son of man suggested the chief agent in that great act of deliverance, whereby Jehovah was to vindicate the righteous and inaugurate a universal reign of justice. The question which cannot be definitely answered, however, is, How far was this interpretation of the term son of man fixed in the mind of Jesus and in the minds of the multitudes to which he spoke? The fact that it is found in two (Enoch and II Esdras) of the few Jewish writings which come from the period gives good ground for believing that it was far more widely held than these chance references indicate. It is also significant that in referring to himself Jesus preferred to use the third person rather than the more direct first person. His purpose in so doing is, perhaps, revealed by the fact that he employed the term Son of man almost exclusively in describing his coming suffering and humiliation. In the light of all these facts, it is probable that he employed the term (1) because it emphasized his close kinship with his fellowmen, (2) because, unlike the term Messiah or Servant of Jehovah, it did not arouse in the minds of his hearers ideas and hopes at variance with his own ideals, and (3) because it suggested that the one who bore it stood in a unique relation to mankind, and was divinely called, through his teaching and suffering, to perform a peculiar service for his fellow-men. At least it is impossible to escape the conviction that with Jesus, as with his later disciples, it expressed the consciousness of his spiritual messiahship. Like the term Son of God, which is used as its equivalent in the Fourth Gospel, it proclaimed his kinship with his disciples to whom "he gave power to become the sons of God" (John 1[12]), and yet was at the same time a declaration of his unique relationship to God, as well as to man.

III. **Jesus' Interpretation of the Extent of His Mission.** Jesus stated definitely that his mission was primarily to "the lost sheep of the house of Israel." In his commission to his disciples, recorded in Mark 3[13-14] and 6[7, 8] he said nothing of the larger world beyond Judaism. Matthew's parallel version (10[5, 6]) states that he expressly enjoined them:

> Go not in the way of the Gentiles,
> And enter no city of the Samaritans.
> Rather go to the lost sheep of the house of Israel.

It is impossible to conceive how a gospel writer, living in the age when Christianity was rapidly sweeping through the Roman Empire, would put such a command on the lips of Jesus unless he regarded it as a true expression of the Master's attitude toward the broad field that opened before him.

The request of the Syro-Phœnician woman appears to have come to Jesus as a surprise. Here for the first time he was squarely confronted by the Gentile problem. His action in granting her request is significant. His deep love and sympathy for all mankind left no other way open. That Jesus had in mind the Gentile world is shown by such sayings as that found in Matthew 8[11] (cf. 24[14] and 26[13]): "I tell you many shall come from the east and the west and sit down with Abraham and Isaac and Jacob in the kingdom of Heaven, but the sons of the kingdom shall be cast out." This type of universalism had already been clearly expressed by many of Israel's earlier teachers (cf. Zech. 8[22, 23] Isa. 49[6] 56[6-8]). While Jesus fully recognized that the kingdom of God was open to Gentile, as well as Jew, he appears to have confined his attention and that of his disciples strictly to the members of his own race. With that directness and enthusiasm which characterized all that he did, he devoted himself to the field immediately at hand This conclusion alone explains the difficulties which his intimate disciples later experienced in turning to the Gentile world and the long controversy which raged between them and Paul, the great apostle to the Gentiles. At the same time Jesus, in predicting the destruction of the temple and in showing the comparative unimportance of ritual, and of many of the current doctrines of his race, demonstrated the insufficiency of Judaism and laid the foundations for a universal world religion. He also addressed himself to the individual and deliberately avoided all distinctively racial questions, thereby placing his mission and message on a universal basis. Thus not by word but rather by his acts and the inner content of his teaching Jesus prepared the way for that universalism which is fully expressed in the Fourth Gospel and realized in the history of Christianity. The author of Matthew is, therefore, in a profound sense justified in saying that Jesus left, as his parting injunction to his followers, the command: "Go then and make disciples of all the nations" (28[19]).

IV. Why Jesus Is the Universal Saviour of Mankind. From what does man need to be saved? This question must be answered to-day, not in the light of metaphysics or abstract theology, but of physiology, psychology, political science, economics, and sociology. Man needs to be saved, in the first place, from the dominance of the baser animal instincts, from childish impulses which he has not outgrown, and from over-developed or misdirected egoism. He needs to be saved from ignorance of himself, of his relation to his fellow-men and to his larger environment which we call God. He must be saved from worry and fear, which undermine his physical, mental, and moral vigor, and from low ideals that thwart the development of the perfect man. He needs deliverance from the palsying effects of past mistakes and sins. The ordinary man to-day is not troubled or oppressed by fear of an angry God. The consequences of his misdeeds haunt him and smite him in a far more direct and intimate way. Man turns to God not for abstract forgiveness, but for help to escape from these fetters, forged by himself or by his ancestors, which bind him to that which is base and mean. In the light of modern psychology, it is apparent that while a man may experience instantaneously what is commonly called conversion, his salvation is not attained in a moment, but is a continuous educational process. It is accomplished not by negations, but by developing within him nobler impulses and ideals and by bringing him into normal relations with his environment and by teaching him how to function, that is, effectively to accomplish his life-work in the environment in which he is placed.

319

This is precisely what Jesus did for the needy men and women who gathered about him during his work in Galilee. And what he did for them then he is able to do for men to-day, for the needs and the processes of salvation are eternally the same. He was able to perform his saving work because he himself had felt many of the same needs and had found the only way of satisfying them. No teacher of the past was more awake to the weakness of human nature than Jesus; but he also saw and proclaimed clearly its divine possibilities. He saw that those possibilities could be realized only as each individual was brought into normal, living touch with the heavenly Father. This was the great lesson taught by his own experience. Not until he had heard in his soul the words: "Thou art my beloved son in whom I am well pleased," did he enter upon his own work as the Friend and Saviour of sinners. Having heard those divine words, he could not remain away from his needy brothers. Jesus' experience in this respect is a type of universal human experience. A man's recognition of his sonship to God opens his eyes at once to the fact that all men are his brothers. Herein lies the miracle of the religious life. It is the eternal mystery of conversion. When once a man enters fully into this filial attitude toward God and fraternal relation with his fellow-men, he suddenly finds himself saved from the dominance of his passions, his selfish impulses, from worry and fear. Even the consequences of his past sins no longer master him, but a great, alluring field of service opens before him. With this self-forgetting service there comes peace and the joy and exultation that crown worthy achievement.

Jesus meets men on the common level of universal human experience, and, having won their confidence, he introduces them not to a metaphysical God, but to a heavenly Father whose heart throbs with solicitude and love for his earthly children. Then Jesus bids each take up his cross and follow him calmly, joyfully, and successfully along the tortuous path of daily experience that leads to the true heaven that exists both here on earth and in the life beyond. He also initiates him into that universal fraternity in which all are bound together by a common love to a common heavenly Father. Jesus is the Saviour of men because he was the intrepid pioneer, the dauntless explorer in the boundless world of religious truth and experience, the successful discoverer of God, the elder brother, who, as the teacher of his fellowmen, is able to show them the true goal and value of life and the art of living. Fellowship with God, discipleship with Jesus, and brotherhood with man—this is a trinity which Christianity presents to the world to-day as the supreme object of faith and endeavor.

V. Reasons Why Christianity Is a Conquering World Religion.
A study of the life and teachings of Jesus is incomplete without a brief
review of the chief reasons why the faith which he proclaimed by word
and life meets the universal needs of humanity. The first reason is
historical: Christianity sprang from Judaism, the noblest pre-christian
ethical religion. It was the culmination of a genetic development extending through many centuries. It had a broad and varied national
background and therefore is closely and vitally related to humanity
and human needs. It assimilated and combined the essential elements
in the teachings of Israel's prophets, priests, and sages, and fulfilled
the noblest spiritual aspirations of the Hebrew race. As a learned
Jewish scholar (Abrahams) has recently said, "Jesus did what Judaism
was unable to do: He syncretized and harmonized the prophets and the
law, the spirit and the letter, idealism and pragmatism."

By virtue of its genesis and spirit Christianity is also a growing
religion, capable of assimilating that which is best in the spiritual
thought and experience of each succeeding age. It simply and satisfactorily unites religion and ethics by emphasizing religion and by giving to ethics the inspiration of a strong personal faith. It appeals to
the individual will through both the reason and the emotions. Thereby
it touches and completely commands the whole man: his intellect, his
feelings, his faith, and his acts. It sets before men a worthy goal: in
the present life, true happiness, won through self-denial and service
and preserved by faith that frees men from the harassing fears and
worries of life. For the future it holds out the sure promise of individual peace and joy and growth, since the object of its faith is "the
God of the living," whose beneficent rule is revealed in every phase of
human experience.

Christianity is the only thoroughly democratic religion known to
man. It appeals alike to all classes: the rich and the poor, the strong
and the weak, the learned and the ignorant. It proclaims God to be not
only the one supreme Ruler of the universe, but the Father of each individual, a God of justice yet a God of love, constantly watching over and
guiding even the humblest of his children. Christianity offers the only
satisfactory solution of the problem of evil, for it shows on the one hand
that temptation and suffering are indispensable factors in the development of the individual and the race; on the other hand it teaches that
God himself suffers in all the pains that come to his children.

Christianity is pre-eminently a social religion. It emphasizes not
the racial but the universal bonds of human brotherhood. It aims

321

by training the individual conscience and will, to establish a closely knit, world-wide fraternity. It glorifies humanity and all normal human relations. It is in no sense ascetic. Instead of taking men out of the world, it seeks to develop perfect, godlike men in the midst of society, and through them to solve the problems of society.

Christianity wins and transforms men by the influence of personality upon personality. It is a spiritual force emanating from God himself, finding concrete and noblest expression in Jesus, but rendered continuously effective through his apostles and his faithful followers in all ages. It is an ever-broadening wave of direct personal influence, destined ultimately to touch and transform all men, so that they, like Jesus, shall become godlike. The central figure in Christianity is the Son of man, "tempted in all points like as we are, yet without sin." In the midst of life he realized the goal of all life: perfect humanity, which is at the same time divine. The key-stone, therefore, of Christianity is Jesus, our elder brother, our example, our Teacher, our Master, and our Saviour.

APPENDIX

I

A PRACTICAL REFERENCE LIBRARY

Books for Constant Reference. The number of books on the life and teaching of Jesus is legion. It is exceedingly difficult to single out from a library of a thousand or fifteen hundred volumes the few that are of pre-eminent value. Moffatt's *Introduction to the Literature of the New Testament* is the most comprehensive, thorough-going, and, on the whole, most satisfactory introduction to the gospels, as well as to the other New Testament books. It presents the data and the bibliography needful for the scientific investigation of the many problems that gather about the gospels. At the same time its spirit and method are constructive, so that here the general reader will find clearly set forth the positive results of New Testament scholarship. Several excellent harmonies are available: Stevens's and Burton's *Harmony of the Gospels*, Huck's *Synopsis of the First Three Gospels*, and Wright's *Synopsis of the Gospels*. The general reader will find the brief commentaries on the different gospels in the New Century Bible exceedingly convenient and, on the whole, satisfying. For the student, the volumes in the International Critical Commentary are the best, although many will prefer to substitute for Allen's *Matthew*, Plummer's *Matthew*. Professor Bacon's introduction and commentary on Mark, entitled *The Beginnings of the Gospel Story*, is both suggestive and stimulating. The two volumes on *The Synoptic Gospels* by the reformed Jewish scholar Montefiore contain a wealth of fresh material.

No one of the many lives of Jesus occupies a pre-eminent place. The voluminous *Life of Jesus* by Oscar Holtzmann contains much valuable material, but it lacks unity and many of its conclusions will not command acceptance. Stapfer's three volumes, entitled *Jesus Christ Before His Ministry*, *During His Ministry*, and *The Death and Resurrection of Jesus Christ*, contain a brilliant, popular interpretation of the chief facts about Jesus' personality and work. Among the many excellent discussions of the teachings of Jesus, that by Stevens, *The Teaching of Jesus*, is the briefest and yet one of the most satisfactory. A more detailed interpretation of Jesus' teachings in the light of the New Testament as a whole is found in Clarke's fascinating *Outlines of Christian Theology*. More scientific and critical, yet untechnical, are Brown's *Christian Theology in Outline* and *The Essence of Christianity*. The social teachings of Jesus are ably interpreted by two leaders in the modern social movement, Peabody in his *Jesus Christ and the Social Question*, and by Rauschenbusch in his *Christianity and the Social Crisis* and in his *Christianizing of the Social Order*. For the larger interpretation of the personality of Jesus, Bushnell's *The Character of Jesus* remains the message of a modern prophet to the present age.

Additional Books of Reference: Introductions. The reader who is not in touch with the results of modern New Testament historical research will find the little volume by Wrede on the *Origin of the New Testament* a delightful portal to this new world. Hill's *Introduction to the Life of Christ* deals in a conservative yet scholarly manner with the extra-biblical, as well as the gospel records of the life of Jesus. The introductions to the New Testament by Bacon and by Peake present the modern conclusions regarding the origin and history of the New Testament books in brief, popular form. A more voluminous treatment of the same themes is found in Jülicher's vivid, illuminating *Introduction to the New Testament*. While it does not contain the minute data so ably tabulated in Moffatt's *Introduction*, it is parallel to and in many ways supplements the latter. The *Oxford Studies in the Synoptic Problem* contain a series of suggestive papers by Professor Sanday and his colleagues on the different phases of that problem. Professor Burkitt of Cambridge, in his little hand-book on *The Earliest Sources for the Life of Jesus*, and in his larger work on *The Gospel History and Transmission*, sets forth the results of his brilliant, although not always convincing, scholarship.

Harmonies. In addition to the harmonies already mentioned, the critical Greek student will find Rushbrook's *Synopticon* indispensable. Tatian's *Diatessaron*, which represents an early attempt to combine the four gospels, is made available for English readers in Hill's *The Earliest Life of Christ* or Hogg's *Ante-Nicene Christian Library*.

Commentaries. To the commentaries mentioned above should be added two which lack at points the critical historical basis and yet are rich in their spiritual and interpretative values; Robertson's *The*

APPENDIX

Gospel According to Matthew and Menzies' *The Earliest Gospel*. Students will also find three German commentaries especially valuable, for they each make their distinctive contribution to the interpretation of the gospels. Wellhausen's critical translation and interpretation, contained in his *Evangelium Matthaei, Marci,* and *Lucae,* reveal the same keen insight and suggestiveness that have enriched in many ways the interpretation of the Old Testament. Holtzmann, *Die Synoptiker,* in the *Hand-Commentar zum Neuen Testament,* is concise and illuminating. Johannes Weiss's *Die Schriften des Neuen Testaments* is based on the results of modern critical scholarship, but emphasizes especially the historical and religious interpretation of the New Testament books.

Lives of Jesus. Keim's *History of Jesus of Nazareth* still remains one of the most stimulating interpretations of the personality of the great Teacher and especially of his forerunner, John the Baptist, although many of its conclusions are no longer tenable. Briefer, and yet of the same general character, is Bousset's *Jesus.* Even though many of his positions are extreme, Schmidt, in *The Prophet of Nazareth,* has shed new light on the central figure of all history. Even Renan's *Life of Jesus,* although unhistorical and unscientific in its method, still makes upon the mind of the thoughtful reader the profound impression of the reality of Jesus and that he must be interpreted in the light of the age in which he lived. Thompson's *Jesus According to St. Mark* is a fresh, frank discussion of Jesus' personality and work as recorded in the oldest narrative gospel, but it lacks proportion and completeness. Robertson's *Epochs in the Life of Jesus,* although uncritical, shows a deep spiritual appreciation of the inner experiences of Jesus. Hitchcock's *The Psychology of Jesus* has the faults and the virtues of a pioneer volume in a field which promises rich results. Garvie's *Studies in the Inner Life of Jesus* contains many flashes of clear insight, but its apologetic and theological tone and point of view impair its usefulness for the ordinary reader. Watson, in his *Life of the Master,* and Rhees, in his *Life of Jesus,* have succeeded perhaps better than any others in combining in a brief volume the results of the modern point of view and a brief, constructive presentation of Jesus' personality and work. Among the more popular interpretative and inspirational discussions of Jesus may be mentioned Ross's *The Universality of Jesus,* Crooker's *The Supremacy of Jesus,* Jacobs's *As Others Saw Him,* Leonard's *The Poet of Galilee,* Gilbert's *Jesus,* and Hyde's *Jesus' Way.*

The Teachings of Jesus. To the volumes mentioned above should be added Harnack's critical attempt in *The Sayings of Jesus* to recon-

struct on the basis of the data in Matthew and Luke the original form
of Jesus' utterances, as they were taken by the gospel writers from Matthew's collection of his sayings. Among the older interpretations of
the teachings of Jesus, Bruce's *The Kingdom of God*, Wendt's *Teaching of Jesus*, and Beyschlag's *Theology of the New Testament* are exceedingly useful. Matthews's *Social Teaching of Jesus* is also a useful companion to the volumes by Peabody and Rauschenbusch. Valuable
discussions of every phase of Jesus' life and teachings are found in
Hastings's *Dictionary of Christ and the Gospels*, in his five-volume *Dictionary of the Bible*, and in the *Encyclopædia Biblica*. In this list should
also be included the admirable biblical articles in the eleventh edition
of the *Encyclopædia Britannica*.

II

GENERAL QUESTIONS AND SUBJECTS FOR SPECIAL RESEARCH

The GENERAL QUESTIONS, as in the preceding volumes, follow the
main divisions of the book and aim to guide the student in collecting
and co-ordinating the more important facts presented in the biblical
texts or in the notes.

The SUBJECTS FOR SPECIAL RESEARCH are intended as a guide for
further study in related lines, and aim, by means of detailed references, to introduce the student and the teacher to the more important
passages in the best English books of reference. In class-room work
many of these topics may profitably be assigned for individual research.
The references are to pages, unless otherwise indicated. Ordinarily,
several parallel references are given, that the student may be able to
utilize the book at hand.

INTRODUCTION: RECORDS OF THE LIFE AND TEACH-INGS OF JESUS

I. The Records Outside the Gospels. GENERAL QUESTIONS: 1.
What is Christianity? 2. What is the most irrefutable evidence of
Jesus' work and teaching? 3. Describe the testimony of the Roman
historians regarding Jesus and his earlier followers. 4. Of the Jewish

writers. 5. The nature of the evidence furnished by the Catacombs. 6. Historical value of the uncanonical gospels. 7. Of the writings of the Church Fathers and of the apocryphal gospels. 8. Paul's references to Jesus.

SUBJECTS FOR SPECIAL RESEARCH: 1. Write a life of Jesus based simply on the extra-gospel records. 2. The evidence regarding the authenticity of Josephus's detailed reference to Jesus. Holtzmann, *Life of Jesus*, 13–16; Hill, *Introd. to the Life of Christ*, 6–9. 3. The extra-canonical sayings of Jesus. Hill, *Introd. to the Life of Christ*, 15–20; Hastings, *D. B.*, extra vol., 343–52; Grenfell and Hunt, *Sayings of Our Lord* and *The Oxyrhynchus Papyri*, Pt. I, 1–3; Ropes, *Sprüche Jesu*.

II. The Contents and Characteristics of the Four Gospels.
GENERAL QUESTIONS: 1. Why is it impossible to determine the exact sequence of the events in the life of Jesus? 2. Describe the general plan of the Gospel of Mark. 3. Its distinctive characteristics. 4. Its aim and the class for which it was intended. 5. The characteristics and aim of the Gospel of Matthew. 6. Of Luke. 7. Of the Fourth Gospel. 8. Give a descriptive title to each of the four gospels.

SUBJECTS FOR SPECIAL RESEARCH: 1. The distinctive contribution of each gospel to our knowledge of the life and work of Jesus. 2. Luke's use of medical terms. Hobart, *The Medical Language of St. Luke;* Harnack, *Luke, the Physician*, 175–98. 3. A detailed comparison of the grouping of the material in Matthew and in Luke. *Cf.* standard harmonies of the life of Jesus.

III. The Written Sources Underlying the Gospels.
GENERAL QUESTIONS: 1. How far do Matthew and Luke follow the order of Mark? 2. How much of the material in Mark is quoted by Matthew and Luke? 3. What narratives are recorded in only one of the first three gospels? 4. In what four or five different ways do the authors of Matthew and Luke reproduce the material which they drew from Mark? 5. Describe the general conclusions drawn from the study of the synoptic problem. 6. In what marked respects does the Fourth Gospel differ from the synoptic gospels? 7. What is Papias's testimony regarding the origin of Mark's gospel. 8. The internal evidence regarding its origin. 9. The evidence that Matthew and Luke drew from a common teaching source. 10. The probable character and contents of this teaching source. 11. Its historical value.

SUBJECTS FOR SPECIAL RESEARCH: 1. The evidence that Mark was acquainted with Matthew's collection of the sayings of Jesus. *Ox-*

APPENDIX

ford Studies, 165–183; Moffatt, *Introd. to N. T.*, 204–6; Bacon, *Beginnings of Gospel Story*, xx–xxii; Harnack, *Sayings of Jesus*, 193–227. 2. Original extent and order of this early collection. *Oxford Studies*, 141–64, 185–208; Moffatt, *Introd. to N. T.*, 197–202; Harnack, *Sayings of Jesus*, 127–93. 3. Evidence that different versions of the early collection were used by Matthew and by Luke. *Oxford Studies*, 285–6; Moffatt, *Introd. to N. T.*, 194–7.

IV. **The Literary History and Date of the Gospels.** GENERAL QUESTIONS: 1. How long and how were Jesus' teachings probably transmitted orally? 2. Why were the earliest gospels written? 3. What were the probable dates of Matthew's Aramaic collection of (1) the sayings of Jesus (2) and of Mark's Gospel? 4. Of the Gospels of Matthew and Luke? 5. Of the Fourth Gospel? 6. Trace the literary dependence of the gospels upon their earlier sources and upon each other.

SUBJECTS FOR SPECIAL RESEARCH: 1. Evidence regarding the date of the earliest collection of Jesus' sayings. Moffatt, *Introd. to N. T.*, 203–4; Harnack, *Sayings of Jesus*, 246–9. 2. The reasons for an early or for a late dating of Luke. Moffatt, *Introd. to N. T.*, 512–3; Harnack, *Neue Untersuchungen zur Apostelgeschichte*, 80. 3. The authorship of the Fourth Gospel. Moffatt, *Introd. to N. T.*, 567–70; Bacon, *The Fourth Gospel in Research and Debate;* Sanday, *The Criticism of the Fourth Gospel.*

V. **Historical Background of Jesus' Life and Work.** GENERAL QUESTIONS: 1. Describe the final division of Palestine after the death of Herod the Great. 2. Rome's policy in the treatment of Judea. 3. The threefold duties of the Roman procurators. 4. Organization and functions of the Jerusalem sanhedrin. 5. Character of Pontius Pilate. 6. Of Herod Antipas. 7. Rome's weakness and needs.

SUBJECTS FOR SPECIAL RESEARCH: 1. Rome's provincial policy. Botsford, *Hist. of Rome*, 192–3, 208–10; Arnold, *Roman Prov. Administ.*, ch. III; Mommsen, *Provinces of the Roman Empire.* 2. The strength and weakness of Stoicism. Holtzmann, *Life of Jesus*, 5, 8–21; *Encyc. Brit.*[11], XXV, 943–52. 3. Hillel. Holtzmann, *Life of Jesus*, 509–12; *Encyc. Brit.*[11], XIII, 467–8.

§ CXXI. **Jesus' Birth, Boyhood, and Early Training.** GENERAL QUESTIONS: 1. In what respects do Luke's and Matthew's accounts of Jesus' birth agree and disagree? 2. Describe the testimony of the earliest biblical records regarding the manner of his birth. 3. The probable origin and the significance of the two accounts in Luke

328

APPENDIX

and Matthew. 4. The ultimate basis of the belief in Jesus' divine character. 5. The probable date and place of his birth. 6. The influences of his home at Nazareth. 7. His education. 8. Meaning of his first visit to the temple. 9. His knowledge of the Old Testament. 10. His training as a Master Builder.

SUBJECTS FOR SPECIAL RESEARCH: 1. The claim that Luke 1[34, 35] is secondary. Moffatt, *Introd. to the N. T.*, 268–70; *En. Bib.*, III, 2954–7; Lobstein, *Virgin Birth*, 42–79. 2. The chronology of the life of Jesus. *En. Bib.*, I, 801–9; Hastings, *Dict. of Christ*, 408–16; Schmidt, *Proph. of Naz.*, 240–7.

§ CXXII. **The Personality and Teaching of John the Baptist.** GENERAL QUESTIONS: 1. Describe the sources of our knowledge regarding John. 2. His personality. 3. His aims and methods. 4. His message. 5. What he accomplished.

SUBJECTS FOR SPECIAL RESEARCH: 1. A comparison of the personality and message of Amos and of John the Baptist. 2. Origin of John's symbol of baptism. Hastings, *Dict. of Christ*, I, 863–4; *En. Bib.*, I, 471–2.

§ CXXIII. **Jesus' Baptism and Temptation.** GENERAL QUESTIONS: 1. Describe Jesus' probable motives in going to John. 2. Literary character of the accounts of the Baptism and Temptation. 3. Jesus' inner experience at his baptism. 4. The three different phases of temptation which assailed Jesus.

SUBJECTS FOR SPECIAL RESEARCH: 1. Compare Jesus' vision at the Baptism with that of Isaiah at the temple, and with Paul's vision on the way to Damascus. 2. The different interpretations of the account of Jesus' temptation. Montefiore, *The Synoptic Gospels*, II, 465–70; Holtzmann, *Life of Jesus*, 144–54; Hastings, *Dict. of Christ*, II, 714–6; Ross, *The Universality of Jesus*, 57–67. 3. Jesus' interpretation of his mission as revealed by the story of his temptation.

§ CXXIV. **Jesus and John the Baptist.** GENERAL QUESTIONS: 1. What are the indications that Jesus worked first in Judea? 2. Describe John's arrest and imprisonment. 3. His message to Jesus and the reply. 4. Jesus' tribute to John. 5. John's death.

SUBJECTS FOR SPECIAL RESEARCH: 1. The situation of Machærus, where John was imprisoned and beheaded. Smith, *Hist. Geog. Holy Land*, 569–70; Kent, *Bib. Geog. and Hist.*, 244–5. 2. A comparison of the character and methods of Elijah and of John the Baptist. 3. The qualities in John which appealed most strongly to Jesus. Robertson, *John the Loyal*.

APPENDIX

§ CXXV. **Jesus' Early Work in Galilee.** GENERAL QUESTIONS: 1. Describe the character of the Marcan narrative at this point. 2. The situation of ancient Capernaum. 3. Reasons why Jesus made this the centre of his activity. 4. His aims and methods in his early Galilean work. 5. The reasons why he attracted men to himself. 6. The influence of his personality upon the insane. 7. The reasons why he left the afflicted multitudes at Capernaum.

SUBJECTS FOR SPECIAL RESEARCH: 1. The archæological and historical evidence regarding the site of Capernaum. Masterman, *Studies in Galilee*, 71–89; Kent, *Bib. Geog. and Hist.*, 247–50. 2. Of Chorazin and Bethsaida. Masterman, *Studies in Galilee*, 92–106; Kent, *Bib. Geog. and Hist.*, 250–2. 3. The ancient synagogues of Galilee. Masterman, *Studies in Galilee*, 109–25; Palestine Expl. Fund, *Memoirs*, Vol. I.

§ CXXVI. **Jesus' Popularity and the Beginning of the Pharisaic Opposition.** GENERAL QUESTIONS: 1. Describe the reasons why the Pharisees opposed Jesus. 2. Compare his aims and methods with theirs. 3. What were the four distinct charges that they brought against him? 4. What was his interpretation of the meaning and use of the Sabbath?

SUBJECTS FOR SPECIAL RESEARCH: 1. Compare Jesus' definition of religion with that of the Jewish rabbis of his day. 2. How far did he conform to the demands of the Pharisees? 3. The then current Jewish laws regarding Sabbath observance. Holtzmann, *Life of Jesus*, 224–7; Hastings, *Dict. of Christ*, II, 540–2: *Mishna*, *Shabbath*, and *Erubin*. 4. Was the Puritan Sabbath a realization of the Jewish or the Christian ideal?

§ CXXVII. **The Gospel Miracles.** GENERAL QUESTIONS: 1. Describe the conditions in Jesus' day which led him to perform miracles. 2. The contemporary interpretation of abnormal mental states. 3. Jesus' attitude toward the popular demand for miraculous signs. 4. In what records are most of the Old Testament miracle stories found? 5. Define a miracle. 6. The canons employed by critical historians in interpreting miracles. 7. Describe and illustrate the four distinct types of gospel miracles. 8. What types are best attested? 9. Which are the most significant?

SUBJECTS FOR SPECIAL RESEARCH: 1. How far are the gospel miracles paralleled by mediæval and modern examples? 2. How far are the miracles of Jesus in harmony with the conclusions of modern psychology? 3. Are the gospel miracles as a whole a stumbling-block or an aid to the faith of the modern generation?

APPENDIX

§ CXXVIII. **Call and Training of Jesus' Disciples.** GENERAL QUESTIONS: 1. Why did Jesus gather about him a group of disciples? 2. From what classes were they drawn? 3. The conditions which he imposed upon his immediate followers. 4. The nature of the relationship between Jesus and his disciples. 5. The number and the duties of the ministering women. 6. The character and purpose of his directions to the Twelve. 7. The reason why he sent them out. 8. The nature of their work. 9. The impression which the report of their success made upon Jesus.

SUBJECTS FOR SPECIAL RESEARCH: 1. Peter's character and work as recorded in the New Testament. Hastings, *Dict. of Christ*, II, 349-51; *En. Bib.*, IV, 4559-4626; Thomas, *The Apostle Peter*. 2. Jesus' appreciation of the peculiar needs of women. 3. A sketch of Jesus' appearance and manner as suggested by the earliest records. Thompson, *Jesus According to St. Mark;* Bousset, *Jesus.*

JESUS' FUNDAMENTAL TEACHINGS

§ CXXIX. **The Aims and Methods of the Great Teacher.** GENERAL QUESTIONS: 1. Describe the chief characteristics which made Jesus pre-eminent as a teacher. 2. His attitude toward the teachings of the Old Testament. 3. His methods of interpreting them. 4. His aims as a teacher. 5. The leading characteristics of his method. 6. His use of parable. 7. Of paradox and hyperbole. 8. Of beatitudes.

SUBJECTS FOR SPECIAL RESEARCH: 1. How far did Jesus anticipate the fundamental principles of modern education? 2. Examples of humor in his teachings. Leonard, *The Poet of Galilee*. 3. A comparison of Jesus' aims and methods as a teacher with those of Socrates. *En. Brit.*[11], XXV, 331-8; Graves, *History of Education Before the Middle Ages*, 180-4.

§ CXXX. **God's Attitude toward Men.** GENERAL QUESTIONS: 1. Describe the contemporary Jewish ideas of God. 2. The Old Testament teachings regarding the fatherhood of God. 3. What did Jesus contribute to men's beliefs regarding the nature of God? 4. Contrast his teachings regarding God's readiness to forgive the sinner with those of the Pharisees. 5. Regarding the way in which God will answer prayer.

SUBJECTS FOR SPECIAL RESEARCH: 1. What did Jesus add to the theology of the Old Testament? 2. How far do the current theological doctrines of the church reflect his teachings? 3. From what sources were the variant elements derived? Abbott, *The Evolution of Christianity*, 68–95.

§ CXXXI. **Man's Attitude toward God.** GENERAL QUESTIONS: 1. Describe Jesus' conception of the dignity and possibilities of man. 2. His teachings regarding oaths. 3. Regarding the essentials of true worship. 4. Meaning of the original prayer which he taught his disciples. 5. The essentials in prayer. 6. Teaching of the parable of the Pharisee and tax-collector. 7. Why are humility and the spirit of forgiveness absolutely vital in effective prayer? 8. Jesus' teaching regarding worry. 9. Regarding the ways in which it can be overcome.

SUBJECTS FOR SPECIAL RESEARCH: 1. Early Jewish prayers, *Mishna Berakhoth*. 2. The variations between the versions of the Lord's prayer in Matthew and in Luke. Hastings, *Dict. of Christ*, II, 57–9; Holtzmann, *Life of Jesus*, 262–6. 3. Jesus' appreciation of nature.

§ CXXXII. **The Kingdom of God.** GENERAL QUESTIONS: 1. Describe the growth of the Hebrew conception of God as king. 2. The three current Jewish conceptions of the kingdom of God. 3. Jesus' attitude toward them. 4. Reasons why he gave the kingdom of God a central place in his teachings. 5. Its character as described by him. 6. The conditions of entrance. 7. Jesus' teachings regarding the advantages and disadvantages of wealth.

SUBJECTS FOR SPECIAL RESEARCH: 1. The Rabbinic teachings regarding the kingdom of God. Schechter, *Some Aspects of Rabbinic Theol.*, 57–115. 2. The contrasts between the Jewish and Christian conception of the kingdom of God. 3. The fundamental points of agreement.

§ CXXXIII. **The Obligations of Citizenship in the Kingdom of God.** GENERAL QUESTIONS: 1. Did Jesus place the emphasis on the act or the motive? 2. What were the chief temptations that assailed the Jews of his day? 3. What is the meaning of the parable of the man who pulled down his barns to build larger? 4. Describe Jesus' teaching regarding the right use of wealth. 5. Regarding the use of individual wealth and present opportunity. 6. Of natural gifts. 7. *Résumé* of his teachings regarding the duties of citizenship in the kingdom of God.

SUBJECTS FOR SPECIAL RESEARCH: 1. The teaching of modern psychology regarding the relation of motives and acts. *Cf.* standard psychologies by James, Dewey, Judd, Kirkpatrick, and Angell. 2. Does

Luke overstate Jesus' teaching regarding wealth and poverty? **Pea-**
body, *Jesus Christ and the Social Question*, 192–214.

§ CXXXIV. **Man's Duties to His Neighbor and to Himself.**
GENERAL QUESTIONS: 1. What did Jesus declare were the evil effects
of wrong thinking? 2. What evidence is there that he felt a deep
reverence for the person of another? 3. How did he deal with the
social evil? 4. On what did he base the duty of forgiveness? 5. Describe his teachings regarding uncharitable judgment. 6. The meaning of his law of love. 7. Its practical expression.

SUBJECTS FOR SPECIAL RESEARCH: 1. The effect of a man's thoughts
upon his physical condition and relative efficiency. 2. The physiological effects of anger. *Cf.* standard works on physiological psychology. 3. How far is Jesus' law of love practically applicable in the
modern economic world?

§ CXXXV. **Man's Responsibility to Society.** GENERAL QUES-
TIONS: 1. Describe Jesus' methods as a social teacher. 2. His teachings regarding the importance of the family. 3. Regarding divorce.
4. The duties of the individual citizen to the state. 5. Principles to be
followed in the treatment of criminals. 6. In giving alms. 7. The
responsibility of the strong to the dependent classes. 8. The results
of applying Jesus' social principles in modern life.

SUBJECTS FOR SPECIAL RESEARCH: 1. Jesus and modern socialism.
Abbott, *Christianity and Social Problems*, 100–37; Peabody, *Jesus
Christ and the Social Question*, 13–26. 2. Advances in the treatment
of criminals. Ellis, *The Criminal;* Abbott, *Christianity and the Social
Problems*, 297–328; Reports of the *National Prison Association;* De-
vine, *The Spirit of Social Work*, 109–26. 3. How far are Jesus' social
teachings applicable to modern society?

§ CXXXVI. **The Rewards of the Christian Life.** GENERAL
QUESTIONS: 1. Describe the current Jewish doctrines regarding rewards for right action. 2. Contrast these with Jesus' teaching on the
subject. 3. What was the goal which he set before his followers?
4. His definition of happiness. 5. What did he declare were the conditions of true happiness?

SUBJECTS FOR SPECIAL RESEARCH: 1. The contemporary Jewish
doctrines regarding the rewards of the righteous after death. Charles,
Eschatology, Heb., Jew., and Christian, 162–99. 2. The Platonic and
Stoic ideas of happiness. *Cf.* standard histories of Greek philosophy.
3. Is happiness a valid goal for which to strive? Hilty, *Happiness.*

APPENDIX

THE CULMINATING EVENTS OF JESUS' LIFE

§ CXXXVII. **The Crisis in Galilee.** GENERAL QUESTIONS: 1. Why did Herod Antipas fear Jesus and desire to put him to death? 2. Why would Jesus' death at this time have endangered his cause? 3. Describe the historical facts which probably underlie the stories regarding the feeding of the multitudes. 4. The significance of Jesus' midnight meeting with his disciples on the shore. 5. The basis of Jesus' charges against the scribes and Pharisees. 6. His reasons for warning his disciples. 7. The change in the scene and method of his work.

SUBJECTS FOR SPECIAL RESEARCH: 1. Herod's new capital, Tiberias. Smith, *Hist. Geog. of Holy Land*, 447–50; Hastings, *Dict. of Christ*, II, 729–30. 2. The different interpretations of "the sin against the holy spirit." Hastings, *Dict. of Christ*, II, 786–8; Stevens, *Theol. of N. T.*, 102. 3. Compare Jesus' methods at the different stages in his ministry.

§ CXXXVIII. **Jesus in Retirement with His Disciples.** GENERAL QUESTIONS: 1. Why did Jesus seek refuge in the territory of Tyre? 2. What was the real significance of his reply to the request of the Syro-Phœnician woman? 3. The meaning of Peter's confession. 4. Jesus' twofold purpose in retiring with his disciples. 5. The facts that probably lie back of his threefold prediction of the Passion. 6. The meaning of the Transfiguration (1) to Jesus, (2) to his disciples. 7. The heroism revealed at this crisis.

SUBJECTS FOR SPECIAL RESEARCH: 1. A comparison of the different gospel accounts of the transfiguration. Hastings, *Dict. of Christ*, II, 742–3. 2. The various interpretations of the story. Hastings, *Dict. of Christ*, II, 743–5; Holtzmann, *Life of Jesus*, 341–5; Ross, *The Universality of Jesus*, 68–75.

§ CXXXIX. **Incidents of the Last Journey to Jerusalem.** GENERAL QUESTIONS: 1. Jesus' purpose and hope in going up to Jerusalem. 2. The inhospitality of the Samaritans. 3. His teachings regarding the narrow way of salvation. 4. His response to the request of James and John. 5. The conversion of Zaccheus. 6. The healing of the blind man.

SUBJECTS FOR SPECIAL RESEARCH: 1. The territory and population of Perea. Hastings, *Dict. of Christ*, II, 335–7. 2. The Jewish doctrine of the necessity of a ransom for sin. Schechter, *Some Aspects of Rab. Theol.*, 293–312. 3. The Jericho of Jesus' day. Smith, *Hist.*

334

APPENDIX

Geog. of Holy Land, 266–8; Josephus, *Jew. Ant.,* IV, 6¹; XIV, 4¹; XV, 4 ; XVI, 5²; Hastings, *D. B.,* II, 580–2.

§ CXL. **The Renewal of Jesus' Public Activity in Jerusalem.**
GENERAL QUESTIONS: 1. Describe the way in which Jesus entered Jerusalem. 2. Its meaning to the multitudes and its later interpretation by Jesus' disciples. 3. The facts underlying the story of the barren fig-tree. 4. Jesus' public arraignment of the temple authorities. 5. His rebuke of the leaders of Judaism. 6. His teaching regarding personal immortality. 7. The basis of his stern arraignment of the scribes and Pharisees.

SUBJECTS FOR SPECIAL RESEARCH: 1. The scene of Jesus' triumphal entry into Jerusalem. Kent, *Bib. Geog. and Hist.,* 259–60; Stanley, *Sinai and Pal.,* 190–4. 2. The duties and powers of the temple authorities. *En. Bib.,* IV, 4948–51; Smith, *Jerusalem,* II, 557–8. 3. The distinctive beliefs of the Pharisees and Sadducees. Hastings, *D. B.,* III, 821–8; IV, 349–51; *En. Bib.,* IV, 4321–9, 4234–40; Kent, *H. B.,* IV, 247–54.

§ CXLI. **Jesus' Preparation for His Death.** GENERAL QUESTIONS: 1. Jesus' original prediction regarding the fate of the temple. 2. The different elements incorporated in Mark 13, and their probable origin. 3. How far did Jesus accept the Jewish apocalyptic expectations of his day? 4. The motive and original content of his predictions regarding the future experiences that were to come to his disciples. 5. The significance of his anointing at Bethany. 6. Judas's motives in entering into negotiations with the high priests. 7. The details and significance of Jesus' last supper with his disciples. 8. The spirit and import of his farewell words.

SUBJECTS FOR SPECIAL RESEARCH: 1. The influence of the apocalyptic hopes of the Jews upon the early Christian belief in Jesus' speedy second coming. 2. Historical origin of the modern pre-millenarian and Adventists' doctrines. 3. Modern interpretations of the meaning of the Lord's supper. Hastings, *Dict. of Christ,* II, 63–76; *D. B.,* III, 148–150; Holtzmann, *Life of Jesus,* 460–4.

§ CXLII. **Jesus' Arrest and Trial.** GENERAL QUESTIONS: 1. What was the real issue at stake during Jesus' struggle in Gethsemane? 2. Describe the manner of his arrest. 3. The account of his examination before the high priest. 4. Its object. 5. His trial before Pilate. 6. The character of Pilate as therein revealed. 7. The injustice of Jesus' condemnation.

SUBJECTS FOR SPECIAL RESEARCH. 1. The traditional and probable site of the garden of Gethsemane. Smith, *Jerusalem,* II, 570–1; *En*

APPENDIX

Bib., II, 1712–3; Hastings, *D. B.*, II, 164. 2. A comparison of the Lucan and Marcan accounts of Jesus' trial. 3. The legality of Jesus' trial. Holtzmann, *Life of Jesus*, 471–8; Hastings, *Dict. of Christ*, II, 749–58; Innis, *The Trial of Jesus Christ;* Buss, *The Trial of Jesus: Illustrated from Talmud and Roman Law.*

§ CXLIII. **Jesus' Death and Burial.** GENERAL QUESTIONS: 1. The characteristics of the gospel records of Jesus' crucifixion. 2. Their variant accounts of his last words. 3. The details of the crucifixion. 4. The probable place. 5. The original form of the tablet affixed to the cross. 6. Jesus' death and burial. 7. The probable date of his death. 8. Its meaning for Judaism, for his followers, and for the realization of his mission.

SUBJECTS FOR SPECIAL RESEARCH: 1. The traditional and modern identifications of the place of Jesus' crucifixion. Kent, *Bib. Geog. and Hist.*, 262–3; Hastings, *Dict. of Christ*, I, 655–7; Wilson, *Golgotha and the Holy Sepulchre; En. Brit.*[11], XXIV, 656–8. 2. The institution of crucifixion. Hastings, *Dict. of Christ*, I, 397–8. 3. The various interpretations of the meaning of Jesus' death.

§ CXLIV. **The Living Christ.** GENERAL QUESTIONS: 1. Describe the immediate effect of Jesus' crucifixion upon the disciples. 2. Their sudden recovery of faith. 3. Paul's early testimony regarding the nature of the resurrection appearances. 4. His beliefs regarding the nature of the resurrection of the dead and those of the Jews. 5. The variant gospel accounts of the resurrection. Testimony of the oldest gospel records. 6. The various naturalistic interpretations of the resurrection story. 7. The supernatural explanation. 8. The spiritual interpretation. 9. The established facts.

SUBJECTS FOR SPECIAL RESEARCH: 1. The apostolic teaching regarding the meaning of Jesus' resurrection. Hastings, *Dict. of Christ*, II, 512–14. 2. In the religious thinking of the present generation. Hastings, *Dict. of Christ*, II, 510–12; *Lux Mundi*, 235.

§ CXLV. **Jesus the Saviour of Mankind.** GENERAL QUESTIONS: 1. Describe the picture of Jesus as Saviour and teacher found in the Fourth Gospel. 2. Its definition of that which is essential to salvation. 3. The title by which Jesus designated himself according to the earliest records. 4. Historical content of the term Son of man. 5. Jesus' growing vision of the extent of his mission. 6. Its interpretation in the Fourth Gospel. 7. In the light of modern knowledge and needs, in what sense is Jesus the universal Saviour of mankind? 8. Why is Christianity fitted, both in theory and in practice, to be a conquering world religion?

APPENDIX

SUBJECTS FOR SPECIAL RESEARCH: 1. The history of the term Son of man. Schmidt, *The Prophet of Nazareth*, 94–134; Hastings, *Dict. of Christ*, II, 659–65; *D. B.*, IV, 579–89; Montefiore, *The Synop. Gos.*, I, 93–104. 2. A comparison of the personality and work of Jesus and of Gautama Buddha. Holtzmann, *Life of Jesus*, 525–7; *En. Brit.*[11], IV, 737–42. 3. Of Jesus and of Confucius. Holtzmann, *Life of Jesus*, 522–3; *En. Brit.*[11], VI, 907–12. 4. Of Jesus and of the Greek philosophers, Socrates, Plato, and the Stoics. Holtzmann, *Life of Jesus*, 513–24; *En. Brit.*[11], XXV, 331–8, 942–3; XXI, 808–24.